Libraries in Literature

Libraries in Literature

Edited by
ALICE CRAWFORD
and
ROBERT CRAWFORD

OXFORD
UNIVERSITY PRESS

OXFORD
UNIVERSITY PRESS

Great Clarendon Street, Oxford, OX2 6DP,
United Kingdom

Oxford University Press is a department of the University of Oxford.
It furthers the University's objective of excellence in research, scholarship,
and education by publishing worldwide. Oxford is a registered trade mark of
Oxford University Press in the UK and in certain other countries

First Edition published in 2022

Impression: 1

Published in the United States of America by Oxford University Press
198 Madison Avenue, New York, NY 10016, United States of America

British Library Cataloguing in Publication Data
Data available

Library of Congress Control Number: 2022933700

ISBN 978-0-19-285573-2

DOI: 10.1093/oso/9780192855732.001.0001

Printed and bound by
CPI Group (UK) Ltd, Croydon, CR0 4YY

Acknowledgements

We would like to thank Professor Jane Stabler and the School of English at the University of St Andrews for hosting and making possible the 2019 research colloquium on 'Libraries in Literature' at which all the contributors to this book met and discussed early versions of their chapters. Dr Paul Malgrati helped ensure that all went smoothly at that event. Gratitude is due, also, to everyone who authored a chapter in this volume and who kept faith with the project during the challenging times of the Covid-19 pandemic. The expert and demanding reports provided by the publisher's referees helped us make *Libraries in Literature* both stronger and more capacious, and Jacqueline Norton, our editor at Oxford University Press, ensured that the project was guided to completion.

We gratefully acknowledge the following permissions:

Jorge Luis Borges, excerpts from 'Poem of the Gifts', translated by Alastair Reid, copyright © 1999 by Maria Kodama; translation copyright © 1999 by Alastair Reid; from *Selected Poems* by Jorge Luis Borges, edited by Alexander Coleman. Used by permission of Viking Books, an imprint of Penguin Publishing Group, a division of Penguin Random House LLC. All rights reserved.

Agatha Christie, excerpts from *The Body in the Library*. Reprinted by permission of HarperCollins Publishers Ltd © 1942 Agatha Christie.

Wanda Coleman, excerpts from 'Chapter Two of the Story' from *Bathwater Wine*. Copyright © 1998 by Wanda Coleman. Reprinted with the permission of The Permissions Company, LLC on behalf of Black Sparrow/David R Godine, Publisher, Inc., www.godine.com.

Lynn Davidson, excerpts from 'Muirhouse Library: When Yellow's on the Broom' © Lynn Davidson 2019, from *Islander* (Wellington/Bristol: Victoria University Press/Shearsman, 2019) by permission of Shearsman Books and Victoria University of Wellington Press.

Rita Dove, excerpts from 'Maple Valley Branch Library, 1967' from *On the Bus with Rosa Parks* (New York: Norton, 1999) by permission of W.W. Norton & Co.

Thomas Sayers Ellis, excerpts from 'View of the Library of Congress from Paul Laurence Dunbar High School' from *The Maverick Room*. Copyright © 2005 by Thomas Sayers Ellis. Reprinted with the permission of The Permissions Company, LLC on behalf of Graywolf Press, Minneapolis, Minnesota, graywolfpress.org.

Jackie Kay, excerpts from 'The Year of the Letter: Biography' from *Darling: New & Selected* Poems (Bloodaxe Books, 2007) by permission of Bloodaxe Books, www.bloodaxebooks.com

James Keery, excerpts from 'Modified Bliss' from *That Stranger, The Blues* by James Keery (Manchester: Carcanet, 1996) by permission of Carcanet Press.

Liz Lochhead, excerpts from 'The Choosing' by Liz Lochhead from *A Choosing* (Edinburgh: Polygon, 2011) by permission of Birlinn Press.

William McIlvanney, excerpts from 'In the Library' from *Long Overdue: A Library Reader*, ed. Alan Taylor (London and Edinburgh: Library Association/Mainstream Publishing, 1993) by permission of the Literary Estate of William McIlvanney.

Haki R. Madhubuti, excerpts from 'So Many Books, So Little Time' by Haki R. Madhubuti from *HeartLove: Wedding and Love Poems* (Chicago: Third World Press, 1998) by kind permission of the author and Third World Press.

Philip Metres, excerpts from 'Hearing of Alia Muhammed Baker's Stroke'. Copyright © 2014 by Philip Metres. Reprinted from Split This Rock's The Quarry: A Social Justice Poetry Database and used with kind permission of the author.

Naomi Shihab Nye, excerpts from 'Because of Libraries We Can Say These Things' from *Fuel*. Copyright © 1998 by Naomi Shihab Nye. Reprinted with the permission of The Permissions Company, LLC on behalf of BOA Editions, Ltd, www.boaeditions.org.

Alastair Paterson, excerpt from 'on the library' from *On the Governing of Empires*. Copyright © 2010 Alastair Paterson. Reprinted with permission of Shearsman Books Ltd.

Charles Reznikoff, excerpts from 'XXIII Cooper Union Library' from *The Poems of Charles Reznikoff: 1918–1975*, edited by Seamus Cooney. Copyright © 2005 by The Estate of Charles Reznikoff. Reprinted with the permission of The Permissions Company, LLC on behalf of Black Sparrow/ David R Godine, Publisher, Inc., www.godine.com.

Alberto Ríos, excerpts from 'Don't Go Into the Library', https://poets.org/ poem/dont-go-library, Copyright © 2017 by Alberto Ríos. Used with kind permission of the author.

Dorothy L. Sayers, excerpts from *Gaudy Night* by Dorothy L. Sayers (Hodder & Stoughton), reproduced by permission of David Higham Associates.

Gerald Stern, excerpts from 'Stepping out of Poetry' from *This Time: New and Selected Poems* (New York: W.W. Norton, 1998) by permission of W.W. Norton & Co.

Contents

About the Contributors

Alice Crawford has held positions at the universities of Glasgow, Dundee, and St Andrews where she was Digital Humanities Research Librarian. Her books include *The Meaning of the Library* (Princeton University Press, 2015) and a study of Rose Macaulay.

Robert Crawford is Emeritus Wardlaw Professor of Poetry in the School of English at the University of St Andrews. His books include *Eliot after 'The Waste Land'* (Cape and Farrar, Straus & Giroux, 2022) and *The Scottish Ambassador* (Cape Poetry, 2018).

Nicola Humble is Professor Emerita in the Department of English and Creative Writing, University of Roehampton. Her books include *The Feminine Middlebrow Novel 1920s to 1950s* (Oxford University Press, 2001) and *Culinary Pleasures* (Faber, 2006).

Elisabeth Jay's books include the biography *Mrs Oliphant: A Fiction to Herself* (Clarendon Press, 1995) and *British Writers and Paris: 1830–1875* (Oxford University Press, 2016). She is Emerita Professor of English at Oxford Brookes and joint general editor of Oliphant's works.

Darryl Jones edited M. R. James's *Collected Stories* for Oxford University Press in 2011. His other books include *Horror: A Thematic History in Fiction and Film* (Oxford University Press, 2002). He is Professor of Modern British Literature and Culture at Trinity College Dublin.

Tom Jones's publications include *Poetic Language* (Edinburgh University Press, 2012) and *George Berkeley: A Philosophical Life* (Princeton University Press, 2021). He is a Professor in the School of English, University of St Andrews.

Sara Lodge's books include *Thomas Hood and Nineteenth-Century Poetry* (Manchester University Press, 2005) and *Inventing Edward Lear* (Harvard University Press, 2019). She is Senior Lecturer in English at the University of St Andrews.

J. Louise McCray is completing a book on William Godwin and the reading culture of late eighteenth-century and early nineteenth-century England. Based in Cambridge, she is developing a new project on libraries and Victorian reading culture.

Robyn Marsack was for over fifteen years Director of the Scottish Poetry Library. Her books include studies of Louis MacNeice, and of Sylvia Plath. She was a Royal Literary Fund Writing Fellow at Glasgow University, 2016–18, and is a Fellow of the Royal Society of Edinburgh.

Kylie Murray is a writer and educationalist who has held research fellowships at Balliol College, Oxford, and at Christ's College, Cambridge. She was a BBC/AHRC New Generation Thinker in 2015. Her books include *The Making of the Scottish Dream Vision* (Oxford University Press, 2022).

Chris Perkins is Senior Lecturer in Japanese at the University of Edinburgh. His book on media and memory of the left in Japan, *The United Red Army on Screen*, was published by Palgrave in 2015, and his interests include the politics of belonging in contemporary Japan.

Siân Reynolds's books include *Marriage and Revolution: Monsieur and Madame Roland* (Oxford University Press, 2012). Formerly Professor of French at Stirling University, she has translated many works, including, in 2014, Sophie Divry's *The Library of Unrequited Love*.

Fiona Stafford's books include *Local Attachments* (Oxford University Press, 2010) and *The Long, Long Life of Trees* (Yale University Press, 2016). A Fellow of Somerville College, she is Professor of English Language and Literature at the University of Oxford.

Kristen Treen is Lecturer in American Literature in the School of English at the University of St Andrews. She is completing a monograph on how material remnants of the American Civil War shaped later literary culture.

Edwin Williamson's *Borges: A Life* was published by Viking in 2004, and his other books include *The Cambridge Companion to Jorge Luis Borges* (Cambridge University Press, 2013). He is King Alfonso XIII Emeritus Professor of Spanish Studies at the University of Oxford.

Introduction

Alice Crawford and Robert Crawford

This is a book for the bookish. Concentrating on writing from the post-medieval English-speaking world, but also taking into account a selection of translated works with a significant English-language readership, it focuses on how poets, novelists, and dramatists over several centuries have imagined and reimagined personal, institutional, and public libraries. It is not a book about archives and archivists, or about bookshops, or about libraries in art or film, or even about writers who have written in libraries. It is, straightforwardly, a book about libraries in literature.

As such, it is the first volume to provide a critical and historical account of its subject. Bibliographers and library historians have examined aspects of the topic before, and specialists have addressed the presentation of the library in the work of individual writers from Rabelais to Borges and beyond; but the authors of the following chapters have come together as literary scholars to offer a more comprehensive account. While still necessarily selective, *Libraries in Literature* shows how the library has developed as a cultural trope in imaginative writing. The editors are conscious that this book cannot cover all aspects of its topic, and should not attempt to do so. It is offered as an initial survey and an incitement to further work, not as the final word. Where librarians or specialist book historians might have attended more to technical manuals of library management or to shifts in technology and hierarchy in tracing the development of libraries in literature—focussing, say, on the impact of the British Parliament's 1850 Public Libraries Act, and painstakingly separating out national libraries from university libraries, and public libraries from private or ecclesiastical ones—the contributors to *Libraries in Literature*, while not oblivious to issues of taxonomy, library-school professionalism, and hierarchy, write principally as critics and historians of imaginative writing. We are particularly interested in the way creative writers who address a general audience imagine and metamorphose collections of books, giving libraries of all sorts and conditions a heightened metaphorical presence. As well as being a work of cultural history, this is a book about writerly artistry, about how libraries become part of literary art.

Not unreasonably, people think of libraries as full of books, rather than of books as being full of libraries. Yet for imaginative writers the lure of the library as a resource, a destination for their work, a place of reverie or haunting or even mockery, has long been strong. In fiction, from *Don Quixote* to *Middlemarch* and beyond, the library has been a presence that both shapes and reveals the nature of character; it can function that way in poetry and drama also. Just as in recent times viewers scan the bookshelves behind politicians, broadcasters, and interlocutors in video calls for signs that will reveal the speaker's personality, so in literature for centuries the library has functioned as a marker of individual character traits as well as an institutional carrier of traditions. In the twenty-first-century era of digital searching, big data, and remote reading, the material nature and the representation of textual storage and consumption have become sources of grow-ing fascination. The words 'library' and 'stack' are now part of the vocabulary of computer science, but technological change serves not to erode but to intensify a preoccupation with what one recent cultural history calls *The Meaning of the Library*.[1]

If for some people physical libraries are now the subject of elegy, then for many they are contested spaces under political and economic attack, while remaining potential gateways to knowledge and imaginative engagement. In the earlier twentieth century writers as different as Ortega y Gasset in 'The Mission of the Librarian' and Walter Benjamin in 'Unpacking My Library' dealt eloquently with the civilizing, necessary, and even visionary possibilities of libraries. For Benjamin, a German Jew writing in the 1930s, the personal library could be a way 'to renew the old world'; for Ortega y Gasset in 1934, unsettlingly, 'the librarian of the future' ought to be 'the doctor and the hygienist of reading'.[2] From Ovid (*Tristia*, 3.14) to Philip Pullman in *La Belle Sauvage*, imaginative writers, and not least women writers, have chafed against the exclusiveness of some elite libraries, against over-hygienic librarians, and against an institutional wish to control or censor reading; it is with a certain sly irony that Virginia Woolf, writing about Bloomsbury's greatest library in 1929 in *A Room of One's Own*, poses the question, 'If truth is not to be found on the shelves of the British Museum, where, I asked myself, picking up a notebook and a pencil, is truth?'[3]

Yet, mostly, imaginative writers have sided with the Russian master of the short story Isaac Babel, another threatened 1930s intellectual, who celebrated in a pungent pen portrait 'The Public Library' as a welcoming 'kingdom of books'.[4] Whenever they could, writers have always tended to amass and treasure their own personal libraries. Leah Price's 2011 edited collection *Unpacking My Library:*

---

[1] Alice Crawford, ed., *The Meaning of the Library: A Cultural History* (Princeton: Princeton University Press, 2015).

[2] Walter Benjamin, 'Unpacking My Library', trans. Harry Zohn, in *Illuminations*, ed. Hannah Arendt (London: Fontana Press, 1992), 63; José Ortega y Gasset, 'The Mission of the Librarian', trans. James Lewis and Ray Carpenter, *Antioch Review* 21.2 (Summer 1961): 154.

[3] Virginia Woolf, *A Room of One's Own* (1929; repr., London: Grafton Books, 1988), 26.

[4] Isaac Babel, *Complete Works*, ed. Nathalie Babel, trans. Peter Constantine (New York: W. W. Norton, 2001), 67.

Writers and their Books, in which novelists including Sophie Gee, Philip Pullman, Gary Shteyngart and Edmund White describe and enthuse about their private book hoards, gives a fine, anecdotal flavour of this: 'I started acquiring books as soon as I started earning my own money,' states Junot Díaz, expressing a widely shared sentiment.[5] In recent decades, though, creative authors, sensing that not absolutely every national or local politician prized book hoards so zealously, have rallied to libraries'—and particularly public libraries'—defence, whether collectively in campaigning anthologies such as Susan A. Toth and John Coughlan's *Reading Rooms: America's Foremost Writers Celebrate Our Public Libraries* or individually as in Ali Smith's *Public Library and Other Stories*. In the former volume (which dates from 1991) the tone can be jubilant, but in the latter book (published in 2015) there is no story called 'Public Library'; instead, at a time when libraries in Britain are often under threat, Smith's opening piece puts the very word 'library' under erasure.[6] During the completion of the present book, the closure of many of the world's public and institutional libraries at a time of global pandemic has given readers a heightened awareness not only of their own personal book collections but also of the differences between the vast virtual libraries of twenty-first-century databases and the traditional, tangible, richly olfactory libraries of dusted or dusty tomes, shelves, and sometimes vertiginous bookcases which have fuelled and, on occasion, overawed both readers and writers.

Libraries in Literature is alert to the changing politics of libraries, and to the way technological change has heightened our sense of the attractiveness as well as the limitations of physical book hoards. In Britain and Ireland, Jenny Peachey writes in *Shining a Light*, a 2017 Carnegie Trust report, that about half the population makes use of public libraries, but notes that their use is increasingly 'under pressure'.[7] The contributors to *Libraries in Literature* are certainly aware of such pressure, signs of which are insistent in the front-line accounts by contemporary English novelist Chris Paling in his *Reading Allowed: True Stories & Curious Incidents from a Provincial Library* (2017) and, perhaps more shockingly, in the way that the American academic Jessica Pressman's *Bookishness: Loving Books in a Digital Age* (2020) contains no entry for 'libraries' in its index, where the entry for '*Library*' refers only to Micha Ullman's 1995 memorial to Nazi book-burning. Yet the present volume is not a direct contribution to library usage surveys, administration, technological debate, concerns over the future of the

---

[5] Leah Price, ed., *Unpacking My Library: Writers and Their Books* (New Haven and London: Yale University Press, 2011), 44.

[6] Susan A. Toth and John Coughlan, ed., *Reading Rooms: America's Foremost Writers Celebrate Our Public Libraries with Stories, Memoirs, Essays and Poems* (New York: Doubleday, 1991); Ali Smith, *Public Library and Other Stories* (London: Hamish Hamilton, 2015), 3.

[7] Jenny Peachey, *Shining a Light: How People in the UK and Ireland Use Public Libraries and What They Think of Them* (Dunfermline: Carnegie UK Trust, 2017), 7.

printed book, or protest. Addressed to literary scholars, cultural historians, and librarians, its chapters may attract, also, a wider audience who simply love reading about reading. The appeal of heavyweight histories of reading, book-collecting, and of libraries by academic scholars including Reid Byers, Anthony Grafton, Robert Darnton, Konstantinos Staikos, and the contributors to *The Cambridge History of Libraries in Great Britain and Ireland*; the more essayistic, reflective considerations of libraries and the power of books by Matthew Battles, Stuart Kells, Alberto Manguel, Tom Mole, and others; and the measured silence of photographer Candida Höfer's impressively depopulated *Libraries* or James W. P. Campbell's more sumptuously populated *The Library: A World History*— all these testify in their different ways to a fascination with the cultural importance of libraries.[8] The most recent (2021) account of the evolution of libraries, the impressively wide-ranging and highly readable *The Library: A Fragile History* by Andrew Pettegree and Arthur der Weduwen, attests to this too.[9] *Libraries in Literature* addresses scholarly as well as more general readers. It is an academic book, published by a university press; but it is also an accessibly written volume that can reach readers anywhere who cherish libraries in their own imaginations. To borrow phrasing used by the English writer Richard de Bury in the *Philobiblon*, his fourteenth-century library manual written almost half a millennium before the word 'bibliophile' entered the English language, *Libraries in Literature* is a work preoccupied with the imaginative portrayal of the habitat of the 'lover of books'.[10]

Throughout this volume a number of 'library tropes' recur. It begins with two of them: the exaggerated and satirically subversive depiction of taxonomy set out by Rabelais in his sixteenth-century presentation of the library of St Victor in Paris, and the mind-addling library of Don Quixote presented by Cervantes in the early seventeenth century. Indicating how these tropes function and how they have been inherited by several later writers, this book's opening chapter takes something of a through line across literary history. It is followed by a chapter on

---

[8] See, e.g., Reid Byers, *The Private Library: The History of the Architecture and Furnishing of the Domestic Bookroom* (New Castle, DE: Oak Knoll Press, 2021); Anthony Grafton, *Commerce with the Classics: Ancient Books and Renaissance Readers* (Ann Arbor: University of Michigan Press, 1997), and Anthony Grafton, ed., *Rome Reborn: The Vatican Library and Renaissance Culture* (New Haven: Yale University Press, 1993); Robert Darnton, *The Case for Books* (New York: Public Affairs, 2009); Konstantinos Staikos, *A History of the Library in Western Civilization* (New Castle, DE: Oak Knoll Press, 2004–12); Peter Hoare, ed., *The Cambridge History of Libraries in Britain and Ireland* (Cambridge: Cambridge University Press, 2006); Matthew Battles, *Library: An Unquiet History* (London: Heinemann, 2003); Stuart Kells, *The Library: A Catalogue of Wonders, A Love Letter to Libraries and to Their Makers and Protectors* (Melbourne: Text Publishing, 2017); Alberto Manguel, *The Traveler, the Tower, and the Worm* (Philadelphia: University of Pennsylvania Press, 2013); Tom Mole, *The Secret Life of Books* (London: Elliott and Thompson, 2019); James W. P. Campbell, *The Library: A World History* (London: Thames & Hudson, 2013).

[9] Andrew Pettegree and Arthur der Weduwen, *The Library: A Fragile History* (London: Profile Books, 2021).

[10] *The Philobiblon of Richard de Bury*, trans. Ernest C. Thomas (London: Kegan Paul, Trench & Co., 1888), 168.

'Dramatic Libraries' which, beginning with Marlowe and Shakespeare, covers an equally extensive historical sweep as it indicates how, over several centuries, the apparently undramatic phenomenon that is the library has functioned on the anglophone stage. These two extensive, cross-cutting surveys prepare the way for later chapters which move beyond the early modern period to show, sometimes through wide-scale historical survey and sometimes through more detailed individual case studies, how libraries have been presented in more recent imaginative writing from the early Enlightenment to the present day.

The book's course, then, is generally chronological. Though its selection of material centres on literature available to anglophone readers, and on post-medieval writing, it seeks to combine the relatively familiar—Cervantes, Shakespeare, and George Eliot—with revealing but less frequently discussed creative work, including writings by William Godwin, Margaret Oliphant, and Mary Augusta Ward. The volume's design acknowledges the pronounced growth of interest in libraries in twentieth-century fiction, and not least in crime fiction, but readers may be surprised by the range as well as the depth of creative reactions to libraries on the part of poets as well as novelists. For all that its principal interest is in anglophone texts, *Libraries in Literature* remains alert, too, to a range of international imaginative writing about libraries in other languages which, through the medium of translation, has become part of literature in English—from Rabelais to Murakami. A range of wider international and historical comparisons is encouraged.

In this context, it is clear that from their advent libraries have been bound up with ideological argument. They have been battle-sites of books: not just centres of cultural consolidation, but also emblems of cultural destruction. Modern as well as ancient libraries from Berlin to Timbuktu feature in Kenneth Baker's 2016 volume *On the Burning of Books* and in Richard Ovenden's *Burning the Books* (2020).[11] If ancient Chinese history, as Karen Armstrong points out, involves stories both of 'book burning' and of 'the concentration of intellectual authority in an imperial library' around the third and second centuries BCE, then the Western counterparts of such tropes surely include the development of the great library at Alexandria around the same period—and its subsequent destruction by Julius Caesar in 48 BCE, an event alluded to by writers from the biographer and historian Plutarch in ancient Greek to the poet Don Paterson in modern English.[12] Libraries are vulnerable to external attack, but they are also places in which ideological conflicts are staged. The trope of the library as battle-site, most familiar to anglophone readers in Jonathan Swift's *Battel of the Books*, re-echoes throughout the present volume.

---

[11] Kenneth Baker, *On the Burning of Books* (London: Unicorn, 2016); Richard Ovenden, *Burning the Books: A History of Knowledge Under Attack* (London: John Murray, 2020).
[12] Karen Armstrong, *The Lost Art of Scripture* (London: Bodley Head, 2019), 166.

Yet, though libraries can be places of conflict, each is more usually what Alberto Manguel styles 'a realm of order', a shrine to taxonomy; fascinated by lists, writers have relished responding to this since long before the Middle Ages.[13] No one who loves libraries can nourish a hatred of lists. The set of index lists, the *Pinakes*, attributed to poet and scholar Kallimachos at Alexandria serves as a classical reminder of how writers love not just lists in general but also specific book lists. The medieval Latin poet Alcuin versifies an episcopal library catalogue; in English Sir Thomas Urquhart's seventeenth-century translation of Rabelais presents the catalogue of the library of St Victor with such works as '*The Spur of Cheese*' and '*The Cobbled Shoe of Humility*'; later, in 1711, Joseph Addison catalogues a Ladies Library in his magazine, *The Spectator*; James Joyce in *Ulysses* issues the instruction 'Catalogue these books', and goes on to do so; while more recently Asabuki Ryōji's 'I classify' (which classifies '*books:* by number only') marks just one later twentieth-century creative wink at the Dewey-eyed taxonomic impulse which lies at the heart of most libraries.[14] In the twenty-first century Edward Wilson-Lee's 2018 investigation of Christopher Columbus and the quest for a universal library, *The Catalogue of Shipwrecked Books*, is one of the most recent examples of the catalogue as a way of figuring allure and imaginative relish. The trope of the library as a place of curated order is a persistently recurrent one in the chapters of *Libraries in Literature*, and, as well as offering analysis and historically inflected insight, on occasion this book's contributors display their own unabashed love of listing.

While libraries are places of taxonomic order, repositories, 'shrines' of 'relics', this makes them, too, carefully tended book graveyards.[15] In his late seventeenth-century poem 'On Sir Thomas Bodley's Library' the poet Henry Vaughan presents that famous Oxford library as a place where, thanks to the priestly ministrations of librarians, ancient texts that might otherwise be akin to 'empty Skulls' can be revealed as 'not dead, but full of *Blood* again'.[16] 'It is with Libraries, as with other Cemeteries', writes Swift in *The Battel of the Books*, and the trope of libraries as cemeteries, 'repositories of mouldering learning' as Charles Lamb puts it, becomes a familiar one, as does the notion that libraries may be where the dead can come back to life.[17] It is no accident that a bookroom features in Ann Radcliffe's classic Gothic novel *The Mysteries of Udolpho* or that Count Dracula has a library in his

[13] Alberto Manguel, *The Library at Night* (New Haven: Yale University Press, 2008), 12.

[14] François Rabelais, *Gargantua and Pantagruel*, trans. Thomas Urquhart and Peter le Motteux (London: Dent, 1966), 2 vols, I, 159; Joseph Addison, *Spectator*, No. 37; James Joyce, *Ulysses* (1922; repr. London: Penguin, 1974), 629; Asabuki Ryōji, 'I Classify', in *The Penguin Book of Japanese Verse*, ed. and trans. Geoffrey Bownas and Anthony Thwaite (London: Penguin, 2009), 250.

[15] Francis Bacon, *Works* (London: Newnes, 1902), 282 (*Advancement of Learning*, Book II).

[16] Henry Vaughan, *Poetry and Selected Prose*, ed. L. C. Martin (London: Oxford University Press, 1963), 405 ('On Sir Thomas Bodley's Library').

[17] Jonathan Swift, *Selected Prose and Poetry*, ed. Edward Rosenheim Jr (New York: Holt, Rinehart & Winston, 1968), 159 ('Battel of the Books'); Charles Lamb, *Essays of Elia* (London: Oxford University Press, 1964), 14 ('Oxford in the Vacation').

castle, and readers of the present book will become familiar with the trope of the library as a cemetery or morgue of books.

If mouldering libraries came to fuel the Gothic imagination in M. R. James and beyond, then the idea of the library not as a resting place of the dead who may be disturbed there but as itself a source of disturbance is another recurring figuration of the book hoard. Its *locus classicus* is *Don Quixote*, where Cervantes presents his protagonist's library, stuffed with chivalric romances, as the source of the 'woes' which have conspired to 'crack' Don Quixote's 'brain'.[18] Two centuries later, Walter Scott, who uses the recently coined noun 'bibliomaniac' when he applies it to Don Quixote, has his protagonist Edward Waverley begin as a young man whose reading in 'the library at Waverley-Honour, a large Gothic room' has left him 'like a vessel without a pilot or a rudder'—not mad but certainly at sea and prone to wavering.[19] By Victorian times bibliomania has become so established that readers encounter George Eliot's Mr Casaubon, who teeters on the borderline of scholarship and mental imbalance before having 'a fit in the library', which may have helped audiences agree (in the context of the grand private library in Mary Augusta Ward's *Robert Elsmere*) that 'Most men of letters are mad'.[20]

While such figurations connect the imaging of the expanding library to the image of the mad professor, they also lead to visions of the library as a place of what we might now call 'information overload'. Conscious he could never absorb even a fraction of its contents, Thomas De Quincey from his youth felt 'pain and disturbance of mind' when entering a great library.[21] By 1891 in George Gissing's *New Grub Street* there is a sense of 'the huge library' as oppressively bound to the 'Literary Machine': surely soon 'some Edison' will 'make the true automaton' capable of taking 'old books' and having them 'reduced, blended, modernised into a single one for today's consumption'.[22] John Davidson's similarly modern sense in 1901 of 'automata / That served machines' and people who may 'die crushed under libraries' opens the way to the later sense of infinite libraries and a knowledge surplus in the work of Jorge Luis Borges, Umberto Eco, Haruki Murakami, and more recent writers.[23] Such entrapping and infinite libraries are at the heart of several chapters towards the end of the present book.

Ordered, yet subjected to the imagined as well as actual ravages of disorder and even madness, libraries in literature are often guarded spaces. The medieval

---

[18] Miguel de Cervantes Saavedra, *Don Quixote*, trans. Peter le Motteux (London: Dent, 1970), 2 vols, I, 34.

[19] Walter Scott, *The Antiquary* (London: Dent, 1923), 33; Walter Scott, *Waverley* (London: Penguin, 1981), 47, 48.

[20] George Eliot, *Middlemarch* (1872; repr. London: Dent, 1969), 2 vols, I, 250; Mrs Humphry Ward, *Robert Elsmere* (1888; repr. London: Smith, Elder, 1903), 195.

[21] Thomas De Quincey, *Letters to a Young Man* (Philadelphia: John Penington, 1843), 67.

[22] George Gissing, *New Grub Street* (London: Smith, Elder, 1891), 3 vols, I, 195.

[23] John Davidson, *Poems*, ed. A. Turnbull (Edinburgh: Scottish Academic Press, 1973), 329, 330 ('The Testament of a Man Forbid').

Richard de Bury devotes a chapter to 'due propriety in the custody of Books', and in the sixteenth century Michel de Montaigne, whose library was the place of the 'throne' in his bookish tower near Bordeaux, regarded himself as having 'absolute' authority there; the notion of the library as a special, protected fortress can be taken to extremes—in Robert Burton's *Anatomy of Melancholy* King James VI and I eulogizes the Bodleian Library in Oxford as a 'prison' where he might be 'chained together with so many good Authors and dead Masters'; for Abraham Cowley the Bodleian is a 'sacred Ark', protecting against 'Insatiate Times devouring Flood'. Such notions reach their apogee when the library becomes not an ark but part of an even stranger vessel:

> 'Captain Nemo,' said I to my host who had just thrown himself on one of the divans, 'you have a library here that would do honour to more than one continental palace, and I am lost in wonder when I think that it can follow you to the greatest depths of the ocean.'[24]

If the library aboard the submarine *Nautilus* in Jules Verne's *Twenty Thousand Leagues under the Sea* (1869–70) is the most astounding example of the library as protected space, then the trope of a library with guardians, guards, or gatekeepers recurs throughout literary history: a friend of one twentieth-century fictional American librarian (alluding ironically to a hymn by Martin Luther) declares, 'A mighty fortress is our library', while a male colleague elsewhere proclaims with near-messianic zeal that 'The great librarians have all been religious men – monks, priests, rabbis – and the stewardship of books is an act of homage and faith.'[25] This trope of the library as guarded enclosure or temple of books connects with the depiction of libraries as hoards of contested cultural capital.

If only they can be accessed, however, creative writers know that libraries may be liberating. The Scottish novelist Tobias Smollett in his 1771 *Humphry Clinker* is aware of the recently founded British Museum 'library' as 'a wonder' founded 'for the benefit of the public', and the later British Museum reading room becomes itself a trope for writers as different as Washington Irving and David Lodge.[26] Sensing its potential for pleasure and liberating educational improvement, as the self-styled 'PEASANT' Robert Burns hymns a rural 'circulating library' in

[24] *Philobiblon*, 236; *The Complete Essays of Montaigne*, trans. Donald M. Frame (Stanford, CA: Stanford University Press, 1958), 650 ('Three Kinds of Association'); Robert Burton, *The Anatomy of Melancholy* (New York: Tudor, 1955), 457; Abraham Cowley, *Poems*, ed. A. R. Waller (Cambridge: Cambridge University Press, 1905), 409 ('Mr Cowley's Book presenting it self to the University Library of Oxford'); Jules Verne, trans. anon., *Twenty Thousand Leagues under the Sea* (London: Ward, Lock & Co., n.d.), 58.
[25] Jane Smiley, *Duplicate Keys* (London: Cape, 1984), 66; Martha Cooley, *The Archivist* (Boston: Little, Brown, 1998), 11.
[26] Tobias Smollett, *The Expedition of Humphry Clinker* (1771; repr. London: Dent, 1968), 97 (2 June).

southern Scotland, and a generation later in London Burns's admirer and fellow Scot Thomas Carlyle maintains that 'The true University of these days is a Collection of Books' at around the same time as he helps found the London Library.[27] If the library, as in Dickens's *Hard Times*, can be a place offering 'general access' to speculation about 'human nature', and even, as for the autobiographer Andrew Carnegie, liberation from a 'dungeon', then for Booker T. Washington (who petitioned Carnegie successfully for library funding) it was part of several kinds of emancipation in *Up from Slavery*.[28] For many writers the public library has been an image for liberation in literature. Yet there is also a strain of mockery of the private, club-like, or aristocratic or plutocratic library that is present from Thackeray's *Book of Snobs* through poet J. G. Saxe's 'Sham Library' to the library of *The Great Gatsby* and beyond.

Not all libraries are as public as they may appear, and the history of libraries in literature is in important ways a history of women's struggles to enter a male-dominated domain. Margaret Oliphant's ghost story 'The Library Window' is in part at least a presentation of gendered exclusion from an academic bookroom. 'Fame's great library', as Margaret Cavendish, Duchess of Newcastle, had put it in the seventeenth century, was often hard to enter, particularly for women.[29] Ladies' use of and access to libraries had been mocked by R. B. Sheridan in his play *The Rivals* (1775), though by the early nineteenth century the figure of 'Esther Caterer, Librarian' of Sheffield (whose career and memorial elegy have received recent scholarly attention) could be praised by John Holland, an English poet fond of the work of Robert Burns.

> When gentles came, in studious mood,
> To fash their brains 'mang learning's brood,   *bother; among*
> Or tak' their meal o' mental food,
>   Wi' ready head
> She ken'd where every volume stood.—   *knew*
>   Auld Esther's dead![30]

Early nineteenth-century poetry found a place for Esther Caterer, but it would be almost seven decades before in prose fiction Henry James in *The Bostonians* presented a fictional scene where a man and a woman stroll through a public library and encounter a female professional librarian. As late as Dorothy Sayers's

---

[27] *The Letters of Robert Burns*, ed. J. De Lancey Ferguson, 2nd ed., ed. G. Ross Roy (2 vols; Oxford: Clarendon Press, 1985), II, 108, 107; Thomas Carlyle, *On Heroes, Hero-Worship and the Heroic in History* (1841; repr. London: Oxford University Press, 1963), 213.

[28] Charles Dickens, *Hard Times* (1854; repr. London: Nelson, 1903), 52; Andrew Carnegie, *Autobiography* (Boston: Houghton Mifflin, 1920), 46.

[29] Margaret Cavendish, *Poems, and Phancies* (London: William Wilson, 1664), 210.

[30] On Esther Caterer and John Holland's published poem about her, see Robert Crawford, 'The Library in Poetry', in Alice Crawford, ed., *The Meaning of the Library*, 181–4.

Gaudy Night a library is linked to fears about the status of women's education, while Virginia Woolf in *A Room of One's Own* presents an academic library as a place from which the female writer is shut out. Edith Wharton in the early twentieth century may have co-authored a book on *The Decoration of Houses* which includes a chapter on 'The Library, Smoking Room, and "Den"', but private libraries were mostly the preserve of men, and few young women were wealthy enough to be able to follow the advice of Beatrice Webb's father with regard to any book 'banned' by libraries: 'Buy it, my dear.'[31]

Growing acknowledgement that libraries might interest women as well as men also hastened a sense of libraries as places where couples might meet. When Mr Darcy in chapter 8 of *Pride and Prejudice* states that he 'cannot comprehend the neglect of a family library in such days as these', readers know he is admirable, but there is more to Darcy's point than simply that. The 'delightful library at "Pemberley"', like the library in which Pushkin's Tatyana fingers Eugene Onegin's books, is predominantly the space of the hero, rather than belonging to the heroine. By the era of Edith Wharton's *The House of Mirth* the private-house 'library at Bellomont' is 'never used for reading' but has become 'a quiet retreat for flirtation', and Stephen Dedalus in early twentieth-century Dublin is told, 'Your beloved is here' as he walks among students 'sheltering under the arcade of the library' in Joyce's *A Portrait of the Artist as a Young Man*.[32] Indeed, by the time of Ian McEwan's *Atonement*, with its lovemaking among the shelves, and in Jackie Kay's steamily homoerotic late twentieth-century poem 'Biography', libraries have become places for heightened eroticism. They may even be, as Sean O'Brien puts it in his poem elegizing a lost society from which he felt subtly excluded, the haunts not just of randy readers but also of 'The Beautiful Librarians'.[33] Libraries now are places for book lovers, but for bookish lovers too.

The trope of the erotic library is beguiling, but more subtly striking is the depiction of the library as a space where men and women simply go about their bookish work in a climate of egalitarian mutual respect. In such an atmosphere writers and readers may even come to respect that most routinely stereotyped of figures, the librarian. Though there is a '*Librarius*' mentioned in the cast list of John Mason's 1648 academic masque, *Princeps Rhetoricus*, in which 'Philologicall Books are fetcht forth from the *Trino-Musaeum*, the Triple Library', the word 'librarian' had not then entered the English language; when it did so around 1670, it meant a scribe.[34] Translating Gabriel Naudé's French *Instructions Concerning Erecting of a Library* in 1661, John Evelyn produced the first such work to be

[31] Edith Wharton and Ogden Codman Jr, *The Decoration of Houses* (New York: Charles Scribner's Sons, 1907), 145–54; Beatrice Webb, *My Apprenticeship* (Harmondsworth: Pelican, 1938), 75.

[32] Edith Wharton, *The House of Mirth* (1905; repr. London: Oxford University Press, 1952), 64; James Joyce, *A Portrait of the Artist as a Young Man* (1916; repr. London: Jonathan Cape, 1943), 245.

[33] Sean O'Brien, *The Beautiful Librarians* (London: Picador, 2015), 28.

[34] John Mason, *Princeps Rhetoricus* (London: H. R. [et al.], 1648), 5, 18.

published in English; festooned with quotations from Latin poets including Claudian, Horace, and Virgil, and rejoicing in several lists, this technical work deploys not the word 'librarian' but the older terms 'Library-Keeper', '*Bibliothecary*', and, more grandly still, Evelyn mentions in an appendix the Bodleian Library's 'Proto-Bibliothecary'.[35] Tobias Smollett, in his *History and Adventures of an Atom* (1769), seems to be the first English-language novelist to use the word librarian in fiction, and librarians can be glimpsed in William Godwin's *Caleb Williams* (1794), Mary Robinson's *Walsingham* (1797), Scott's *Guy Mannering*, the American Francis Parkman's forgotten novel *Vassal Morton* (1856), and Dickens's *Bleak House*—but, mostly, they are fleeting presences. Though subsequent chapters of the present book do note some further references to librarians in pre-twentieth-century creative writing, and, though Anthony Trollope on a visit to Boston Public Library noted in 1862 that novels were 'by no means eschewed' and that 'the librarianesses looked very pretty and learned, and, if I remember aright, mostly wore spectacles; the head librarian was enthusiastic', Trollope (who mentions ironically in chapter 23 of his novel *Can You Forgive Her?* the 'great librarian' Charles Edward Mudie, founder in 1842 of a famous Victorian lending library) was unusual as a mid-Victorian creative writer who paid attention to library staff in his work.[36] By the 1890s, however, the situation was altering, and the twenty-first-century scholar Chris Baggs has looked in detail at how George Gissing, who, like Trollope before him, had been impressed by Boston Public Library and by Mudie (inveighed against in Gissing's novel *New Grub Street*), examines both libraries and librarians with a fiction writer's sharp eye.[37]

If literary and critical attention had been given to writers, to readers, and to libraries, then it was principally in poetry and fiction from around 1900 onwards—and especially in much middle-brow fiction—that librarians became a focus of attention. Instances of the gendered librarian stereotype abound: the profession's persistent and sexist 'meme', that of the fierce, spinsterly shusher of the shelves is tellingly familiar. Librarian Signorina Paglietta in Primo Levi's *The Periodic Table* (1985), for example, is 'small without breasts or hips, waxen, wilted, and monstrously myopic: she wore glasses so thick and concave that, looking at her head-on, her eyes light blue, almost white, seemed very far away, stuck at the back of her cranium.' And there are male librarians who fare little better—the miserable Mr Anstey in Philip Larkin's *A Girl in Winter* (1947) is 'a thin, wizened man' who 'resembled a clerk at a railway station who had suffered from

[35] Gabriel Naudé, *Instructions Concerning Erecting of a Library*, trans. John Evelyn (London: G. Bedle, T. Collins, and J. Crook, 1661), 3, 83, 95.

[36] Anthony Trollope, *North America* (2 vols; London: Chapman & Hall, 1862), I, 360.

[37] Chris Baggs, 'The Public Library in Fiction: George Gissing's *Spellbound*', *Library History* 20.2 (July 2004): 137–46.

shellshock'.[38] Fortunately, however, there are even greater numbers of librarians in literature who defy the stereotype and prove themselves not wizened, wilted, or wasted. For a start there are some who are not even human. Famously, Terry Pratchett's Discworld Librarian of the Unseen University is an orangutan; Jasper Fforde's librarian in his *Thursday Next* series is a Cheshire cat; Harry Harrison's Filer 13B-445-K is a robot; and George MacDonald's librarian Mr Raven in *Lilith* (1895) is a shape-shifting ghost.

Amongst human fictional librarians, however, there are plenty who are reassuringly full-blooded and life-affirming. The present book is titled *Libraries in Literature*, not *Librarians in Literature*. But it does contain one chapter whose focus is on librarians in modern fiction, and it is certainly a volume that hopes to find librarians among its readers, so perhaps the editors may be excused for presenting in the next couple of pages of this Introduction not a library catalogue but a librarian catalogue, which may serve both to whet the appetite for further work in this area and to salute those library workers whom some writers too readily patronize or overlook. Here then, just before we set forth the design of our book, is a kind of honour guard of fictional librarians, a resounding blazon of imagined curators of books.

Their totemic representative might be the beautiful Miss Hopkins in John Fante's *The Road to Los Angeles* (1985), whom the young writer Arturo Bandini ogles in the library as she 'float[s] on white legs in the folds of her loose dresses in an atmosphere of books and cool thoughts'; or the virginal Ianthe Broome, distracted from her library index cards to be courted suddenly and simultaneously by two suitors in Barbara Pym's *An Unsuitable Attachment* (1982); or the less virginal Joy Simpson, British Council librarian in Istanbul, enjoying some energetic *wagon-lit* interludes with Philip Swallow in David Lodge's *Small World* (1991); or the lascivious Brian Herrick, Swift scholar and keeper of Marsh's Library in Dublin, who orchestrates and films elaborate sexual charades at his home in Bartholomew Gill's *The Death of an Ardent Bibliophile* (1995); or the young librarian Eleanor Lealand in George Garrett's *The King of Babylon Shall Not Come Against You* (1996), whom her reporter boyfriend describes quite simply as 'wonderful in bed. Just what the doctor ordered.'[39] If anyone remains unconvinced, a quick look at novelist Sarah Title's *Librarians in Love* series should be enough to clinch the matter. There are indeed *plenty* of sexy librarians in literature.

More light-heartedly, if some of the most celebrated Golden Age crime fiction foregrounds the body in the library and the bibliophile aristocrat Lord Peter

---

[38] Philip Larkin, *A Girl in Winter* (London: Faber & Faber, 1947), 16.
[39] John Fante, *The Road to Los Angeles* (Santa Barbara: Black Sparrow, 1985), 47; George Garrett, *The King of Babylon Shall Not Come Against You* (New York: Harcourt, Brace, 1996), quoted in Grant Burns, *Librarians in Fiction: A Critical Bibliography* (Jefferson, NC: McFarland & Co., 1998), 50.

Wimsey rather than any more workaday library staff, we cannot help noticing the veritable army of librarians in literature who pursue the liberating quests of detective work, sloughing off the pencil skirt and pussy-bow blouse of the librarian to don the Inverness cape and deerstalker hat of the librarian sleuth. It seems to be a truth universally acknowledged that anyone good at pernickety tasks like cataloguing and classification is instantly qualified to offer helpful suggestions to detectives cudgelling their brains in the local CID department or police forensics lab. From Jo Dereske's OCD-ish librarian Helma Zukas to Dr Edward George, retired Yale librarian in Charles Goodrum's *Dewey Decimated* (1977), *Carnage of the Realm* (1979), and *The Best Cellar* (1987), librarian sleuths have played no small part in modern fiction, helping, in their diverse ways, to run counter to the trajectory of Dag Solstad's librarian protagonist, T. Singer, who 'decided to say goodbye to the intoxicating days of his youth and become a librarian instead'.[40]

Defying the stereotype, though in a more alarming way, are the many librarians in literature who Go To The Bad. For every librarian who investigates a murder there seems to be another who is him- or herself a murderer. Librarian Anna Welles beats her lover to death with a clarinet in Elsa Lewin's *I, Anna* (1984); London reference librarian Everett Armidy takes a hatchet to his girlfriend's mother in Ernest Raymond's *A Chorus Ending* (1951); and librarian Alice Barton adds the bones of an unpopular benefactor to her museum's bone collection in Ruth Wallis's *Too Many Bones* (1943). If the sinister Malachi of Hildesheim in Umberto Eco's *The Name of the Rose* (1980) is not the mastermind behind the poisoned book plot which claims the lives of seven people in seven days, nevertheless he is up to his neck in the book's general skulduggery.

Whereas the idea of the body in the library had already captured the imagination of crime writers before Agatha Christie gave it classic formulation, a disconcerting variation on the trope occurs when the body in the library happens to be that of the librarian. Modern fictional librarians have been crushed to death beneath collapsed bookshelves, hit on the head by books, strangled at their desks beside piled-up copies of *Publishers Weekly*; they have been discovered fallen from their library windows or down flights of library stairs, stretched out naked and maggot-blown on library tables, floating dead in the Thames, kidnapped by psychopathic bank robbers, shot between the eyes, stabbed to death in their garages while clutching rare and valuable books, and, in a particularly choice example, bludgeoned to death with a bust of Louisa May Alcott.[41]

---

[40] Dag Solstad, *T. Singer*, trans. Tiina Nunnally (New York: New Directions, 2018), 32.
[41] In, respectively: Hazel Holt, *The Cruellest Month* (1991); Jill Paton Walsh, *The Wyndham Case* (1994); Charles Dutton, *Murder in a Library* (1931); Lavinia Davis, *Reference to Death* (1950); Elizabeth Lemarchand, *Step in the Dark* (1977); Bartholomew Gill, *The Death of an Ardent Bibliophile* (1995); Andrew Garve, *The Galloway Case* (1958); Doris Bett, *Heading West* (1995); Richard and Frances Lockridge, *The Distant Clue* (1963); Will Harriss, *The Bay Psalm Book Murder* (1983); and Jane Langton, *The Transcendental Murder* (1964).

No single book—not even *Libraries in Literature*—can tabulate and incorporate, let alone discuss, all such occurrences of libraries and their inhabitants in literary texts, and (though we hope the preceding roll call has whetted the appetite) it would be folly to attempt to do so in the chapters that follow. The topic of libraries and librarians in film, essayed by Laura Marcus elsewhere, is, likewise, one for several separate volumes.[42] Anglophone readers intent on further sleuthing may be guided by the compendious 1998 critical bibliography of *Librarians in Fiction* compiled by scholar-librarian Grant Burns.[43] It is possible, too, to find individual chapters and articles that examine specialist areas of the subject of literary libraries, from Marina Warner's treatment of ancient Persian library culture as it relates to the Epic of Gilgamesh to Robert Crawford's account of libraries in (principally pre-twentieth-century) poetry and from Mary P. Freier's study of 'The Librarian in Rowling's Harry Potter Series' to Margaret-Anne Hutton's post-Derridean examination of the representation of physical and electronic libraries in several contemporary novels.[44] The purpose of the present book is not to duplicate what is already available elsewhere, but rather to offer resonant, fresh examinations of significant texts which present libraries in literature, and to provide for the first time a book-length, necessarily selective overview of the subject that takes in poetry as well as prose, and that recognizes how the topic, while clearly significant from the Renaissance onwards, has expanded impressively in more recent times.

Libraries in Literature, then, opens with chapters that consider work from the early modern period, paying particular attention to creative writers' presentations of the library which have continued to resonate in the modern era. While libraries figure in a surprising range of earlier texts, it is undoubtedly in the nineteenth and twentieth centuries that depictions of them are most frequent. The proportions of this book reflect that. Alert to late medieval and Renaissance literature and its lasting legacies, Chapter 1 establishes Rabelais and Cervantes as among the most influential of all the creative writers who bring their imaginations to bear on the topic of the library. Chapter 2 demonstrates how, often in a subtle fashion, libraries have featured in several centuries of English-language drama from the late sixteenth century onwards. Tom Jones in Chapter 3 looks principally at Swift and the library as a sometimes dramatic battle-site of books, but draws attention, also, to the very different character of the eighteenth-century *Spectator*'s Ladies Library.

---

[42] Laura Marcus, 'The Library in Film: Order and Mystery', in Alice Crawford, ed., *The Meaning of the Library*, 199–219.

[43] Grant Burns, *Librarians in Fiction: A Critical Bibliography* (Jefferson, NC: McFarland & Co., 1998).

[44] Marina Warner, 'The Library in Fiction', and Robert Crawford, 'The Library in Poetry', in Alice Crawford, ed., *The Meaning of the Library*, 153–75 and 176–98; Mary P. Freier, 'The Librarian in Rowling's Harry Potter Series', *CLCWeb: Comparative Literature and Culture* 16.3 (2014): 1–9; Margaret-Anne Hutton, 'Shelving Books?: Representations of the Library in Contemporary Texts', *Comparative Critical Studies* 14.1 (2017): 7–27.

Attending further to the gendering of literary attitudes towards libraries, to libraries as sociable spaces, and to ongoing book battles, Fiona Stafford considers, in Chapter 4, ways in which the library functions in the fiction of Jane Austen. She then examines aspects of George Crabbe's substantial poem *The Library* and the less familiar eighteenth-century poem *The Country Book-Club* by Charles Shillito. Stafford's specific focus on these three late eighteenth- and early nineteenth-century verse and prose writers is counterpointed by Louise McCray's rather different selection of late eighteenth- and nineteenth-century portrayals of libraries in prose fiction. Offering a panoptic awareness of nineteenth-century intellectual reading culture, McCray concentrates in Chapter 5 on fictional libraries in the context of identity formation; her chapter includes re-examinations of work by William Godwin, Walter Scott, George Eliot, and, in the late Victorian era, Mary Augusta Ward.

While they are cognisant of ongoing arguments over exclusivity, access, and gender in relation to libraries, the late Victorian and Edwardian periods are notable in particular for their library ghost stories. Several of the finest of these are examined by Elisabeth Jay and Darryl Jones in Chapters 6 and 7. Where Jay deals expertly with the less well-known but fascinating tale of 'The Library Window' by Margaret Oliphant, Jones offers fresh insight into the role of the library in the haunted, haunting stories of M. R. James, who brings a new frisson to the established trope of the library as a cemetery of books. Though it may seem very different to that of James, Oliphant's attitude to the aspiring female intellectual in some ways prefigures the pointed treatment of the politics of gender in the library crime fiction of Agatha Christie and Dorothy Sayers, discussed by Nicola Humble in Chapter 8. Humble's brief discussion of Sayers's attitude towards the figure of the librarian in *Gaudy Night* precedes Alice Crawford's overview of librarians in modern fiction throughout the twentieth century in Chapter 9; again, gender (often inflected by issues of social class) is a significant presence in this chapter, which includes consideration of the subtle and perhaps surprisingly sympathetic account of a young female librarian by Philip Larkin, and culminates in looking at aspects of A. S. Byatt's best-known novel, *Possession*, and at contemporary crime fiction.

The business of being a librarian and considerations of gender are also to the fore in Chapter 10 where Kristen Treen surveys libraries in American literature, beginning with Benjamin Franklin's sense of the importance of accessible book collections as democratic resources, and going on to examine libraries' sometimes disruptive potential for later writers from Ralph Waldo Emerson to Richard Wright.

Though much of the focus of *Libraries in Literature* is on fiction, Robyn Marsack in Chapter 11 surveys the persistent, nuanced sense of 'modified rapture' in poems dealing with libraries and librarians over the last century or so. Beginning in nineteenth-century America, Marsack's chapter ranges widely across modern anglophone verse. While some poets, including T. S. Eliot (after whom a wing of the London Library is named), have championed libraries in their non-fictional prose, Marsack's focus is on those who have taken libraries into the heart of their imaginative work. Issues of gender, class, and race, present in several of the preceding chapters considering fiction, are returned to by Marsack, who notes with a certain wry amusement the English poet and librarian Philip Larkin's stubborn determination not to engage with the work of the world's most cele-brated modern writer-librarian, Argentina's Jorge Luis Borges.

Borges's literary preoccupation with libraries is not only the subject of Edwin Williamson's shrewd examination in Chapter 12 but also an influential presence in the two chapters that follow. Kylie Murray in Chapter 13 looks in detail at the celebrated portrayal of library and scriptorium in Umberto Eco's *The Name of the Rose*, that sophisticated crime novel which pays explicit tribute to Borges, while Chris Perkins in Chapter 14 highlights how Borges's international reception helped condition the widely read Japanese novella *The Strange Library* by Haruki Murakami.

It would have been possible to return at the end of *Libraries in Literature* to the Swiftian theme of libraries and martial combat by considering the visceral wartime horrors of Antonio Iturbe's 2012 fact-based fiction *The Librarian of Auschwitz*. But, while maintaining an awareness that in literature as in life the history of libraries can be, as Matthew Battles puts it, 'unquiet', the volume returns instead, in Chapter 15, to the idea that the reimagining of the library can be linked to disruptive forces in terms of the redefinition of gender.[45] Sara Lodge's consider-ation of libraries in fairy tale and fantasy opens with E. Nesbit at the beginning of the twentieth century, but devotes most of its attention to much more recent fiction. And it is with twenty-first-century fiction that the book concludes. In a final coda which discusses Sophie Divry's *The Library of Unrequited Love*, Mikhail Elizarov's *The Librarian*, and Salley Vickers's *The Librarian*, we see that no one-size-fits-all notion of the library will accommodate the treatment of the topic in the contemporary novel. Translator Siân Reynolds highlights the French novelist Divry's preoccupation with ideas of ordering, gender, incarceration, and bookish conflicts; Elizarov's story takes us to a violent post-Soviet dystopia in which warring gangs known as 'libraries' fight to the death over talismanic texts; and Vickers's confusing English tale lures us into the realm of 1950s faux idealism to suggest that libraries can be catalysts for social reform, the books powerful drivers of change. Each of these three remarkably different recent novels seems to articulate through the imaging of libraries deep truths about its particular society, demonstrating that the library in literature can still function in the twenty-first century as a resonant symbol of irreducible cultural complexity.

---

[45] Matthew Battles, *Library: An Unquiet History* (London: Heinemann, 2003).

1

Rabelais, Cervantes, and Libraries in Fiction

Robert Crawford

Rabelais and Cervantes established the most abiding images of libraries in fiction. This chapter examines how they did so, and how, shaped and reshaped, their versions of the library have continued to resonate in the works of novelists over succeeding centuries. Later chapters of the present volume will focus on shorter chronological periods and, usually, on fewer texts. What this opening chapter offers is a 'through line' that runs from the mid-sixteenth century until recent times. It shows how two foundational imaginative visions of the library—that of Rabelais which subverts order and decorum through verbal extravagance and ludic disruption, and that of Cervantes which shows the library as coming to overwhelm its owner's mind—establish themselves and stimulate successive fiction-makers' imaginations.

Translating the Roman philosopher Boethius's *De Consolatione Philosophiae*, Chaucer has the character of Philosophy tell the writer that she is seeking not 'the walles of thi lybrarye apparayled and wrowt with yvory and with glas' but, instead, the fundamentals of the writer's mind.[1] Though this quotation is still regarded as the earliest use of the word 'library' by an English-language writer, Chaucer says little about libraries in his imaginative work. The narrator of his 'Legend of Good Women', who is often taken to represent the poet, characterizes his own library as 'sixty bokes olde and newe', which is considerably more than the single shelf of volumes at the bedhead of the scholar in Chaucer's 'Miller's Tale', but hardly sounds like the contents of a grand 'lybrarye apparayled and wrowt with yvory and with glas'.[2] Though modern readers can turn to the *Philobiblon [Book Lover]* of the fourteenth-century Richard de Bury, Bishop of Durham, to find a Latin work that praises books, sets forth rules of what we now call 'library science', and praises 'the library of wisdom' ('sapientiae libraria'), it is from mid-sixteenth-century subversive French prose rather than from solemn English praise that the library enters early modern fiction; then, not long afterwards, at the start of the

---

[1] *OED*, 'library'.
[2] *The Riverside Chaucer*, 3rd ed., ed. L. D. Benson, (Oxford: Oxford University Press, 1987), 597.

seventeenth century, the sophisticated Spanish prose of Cervantes makes classic the library not as a place of wisdom and love of books but as a site of madness and destruction.[3]

The subversive turn of these overflowing libraries that, more than any other imagined book hoards, establish libraries as a recurring presence in English fiction is not so surprising if we bear in mind that imaginative writers are not just lovers of books, learning, and libraries but also people who see these as material for entertainment. Richard de Bury, Bishop of Durham, represented a reverential attitude towards the library. In France the pioneering sixteenth-century essayist Michel de Montaigne (whose work was soon translated into English by John Florio) offered in book 3, chapter 3 of his *Essais* a brief account of his circular domestic library with its five tiers of shelves 'in the third storey of a tower' as a place of quiet solitude, studious 'pleasure', and extended contemplation.[4] Montaigne would influence the polymathic English essayist Francis Bacon, who described libraries in *The Advancement of Learning* as 'the shrines where all the relics of the ancient saints, full of true virtue, and that without delusion or imposture, are preserved and reposed'.[5] Yet the much more uproarious sixteenth-century French Benedictine François Rabelais, whose work both Montaigne and Bacon enjoyed, had already expressed a very different pronounced irreverence towards the 'sapientiae libraria'. In his expansive narrative of two giants, *Gargantua and Pantagruel* (published over several decades from the 1530s to the 1560s), Rabelais generated much comedy in which scale—gigantism—is crucial: his gargantuan Gargantua eats a lettuce salad so huge that it contains six pilgrims, and plays around 200 card games and board games, all of which Rabelais lists. Rabelais also used *Gargantua and Pantagruel* to mock systems of education; Gargantua's first schoolmaster, the 'sophister' Thubal Holoferne, is an absurd pedant whose name surely gives rise to that of the orotund rhetorician Holofernes in Shakespeare's *Love's Labour's Lost*. Holoferne shapes Gargantua's reading, and Rabelais enumerates some of the learned commentaries which Gargantua is encouraged to pore over. Later, in a work which delights repeatedly in comically excessive lists, Rabelais mocks, too, a Limousin scholar who bamboozles Pantagruel with his jargon, before, in the ongoing course of his education, Pantagruel proceeds to Paris and 'the library of *St Victor*, a very stately and magnifick one', whose extended 'Repertory and Catalogue' Rabelais presents to the reader with considerable relish.[6]

---

[3] *The Philobiblon of Richard de Bury*, ed. Andrew Fleming West, 3 vols (New York: Grolier Club, 1889), I, 16.

[4] Montaigne, *Essays*, trans. J. M. Cohen (Harmondsworth: Penguin, 1971), 262.

[5] Francis Bacon, *Essays or Counsels Civil and Moral, with Other Writings* (London: George Newnes, 1902), 282 ('Of the Proficience and Advancement of Learning', Book II).

[6] *The First Book of the Works of Mr Francis Rabelais, Doctor in Physick, containing Five Books of the Lives, Heroick Deeds, and Sayings of Gargantua, and his Sonne Pantagruel . . . faithfully translated into English* [by Thomas Urquhart] (London: Richard Baddeley, 1653), 36.

Situating it in an actual library building, Rabelais details for the first time in literature a fictional book collection. In the first (1532) edition of his work, this lover of lists presented a library catalogue of forty-three titles. By 1537, with evident gusto, he had extended this list to almost 140, and even added such occasional librarianly touches as volume numbers and details of bindings. Sir Thomas Urquhart, the verbally flamboyant Scottish polymath who would publish the classic English translation of Rabelais in 1653, nearly matched the French original in his own love of language, libraries, and lists. Urquhart's 1652 *Ekskubalauron*, after listing 153 ancestral Urquhart chiefs (and 142 'mothers of the chiefs'), goes on to celebrate books, authors, and book learning in various forms, including that of a 'Scottish man named Cameron', who

> was commonly designed, because of his universal reading, by the title of 'The Walking Library'; by which, he being no less known then by his own name, he therefore took occasion to set forth an excellent book in Latine, and that in folio, intituled *Bibliotheca Movens*, which afterwards was translated into the English language.[7]

Though Cameron 'the walking library' and Urquhart would both feature in the late twentieth-century work of the novelist Alasdair Gray, no one has ever found a copy of the *Bibliotheca Movens*.[8] Urquhart, who was probably working on his Rabelais translation while writing his *Ekskubalauron*, may well have made it up. Yet his idea of a 'walking library' has some classical precedents, while modern digital searching reveals that the phrase is found in over forty seventeenth-century English-language books; Urquhart's attraction to the title and concept of this perhaps fictitious *Bibliotheca Movens* hints at just why he was the ideal translator of the work of the inventor of a great fictional library.[9]

By the time Urquhart's Rabelais translation was published in 1653, the inventory of the library of St Victor's imagined stock had gone beyond 140, beginning with:

The for Godsake of salvation.
The Codpiece of the Law.
The Slipshoe of the Decretals.
The Pomegranate of vice.
The Clew-bottom of Theologie.
The Duster or foxtail-flap of Preachers, Composed by *Turlupin*.
The churning Ballock of the Valiant...

---

[7] Sir Thomas Urquhart of Cromarty, *The Jewel*, ed. R. D. S. Jack and R. J. Lyall (Edinburgh: Scottish Academic Press, 1983), 56, 155.

[8] Alasdair Gray, *Unlikely Stories, Mostly* (Edinburgh: Canongate, 1983), 150.

[9] On classical precedents see Yun Lee Too, *The Idea of the Library in the Ancient World* (Oxford: Oxford University Press, 2010), ch. 3, 'The Breathing Library: Performing Cultural Memories'.

At the end of his long list, Rabelais (as translated by Urquhart) added the words, 'Of which Library some books are already printed, and the rest are now at the Presse, in this noble City of *Tubinge* [Tübingen].'[10] That last sentence makes it absolutely clear to the reader that at least some of the books in this library do not exist beyond the catalogue.

Pointing out that the twelfth-century Hugh of Saint-Victor 'is credited with establishing key groundwork for medieval and even modern library classification', the twenty-first-century scholar Brett Bodemer shows how in certain instances Rabelais has altered the titles of actual books. So, for instance, Rabelais morphs the Latin *Ars praedicandi* ['The Art of Praying'], title of a volume in the surviving 1514 catalogue of the library of the Abbey of Saint-Victor, to *Ars pettandi* ['The Art of Farting']. Most of the time, though, the author of *Gargantua and Pantagruel* just makes up his books, jumbling them in a no-order subversion of structure, and making sure to include no less than thirty titles that have to do with shitting or syphilis and over twenty pertaining to food. Their titles containing words such as 'codpiece', 'bottom', and 'ballock', these volumes are self-evidently scandalous; in one sense they are like the grotesques often found carved in medieval cathedrals, but their note of base, materialist scandal in the context of a sacred library brings its own frisson; centuries later the idea of the medieval ecclesiastical library as the location of a scandalous book would fascinate Umberto Eco, who included Rabelais in his own *Vertigine della Lista* (2009), but for readers of *Gargantua and Pantagruel* it is the gargantuan extensiveness of the catalogue that may be most striking. While many of the entries may be related in their subversive tone, they are all the more arresting for their uproarious jumbled-up-ness. As Bodemer puts it, such Rabelaisian humour 'scorns the paradigm of the medieval library catalog by denying any coherence to a form whose whole point is structural coherence'.[11] With lasting consequences for later fiction, Rabelais carnivalizes the library.

In several forms, this presentation of a library of invented books appealed to English-language writers. Though Anne Lake Prescott points out that it is often hard to know how far Renaissance English writers read Rabelais in detail, she finds an early allusion to his nonsensical library in a 1593 text by Gabriel Harvey, and points out that Laurence Whitaker's 1611 mention of nonsensical titles in 'la Librairie de l'Abbaye St. Victor' is a clear reference to 'Europe's first imaginary library'. Whitaker's text dates from around the time that John Donne, whose 'most likely model' was Rabelais, completed his *Catalogus librorum aulicorum incomparabilium et non vendibilium* ['Catalogue of incomparable courtly books that are

---

[10] *The First Book of the Works of Mr Francis Rabelais*, trans. Urquhart, 36, 49.
[11] Brett Bodemer, 'Rabelais and the Abbey of Saint-Victor Revisited', *Information & Culture* 47.1 (2012): 8, 5, 12–13.

not for sale'].[12] As is clear in a recently rediscovered manuscript of this text, which may date from 1604, Donne differs from Rabelais in that he numbers each title in his library catalogue, so that it seems they have what modern librarians term 'call numbers'. Yet, even if attributed to real authors, Donne's invented book titles in this mock library catalogue can be distinctly Rabelaisian: to the Italian polymath Hieronymus Cardanus Donne attributes book number 10 in his catalogue, *De nullubietate crepitus* ['On the nowhere-ness of farting'], while Donne's fellow poet and courtier the polymath Sir John Harington (a Rabelais enthusiast whose actual writings included proposals for the earliest flush toilet) is credited in Donne's *Catalogus librorum* with a book (number 23) that explains how Noah's Ark was kept free from inordinate amounts of faeces.[13]

Such jokes found a ready audience among the learned, and several manuscript copies of what Donne calls in a letter his *Catalogus librorum satyricus* (and is sometimes termed in English 'The Courtier's Library') seem to have circulated long before the work found its way into print in 1650.[14] Even the learned King James VI and I was assumed to have a taste for what Francis Bacon, addressing his monarch in a 1623 Latin text, terms a volume found 'inter libros famosissimae illius bibliothecae Sancti Victoris; quorum catalogum excepit magister Franciscus Rabelesius'—words which were 'interpreted' into English by Gilbert Watts in 1640 as meaning 'amongst the Books of that famous Library of *S. Victor*, a Catalogue whereof *M. Fra. Rabelais* hath collected'.[15] Rabelais's fictional library of crazy books was establishing itself as a *locus classicus*, a trope of the library in imaginative literature; it has never lost that status.

Nor has it ceased to provide a model for other writers' imaginings and reaminginings of their fictional libraries. In the seventeenth century these included the little-discussed 'Bibliotheca Fanatica' which purports to catalogue the library of the 'Colledge of Bedlam' and includes such Rabelaisian gems as 'The Art of Pimping' as well as 'Fistula in Ano, and the Ulcer of the Rump'.[16] Better known is the work of Sir Thomas Browne, who had invoked Rabelais and 'Pantagruel's Library' in his *Religio Medici*, relishing in particular one of its spoof book titles, 'Tartaretus *De modo Cacandi* [*On how to Shit*]'.[17] Browne's *Musaeum Clausum, or Bibliotheca Abscondita* presents 'his own fantasy library', as Anne Lake Prescott

---

[12] Anne Lake Prescott, *Imagining Rabelais in Renaissance England* (New Haven: Yale University Press, 1998), 72, 168, 173.

[13] These titles and their numbers are taken from the diplomatic Latin text published in Daniel Starza Smith, Matthew Payne, Melanie Marshall, 'Rediscovering John Donne's *Catalogus librorum satyricus*', *Review of English Studies*, 69.290 (June 2018): 479, 481.

[14] For a fuller account, see the article cited in the previous note.

[15] Francis Bacon, *De dignitate et augmentis scientiarum* (1623; repr. Turnhout: Brepols Library of Latin Texts—Series B, 2010), Liber VI, 650; Gilbert Watts, trans., *Of the Advancement and Proficience of Learning... by... Francis Bacon* (Oxford: Robert Young and Edward Forrest, 1640), 257.

[16] *Bibliotheca Fanatica; or, The Phanatique Library* (n.p., 1660), 5.

[17] [Thomas Browne,] *Religio Medici*, 8th ed. (London: R. Scot et al., 1682), 52.

terms it.[18] Like Donne, Browne numbers his catalogue entries, but, while they are clearly the imaginings of a lover of libraries, these entries are markedly less Rabelaisian in tone:

> 19. *Duo Casaris Anti-Catones*, or the two notable Books writ by *Julius Caesar* against *Cato*; mentioned by *Livy, Salustius* and *Juvenal; which the* Cardinal of *Liege* told *Ludovicus Vives* were in an old Library of that City.
>   *Mazhapha Einok*, or, the Prophecy of *Enoch*, which *Ægidius Lochiensis*, a learned Eastern Traveller, told *Peireschius* that he had found in an old Library at *Alexandria* containing eight thousand volumes.[19]

This *Bibliotheca Abscondita* [hidden library] is a fictional library of lost books, part of a larger museum that is, as Claire Preston points out, 'a forlorn compendium of regret'.[20] While Browne was aware of Rabelais's subversive excess, he imagines the library instead as a reclusive place of scholarly melancholy, a meditative space that can seem to share some aspects with Montaigne's solitary bookroom. Montaigne, who emphasizes the importance of walking about in his library, had regarded his bookish refuge as a place of isolated pleasure, but also as a site menaced by temptations of excessive and harmful inactivity.

Clouded with its own sadness, Browne's vision of the library might be set beside that of Richard Burton, whose *Anatomy of Melancholy* (first published in 1621, then subsequently expanded) argues that 'all the world is melancholy, or mad', even if Rabelais might be the appropriate 'physician'; and which, in the context of an extended, list-strewn account of 'great Libraries' and of King James's 1605 visit to Oxford's 'famous Library, renewed by Sir Thomas Bodley', recounts that monarch's statement that if he had to 'be a prisoner', then he 'would desire to have no other prison than that Library, and to be chained together with so many good Authors and dead Masters'. Burton then follows up with a passage exalting and defending 'Libraries & Books'. Yet, overall, he presents these under the aegis of melancholy, and even madness: he loves bookishness, but cautions against 'overmuch study', lest a man 'overstretch his wits, and make a skeleton of himself'. Where Montaigne in his library had registered the risks of sedentary inactivity, Burton obsesses over such dangers. And he warns not least against those fiction lovers who 'read nothing but Play-books, idle Poems, Jests, Amadis de Gaul, the Knight of the Sun, the Seven Champions, Palmerin de Oliva, Huon of Bordeaux, &c. Such many times prove in the end as mad as Don Quixote.'[21]

[18] Prescott, *Imagining Rabelais*, 178.

[19] Thomas Browne[e], *Certain Miscellany Tracts* (London: Charles Mearne, 1684), 199–200.

[20] Claire Preston, 'Punctual Relations: Thomas Browne's Rhetorical Reclamations', *Studies in Philology* 115.3 (Summer 2018): 602.

[21] Robert Burton, *The Anatomy of Melancholy*, ed. Floyd Dell and Paul Jordan-Smith (New York: Tudor, 1955), 101, 455, 457, 458, 459.

Mention of Don Quixote summons up the other fictional library that, along with Rabelais's inventions, does most to shape depictions of libraries in English fiction. Don Quixote, a compulsive reader of romances driven mad by his own library (which, very unusually among Spanish Renaissance libraries, seems to contain almost nothing but such alluring fictions), was familiar to English readers from early in the seventeenth century.[22] In his 'Execration upon Vulcan', a substantial, sophisticated and eloquent poem that catalogues many books in iambic pentametric rhyming couplets as it inveighs against the Roman god of fire after the burning down of his personal library in 1623, Ben Jonson writes that his 'serious follies' might have led him to deserve such a punishment if he had 'begot' a book 'compiled from Amadis de Gaul, / The Esplandians, Arthurs, Palmerins, and all / The learned library of Don Quixote'.[23]

Jonson had done no such thing, but his familiarity with Don Quixote was shared with that of other English readers, whether or not they knew Spanish. Cervantes's narrative had been translated into English over a decade earlier by Thomas Shelton: 'the world's first translation of Don Quixote'.[24] Cervantes's 1605 Spanish masterpiece (a copy of which had entered the Bodleian Library in the year of its first publication) appealed to an audience in England where since the late 1570s 'English versions of Spanish chivalric books'—including some of the romances that lined the shelves of Don Quixote's library—had become 'quite prominent'.[25] From early on, then, the image of Don Quixote as a man not only shaped but actually driven mad by the books in his library established itself as the commonplace that it clearly was by the time of Burton's Anatomy of Melancholy.

Cervantes's presentation of his protagonist as exemplifying strains and contradictions between the bookish contemplative and the man of action clearly appealed, like Hamlet, to Renaissance imaginations which liked to ponder such issues. In his 1595 Defence of Poesie Sir Philip Sidney had told how, when barbaric Goths were ransacking a city, they had 'taken a faire Librarie', and

one hangman belike fit to execute the frutes of their wits, who had murthered a great number of books, woulde have set fire in it. No said an other verie grauely, take heed what you do, for while they are busie about those toyes, wee shall with more leisure conquere their Countries.[26]

---

[22] On the unusual nature of Don Quixote's library see Edward Baker, 'Breaking the Frame: Don Quixote's Entertaining Books', *Cervantes: Bulletin of the Cervantes Society of America* 16.1 (1996): 12–31.

[23] Ben Jonson, *Poems*, ed. Ian Donaldson (London: Oxford University Press, 1975), 194.

[24] Sandra Forbes Gerhard, *'Don Quixote' and the Shelton Translation* (Madrid: Studia Humanitatis, 1982), 1.

[25] Leticia Alvarez-Recio, 'Translations of Spanish Chivalry Works in the Jacobean Book Trade: Shelton's *Don Quixote* in the Light of Anthony Munday's Publications', *Renaissance Studies* 33.5 (2018): 692.

[26] Philip Sidney, *The Defence of Poesie* (London: William Ponsonby, 1595), n.p.

Enthralled by his own 'toyes'—the books of his library—Don Quixote makes a less than convincing conqueror as he sallies forth in antique armour. The burning of his volumes takes place in chapter 6 of Part I of *Don Quixote*, which is headed in the original Spanish 'Del donoso y grande escrutinio que el cura y el barbero hicieron en la librería de nuestro ingenioso hidalgo', and which Shelton translates as 'Of the pleasant and curious search made by the Curate and the Barber, of *Don Quixotes* Library'.[27] This chapter involves mild satire directed at the practices of the Spanish Inquisition and at such famous book burnings as that bonfire of the vanities instigated by the religious ascetic Savonarola in early Renaissance Florence. Yet it is not the Catholic Church in the person of the local curate who initiates the burning of Don Quixote's books; instead, it is his niece, and she does so hoping that it may cure his madness, or at least prevent others from succumbing to it. Inveighing against her uncle's binge-reading of 'those accursed books of Knighthood' which have addled his wits, she wants them 'recommended to *Sathan* and *Barrabas*', and she blames herself for not having spoken sooner to her uncle's friends the local barber and curate about Don Quixote's predicament so that they might have 'burnt all those excommunicated books; for hee had many that deserued the fire as much as if they were Hereticall'.[28]

The books that are burned are not actually heretical, then, but are treated as such. The instigator of the burning is not a priest but a concerned close relative who still has some hope that her uncle 'be cured of his Knightly disease'; the person who eventually burns Don Quixote's book hoard is another woman who knows him well, his housekeeper.[29] As the curate examines Don Quixote's library, it is clear that he too admires many of its volumes and has enjoyed their contents; the same is true of the barber. Both of these lovers of poetry and fiction start to select favourite books (including work by Cervantes himself) to hold back from the flames, but eventually they tire of being so selective and order all the rest to be burned. The housekeeper, however, simply burns the lot. Cervantes's treatment of Don Quixote's library is subtle and complex. As the contents of the book collection are examined and many titles supplied to the reader, there is an evident sense of imaginative connoisseurship and delight in these rather old-fashioned romances (none of which, modern scholarship points out, post-dates 1591), as well as a well-intentioned determination to burn them. Not since Rabelais's narrative of gigantism had a fiction included so many book titles and details of books. After the contents of his library are torched, and the library itself is walled up, Don Quixote is told by his niece that a great enchanter has done the deed. Later, in an attempt at a rationalizing afterthought that might explain his

[27] *The History of the Valorous and Wittie Knight-errant, Don-Quixote Of the Mancha* [trans. Thomas Shelton] (London: Edward Blount and W. Barret, 1612), 37.

[28] *The History of the Valorous and Wittie Knight-errant*, 34–5.

[29] *The History of the Valorous and Wittie Knight-errant*, 43.

celebrated riding into battle against windmills, Don Quixote tells his faithful, commonsensical, and illiterate servant Sancho Panza that this action was undertaken to revenge himself on the ogre 'who robbed my Studie and books', and that it was this same ogre who 'transformed these *Giants* into Mils'.[30]

So, at one point, the loss of his library is directly linked by the protagonist to the best-known moment in *Don Quixote*, the tilting at windmills; but the narrative makes it very apparent, too, that while Don Quixote's library no longer exists in terms of physical texts, the protagonist himself, who quotes from and alludes endlessly to the contents of his lost volumes (and whose quotations and allusions are often recognized by those he meets) is himself a *bibliotheca movens*, a living incarnation of his library. Though he had learned from earlier fictions including Mateo Alemán's long picaresque novel *Guzmán de Alfarache*, Cervantes moved beyond these in his making the protagonist the product of a lovingly assembled library. As much as it makes manifest the destruction of romances and works of fiction, *Don Quixote* celebrates them. An examination of the nature of fiction lies at the heart of the celebrated discussion of Don Quixote's books set forth by a Canon of Toledo, whom modern scholars sometimes regard as Cervantes's 'spokesman'.[31]

The great arc of the completed *Don Quixote* returns to the matter of the burning of 'all *Don-Quixotes* library' in the extended consideration of the status of fiction and romance that forms part of the novel's conclusion.[32] As is clear from his works—including his final romance, *The Travails of Persiles and Sigismunda*, as well as *Don Quixote*—Cervantes had a remarkably sophisticated understanding of fictional creation and a wish to celebrate and analyse as well as critique it. While the present chapter is not the place to present an extended consideration of the discussion of fiction that is part of *Don Quixote*'s conclusion and that forms 'Cervantes' most complete and profound statement of a theory of literature', it is wholly appropriate to emphasize that the way *Don Quixote* presents a protagonist shaped by reading, formed and possessed by his library, is fundamental not just to *Don Quixote* itself but also to the development of the novel as a form.[33]

Scholars including Ronald Paulson and J. A. G. Ardila have tracked Cervantes's influence on English fiction.[34] What matters most in the present context is that this Spanish writer establishes in the novel the foundational trope of the library as

---

[30] *The History of the Valorous and Wittie Knight-errant*, 53.

[31] Anthony J. Close, 'The Legacy of Don Quijote and the Picaresque Novel', in Harriet Turner and Adelaida López de Martínez, eds., *The Cambridge Companion to the Spanish Novel* (Cambridge: Cambridge University Press, 2003), 22.

[32] *The History of the Valorous and Wittie Knight-errant*, 552.

[33] Alban K. Forcione, *Cervantes, Aristotle, and the Persiles* (Princeton: Princeton University Press, 1970), 91.

[34] Ronald Paulson, *Don Quixote in England* (Baltimore: Johns Hopkins University Press, 1998); J. A. G. Ardila, ed., *The Cervantean Heritage: Reception and Influence of Cervantes in Britain* (Oxford: Legenda, 2009).

a structure that forms and controls intellectual development and human conduct. As an implied or actual presence in fiction, such a trope of the library will be revised and revisited from Cervantes's time to our own by fiction-makers as different as Walter Scott and Gustave Flaubert, George Eliot, G. K. Chesterton, and Jorge Luis Borges. Each of these authors, like many other novelists, has engaged directly and ambitiously with imagining the governing power of libraries.

Though the greatest and most influential early fictional libraries were those of Rabelais and Cervantes, other references in once-popular early modern European fictions make it clear that libraries were evident markers of prestige, whatever their cultural background or location. In the French writer Madeleine de Scudéry's first prose romance, *Ibrahim* (1641), readers encounter in a spacious gallery in the Turk Ibrahim's palace:

> vne Bibliotheque, de tous les liures curieux des langues Orientales, & de tous les rares & de tous les beaux, de la Greque, de la Latine, de l'Espagnole, & de l'Italienne. Mais comme le grand Visir, ioignoit tousiours la magnificence à la curiosité, tous ses liures estoient couuerts de lames d'or, esmaillées de blanc & de vert, & rangez sur des Tablettes d'Ebene, bordées d'vne dentelle d'orpheurerie, esmaillée des mesmes couleures.[35]

Just over a decade later, in his translation of de Scudéry's 'excellent new romance', Henry Cogan Englished this as:

> a Library of all the curious Books of the Orientall Languages, and of all the choicest and rarest in the Greek, Latin, Spanish, and Italian; but whereas the grand Visier did always joyn magnificence to curiosity, all his Books were bound up in plates of Gold, enamelled with white and green, and placed in order upon shelves of Ebony, which were bordered with a dentile of Goldsmiths-work, enamelled with the same colours.[36]

In both the original and in translation, de Scudéry's description continues with a detailing of the pictures, furniture, and curiosities within this library. An age with a taste for cabinets of curiosities relished such things, but increasingly fiction was asserting that a personal library was not only an ornamental asset but a prime resource. It was in female as well as male novelists' interest to encourage such attitudes, and, in *The Luckey Mistake*, the first of her fictions to call itself a 'novel', the pioneering English fiction writer, poet, and dramatist Aphra Behn did so,

---

[35] [Madeleine de Scudéry,] *Ibrahim, ou l'Illustre Bassa, Premiere partie* (Paris: Antoine de Sommaville, 1641), 421.

[36] [Madeleine de Scudéry,] *Ibrahim, or, The Illustrious Bassa, An Excellent New Romance*, trans. Henry Cogan (London: Humphrey Moseley et al., 1652), 53.

asserting that 'perfect Tranquillity of Life' was 'no where to be found, but in retreat, a faithful Friend and a good Library'.[37]

Yet libraries retained their potential for danger. Jonathan Swift, whose Dublin student career was interrupted by the events surrounding the 1690 Battle of the Boyne (in effect a sectarian civil war fought out in Ireland, and won by the forces of Britain's King William III, whose victory is the subject of Swift's earliest surviving poem), published in 1710 his 'Battel of the Books'. Where Cervantes had linked bookishness and battling, Swift, whose great library book battle is examined in detail in Chapter 3 of the present volume, populated the British monarch's Royal Library itself with armed troops, some of them mounted on horseback, and offered an account of their absurd but bloody contest. This stylized civil war among the shelves is fought out with amounts of wind, ordure, and a Rabelaisian gusto sensed elsewhere in Swift's *A Tale of a Tub*. Its author's engagement with the seventeenth-century French 'querelle des anciens et modernes' developed into the full-scale library book battle which came to form a preface to that work when it was published in 1704. At the very start of *A Tale of a Tub* Swift also winks towards the library cataloguer Rabelais by providing a catalogue of his own forthcoming books; these include *A modest Defence of the Proceedings of the* Rabble *in all Ages*, and, even better, *A general History of* Ears.[38]

Elsewhere, in *Gulliver's Travels*, Swift's comedy, like that of Rabelais, depends on exaggerations of scale but has a more modern scientific inflection and involves miniaturization as well as gigantism. Where Rabelais had mocked both academics and a library, *Gulliver's Travels* too mocks these: as well as parodying the real-world scientists of London's Royal Society, Swift's fictional Academy at Lagado draws on Rabelais's cogitating officers in Quintessence at the court of Queen Whim in *Gargantua and Pantagruel*, but in *Gulliver's Travels* the giant King's royal library of a thousand vast volumes in Brobdingnag also involves a Rabelaisian comedy of scale. The human Gulliver needs to climb a huge library ladder in order to read a single book:

> I first mounted to the upper step of the ladder, and, turning my face towards the book, began at the top of the page, and so walking to the right and left about eight or ten paces, according to the length of the lines, till I had gotten a little below the level of mine eyes, and then descending gradually until I came to the bottom. After which I mounted again, and began the other page in the same manner, and so turned over the leaf, which I could easily do with both

[37] Aphra Behn, *The Luckey Mistake* (London: R. Bentley, 1689), 1.
[38] Jonathan Swift, *Selected Prose and Poetry*, ed. Edward Rosenheim, Jr (New York: Holt, Rinehart & Winston, 1968), [8].

my hands, for it was as thick and stiff as a pasteboard, and in the largest folios not above eighteen or twenty feet long.[39]

Here, in a parody of library furniture and customs, the narrator has to climb a ladder not to access a high shelf but simply to get to the top line on a page; the book becomes a physical environment that this reader must walk across and climb through. Drawing on such familiar tropes as having one's head in a book, getting lost in a book, and turning over a new leaf, Swift's reimagined library offers texts that are at once monstrous and familiar in their order and requirements. In a parody of what we now term 'close reading', Gulliver is dwarfed by a library, and then, just as much as Don Quixote, risks being overwhelmed by his reading matter.

Gulliver peruses his giant book not in the King's library but in an affectionate giantess's chamber. Because of their power to shape and influence their readers' minds, libraries remained places of potential endangerment; yet now they were less likely to lead to potential madness of the Don Quixote sort than to the enchanting perils of love and infatuation. In the *Secret Memoirs* of Mary de la Rivière Manley's *The New Atlantis*, a randy Duke introduces an impressionable young woman, Charlot, to his 'noble Library in all Languages', which contains 'a Collection of the most valuable Authors, with a mixture of the most Amorous'. Soon she is seduced not only by the Duke but also by the books he has 'recommended to her'. This involves 'the most dangerous Books of Love, *Ovid, Petrarch, Tibullus*, those moving Tragedies that so powerfully expose the force of Love, and corrupt the Mind...Her Memory was prodigious, she was indefatigable in Reading.'[40]

Just as novelists depicted the library's seductive power, so other writers sought to investigate and regulate it. One investigation of a lady's library appeared in *The Spectator* magazine in 1711, itemizing a library which included novels as well as poetry and other texts. While this work will be discussed by Tom Jones in Chapter 3 of the present book, it is worth noting here that it also gave rise to a three-volume book of advice on good conduct, *The Ladies Library*, supposedly written by a lady and published by Richard Steele, which went through several successive editions. Eighteenth-century ladies needed defending by libraries from libraries. Part of the seduction technique of the rapacious master in Samuel Richardson's *Pamela* (1741) involves inviting the heroine to step into his library, though the heroine in Charlotte Lennox's 1751 *Life of Harriot Stuart* makes readers aware of the value of a library belonging to a noblewoman, rather than a rapacious nobleman. Lennox regendered Cervantes's protagonist in *The Female*

---

[39] Jonathan Swift, *Gulliver's Travels* (1726; repr. London: Oxford University Press, 1974), 162.
[40] Mary de la Rivière Manley, *Secret Memoirs and Manners of Several Persons of Quality* (London: John Morphew et al., 1709), 20, 21.

Quixote (1752), where a marquis's daughter, Arabella, is given early access to her father's 'library... in which, unfortunately for her, were great store of romances'. Soon Arabella is embroiled in a comical yet perilous relationship with her male cousin Glanville, which takes the form of an 'Adventure of the Books' (not least 'voluminous Romances' authored by de Scudéry) from 'her Library' and to a relationship presented 'in the Language of Romance'. Eventually, after entertaining several romantic delusions, the bookish heroine sees beyond the library's influence and marries Glanville, one of whose saving graces has been that from the start he was worried in case Arabella might make him read too many of those 'voluminous Romances'.[41]

While Henry Fielding expressed indebtedness to Cervantes, and Tobias Smollett (whose Miss Williams in *Roderick Random* grows similarly addicted to romances) admired Rabelais and translated *Don Quixote*, it was Lennox who was most closely attuned to Cervantes's innovative fictional presentation of the library. Her *Female Quixote* encouraged a sense of the library in English fiction as a risky but also exciting place for ladies, a theme that would play into eighteenth-century anxieties about the growing power of circulating libraries and women's fondness for devouring those libraries' collections of romantic novels. If Sarah Fielding, whose 1759 novel *The History of the Countess of Dellwyn* is prefaced by a sophisticated examination of the power of fiction, believed that a person's character could be deduced from their library, then, like Laurence Sterne, whose narrator's Uncle Toby obsessively develops a library in *The Life and Opinions of Tristram Shandy* (1760), she too was also conscious of the self-deluding power that Cervantes had highlighted in *Don Quixote*. A seduced girl in Henry Mackenzie's 1771 *The Man of Feeling* also has her life conditioned by her reading: 'My mother's books were left behind at the different quarters we removed to, and my reading was principally confined to plays, novels, and those poetical descriptions of the beauty of virtue and honours, which the circulating libraries easily afforded.'[42] For some eighteenth-century readers, the very mention of a circulating library sounded a note of caution. As the pioneering American novelist William Hill Brown put it in his preface to *The Power of Sympathy* (1789), dedicated 'To the young Ladies of United Columbia', 'Novels have ever met with a ready reception into the Libraries of the Ladies, but this species of writing hath not been received with universal approbation.'[43]

Elaborate descriptions of libraries are rare in eighteenth-century English fiction; an exception is the extended account of the philosophers' library at Ulubrae in

---

[41] Charlotte Lennox, *The Female Quixote*, 2nd ed. (2 vols, London: A. Millar, 1752), I, 4, 70, 76; see also Susan Stavely, 'Don Quixote in Eighteenth-Century England', *Comparative Literature* 24.3 (Summer 1972): 193–215.

[42] Henry Mackenzie, *The Man of Feeling* (1771; repr. Berwick: John Taylor, 1780), 99.

[43] William Hill Brown, *The Power of Sympathy* (2 vols, Boston: Isaiah Thomas, 1789), I, [Dedication and] 'Preface'.

Thomas Amory's eccentric novel *The Life of John Buncle, Esq.*, a book so eclectic in its assemblage of knowledge that it might have delighted Sir Thomas Urquhart. Indeed, the essayist William Hazlitt would contend that 'The soul of Francis Rabelais passed into...the author of...*John Buncle*'.[44] Over several pages, Amory has his protagonist Buncle browse at length in this learned library, citing not just titles but volume, chapter, and page numbers. Several times during his library trawl, Buncle mentions the learned Renaissance religious historian Isaac Casaubon, whose surname will recur a century later in the context of the much better known fictional library in George Eliot's *Middlemarch*. The idea that a man might lose his wits not just in a library of romances but also in a library of religious texts was reinforced by Richard Graves's 1773 *The Spiritual Quixote*, a satire on Methodism in which the protagonist Geoffry Wildgoose energetically reads him-self silly.

In the later eighteenth century the growth of a taste for all things Gothic meant that any novel at all touched by this fashion had to include a (preferably haunted) house or castle which routinely featured a library: that library might be the gloomy, deserted bookroom of Charlotte Smith's *Emmeline, the Orphan of the Castle* (1788), or the library of the same author's *The Old Manor House* (1793) in which a young protagonist is shaped by his reading, or the paternal library in Ann Radcliffe's *The Mysteries of Udolpho* where the melancholy Emily sits in her late father's chair, pondering one of his books as 'her thoughts dwelt on the probable state of departed spirits'.[45] In William Godwin's *Caleb Williams* (1794) terror and a library are again fused. Linking 'horrors' to 'a circulating library', Jane Austen might spoof this sort of fiction in *Northanger Abbey* and elsewhere, but its Gothic legacy persists in *Jane Eyre*, in *Dracula*, and beyond.[46] More immediately, it was joined to a long-standing engagement with the library of *Don Quixote* in the first novel by the writer who did more than any other to influence the global develop-ment of the nineteenth-century novel, the Cervantes-loving Walter Scott.

Shaped by the libraries of his own childhood, and having had to renounce his hopes of a career as a military man of action, Scott in his teens had embarked on translating *Don Quixote*. In the spring of 1810, casting his eye over the history of English fiction, and saluting, among others, Charlotte Smith and Ann Radcliffe, he had written nostalgically of 'the circulating library' of his youth.[47] He recalled, later, how as a boy, 'reading without compass or pilot', he had sampled the 'romances of chivalry', work by de Scudéry, and more recent novels in what was left of the poet Allan Ramsay's Edinburgh circulating library.[48] In the summer of

---

[44] Hazlitt, cited in Huntington Brown, *Rabelais in English Literature* (Paris: Société d'édition 'les belles lettres', 1933), 181.

[45] Ann Radcliffe, *The Mysteries of Udolpho* (1794; repr. London: Dent, 1973), 98.

[46] Jane Austen, *Northanger Abbey* (1818; repr. Boston: Little, Brown, 1903), 135.

[47] [Walter Scott,] 'Maturin's Fatal Revenge', *Quarterly Review* 3.6 (May 1810): 340.

[48] Walter Scott, 'General Preface' (1829), in *Waverley* (New York: Dutton, 1906), 6.

1810 Scott had written several chapters of *Waverley* (1814), whose 'very bookish' protagonist, Edward Waverley (whose surname echoes that of a character in Charlotte Smith's *Desmond*), spends much of his boyhood in 'the library at Waverley Hall, a large Gothic room, with double arches and a gallery', which contains a 'miscellaneous and extensive collection of volumes'—poetry, 'numerous collections of *novelle*', prose 'romances so well written as hardly to be distinguished from memoirs', and Spanish books that 'contributed to his stock of chivalrous and romantic lore'. So, pursuing his unstructured, wavering 'studies', Waverley 'in the corner of the large and sombre library, with no other light than was afforded by the decaying brands on its ponderous and ample hearth ... would exercise that internal sorcery by which past or imaginary events are presented in action, as it were, to the eye of the muser'. Scott's fledgling hero is seen as living in an 'ideal world', a fantasy kingdom of knightly imaginings 'as brilliant and fading as those of an evening sky'.[49]

Scott may have been piqued when in September 1810 his ambitious publisher friend James Ballantyne commented on the draft chapters of *Waverley* that the protagonist's 'studies' lacked 'the connection betwixt the studies of Don Quixote and the Female Quixote, and the events of their lives'.[50] In the published text, the first sentence of chapter 5 cautions the reader against simply expecting 'in the following tale, an imitation of the romance of Cervantes', and makes it clear that 'My intention is not to follow the steps of that inimitable author'.[51] Yet Scott has already done more than enough to invoke the influence of the library of Don Quixote; where *Waverley* differs is in its allowing its young English hero to learn how to move beyond the pervasive influence of the library and come to terms with the outside world, including the world of martial exploits, while remaining commendably sane. Waverley is certainly shaped by his time in the library, but not driven mad by it. Scott takes the model of the Cervantean library, but recasts it in the light of Scottish Enlightenment rationality. His novel is powered by the proto-anthropological and sociological ideas of Enlightenment thinkers and uses these to critique as well as to exploit the heightened chromatics of Romanticism. Travelling through Scotland, Waverley compares and learns from different kinds of society—principally Lowland Scotland and Highland Scotland—and so is educated by a life beyond bookshelves. His library makes him a bookish dreamer in the early chapters, but, thanks to his maturing beyond its bounds, it is deprived of the power to overwhelm him.

Throughout his fiction and career Scott, who built his own splendid library as part of his manorial home at Abbotsford, and who authored a catalogue of its treasures and relics, was fascinated by libraries and undeniably registered their

---

[49] Walter Scott, *Waverley*, ed. P. D. Garside (Edinburgh: Edinburgh University Press, 2007), 14, 15, 16, 19.
[50] Scott, *Waverley*, 377 (Garside, 'Essay on the Text').   [51] Scott, *Waverley*, 20.

allure. Depicted by many artists from the seventeenth century onwards, and chosen as a set piece by the illustrators of successively reprinted translations of *Don Quixote*, the library at La Mancha maintained its hold on writerly and readerly imaginations.[52] Scott both recalled it and moved beyond it. The way his example encouraged library depictions in later English-language fictions may be sensed in episodes as different as those of chapter 10 of Thackeray's *Vanity Fair* (where young ladies read in an old country-house library a diverse array of not entirely suitable books) and chapter 41 of Herman Melville's *Redfern*, which depicts random reading in a library on board a warship. Though there are many libraries in nineteenth-century fiction, some of which will feature in later chapters of the present book, by no means all Victorian novelists focus on the topic. In chapter 8 of *Hard Times* Dickens is happy to mock the industrialist Gradgrind's anxiety over the fact that the workers of Coketown read fiction rather than factual books in the Coketown library, but Dickens's most sympathetic characters tend to be too poor to have substantial libraries of their own.

At home, however, following a fashion encouraged by the poet and journalist Thomas Hood, whose creation of a library of over eighty fake book titles (such as 'Cursory Remarks on Swearing') for Chatsworth House shows a certain Rabelaisian abundance, the increasingly prosperous Dickens created for his private amusement a mock library of more than sixty imitation book spines, whose titles he tabulated in a letter; they included 'Bowwowdom. A Poem' and 'Growler's Gruffology, with Appendix. 4 vols.'[53] Such japes seem pallid in comparison with Rabelais's invented library books, but, appealing to Victorian taste, they continued, albeit in chastened form, aspects of the Rabelaisian tradition. More solemnly, in 'Amos Barton', the first of the tales in George Eliot's 1858 *Scenes of Clerical Life*, a library's stock is modified to combat ecclesiastical dissent; and in Eliot's historical novel *Romola*, set in the Florence of Savonarola's bonfire of the vanities, the heroine's elderly father worries over what will happen to his extensive learned library. It is in *Middlemarch*, though, that Eliot, who grew up aware of both Cervantes and Scott, makes the library a compelling emblem of intellectual obsession and entrapment.

The most important library in *Middlemarch* is, like that of Scott's Waverley Manor, the library of a 'manor-house'. Its most avid reader, the house's owner, is, like Don Quixote, the young Edward Waverley, and several other Scott characters, a figure overcome to the point of possession by what he reads. Unlike Waverley, though, George Eliot's Edward Casaubon, the ageing scholar, is unable to escape his library's potentially lethal grip. The novel's heroine, Dorothea Brooke, 'full of

---

[52] Among the earliest paintings of Don Quixote's library is an oil by John Michael Wright (1617–94), now in the Victoria and Albert Museum.

[53] Walter Jerrold, *Thomas Hood: His Life and Times* (New York: John Lane, 1909), 260; *The Letters of Charles Dickens*, ed. Madeline House and Graham Storey (Oxford: Clarendon Press, 1965–2002), VI, 851.

hope and action', sets about 'getting down learned books from the library and reading many things hastily' so 'that she might be a little less ignorant in talking to Mr Casaubon', who guides her reading and whom she agrees to marry.[54] Linking Casaubon to that famous passage from Burton's *Anatomy of Melancholy* about the ill health of scholars, Eliot presents her Dorothea as initially entranced by 'the dark book-shelves in the long library' of Casaubon's house, where he spends 'laborious uncreative hours' reading and reading in preparation to author a great *Key to All Mythologies*—a book that, throughout the novel, remains 'still unwritten'.[55] Honeymooning with Dorothea in Italy, Casaubon spends 'every day' reading 'in the Library of the Vatican', as she tells his cousin Will, with whom she falls in love. It is Will who explains to her that Casaubon's scholarship is out of date. Returned from honeymoon, Casaubon complains 'of palpitation' and heads for his library, where he sits alone while Dorothea feels 'dreary oppression'.[56] She has established a pattern of life in which 'she should take her place at an early hour in the library and have work either of reading aloud or copying assigned her,' but Casaubon sometimes heads to the library before breakfast and eats there alone before she joins him. Though Dorothea, in an image which summons up female subservience to a difficult learned man, 'had thought that she could have been patient with John Milton', her husband's bad temper wears her down. After she sees him 'on the library-steps clinging forward as if he were in some bodily distress', it emerges that, as one of the servants puts it, 'Mr Casaubon had "had a fit in the library"'. 'Good God! This is just what might have been expected,' is a visitor's first thought.[57]

The library in *Middlemarch* is an image of entrapping futility. As the modern intellectual historian Colin Kidd shows in *The World of Mr Casaubon*, Eliot alludes to or mentions in her novel many of the specific texts which matter to her fictional Casaubon—in effect the books from his library.[58] Yet the narrative of her novel and her characterization let Eliot present knowledge as something greater and more vital than merely that of the 'brown library'.[59] Casaubon, who hopes marriage to Dorothea may let him leave behind in the world 'a copy of himself', fails to appreciate this, conscious only that he 'had not yet succeeded in issuing copies of his mythological key'. Eliot's use of the words 'copy' and 'copies' here emphasize the way Casaubon regards himself and his world only in terms of books. After a doctor has 'forbade books, the library' is 'out of the question', but Casaubon cannot refrain from immuring himself there.[60] On a rare occasion when he does not, Dorothea meets Will in the same library, and, later, after Casaubon (who is now, on occasion, taking dinner alone among his bookshelves, and at

---

[54] George Eliot, *Middlemarch* (1872; repr. Edinburgh: Blackwood, 1881), 22.
[55] Eliot, *Middlemarch*, 51, 61, 206.   [56] Eliot, *Middlemarch*, 151, 201, 202.
[57] Eliot, *Middlemarch*, 207, 208, 209.
[58] Colin Kidd, *The World of Mr Casaubon* (Cambridge: Cambridge University Press, 2014).
[59] Eliot, *Middlemarch*, 565.   [60] Eliot, *Middlemarch*, 205, 212.

other times asking Dorothea to act as his amanuensis there) grows 'more haggard' and dies, it is ultimately in her late husband's library that Dorothea again meets Will. This reunion in the library leads to their eventual marriage, even at the cost of Dorothea's renouncing her substantial inheritance from Casaubon.[61] It leads to her escape from the bookroom.

Written by nineteenth-century England's most commandingly intellectual novelist, *Middlemarch* is a text in which fiction is deployed to critique the world of the scholarly library. Though we are told several of the authors he reads, none of the texts that matter in Casaubon's library is a novel. Yet *Middlemarch* mentions Walter Scott several times and takes the epigraph to its second chapter from *Don Quixote*. Twice (once, negatively by Casaubon, and once more positively by another character) Dorothea is related to the 'Quixotic'.[62] However, it is she who, after enduring the desiccation of Casaubon's library, escapes from it. Eliot, so alert to *Don Quixote*, is playing with tropes of the library from earlier fictions, but is also altering them as she examines 'reality and illusion'.[63] The library in her novel may represent entrapment, the place where Casaubon fails (as the twenty-first-century critic Ian Duncan puts it) 'to recover a vital relation to meaning', but Eliot's fiction also shows the way of liberation.[64] As a profoundly bookish writer, she knows and shows how the library—not just Casaubon's library but even the library that spurs her modern scientific investigator Lydgate—is not, and cannot be, enough.

Later chapters of the present volume will discuss many of the libraries that appear in novels after *Middlemarch*, but this first chapter will conclude by indicating how the inheritance of Rabelais and Cervantes continued to condition the presentation of libraries in the work of authors not treated elsewhere in this volume. Surprisingly, perhaps, libraries rarely feature extensively in fiction until well into the twentieth century, though, as John Sutherland and others have shown, public libraries were an important part of the Victorian and post-Victorian social landscape, and are to be glimpsed in Andrew Carnegie's *Autobiography*, in Arnold Bennett's *The Old Wives' Tale*, and in Jack London's *Martin Eden*. The same is true of librarians themselves, even with regard to the grandest libraries. It is these grand libraries, rather than their librarians, that are sometimes insistent presences. More than any other late Victorian novelist, George Gissing portrays the atmosphere inside the British Museum reading room, the splendid circular national bookroom that preceded the present-day British Library. For Marian, the struggling female writer in George Gissing's 1891 *New Grub Street*, the reading room is as oppressive as Casaubon's library had been

---

[61] Eliot, *Middlemarch*, 317.   [62] Eliot, *Middlemarch*, 311, 566.

[63] Chester Mills, 'Eliot's Casaubon: The Quixotic in *Middlemarch*', in Ardila, ed., *The Cervantean Heritage*, 176.

[64] Ian Duncan, *Human Forms: The Novel in the Age of Evolution* (Princeton: Princeton University Press, 2019), 181.

for Dorothea Brooke: 'This huge library, growing into unwieldiness, threatening to become a trackless desert of print – how intolerably it weighed upon the spirit!' Gissing's tone is very different from that of Cervantes, but he continues and develops the idea that a library's books can overwhelm their reader. Sensing herself part of a huge 'Literary Machine' for producing volume after volume, Marian raises her eyes from her library desk:

> The fog grew thicker; she looked up at the windows beneath the dome and saw that they were a dusky yellow. Then her eye discerned an official walking along the upper gallery, and in pursuance of her grotesque humour, her mocking misery, she likened him to a black, lost soul, doomed to wander in an eternity of vain research along endless shelves. Or again, the readers who sat here at these radiating lines of desks, what were they but hapless flies caught in a huge web, its nucleus the great circle of the Catalogue? Darker, darker. From the towering wall of volumes seemed to emanate visible motes, intensifying the obscurity; in a moment the book-lined circumference of the room would be but a featureless prison-limit.[65]

While in English this vision of the library fuses vestiges of the Cervantean heritage with Casaubon's 'eternity of vain research', and would bequeath visions of the British Museum reading room to David Lodge (whose 1965 comic novel about library researcher Adam Appleby, *The British Museum is Falling Down*, is steeped in lore about the great circular reading room and festooned with epigraphs about it from previous writers) and to others, more widely in world literature the vision of the library as an all-encompassing prison-like space would be explored by Jorge Luis Borges, Umberto Eco, and Haruki Murakami.

Yet alongside a lineage of darker visions there continues a more frolicsome tradition of fictional libraries which owes much to Rabelais. Taking its epigraph from a fictional book by the imagined author and book collector John Charteris, American fantasy novelist James Branch Cabell's *Beyond Life* (1919) mentions both 'Don Quixote' and 'Rabelais as foundation'. With its 'flagrantly irregular' bookcases, Charteris's extensive library at Willoughby Hall, Fairhaven, is presented in detail, with considerable listing of its treasures. These include 'The Complete Works of David Copperfield', 'The Works of Arthur Pendennis', and other books supposedly authored by 'the most gifted writers of Bookland'. Cabell's narrator runs his eye over titles from '*The Nungapunga* by G. B. Torpenhow' to '*An Essay upon Castramentation*', before his eye is caught by '*Cannonmills, The Rising Sun*' and other works 'of Stevenson's I never heard of'. Charteris has managed to purchase, too, Milton's *King Arthur*, 'the last six books of *The Faery*

---

[65] George Gissing, *New Grub Street* (3 vols. London: Smith, Elder, 1891), I, 195, 196.

Queen and the latter *Canterbury Tales*'; he boasts that 'The main treasure of my library, though, is that unbound collection of the Unwritten Plays of Christopher Marlowe.' With its evident awareness of Cervantes and Rabelais, and its compendious sense of 'the world's library', Cabell's fiction looks forward not just to Borges but also to the fantastic libraries of Terry Pratchett (whose Unseen University Library in *The Last Continent* (1998) contains potentially all books yet to be written) and Neil Gaiman, whose *Sandman* graphic novels series includes a compendious Dream Library of imagined volumes.[66] The libraries of unpublished books in Richard Brautigan's *The Abortion: An Historical Romance 1966* (1971) and in David Foenkinos's *Le Mystère Henri Pick* (2016; English translation, 2020) take matters even further.

If these libraries point towards vastness and the World Wide Web era of textual totality, modern fiction has also turned the Rabelaisian subversion of library cataloguing in other imaginatively productive directions. After the imperative 'Catalogue these books' in Joyce's *Ulysses* comes a jumbled list which juxtaposes '*Thom's Dublin Post Office Directory*, 1886' with 'Denis Florence M'Carthy's *Poetical Works* (copper beechleaf bookmark at p.5)'. In its way, Leopold Bloom's home library mocks what the narrative calls 'The necessity of order' just as much as had Rabelais's famous book catalogue. Including a '13 days overdue' volume that is 'property of the City of Dublin Public Library', Bloom's list, however, clearly belongs to the modern world of book circulation rather than to the library of a medieval abbey.[67] If *Ulysses* also includes a list of the 'World's Twelve Worst Books', then *Finnegans Wake* is more thoroughgoingly Rabelaisian when it unleashes a list of about 130 jumbled but consistently risqué titles such as *Cock in the Pot for Father*, *A New Cure for an Old Clap*, and *In My Lord's Bed by One Whore Went Through It*. Joyce owned a copy of Urquhart's Rabelais translation, as well as a study entitled *La Langue de Rabelais*, and the scholars Claude Jacquet, Norman Silverstein, and Joanne E. Rea have shown with great attentiveness how Rabelaisian wording is echoed in *Ulysses* and *Finnegans Wake*.[68] Yet their minute focus on verbal details risks missing Joyce's clear redeployment of the Rabelaisian library catalogue as a satirically subversive fictional form that serves to emphasize, not least, the insistently material presence of sexuality on the shelves. Joyce, like Rabelais, makes the library catalogue into a poem. In so doing he encourages the several book-listing poems entitled 'The Alexandrian Library' by Don Paterson in our own day.

Many of the instances of the lingering influence of Cervantes and Rabelais cited so far have been drawn from the work of well-known novelists, but several are

---

[66] James Branch Cabell, *Beyond Life* (1919; repr. New York: R. M. McBride, 1921), 284, 5, 11, 12, 13, 40.
[67] James Joyce, *Ulysses* (1922; repr. Harmondsworth: Penguin, 1974), 629.
[68] Claude Jacquet, *Joyce et Rabelais* (Paris: Didier, 1972); Norman Silverstein, 'Deconstructing the Rabelaisian Element of *Finnegans Wake*', *James Joyce Quarterly* 11.4 (Summer 1974): 414–19; Joanne E. Rea, 'Joyce and "Master François Somebody"', *James Joyce Quarterly* 18.4 (Summer 1981): 445–50.

today less familiar. Sometimes, when it comes to the specific topic of libraries in literature, these less often discussed texts can be significant in the way they continue or redirect an imaginative lineage. A final case in point, exceptional in its extended portrayal of a librarian yet clearly indebted to much older traditions, is G. K. Chesterton's last and now little-read novel, *The Return of Don Quixote* (1927). Like his friend and fellow Catholic writer Hilaire Belloc, Chesterton had a marked taste for the Middle Ages, for libraries, and for the allure of a romanticized past. In *The Return of Don Quixote* a group of upper-class people are searching without success for someone to play the part of a medieval troubadour in their amateur dramatic production. They turn in desperation (since a 'librarian' seems to them even 'lower and viler than a knife-boy') to Michael Herne, librarian to Lord Seawood. Appearing at first like a minor Casaubon, Herne, whose preoccupation is 'the Palaeo-Hittites', but who has 'never written a book about his Hittites', is presented as a 'librarian ... of the sort that is remote from the daylight, and suited to be a shade among the shades of a great library'. Described at some length in a chapter called 'The Ladder in the Library', Herne's church-like library is part of what was once Seawood Abbey. It is, however, far less like Rabelais's Abbey of Saint-Victor and much more like Don Quixote's bookroom: so much so that sitting atop his high library ladder, 'his head entirely invisible behind the leather wall' of a 'large volume', Herne is regarded by some of the other characters as 'Mad'. Yet in a later chapter ('The Lunacy of the Librarian'), Herne emerges as an impressive actor—'a librarian [who] can act a King'. He comes to be recognized for leadership qualities full of political possibility. By the book's final chapter, 'The Return of Don Quixote', Herne (part belated defender of the Arts and Crafts Movement, and part twentieth-century charismatic leader) has emerged as champion of the finest medieval values against the 'millers' and 'windmills' that are 'the mills and manufactures that have darkened and degraded modern life'.[69] This librarian-turned-Don Quixote, rather than his revolutionary socialist opponent, is seen as a political saviour and as a fit partner for the book's heroine. Chesterton's whimsical fiction is in more than one way quixotic, and it may be unconvincing, but, written by one of the modern English popular writers whom Borges most admired, it certainly reinscribes the story of *Don Quixote* in a modern context. It is also among the first novels in English to have a librarian as a central character and to grant to this librarian (whose gender is surely a pertinent factor) a sense of significant power. Chapter 9 in the present book will examine how issues of agency for librarians—and particularly female librarians—are treated in a range of twentieth-century novels. In almost all earlier fiction, however, and not least in that of Rabelais and Cervantes, the cynosure of attention and the site of true authority is not any mere librarian but, instead, the library itself.

---

[69] *The Collected Works of G. K. Chesterton, VIII, The Return of Don Quixote* (San Francisco: Ignatius Press, 1999), 62, 66, 67, 73, 154, 245.

2

Dramatic Libraries

Robert Crawford

Libraries in English-language drama represent power. Though the power can be primarily intellectual, it is also, particularly in the nineteenth and twentieth centuries, economic. So often associated with stillness and contemplation, and linked, especially in modern times, to disciplined silence, libraries might seem the most unpromising locations for dramatic action. On stage, they are most often invoked through allusion rather than through full representation. Yet from the Renaissance onwards there are a small but significant number of plays—some well known, and others not—in which the library is a key location, a place where power is maintained and, repeatedly, challenged. This chapter will focus on such plays, while indicating also aspects of the wider presentation of libraries in the theatres of the English-speaking world.

The 'study' in which, at the start of the 1590s, Christopher Marlowe presents his seated protagonist Doctor Faustus is clearly a bookroom, and Faustus, 'grac'd with doctor's name' and 'glutted now with learning's golden gifts', is evidently an obsessive reader. 'Sweet Analytics, 'tis thou hast ravish'd me!' he exclaims in his opening speech, manifesting a desire to 'live and die in Aristotle's works'. Yet even as Faustus resolves to 'settle' in his 'studies', this most bookish of speakers offers the audience a verbal inventory of his bookshelves, ranging far beyond Aristotle to the ancient Greek medical writer Galen, to the Latin legal writer Justinian, and the biblical translator Jerome, before going on to enthuse about 'metaphysics of magicians' and the 'heavenly' properties of 'necromantic books'.[1] Apparently reading aloud from a selection of his favourite texts, Doctor Faustus delivers quotations in Latin as well as his own heady vernacular rhetoric. Every inch a university man, 'John Faustus of Wertenberg' (Wittenberg) converses with scholars, and although, in the style of older medieval drama, he is advised by a good angel to 'lay thy damned books aside', his book-fuelled quest for learning spurs his assertion that 'A sound magician is a mighty god', and leads both to his pact with the devil and to his eventual damnation.[2]

'These books' which Faustus's friend Valdes praises propel the learned protagonist towards powers in which, as 'conjuror laureat', he delights; but ultimately

---

[1] Christopher Marlowe, *Plays and Poems*, ed. M. R. Ridley (London: Dent, 1973), 121.
[2] Marlowe, *Plays and Poems*, 133, 123, 122.

they hurry him to hell. 'Take this book', Mephistophilis urges Faustus, and no words are more dangerous to Faustus than his own, 'Nay, let me have one book more'.[3] The pleasures which Faustus savours as a result of his pact with the devil are often bookish ones: 'Have not I made blind Homer sing to me', he boasts, having called back to life a favourite epic author; travelling miraculously with Mephistophilis, he visits 'Maro's golden tomb'—the resting place of another epic poet, Virgil. The sheer learned bookishness of the play is hard to exaggerate. Its most famous lines—'Was this the face that launch'd a thousand ships? / And burnt the topless towers of Ilium?'—are a further allusion to the Troy story given classic literary formulation by Homer. Even in the more knockabout scenes, the audience hears Robin the Ostler boast of having stolen 'one of Doctor Faustus' conjuring books'; but when the conjuring with 'Doctor Faustus' book' leads to frightening results, Robin begs, 'Good devil, forgive me now, and I'll never rob thy library more.'[4]

Though it is from the books of his library that Faustus derives the power which hastens him on the road to damnation, he eventually reaches a point where he wishes, 'O, would I had never seen Wertenberg, never read book!' Too late, he resolves, 'I'll burn my books!' The play's final choral passage laments that 'burned is Apollo's laurel-bough, / That sometime grew within this learned man', and the audience is warned that 'forward wits' must resist the 'deepness' that entices them 'To practise more than heavenly power permits'.[5] The power of hoarded books in *Doctor Faustus* has led the protagonist too far. The library can be empowering; but bookishness must also be curbed.

If Shakespeare's Hamlet is another tragic student of the University of Wittenberg who struggles to align his scholarly inclinations with the demands of moral conduct, then the theme of a divide between the seclusion of the bookish scholar and the public show of the courtly man of action was also evident elsewhere in Elizabethan drama. In John Lyly's 1584 *Sapho and Phao*, which was acted before Queen Elizabeth, the 'Schollerlike' Pandion who has come from 'universitie to the court' is told, 'you must learne to turn your library to a war drope [wardrobe], & see whether your rapier hang better by your side, then the penne did in your eare'.[6] Yet the library might serve, too, as a metaphor for powerful concentration which extended beyond the purely scholarly: 'His looks shall be my only Librarie,' says Dido of her lover Aeneas in Marlowe's 1594 *Tragedie of Dido Queene of Carthage*.[7] A related notion of 'women's eyes' as 'the books, the academes, / From whence doth spring the true Promethean fire' is important in *Love's Labour's Lost*, in which Shakespeare, a few years later, has the

---

[3] Marlowe, *Plays and Poems*, 127, 135.
[4] Marlowe, *Plays and Poems*, 136, 140, 154, 143, 144, 145.
[5] Marlowe, *Plays and Poems*, 155, 158.
[6] [John Lyly], *Sapho and Phao* (London: Thomas Cadman, 1584), [7–8].
[7] Marlowe, *Plays and Poems*, 348.

King of Navarre resolve to turn his 'court' into 'a little academe' dedicated to 'study', only to have this aim questioned by his noble courtier Berowne, who resolves 'to study so, / To know the thing I am forbid to know', and, reluctant 'painfully to pore' over 'others' books', prefers erotic rhetoric and dedication to those 'books' that are 'women's eyes'.[8]

In *Love's Labour's Lost*, though the word 'library' is never used, its presence is implied throughout. The play exults in a frolicsome fascination with bookishness—whether that of courtiers addicted to poetry and rhetoric, or that of the absurdly pedantic Holofernes, who seems to have 'eat paper' and 'drunk ink'. Sprinkling his speeches with Latin tags, he delivers such orotundly bookish lines as 'I will overglance the superscript'. This comedy of learned men seems to suggest that authority derived from the library is rhetorically beguiling, but ultimately insufficient in the face of love. However 'fruitful', Berowne's 'brain', like the pedantic intelligence of the schoolteacher Holofernes, must be chastened and governed, kept under control.[9] As Neil Rhodes argues when he asks, 'Did Shakespeare Study Creative Writing?', the playwright both drew on and reacted against the rhetorical manuals and copious bookishness of his era.[10] Several centuries afterwards, T. S. Eliot, at a time when writers frequented the great library in the reading room of the British Museum, argued that 'Shakespeare acquired more essential history from Plutarch than most men could from the whole British Museum'; but Shakespeare was well aware of libraries as potent repositories.[11] In his first play, *Titus Andronicus*, the protagonist gives his mutilated daughter full access to his books—'choice of all my library'—so that she may 'beguile' her 'sorrow' until 'the heavens / Reveal' her violator.[12] Yet, using the library's power, Lavinia (whose tongue has been ripped out) immediately indicates a particular volume there, and directs Titus's attention to the story of raped Philomela in Ovid's *Metamorphoses*. As a result of Lavinia's harnessing the power of the library to express in detail what she could not otherwise articulate, the already bloody drama accelerates towards its even bloodier conclusion. The library here leads to violence, its bookish power opening the way to a bloodbath.

Shakespeare's last word on the library, however, points in the opposite direction. Yet it still maintains a strong sense of the library as a source of power. In *The Tempest* the bookish Milanese Duke Prospero, 'reputed . . . for the liberal Arts' and 'secret studies', tells how he was usurped by his wicked, worldly brother Antonio, who took advantage of Prospero's Montaigne-like scholarly seclusion ('Me, poor man, my library / Was dukedom large enough'). Yet after the usurpation 'a noble

---

[8] William Shakespeare, *Love's Labour's Lost*, ed. Richard David (London: Methuen, 1968), 106, 3, 6, 7.

[9] Shakespeare, *Love's Labour's Lost*, 75, 85, 182.

[10] Neil Rhodes, *Shakespeare and the Origins of English* (Oxford: Oxford University Press, 2004), ch. 2.

[11] T. S. Eliot, *The Sacred Wood* (1920; repr. London: Methuen, 1960), 52.

[12] William Shakespeare, *Titus Andronicus*, ed. J. C. Maxwell (London: Methuen, 1968), 76.

Neapolitan', Gonzalo, made sure that Prospero was still able to access his sources of book-derived strength:

> Knowing I lov'd my books, he furnish'd me
> From mine own library with volumes that
> I prize above my dukedom.[13]

So it is that, even in exile on a remote island, Prospero has been able to perfect 'mine Art', which appears a form of magic learned from 'my book'. Caliban, the island native who resents Prospero's presence, seeks to seize 'his books', and urges his confederates,

>   Remember,
> First to possess his books; for without them
> He's but a sot, as I am, nor hath not
> One spirit to command; they all do hate him
> As rootedly as I. Burn but his books.

Prospero's triumph over Caliban and his usurping brother comes as a result of the 'so potent art' which he has derived from the books of his library. If, at the play's conclusion, he resolves to 'drown my book', it is because he—and the play's audience—know the book has now accomplished its powerful work, and that this volume, metonymic of Prospero's 'own library', can now be relinquished.[14] From this perspective, Prospero emerges as a figure who may be set against Faustus. Where the latter gives way to the power of his library, Prospero remains in control and relinquishes it. Yet in both cases the library is a source of extraordinary authority.

The library's intoxicating potency is paid a backhanded compliment in several plays where its volumes' powers are juxtaposed with the power of strong drink. In 1630 Thomas Randolph has a 'Wild-man' inveigh against 'the learned Library' with its 'Philosophicall volumes' as 'bookes of the blacke Art'. While it sounds as if he has grown up familiar with Marlowe's Doctor Faustus, what this Wild-man sets against a 'whole *Vatican*' library of dubious books is neither book burning nor the curbing of literary power, but instead a potent countering force. The play tells us of a 'Pewter Librarie' of tankards, and Randolph's drama's full title sums up its moral: *Aristippus, Or The Iouiall Philosopher: Demonstrativelie prouing, That Quartes, Pintes, and Pottles, Are sometimes necessary Authours in a Scholers Library*.[15] This trope of a counter-library of drinks and drinking vessels would

---

[13] William Shakespeare, *The Tempest*, ed. Frank Kermode (London: Methuen, 1964), 14, 16, 20.
[14] Shakespeare, *The Tempest*, 28, 77, 81–2, 116.
[15] Thomas Randolph, *Aristippus* (London: John Marriott, 1630), 22.

be repeated in several later plays. In Randolph's *The Muses Looking Glass* (1638) a character promises to open a school 'For th'education of young Gentlemen / To study how to drink' and pursue other vices; it will be equipped 'With a large Library of Drapers bookes' and will, he is assured, 'put down *Bodlies* and the *Vatican*'.[16] 'I like no Library but a well-fill'd Cellar', maintains a character in Thomas Fuller's 1661 *Andronicus*, trying to sound reassuring.[17] If some plays invoked a counter-library of drink (or even a 'lascivious library' of alluring women), their use of such invocations implies that the power of actual libraries was taken for granted.[18] To emphasize the glory of his protagonist and her lover, Thomas May's 1639 *Tragedie of Cleopatra Queen of Ægypt* mentions Antony's bestowing on Cleopatra the 'famous Library of Pergamus, / In which there were two hundred thousand Books'.[19]

Libraries could be linked to glory as well as to power, but by the mid-seventeenth century audiences were growing used to more mischievous treatments of libraries too. Cambridge graduate Henry Glapthorne's *Wit in a Constable* (1640) alludes to '*Faustus*', and opens with a young Cambridge man who 'loves to be esteem'd a doctor by / His volumnes' discussing his personal library at considerable length; he has enough 'fancy volums', as his servant (who has 'spent two dayes in sorting Poets from Historians') puts it, 'to furnish a new Vatican'.[20] Moving to London, however, and falling in love, make the scholar realize that love may be more important than libraries, and 'wit' may be found beyond books. In this sometimes winningly bookish play Glapthorne draws on Shakespeare's *Much Ado about Nothing* and on other Renaissance drama, but his jokes about libraries are often his own, for all he is clearly aware of both *Don Quixote* (referenced in Act I, scene i) and *Gargantua and Pantagruel* (Act I, scene ii). While Glapthorne's scholar has a taste founded on learned tomes, the servant who is charged with arranging (and later selling off) his library prefers more popular ballads and tales. That servant was hardly alone in harbouring such tastes. Pyle, the 'rich haughty widow of Byz[antium]' in William Cartwright's *The Siege* (which dates from around the same time as Glapthorne's play), speaks of her wish to 'found a Library, which shall / Be only stor'd with Play-books and Romances'.[21] If this sounds closer to the protagonist's library in *Don Quixote*, by that time a popular book in Britain, than it does to the libraries of Faustus or Prospero, then it also presages a sense of the female appetite for romances, fiction, and plays which would be regarded as absurdly destabilizing by later generations. For James Shirley

---

[16] Thomas Randolph, *The Muses Looking Glass* (London: William Roybould, 1638), 42.
[17] Thomas Fuller, *Andronicus* (London: Richard Hall et al., 1661), 4.
[18] Thomas Jordan, *Fancy's Festivals* (London: Thomas Wilson, 1657), [14].
[19] Thomas May, *The Tragedie of Cleopatra Queen of AEgypt* (London: Thomas Walkly, 1639), [15].
[20] Henry Glapthorne, *Wit in a Constable* (London: F[rancis] C[onstable], 1640), [8, 10, 5, 6].
[21] William Cartwright, *Comedies, Tragi-comedies, with Other Poems* (London: Humphry Moseley, 1651), [96,] 118.

in 1659 there seems to be reassurance offered by a character who maintains that 'My Lady keeps no Library, no food / For booke-worms'.[22] Twenty years later, it was the remarkable female dramatist Aphra Behn who (in her comedy *Sir Patient Fancy*) had her protagonist mock 'the intolerable Lady, Madam Romance, that walking Library of Profane Books'.[23] Shakespeare's Holofernes, too, had been a walking library, a kind of human book, but by the later seventeenth century such figures of fun could be regendered.

Books, after all, could addle the female brain as well as the male one. '*Don Quixot's Library*' was a familiar reference point by the 1660s, and need not even be mentioned explicitly in order to be summoned up.[24] Just as when a character called Sancho in Colley Cibber's later comedy *Love Makes a Man* enters with 'a Wagon Load of my Master's Books', so the audience is presumed to understand the allusion when another Spanish character named 'Sancho' is urged by a fellow Spaniard in William D'Avenant's final (1668) comedy, *The Man's the Master*, 'Let's visit his Library. Yet, now I think on't, I have had my head twice crackt with reaching down great Books from high Shelves. Well, 'tis strange how since my childhood I ever lov'd huge great Books...'[25] Sometimes regarded as Shakespeare's godson, D'Avenant had already recast a version of *The Tempest*. His own *The Tempest, or The Enchanted Island, A Comedy*, transposes to the prose of Act I, scene i, Prospero's tribute to Gonzalo, 'of his gentleness (knowing I lov'd my Books) he furnish me from mine own Library, with volumes which I prize above my Dukedom'.[26] D'Avenant can be seen as invoking both the inheritance of Prospero's library and that of Don Quixote.

In the following century the idea of the readers who lose their minds to reading would come to be associated particularly with blue-stockinged women. Before then, however, at the start of the decade when he would suffer from mental instability of his own, Nathaniel Lee, who summoned up echoes of Jacobean drama in his 1680 *Caesar Borgia*, became the first English writer to introduce a motif which would feature in later crime fiction: the trope of the body in the library. In Lee's play the character of Machiavelli recounts how,

This morning, being early in the *Vatican*,
Far in the Library, at the upper end,
Methought I saw two stately Humane Forms,
Lying at a distance, wrapt in Linen Shrouds...

---

[22] James Shirley, *Honoria and Mammon* (London: The Author, 1659), 2.
[23] Aphra Behn, *Sir Patient Fancy* (London: Richard and Jacob Tonson, 1678), 19.
[24] John Wilson, *The Cheats* (London: G. Bedell et al., 1664), [1].
[25] Colley Cibber, *Love Makes a Man* (London: Richard Parker et al., 1701), 2; William D'Avenant, *The Man's the Master* (London: Henry Herringman, 1669), 19.
[26] William D'Avenant, *The Tempest* (London: Henry Herringman, 1670), 6.

This turns out to be a vision of two corpses. One, 'pale, ghastly, cold and dead', is that of the Pope; the other, 'Swoln black, and bloated', is what remains of Caesar Borgia.[27] The contrast of the calm of a library juxtaposed with slaughtered bodies would prove irresistible to more than one future novelist, though it remained rare on stage.

More common, oddly enough, are what can sound like dramatizations of library catalogues. The prolific playwright Robert Wild offers one of these in his 1689 comedy *The Benefice*, where, after the character of Invention asks, 'May I be so bold as to peruse your Library?', audiences listen as Invention '*takes up the Books, looks at them, and speaks*', offering critical remarks and appraisals of various authors including Plautus, Ben Jonson, Shakespeare, Beaumont and Fletcher, and Thomas Randolph.[28] Though some onstage characters were interested in the contents of the books in a library, libraries in the theatre were also coming to function as markers of cultural power, or, to put it more straightforwardly, of social class. This could lend itself to mockery. In architect and dramatist John Vanbrugh's 1696 comedy of sexual intrigue *The Relapse*, the character of Sir Novelty Fashion (brought to prominence in an earlier play by Colley Cibber) is 'newly created Lord Foppington' and tells Amanda ('wife to Loveless') about his 'private Gallery', where he likes to stroll and which 'is furnish'd with nothing but Books and Looking-glasses'. Amanda replies, 'Nay, I love a neat Library too; but 'tis I think the Inside of the Book, shou'd recommend it most to us.' This disconcerts Lord Foppington, who retorts in his affected accent, 'That I must confess I am nat altogether so fand of. Far to mind the inside of a Book, is to entertain ones self with the forc'd Product of another Man's Brain. Naw I think a Man of Quality and Breeding, may be much better diverted with the Natural Sprauts of his own.'[29]

If libraries of the rich, such as that of Mr Graspall ('so fine a Library') in Eliza Haywood's 1724 comedy *A Wife to be Lett*, were markers of economic and social prestige, and the question of 'Choice of a Library' (raised in Thomas Odell's 1729 farce *The Smugglers*) could be answered showily, then, even if it is possible to find the occasional joke about a horse in a library, there is something of a disconnect between the libraries of late seventeenth- and eighteenth-century drama and the most strikingly imaginative contemporary prose text to feature the library, Swift's *Battel of the Books*.[30] Where there are clashes between kinds of library onstage, they tend not to involve ancient texts versus modern ones so much as scandalously entertaining texts (for example, the Earl of Rochester's notorious erotic poems)

---

[27] Nathaniel Lee, *Caesar Borgia* (London: R. Bentley et al., 1680), 61.
[28] Robert Wild, *The Benefice* (London: R. Janeway, 1689), 8, 9.
[29] John Vanbrugh, *The Relapse* (London: Samuel Briscoe et al., 1697), 28.
[30] Eliza Haywood, *A Wife to be Lett* (London: Dan Browne junr. Et al., 1724), 24; Thomas Odell, *The Smugglers* (London: John Clarke et al., 1729), 13; for a joke about a horse in a library see Thomas Baker, *An Act at Oxford* (London: Bernard Lintot, 1704), 7.

versus solemnly professional tomes (such as law books), as in Act 2, scene 2, of Henry Fielding's *The Temple Beau* (1730), in which a father demands to inspect his son's library; or else activities quite other than reading are hinted at, as in John Kelly's 1732 *The Married Philosopher*, in which the young protagonist assures an enquirer that female visitors are 'Ladies of undoubted Honour, Lovers of Learning, who sometimes favour me with a Visit, purely to turn over my Library'.[31]

By the mid-eighteenth century another sort of library, familiar in society for several decades, begins to feature on stage: the circulating library. It is mentioned in the context of a possibly dubious '*French* Book' in Samuel Foote's 1757 comedy *The Author*, and it features at greater length in George Colman the Elder's *Dramatic Novel of One Act* entitled *Polly Honeycombe* (1760).[32] Having some fun with the increasingly strong linkage between the novel and female readers, Colman (whose preface includes 'Criticism' drawn from 'a Letter from my Mother') sets out in place of a list of *dramatis personae* a considerable extract from 'the Catalogue of the Circulating Library'. This substantial list (a treasure trove for modern book historians) begins with the letter *A*: *Accomplished Rake, or the modern fine Gentleman*; *Adventures of Miss Polly B-ch-rd and Samuel Tyrrel, esq.*; *Adventures of Jerry Buck*; *Adventures of Dick Hazard* .... As it unrolls, even twenty-first-century readers realize that its titles—which include Fielding's *Adventures of Joseph Andrews* and Tobias Smollett's *Adventures of Roderick Random*—are those of actual books.[33] This incorporation of what appears to be a mid-eighteenth-century circulating library's stock list prepares us for a play whose prologue, alluding to a 'dread Sorceress' called '*Romance*', to a 'mad Sublime', and to 'Cervantes', introduces a bevy of giddily intoxicated female readers of fiction, headed by Polly Honeycombe, who, invoking the heroines of her favourite fictions, hopes she has 'out-topped them all – Miss Howe, Narcissa, Clarinda, Polly Barnes, Sophy Willis, and all of them'. She asks her beloved Mr Scribble, 'D'ye think I am as handsome as Clarissa, or Clementina, or Pamela, or Sophy Western, or Amelia, or –.' And Mr Scribble reassures her, 'Handsome! – you are a constellation of all their beauties blended together – Clarissa and Sophy, and the rest of them, were but mere types of you.' Here, 'downright raving – Mad as a March hare –', and fit only for 'Bedlam' in her father's view, is a young woman whose wits have been addled by the fare of the modern circulating library to which she has become addicted. Denouncing 'These damn'd Story Books!', it is Polly's father who has the last word: 'a man might as well turn his Daughter loose in Covent-garden, as trust the cultivation of her mind to A CIRCULATING LIBRARY.'[34]

---

[31] John Kelly, *The Married Philosopher* (London: T. Worrall et al., 1732), 22.
[32] Samuel Foote, *The Author* (London: P. Valliant et al., 1757), 4.
[33] George Colman [the Elder], *Polly Honeycombe* (London: T. Becket et al., 1760), vii, vi, ix, ix–xiii.
[34] Colman, *Polly Honeycombe*, xiv, 18, 28, 41, 43, 44.

Yet, given that David Garrick wrote for Polly a final, laughing 'Epilogue', this isn't quite the last word in *Polly Honeycombe*. Garrick's epilogue lets Polly plead the subversive case for women's unfettered reading:

> *Leap these old bounds, and boldly set the pattern,*
> *To be a Wit, Philosopher, and Slattern –*
> *O! did all Maids and Wives, my spirit feel,*
> *We'd make this topsy-turvy world to reel...*[35]

Though this humorous speech may not quite leave the audience reeling, it does herald the shape of things to come.

That the idea of a gentleman's library was being disturbed in the era of the new circulating libraries beloved of female readers may be hinted at in the very first speech of F. C. Sheridan's 1763 comedy *The Discovery*. The play opens in 'a Library' in the home of Lord Medway, who sits reading at a table and looks up, disconcerted, as his wife enters: 'How's this, madam? Pursue me into my study! My sanctuary! I thought this place, at least, was to be considered by your Ladyship as inviolable.'[36] There is no mention here of a circulating library, but clearly the phenomenon was upsetting the previously gendered control of reading more widely in society. In William Whitehead's *A Trip to Scotland* (1770) we hear of 'a fine scholar' whose 'aunts' maintain that she 'read through a whole circulating library once, in half a year'.[37] The second scene of R. B. Sheridan's famous comedy *The Rivals* opens on a scene in a room in Mrs Malaprop's lodgings where Lucy is speaking about searching for a book among several circulating libraries: 'I don't believe there's a circulating library in Bath I ha'nt been at.'[38] A discussion then ensues about such titles as *The Reward of Constancy*, *The Fatal Connection*, *The Mistakes of the Heart*, and *The Delicate Distress*. These are hardly the books of Doctor Faustus or Prospero, but evidently the circulating libraries from which they come are institutions that exercise substantial power over their patrons. The concern seems to be that female readers are being led astray. 'Why,' exclaims a character in Samuel Foote's comedy *The Lyar* (1764), 'he will tell you more lyes in an hour, than all the circulating libraries, put together, will publish in a year.'[39]

If circulating libraries gave way to anxious reactions to their frequently female customers, then these reactions too could be mocked. Richard Cumberland's 1785 comedy *The Natural Son* includes a discussion of 'the library' and upper-class female literary taste, during which it is explained that 'Doctor Calomel...has

---

[35] Colman, *Polly Honeycombe*, [46].
[36] Frances Chamberlaine Sheridan, *The Discovery* (London: T. Davies et al., 1763), 1.
[37] William Whitehead, *A Trip to Scotland* (London: J. Dodsley et al., 1770), 9.
[38] Richard Brinsley Sheridan, *The Rivals* (London: John Wilkie et al., 1775), 5.
[39] Samuel Foote, *The Lyar* (London: G. Kearsly et al., 1764), 23.

wrote a book purposely to dissuade people from reading'.[40] By this point in the eighteenth century *The Ladies Library*, a three-volume conduct book 'published by Sir Richard Steele' (who had written about the topic in *The Tatler*) and supposedly 'Written by a Lady' (but sometimes ascribed to George Berkeley), had gone through at least seven editions, warning female readers to avoid 'gallant writers' whose works 'lead the heart to love'.[41] Such counsels, even when set beside the more learned disquisitions on Rhetoric and Belles Lettres by university teachers of English literature headed by the Reverend Hugh Blair in Edinburgh, were no match for the power of the circulating libraries, as several dramas attest. What amused German audiences in August Friedrich von Kotzebue's *The Writing Desk* was readily translatable for anglophone audiences amused at the suggestion that 'the *Liaisons Dangereuses*...must be taken away' from a young lady's book collection because that author was 'at times inclined to moralise'. When offered two alternative, more improving books 'from the circulating library', the young lady's response is, 'I don't like to read them.'[42]

Throughout the English-speaking world and beyond, women were not only using circulating libraries but also developing more intimate book collections that were frequently based on their own taste for fiction. Stepping into the 'closet' of an American lady called Charlotte, the character tellingly named Manly in Harvard law graduate Royall Tyler's 1790 comedy *The Contrast* notes that 'this is what I believe she calls her little library'.[43] 'I have so accustomed myself to the reading of *Novels*, that I fear I have lost the capacity of deriving instruction from other books,' confesses Mrs Loveless in another play of the period. Mr Loveless, however, is all too keen to 'set about the selection' of 'a library' suitable for a lady.[44] Knowing that personal as well as commercial and educational libraries exercised power and influence, men and women sometimes tussled over their regulation, both onstage and off. The title of the drama in which these Lovelesses appear is *The Reformation*, and the title alludes not least to efforts to reform literary taste. The play was published in London around 1785 (and then at New Haven in 1791) in a compendium of *Dramatic Pieces, Calculated to Exemplify the Mode of Conduct Which Will Render Young Ladies Both Amiable and Happy, When Their School Education is Completed*. Some libraries in plays (such as the nursery library mentioned in *The Good Mother-in-Law*, which appears in the same compendium) are manifestly designed to further such aims; others endangered or subverted them. Marianne, glimpsed in 'A Library in Lady Waitfor't's

[40] Richard Cumberland, *The Natural Son* (London: C. Dilly et al., 1785), 2.
[41] *The Ladies Library* (3 vols; London: J. Tonson, 1714), I, 25.
[42] Charles Smith, *The Writing Desk...from the German of Kotzebue* (New York: Charles Smith, 1801), 47.
[43] Royall Tyler, *The Contrast* (Philadelphia: Thomas Wignell, 1790), 70.
[44] [Anon.,] *The Reformation*, in *Dramatic Pieces, Calculated to Exemplify the Mode of Conduct Which Will Render Young Ladies Both Amiable and Happy, When Their School Education is Completed* (3 vols; London: John Marshall [c.1785]), II, 71, 70.

House' in Frederick Reynolds's 1793 London comedy *The Dramatist*, is discussing exciting romantic plays with the playwright Vapid. 'Lord! I don't care about fine morals', exclaims Marianne, before discussion turns to such other dramatists as 'Mr Poet' and 'our friend Ennui'. Seated among Lady Waitfor't's books, Marianne is suffering from 'a sudden touch of the dramatic mania'.[45] Clearly, she is in danger in the library.

By this time dramatic libraries were not only places familiar to audiences for exercising power over the characters who passed through them; they were also zones of dark allure. The fashion for all things Gothic which brought novel readers Ann Radcliffe's *The Mysteries of Udolpho* (1794)—in which the young heroine feels 'a sudden terror of something supernatural' while sitting in her late father's library—also brought to the stage Miles Peter Andrews's *The Mysteries of the Castle*, in which, listening at the door of her friend's 'father's library', a young heroine hears about 'an old Castle, and then the words "Carlos and murder"'.[46] Nowhere onstage did the Gothic library promise a more Gothic intensity than in George Colman the Younger's play *The Iron Chest*, based upon the novel *Caleb Williams* by William Godwin. Godwin had a marked interest in the formative effect of reading, but his novel's sinister iron chest is located in an apartment off the library; in Colman's play it is the library itself which houses the chest and becomes a prominent dramatic location. Seldom can asking one's servant to walk to a library bookcase and hand over a volume from a shelf have produced such overwrought musings as those of Sir Edward Mortimer at his writing table:

Books
(My only commerce, now,) will sometimes rouse me
Beyond my nature. I have been so warm'd,
So heated by a well-turn'd rhapsody,
That I have seemed the hero of the tale,
So glowingly described. Draw me a man
Struggling for Fame, attaining, keeping it,
Dead ages since, and the Historian
Decking his memory, in polish'd phrase,
And I can follow him through every turn
Grow wild in his exploits, myself himself,
Until the thick pulsation of my heart
Wakes me, to ponder on the thing I am.[47]

---

[45] Frederick Reynolds, *The Dramatist* (London: T. N. Longman et al., 1793), 21, 22, 23, 24.
[46] Ann Radcliffe, *The Mysteries of Udolpho* (1794; repr. London: Dent, 1973), 98; Miles Peter Andrews, *The Mysteries of the Castle* (London: J. Woodfall et al., 1795), 50.
[47] George Colman [the Younger], *The Iron Chest* (London: Cadell and Davies, 1796), 31.

In this overwrought atmosphere audiences witness in the library a deadly struggle as a pistol-wielding Sir Mortimer, after dashing his book to the floor, tries to defend the iron chest that lies at the heart of his library, and which the suspicious investigator Wilford is trying to open. No wonder that in Act II, scene ii, Wilford exclaims of Sir Mortimer, 'I'd rather step into a Lion's den / Than meet him in the Library!' Eventually, and somewhat predictably, the chest is discovered to contain the bones of a murder victim. The library's power in the Gothic era was nothing if not Gothic; but, while differently inflected in the Romantic period, its power as a zone of torment and danger is in some ways reminiscent of the hellish Renaissance library of *Doctor Faustus*. 'Last night, when I was writing for him, in the library,' recalls Wilford of Sir Mortimer, 'I could not help fancying I was shut up with the devil.'[48]

American John Stokes's 1821 drama *The Forest of Rosenwald* opens in 'a gothic library', and such settings remained persistent.[49] Yet if in *The Iron Chest* and elsewhere the fashion for the Gothic could make the library all too dramatic, then gentler, but still pointed, mockery of female taste for fiction and circulating libraries continued. In Irish writer Thomas Moore's 1811 comic opera *M. P. or The Blue-Stocking*, several scenes take place in 'A Circulating Library' run by a man called Leatherhead. This busy library's stock extends from *Tricks upon Travellers* and *Road to Ruin* to 'Ovid's *Art of Love*', and mocking mention is made of such recent works as Walter Scott's 'the *Lady of the Lake* to be delivered at the *Lying-in Hospital*', and (in a risqué joke) a modern novel by Sydney Owenson—'how the *Wild Irish Girl* has been tossed and tumbled by Captain O'Callaghan'.[50] If a few of this library's readers are men, most are women. The play's jokes are ambitiously bookish, taking in Johnsonian criticism of the metaphysical poets Donne and Cowley as well as mockery of 'Lady Bab Blue's library', the book collection of a 'lady of learning' whose tastes run from the Roman historian Sallust to scientific tomes and Eliza Haywood's popular 1751 novel about a strong-minded wife, *The History of Miss Betsy Thoughtless*. Provocatively, Lady Bab complains that a man who is rearranging her library books has placed '*Sir Isaac Newton* in the corner with *Betsy Thoughtless*'.[51] Though the library and character of the polymathic bluestocking are mocked in this play and in others of the early nineteenth century, it does pay a back-handed tribute to the power exercised by both the commercial circulating library and the private library of a woman wealthy enough to be able to develop her intellectual passions.

[48] Colman, *The Iron Chest*, 51, 20.
[49] John Stokes, *The Forest of Rosenwald* (New York: E. Munden, 1821), 1.
[50] Thomas Moore, *M. P. or the Blue-stocking* (London: J. Power et al., 1811), 19, 21.
[51] Moore, *M. P. or the Blue-stocking*, 39, 57.

Yet as the nineteenth century progresses, a new type of library appears on stage: a library that is entirely fake. An early example of this occurs in Emmeline Stuart-Wortley's five-act comedy *Moonshine* (1843), in which Mr Montague de Batenbille, M. P., tells two titled ladies,

> My father possesses the finest library in Europe; universally allowed to be so; it is quite perfect and complete, and of enormous dimensions: – three chimney pieces – two magnificent tables – luxurious reading chairs; it has, indeed, no books, but the cases are very fine and ample, and there are some false backs, put up with Morocco bindings, that answer all the purposes of books most satisfactorily.[52]

While it can be linked to the collections of faux books made by Thomas Hood and Charles Dickens which were mentioned in Chapter 1 of the present volume, this library in *Moonshine*, which signals the power of opulence but contains no real books, can be seen, too, as a forerunner of many libraries in later nineteenth- and early twentieth-century dramas that make use of the private library simply as a setting to indicate social class and economic power. Where earlier stage depictions of libraries had included quite specific references to particular books, now the individual books count for nothing: it is the look that matters. While a few little-known dramas might feature rather undramatic scenes of book-reading, the scholarly library could be used in this era as an indicator of boredom: 'Pshaw! Wed me to a musty library!' exclaims a young woman disgustedly in James Sheridan Knowles's *The Hunchback* (1832).[53] 'Dark, and not very cheerful' sums up the library in William Bayle Bernard's mid-nineteenth-century comedy *The Tide of Time*.[54] While a curiosity such as Samuel Woodward's 1831 'dramatic medley' which brings to America classical muses to celebrate *The Ninth Anniversary of the New York Mirror* and includes a Librarian and a versified library catalogue of American literature, on the whole libraries onstage were becoming places associated less with books and more with men reading news-papers or smoking. 'I think you might take that cigar into the library,' Mrs Naggleton advises her husband in Shirley Brooks's genteel Victorian comedy *The Naggletons*.[55]

Seeking to present an atmosphere of upper-class opulence, later nineteenth-century plays sometimes specify specific items of library furniture, but almost never specific books. The 'Fairy Library' in James Robinson Planché's 1852 'fairy extravaganza' *The Good Woman in the Wood* is a rare exception that helps prove

---

[52] Emmeline Stuart-Wortley, *Moonshine* (London: W. S. Johnson, 1843), 35.
[53] James Sheridan Knowles, *The Dramatic Works* (London: Routledge, 1859), 242.
[54] William Bayle Bernard, *The Tide of Time* (London: Thomas Hailes Lacy, 1859), 40.
[55] Shirley Brooks, *The Naggletons* (London: Bradbury, Agnew, 1875), 65.

this rule.[56] As if anticipating the milieu of *The Great Gatsby*, in American dramatist Lester Wallack's 1863 *Rosedale* Mr Bunberry Kobb makes clear with regard to the selection of books for his plush library, 'I left it to the bookseller—gave him the size of the shelves to an inch; wait till you see them—quite full—all bound alike—devilish expensive, too.'[57] By the time of Oscar Wilde's 1899 *An Ideal Husband* the well-appointed private library is a place for newspapers and idle chat, not direct engagement with books. With its Americans in Europe, Richard Harding Davis's 1906 farce *The Galloper* specifies in great detail the hotel 'reading room' set for its opening scene, detailing writing table, 'long library table' on which are ranged 'periodicals and the illustrated papers of different countries', photographs 'of the Acropolis' and 'classic Greek statues', but paying no attention to any volumes.[58] Books in plays' library scenes are now most often general props. Clyde Fitch's 1915 American drama *The City* specifies particular artworks and furniture that feature in the library in which the opening scene is set, but that scene is oblivious to particular books. The same is true for *The Witching Hour* by Fitch's American contemporary Augustus Thomas, which also opens in a library; and for Edward Sheldon's 1917 *Romance*. Such libraries, functioning as wallpaper rather than as collections of specific titles, still testify to a kind of power, but that power is simply economic. Generally, libraries as locations where people engage significantly with books fade from the twentieth-century theatre, even as they remain significant in twentieth-century fiction and, at times, in the new medium of cinema. The most dramatic libraries in modern live theatre are likely to be those in revivals of much older plays.

It is appropriate, though, to end this chapter with a resonant exception. Tom Stoppard's *Travesties* (1974) is the most remarkable play set in a library in the last hundred years, and may be unique in modern drama for the use it makes of its bookroom setting. Its opening stage direction makes clear that one of the play's two locations is 'a section of the Zurich Public Library', and, though only tall bookcases and a librarian's desk are specified as required by this setting, some performances have made much of the all-pervading bibliophilia of the play.[59] The 2018 London and Broadway production directed by Patrick Marber, for instance, featured a set designed to suggest what critic Ben Brantley called in *The New York Times* 'a ransacked library of the mind'. Marber had Stoppard's sometimes confused memoirist Henry Carr sitting in an armchair surrounded by piles of books, and then 'standing among a scattered wreckage of books and loose papers' in the 'room' which, as the play's other location, alternates with the more ordered

---

[56] James Robinson Planché, *The Good Woman in the Wood* (London: Thomas Hailes Lacy [, 1852]), 26.

[57] Lester Wallack, *Rosedale* [1863], in Isaac Goldberg and Hubert Heffner, ed., *Davy Crockett and Other Plays* (Princeton: Princeton University Press, 1940), 6.

[58] Richard Harding Davis, *Farces* (New York: Charles Scribner's Sons, 1906), 137, 138.

[59] Tom Stoppard, *Travesties* (London: Faber & Faber, 1974), 1.

reading space of the Public Library.[60] Featuring James Joyce, V. I. Lenin, and the Dadaist Tristan Tzara, all of whom lived and worked in Zurich, *Travesties* also includes local librarian Cecily Carruthers. Joyce, who had a fondness for the lions of the Zurich Zoo, is the first of the characters to call her a 'librarianness', though this word which seems to fuse together 'librarian' and 'lioness', is later applied to her by Tzara too. In the play's first scene, Cecily appears thoroughly stereotyped, as she emerges from what Joyce in an apparently improvised limerick calls 'her niche', and, disapproving of 'garrulity in the Reference Section', tries to control her remarkable readers with the repeated injunction, 'Shhhh!' Tzara thinks her 'rather pretty, and well-bred', but fears 'her views on poetry are very old fashioned and her knowledge of the poets, as indeed of everything else, is eccentric, being based on alphabetic precedence'. Used to 'working her way along the shelves', Cecily, it transpires, has read such poets as William Allingham, Anon, Matthew Arnold, Hilaire Belloc, William Blake, Elizabeth and Robert Browning, Lord Byron, and other writers of verse, but seems not to have read the work of any poet whose surname begins with a letter of the alphabet beyond 'G'.[61]

In a play which repeatedly juxtaposes ideas of revolutionary anarchy with declining traditional mores, the orderliness of the library may be viewed as representing the old order in literature, politics, and art. However, Cecily, the representative of the library who is in some ways a caricature—even a travesty—of a conventional librarian, is also presented as helping Joyce, Tzara, and Lenin in the creation of their writings as books in this bookish drama are refashioned from older books. Cecily's remark that 'Intellectual curiosity is not so common that one can afford to discourage it' not only signals her librarianly professionalism but also presages a certain transformation in which, having absorbed a good deal from her library's early twentieth-century patrons, she berates the bumbling Englishman Carr as a 'bourgeois intellectual humbugger' and a 'patronising Kant-struck prig' who discourses on 'classes' while all the time 'trying to imagine how I'd look stripped off to my knickers'. Though Carr maintains that this is a lie, a stage direction makes clear that 'apparently it isn't'. Then, to the sound of a band from 1974 'playing "The Stripper"', Cecily mounts her desk while cabaret-style lights play across her body and she does a striptease.[62] Eventually, we discover that she has married Carr, and the veracity of Carr's memories of the Zurich Public Library capers of his youth is called seriously—or, more accurately, absurdly—into question.

In this Zurich-set play of epoch-changing political, sexual, literary, and artistic energies, the Public Library is the place where these energies are both fuelled and released. Twenty-first-century critics might argue over how much the often

---

[60] Ben Brantley, 'Screwball Eggheads Tear Up the Library in "Travesties"', *New York Times*, 25 April 2018, Section c, 5.
[61] Stoppard, *Travesties*, 31, 32.   [62] Stoppard, *Travesties*, 64, 66.

stereotypical presentation of Cecily owes to sexist attitudes of the 1970s, and just how central the library setting really is to this drama of untethered ideas. At once theatrical and metatheatrical, the shifting onstage antics and allusions to offstage events, texts, and ideological forces make *Travesties* a work that is challengingly complex to discuss as it mixes the ludic with hints of nostalgia and menace. Yet what is surely undeniable is that, almost uniquely in modern theatre, it offers its audience a vision of the library not just as a kind of accidental backdrop or a marker of social prestige but as a place of both latent and actual power where the modern world can be born.

3

Battle-Sites of Books

Tom Jones

In 1704, Jonathan Swift published *A Tale of a Tub. Written for the Universal Improvement of Mankind. To which is added, An Account of a Battel between the Antient and Modern Books in St. James's Library*. The volume also included, as its third part, 'A Discourse Concerning the Mechanical Operation of the Spirit. In a Letter to a Friend. A Fragment'. In Swift's battle of the books the library becomes a site of contest. The library is not just the setting for (part of) the action of the text. It is a place, an institution, and a concept, the definition of which is important strategic territory in the conflict in which Swift is engaging. How the book, its constituent technologies, and the related technology of storing books can best contribute to humanity is the contest the present chapter discusses. Swift explores this question in the context of a book written as a means of conservative social regulation, and this chapter will conclude by moving towards discussion of the growing phenomenon of ladies' libraries, and in particular an anthology called *The Ladies Library*, again in the context of social regulation. To begin with, though, I will establish the background of Swift's 'Battel'.

Jonathan Swift, a young graduate of Trinity College Dublin, had to leave Ireland in 1689 on account of the War of the Two Kings, during which supporters of the deposed monarch James II clashed with the newly enthroned King William III. William Temple, the retired diplomat and essayist, was a friend of the Swift family and employed Swift as his secretary. Swift lived with Temple and his family at Moor Park in Surrey between 1690 and 1694 and again from 1696 until 1699, when Temple died.[1] The *Tale* was composed during this second period, mostly in 1697. One of Swift's tasks as secretary was the publication of Temple's essays, letters, and memoirs, a process that continued after Temple's death. Swift saw three volumes of Temple's *Miscellanea* through the press. The first essay in the *Miscellanea. The Second Part* of 1690 was 'A Essay upon the Ancient and Modern Learning', written in 1689.[2] Temple defends the ancients from the challenge that

---

[1] Irvin Ehrenpreis, *Swift: The Man, His Works, and the Age, I: Mr Swift and his Contemporaries* (London: Methuen, 1962), 88–93, 169.

[2] *The Cambridge Edition of the Works of Jonathan Swift*, ed. Claude Rawson, Ian Higgins, James McLaverty, and David Womersley, I, *A Tale of a Tub and Other Works*, ed. Marcus Walsh (2010), introduction lxxiv–lxxv. Further references in this chapter will be made parenthetically by page number in the main text.

moderns have excelled them in every intellectual field. The capacity of ancient literature to communicate the character (wit, force, genius, race) of its creators is one of Temple's chief concerns. He makes the claim that the texts known as the Epistles of Phalaris are genuine productions of a tyrant of the era of Cyrus and Pythagoras, rather than accepting the attribution to Lucian that had been suggested. He thought they 'have more Race, more Spirit, more Force of Wit and Genius, than any others I have ever seen, either ancient or modern':

> he must have little skill in Painting, that cannot find out this to be an Original; such diversity of Passions, upon such variety of Actions, and Passages of Life and Government, such Freedom of Thought, such Boldness of Expression, such Bounty to his Friends, such Scorn of his Enemies, such Honour of Learned men, such esteem of Good, such Knowledge of Life, such contempt of Death, with such Fierceness of Nature and Cruelty of Revenge, could never be represented, but by him that possessed them; and I esteem *Lucian* to have been no more capable of Writing, than of acting what *Phalaris* did. In all one Writ, you find the Scholar or the Sophist; and in all the other, the Tyrant and the Commander.[3]

Texts, Temple suggests, will reveal qualities of the character of the person that produced them. They are revelations, not representations. An attempt to represent the qualities that an original production displays would not be convincing. For Temple, then, the letters are a means by which he and other appropriately qualified readers can identify the attributes of a certain type of ancient nobility, and respond to it in their own lives and practice.

Temple's essay initiates a local phase in the conflict between the ancients and the moderns. William Wotton, a young Fellow of the Royal Society, responded to Temple's essay in his 1694 *Reflections upon Ancient and Modern Learning*, giving some ground to the ancients but emphasizing the progress of modern mathematical and physical sciences, and philological and historical learning. A group from Christ Church, Oxford, including Charles Boyle, produced a new edition of the Epistles of Phalaris in 1695, not explicitly stating their authenticity, but clearly in keeping with Temple's attitude. That edition contained the allegation that Richard Bentley, keeper of the King's Library at St James's Palace, had not allowed the editors to consult a manuscript of the epistles. Bentley responded with a 'Dissertation upon the Epistles of Phalaris' that was appended to the second edition of Wotton's *Reflections* in 1697 and set out his arguments against the authenticity of the letters. There were further sallies on each side before Temple's 'Some Thoughts upon Reviewing the Essay of Antient and Modern Learning' was

---

[3] William Temple, *Miscellanea. The Second Part*, 4th ed. (London: Ri. and Ra. Simpson, 1696), 59.

published after the author's death by Swift in 1701 in *Miscellanea. The Third Part*. Swift himself published the *Tale* in 1704, with Bentley and Wotton featuring throughout, as well as in the 'Battel'.

The battle of the books is ostensibly over who can claim the greatest advances in the various branches of human knowledge. It was an old debate, given a new form in England at the turn of the eighteenth century. Joseph Levine, the great recent historian of the battle, has pointed to a generally accepted division whereby imitative disciplines such as the arts were granted to the ancients, and disciplines that were more cumulative to the moderns.[4] Within the humanities, the battle is actually between the modern scholarly science of exhuming classical texts and the ancient tradition of imitating them as exemplars. Levine suggests that

> the very instruments of classical scholarship, the commentary, dictionary, index, above all, the footnote, all new and modern in their time, appeared to impede the desire for elegance and for eloquence.... the very advances in philological and archaeological learning, the real addition to the understanding of classical authors that resulted, began to threaten the confidence in imitation and in the ancient wisdom[.][5]

The battle involved humane knowledge understood either as taking on the character of the ancients or as the dispassionate consideration of the material evidence as a discrete historical entity.

'The Battel of the Books' sets some of its action in the Royal Library, where Bentley was keeper. Documentation of royal library holdings reaches back into the fourteenth century, and relates to various library sites (at Eltham, Richmond, and Whitehall, for example). James I made St James's Palace the residence of his son, Henry Frederic, who was a collector, and built a new library, probably under the supervision of Inigo Jones.[6] Bentley was appointed in 1694 and revived the deposit rights of the library, which it had been granted in 1666, bringing in at his own estimate 1000 volumes. Bentley was not happy with the physical resources of the library in terms of space and the preservation and extension of the collection.[7] Humfrey Wanley and John Evelyn both remarked on the disorderliness of the library in the period immediately prior to Bentley's appointment.[8] In 1697,

---

[4] Joseph M. Levine, *The Battle of the Books: History and Literature in the Augustan Age* (London and Ithaca: Cornell University Press, 1991), 2.

[5] Joseph M. Levine, 'Ancients and Moderns Reconsidered', *Eighteenth-Century Studies* 15.1 (Autumn 1981): 82–3.

[6] I am entirely indebted here to Joanna Frońska, *The Royal Collection of Manuscripts*, https://www.bl.uk/catalogues/illuminatedmanuscripts/TourRoyalGen.asp, accessed 9 May 2019.

[7] Raymond Irwin, *The Heritage of the English Library* (London: George Allen & Unwin, 1964), 241. See also K. W. Humphreys, *A National Library in Theory and Practice (The Panizzi Lectures, 1987)* (London: British Library, 1988), 6–7.

[8] Mark McDayter, 'The Haunting of St. James's Library: Librarians, Literature, and the "Battle of the Books"', *Huntington Library Quarterly* 66.1/2 (2003): 7–8.

Bentley made a proposal for a new building that included meeting space and an ambitious acquisitions policy, funded by a duty on imported paper, all on the presumption that the library was for public use.[9] Bentley inherited a stagnant collection in a poorly appointed space, but was imagining, and in part implemented, improvements that would facilitate the type of modern philological research in which he himself was engaged.[10]

The library in which the 'Battel' that takes place, then, was far from the ideal of its keeper. The statement on the title page (and section title) that the 'Battel' was fought in St James's library must, in any case, be qualified. The bookseller's address to the reader says that the books in St James's library themselves took up the quarrel between Temple and Boyle on the one side, Wotton and Bentley on the other. But the main text begins the action quite elsewhere: 'This Quarrel first began ... about a small Spot of Ground, *lying* and *being* upon one of the two Tops of the Hill *Parnassus*; the highest and largest of which, had it seems, been time out of Mind, in quiet Possession of certain Tenants, call'd the *Antients*; And the other was held by the *Moderns*' (144). The ancients refer to themselves as aborigines, and the moderns as colonists to whom they have granted some land. They refuse the modern demand to exchange peaks, but offer to help the moderns raise their peak to the height of the ancients' (144–5). The moderns' refusal initiates a war. The first battle, then, is set in 'Parnassus', a place standing in for an indefinite abstraction, probably something like 'the total stock of human intellectual endeavour'.

We are told that the war was not easily ended, and that it was fought in ink (quills as spears). Controversial pamphlets are published by both sides in order to claim victory in any encounter that does not have a clear issue. From this point the physical space of the—or at least a—library comes into view as the place where these controversial publications are collected. 'In these Books', our author tells us, 'is wonderfully instilled and preserved, the Spirit of each Warrier, while he is alive; and after his Death, his Soul transmigrates there, to inform them' (145). Here Swift reifies, a strategy central to the 'Battel' and the *Tale* at large.[11] The books of controversy are kept isolated and bound in place by chains in the library to prevent them fomenting social disorder (146). The violent controversy between books supporting either side in the dispute over the peaks of Parnassus disrupts the peace that could otherwise have been kept in libraries.

Before continuing with the 'Battel', it is worth noting the opening of the *Tale* here, which itself posits a connection between publishing and social order. The narrator reports in the 'Preface' on the reason for writing his book. It is a moment

[9] Irwin, *Heritage of the English Library*, 242.
[10] For an account of Bentley's work as librarian and his contributions to the battle see Kristine Louise Haugen, *Richard Bentley: Poetry and Enlightenment* (Cambridge, MA: Harvard University Press, 2011), 105–23.
[11] McDayter, 'The Haunting of St. James's Library', 18.

at which Swift's voice might come through his ironized narrator: 'The Wits of the present Age being so very numerous and penetrating, it seems, the Grandees of *Church* and *State* begin to fall under horrible Apprehensions, lest these Gentlemen, during the intervals of a long Peace, should find leisure to pick Holes in the weak sides of Religion and Government.' Something must be done, and the relation of a seaman's anecdote of distracting whales from ruining ships by casting them a tub to play with is taken as the prompt. 'The *Whale* was interpreted to be *Hobs*'s *Leviathan*, which tosses and plays with all other Schemes of Religion and Government...This is the *Leviathan* from whence the terrible Wits of our Age are said to borrow their Weapons. The *Ship* in danger, is easily understood to be its old Antitype the *Commonwealth*.' The tub itself is just a tub. 'And it was decreed, that in order to prevent these *Leviathans* from tossing and sporting with the *Commonwealth*, (which of it self is too apt to *fluctuate*) they should be diverted from that Game by a *Tale of a Tub*. And my Genius being conceived to lye not unhappily that way, I had the Honor done me to be engaged in the Performance' (25). That is, the *Tale* is a device to distract modern wits from their chief business of using Hobbesian means to trouble the state and established religion. This is a plausible description of Swift's satiric aim; it is also an indication of where, for him, literary culture might sit in relation to social order. Swift's intervention in the dispute between the ancients and the moderns has a pronounced social regulatory character that is deeply conservative.[12] I will suggest below that this conservative social regulatory function is shared with the production of *The Ladies Library* by George Berkeley, with Richard Steele, in 1714.

Returning to the 'Battel', the figure of Bentley bridges the different conceptual spaces of the text, 'Parnassus' and 'St James' library'. He attempts to knock two ancient chiefs from a pass on their summit, and on failing to do so retaliates against the ancients by ensuring that any book which advocated for them 'was buried alive in some obscure Corner' of the King's library. St James's library comes more firmly into view. The parties begin to organize themselves, and Temple, who, 'having been educated and long conversed among the *Antients*, was, of all the *Moderns*, their greatest Favorite, and became their greatest Champion' (148), informs the ancients of the moderns' intention to make war. No books have yet exchanged blows, and before they do so an extended exchange between a spider and bee, representatives of the moderns and ancients respectively, occurs within the conceptual space of the library, and is interpreted (in a surprisingly redundant fashion) by Aesop, another chief ancient whose authenticity had been defended by Temple and challenged by Bentley.[13] There then follow the mock-epic encounters

---

[12] Randy Robertson, 'Swift's "Leviathan" and the End of Licensing', *Pacific Coast Philology* 40.2 (2005): 44 ('the Tale's narrative chaos is in the service of national order') and 50.

[13] The bee asks on p. 151, '*Whether is the nobler Being of the two, That which by a lazy Contemplation of four Inches round; by an over-weening Pride, which feeding and engendering on it*

between specific paired ancients and moderns for which the text is best known, and in which the ancients come off best even if there are some consolations for some moderns.[14]

The setting within the library is not consistently maintained. Phalaris and Aesop are sleeping by an oak when Bentley seizes their armour; he takes his way until he arrives at one of the streams of Mount Helicon. The library, then, contains or is contained by the geography of ancient Greece with which the text started. The setting of the 'Battel' is a conceptual blend of the geography of ancient Greece, conceived as an analogy for all human knowledge, and the space of a particular library. That library is itself conceived as a site of conflict in which ancient and modern texts compete with one another, as do ancient and modern attitudes towards the study of texts. The 'Battel' reifies by imagining that the intellectual controversy was played out by the physical books in the physical library. But libraries are never just physical spaces. Conceptions of what knowledge is, how it might be organized, communicated, and acquired are bound up in the architecture of libraries.[15] The 'Battel' takes place in, or one might say for or over, the *concept* of the library and its relation to humanity—how best to acquire knowledge about humans, and how best to become human, in part through the acquisition of such knowledge.

The *Tale* and its companion pieces make up a mock book.[16] (In this context we might think of the mock book as a book that dares its reader to consider it worth preserving in a library.) Swift acquired the intimacy with the book trade necessary for producing such an intricate parody of the modern book by publishing Temple's works in the 1690s.[17] The *Tale* is also a response to the lapse of the Licensing Act in 1695 and the consequent increase in publishing activity.[18] In the world that Swift parodies, books are conceived of as productions or products, rather than performances. Engaging with books is conceived of as the mastery of (physical) material, rather than the adoption of exemplary character. Swift

---

self, turns all into Excrement and Venom; producing nothing at last, but Fly-bane and a Cobweb: Or That, which, by an universal Range, with long Search, much Study, true Judgment, and Distinction of Things, brings home Honey and Wax.'

[14] Cowley is defeated by Pindar, p.160, but half the leaves of the volume are 'turned into Feathers, and being gilded before, continued gilded still; so it became a *Dove*' which Venus 'harness'd ... to her Chariot'.

[15] Lee Fallin, 'Beyond Books: The Concept of the Academic Library as Learning Space', *New Library World* 117.5/6 (2016): 310; Werner Oechslin, '"Mentalmente architettato" – Thoughts in Physical Form: Immutable or Dynamic? The Case of the Library', in *Collection, Laboratory, Theatre: Scenes of Knowledge in the 17th Century*, ed. Helmar Schramm, Ludger Schwarte, and Jan Lazardzig (*Theatrum Scientiarum*, English ed. Vol. 1) (Berlin: de Gruyter, 2005), 122–45.

[16] Marcus Walsh, 'Swift's *Tale of a Tub* and the Mock Book', in *Jonathan Swift and the Eighteenth-Century Book*, ed. Paddy Bullard and James McLaverty (Cambridge: Cambridge University Press, 2013), 101–18.

[17] Michael Treadwell, 'Swift's Relations with the London Book Trade to 1714', in *Author/Publisher Relations During the Eighteenth and Nineteenth Centuries*, ed. Robin Myers and Michael Harris (Oxford: Oxford Polytechnic Press, 1983), *Publishing Pathways*, 6–7.

[18] Robertson, 'Swift's "Leviathan"', 42.

presents a world in which commentary, dictionary, index, and footnote (to repeat Levine's list) have supplanted almost all other textuality.[19] Noting that, in the 'Battel', Bentley's 'Armour was patch'd up of a thousand incoherent Pieces' (160), Stephen Zwicker suggests that 'we might take the figure skimming indices as an emblem of the technologies of reading c. 1700'. Zwicker's point is that modern book technology is presented as removing the active labour that was required of the reader drawing on the ancients for examples to imitate. The index permits efficient assembly of materials without an underlying labour corresponding to or enabling the transformation of character.[20] Paddy Bullard contrasts the physical commitment to the book and page required of Gulliver in the King's library at Brobdingnag, already discussed by Robert Crawford in Chapter 1.[21]

Swift distrusted these forms of economizing book technology. The teller of the *Tale* laments that 'no famous *Modern* hath ever yet attempted an universal System in a small portable Volume, of all Things that are to be Known, or Believed, or Imagined, or Practised in Life'. (He acknowledges that some think of Homer as presenting 'a compleat Body of all Knowledge Human, Divine, Political, and Mechanick' but finds him wanting in Cabbala, mechanics, common law, and 'the Doctrine as well as Discipline of the Church of *England*' (83).) The teller, however, has 'a certain curious *Receipt*, a *Nostrum*' to assist any modern taking the task on: boil down '*correct Copies . . . of all Modern Bodies of Arts and Sciences whatsoever, and in what Language you please*'; add opiates and '*three Pints of Lethe*'; evaporate and distil until

> *what remains will amount to about two Drams. This you keep in a Glass Viol* Hermetically *sealed. . . . Then you begin your Catholick Treatise, taking every Morning . . . three Drops of this* Elixir, *snuffing it strongly up your Nose. It will dilate it self about the Brain (where there is any) in fourteen Minutes, and you immediately perceive in your Head an infinite Number of* Abstracts, Summaries, Compendiums, Extracts, Collections, Medulla's, Excerpta quaedam's, Florilegia's *and the like, all disposed into great Order, and reducible upon Paper.*   (82)

The index as distillation or digest is mocked. The moderns 'have discovered a shorter, and more prudent Method, to become *Scholars* and *Wits*, without the Fatigue of *Reading* or of *Thinking*'. The 'choicer, the profounder, and politer Method' is 'to get a thorough Insight into the *Index*, by which the whole Book is governed and turned, like *Fishes* by the *Tail*. . . . Thus Physicians discover the State of the whole Body, by consulting only what comes from *Behind*. Thus Men catch

---

[19] Marcus Walsh, 'Text, "Text", and Swift's *Tale of a Tub*', *Modern Language Review* 85.2 (1990): 296.

[20] Steven N. Zwicker, 'The Constitution of Opinion and the Pacification of Reading', in *Reading, Society and Politics in Early Modern England*, ed. Kevin Sharpe and Steven N. Zwicker (Cambridge: Cambridge University Press, 2003), 297–300.

[21] Paddy Bullard, 'What Swift Did in Libraries', in Bullard and McLaverty, *Jonathan Swift*, 80.

Knowledge by throwing their *Wit* on the *Posteriors* of a Book, as Boys do Sparrows with flinging *Salt* upon their *Tails*' (96). The consulter of indexes is an investigator of others' dirty remains. If the index is a digest of the whole book, a way of bypassing the (truly productive) labour of reading and thinking, it is one that involves its practitioner in muck. This association between modern forms of book production and the excremental is one I shall explore further below. It is also important to note the social and political attitudes that are associated with the forms of knowledge and book production and consumption seen in Brobdingnag. Brobdingnagian law is of very limited extent, no law containing more words than there are letters in the alphabet. Brobdingnagian culture could, reading against the grain, be seen as an implausible act of concentration, just like the narrator's nostrum. Brobdingnagian libraries must be of such limited extent (the King's is the largest at 1000 volumes) partly because laws are economically expressed, interpreted in only one sense, and any act of commentary upon them a capital crime.[22] The economical character of this culture is authoritarian, and determined to weed out the canker of meddling professionals such as lawyers and, one might presume, other textual commentators that the true judge deems unqualified.

The target of Swift's pastiche in the *Tale* is, however, clear enough. Wotton notes that printing has improved the production of knowledge by cheapening book production, increasing diffusion, and easing consumption. Books may also 'be printed with Indexes, and other necessary Divisions, which, though they may be made in *MSS.* yet they will make them so voluminous and cumbersome, that not one in Forty who now mind Books, because they love Reading, would then apply themselves to it.'[23] The physical ease of finding matter of particular concern makes reading more popular, less exclusive, more functional. In the sociology of knowledge and genius that the moderns are proposing, diffusion is a good thing, prompting emulation and advance; the ancients maintain the value of an exclusive access to and imitation of the exemplar tradition.[24] Bullard has noted that Swift likely inherited his dislike of excessively large modern libraries from Temple, and that he conceived of the resulting specialization of knowledge as a constraint on active participation in civil life.[25]

If the difference between the use of books envisaged by the ancients and moderns is the difference between the acquisition of character through transformative

---

[22] *The Cambridge Edition of the Works of Jonathan Swift*, XVI, *Gulliver's Travels*, ed. David Womersley (2012), Book II, ch. 7.

[23] William Wotton, *Reflections Upon Ancient and Modern Learning* (London: J. Leake for Peter Buck, 1694), 171–2.

[24] One could parse these attitudes into David Hume's analysis that monarchies promote imitation and the polite arts, republics emulation and the sciences; 'Of the Rise and Progress of the Arts and Sciences', in *Essays Moral, Political and Literary*, ed. Eugene F. Miller, rev. ed. (Indianapolis: Liberty Fund, 1987), 125–6.

[25] Bullard, 'What Swift Did in Libraries', 66. The management of Swift's personal library is described on pp. 71–2.

encounter and the accessing of information through efficient material systems, there is a corresponding difference in conceiving the library. Wotton contends with Temple's notion that the Ptolemaian library contained 600,000 volumes, each of which was a masterwork of antiquity. As well as questioning the numbers, Wotton notes that 'he that raises a Library, takes in Books of all Values; since bad Books have their Uses to Learned Men, as well as good ones'.[26] Temple, in the extended citations Wotton makes from him, criticizes the separation of university book learning from the practical induction into a way of life that was characteristic of ancient knowledge, and the mechanical industry of the scholar:

> The Moderns gather all their Learning out of Books in Universities, which are but dumb Guides, that can lead Men but one Way, without being able to set them right if they should wander from it.... To pore in old *MSS.* to compare various Readings; to turn over *Glossaries*, and old *Scholia* upon Ancient Historians, Orators and Poets; to be minutely critical in all the little Fashions of the Ancient *Greeks* and *Romans*, the Memory whereof was, in a manner, lost within Fifty or an Hundred Years after they had been in use; may be good Arguments of a Man's Industry, and Willingness to drudge; but seem to signifie little to denominate him a great Genius, or one who was able to do great Things of himself.[27]

Temple draws from Wotton an over-egged defence of the modern philological scholar: 'There are Thousands of Corrections and Censures upon Authors to be found in the Annotations of Modern Criticks, which required more Fineness of Thought, and Happiness of Invention, than, perhaps, Twenty such Volumes as those were, upon which these very Criticisms were made.'[28] The modern book and library enable the kind of critical philological intervention that Wotton admires by providing economical means of accessing information. Such achievements are no indication of great character or the capacity for active life, as Temple believes ancient texts are.

Both these models, of ancient reader and modern critic, are exclusively masculine. There is very little space for female figures in 'The Battel of the Books', but femininity plays a vital conceptual role in the text. '*Afra* the *Amazon*' (Aphra Behn) is amongst those (some unnamed) slain by Pindar before his less one-sided encounter with Abraham Cowley. The goddess Dulness makes a brief appearance, transforming herself into the figure of Horace to distract Thomas Creech and lead him safely out of combat and back to his father, John Ogilby. The goddess Diffidence operates unseen on Dryden and encourages him to accept an exchange of gifts with Virgil (all 158–9). It is the goddess Criticism, however, who is the

---

[26] Wotton, *Reflections*, 84.   [27] Temple, cited in Wotton, *Reflections*, 86–7, 316.
[28] Wotton, *Reflections*, 317–18.

presiding deity of the moderns. Momus, fearing the worst for the moderns, flies to Criticism—daughter and wife to Ignorance, daughter of Pride, sister to Opinion, mother of Noise, Impudence, Dullness, Vanity, Positiveness, Pedantry, and Ill Manners. She has

> Claws like a Cat: Her Head, and Ears, and Voice, resembled those of an *Ass*; Her Teeth fallen out before; Her Eyes turned inward, as if she lookt only upon herself: Her Diet was the overflowing of her own *Gall*: Her *Spleen* was so large, as to stand prominent like a Dug of the first Rate, nor wanted Excrescencies in form of Teats, at which a Crew of ugly Monsters were greedily sucking[.]   (154)

She is rendered monstrous particularly in her sexed and gendered characteristics, her reproductive capacity.[29] Criticism declares her powers of raising juniors above their seniors, and enabling judgement without knowledge. She flies in her goose-drawn chariot to her favoured isle of Britain, dispensing goods to the 'Seminaries of *Gresham College* and *Covent-Garden*' as she goes. She is immediately taken up in defence of Wotton, her child (by unknown father), and appears to him as an octavo of the works of Bentley (155).

The engraving that accompanies the 'Battel' in the 1710 edition of the *Tale* shows just one female figure, Fame, hovering above the battle scene, blowing from one raised trumpet, holding the other down and behind her. Some illustrations of Ripa's *Iconologia*, the early seventeenth-century handbook of emblems, depict Fame similarly.[30] Samuel Butler's Fame 'boards / Her self on Air' and has wings on her shoulders.

> Two Trumpets she does sound at once,
> But both of clean contrary tones.
> But whether both with the same Wind,
> Or one before, and one behind,
> We know not; only this can tell,
> Th' one sounds vilely, th' other well.
> And therefore vulgar Authors name
> Th' one good, th' other Evil *Fame*.[31]

---

[29] For maternity in Swift see Louise Barnett, *Jonathan Swift in the Company of Women* (Oxford: Oxford University Press, 2007), 110–24.

[30] A 1644 French illustration of 'Renommée' from a version of Ripa's text is reproduced by Valerie Mainz, *Days of Glory? Imaging Military Recruitment and the French Revolution* (Basingstoke: Palgrave Macmillan, 2016), 216.

[31] Samuel Butler, *Hudibras* (London: W. Rogers, 1684), II.i, 226–7. According to an anecdote related by Laetitia Pilkington (who herself knew Shakespeare by heart), Swift, if provided with any line of the poem, could continue to recite it from memory. See Brean Hammond, 'Swift's Reading', in *The Cambridge Companion to Jonathan Swift*, ed. Christopher Fox (Cambridge: Cambridge University Press, 2003), 76.

Figure 3.1. George II in the Library of St James's Palace, *c*.1738, by Charles Philips (1703–47). Marble Hill House. Image PLB/J920095, © Historic England Archive and used with permission.

Charles Philips's portrait of George II standing, with his dogs, by the entrance to the St James's Palace library shows a life-size statue of a female figure mounted on a plinth just within (Figure 3.1). Her spear, plumed helmet, and attitude recall widely reproduced and imitated depictions of Minerva or Pallas Athena, goddesses of wisdom and the various arts. Criticism and Fame are, in their different ways, travesties of Minerva, the protectress of wisdom, guarding the library entrance. They feminize the object of Swift's antagonism, finding female animating principles and motivations behind the modern, mechanistic scholarship. Though mostly written under William and Mary, the *Tale* was published, and went into its further, expanded editions, in the reign of Anne, who was so often depicted as a benevolent female power behind the scenes, banishing discord and bringing peace in Pope's *Windsor-Forest*, for example, a poem begun in the early and finished in the last years of her reign.

Criticism is figured through monstrous femininity in the 'Battel'. In the *Tale* it is figured through excrement. The *Tale*'s '*Digression concerning* Criticks' distinguishes three kinds, the first two of which have long been extinct. These critics (true in Swift's sense) are either 'the Restorers of Antient Learning from the Worms, and Graves, and Dust of Manuscripts' (that is, textual editors), or, primarily,

> such Persons as invented or drew up Rules for themselves and the World, by observing which, a careful Reader might be able to pronounce upon the productions of the *Learned*, form his Taste to a true Relish of the *Sublime* and the *Admirable*, and divide every Beauty of Matter or of Style from the Corruption that Apes it: In their common perusal of Books, singling out the Errors and Defects, the Nauseous, the Fulsome, the Dull, and the Impertinent, with the Caution of a Man that walks thro' *Edenborough* Streets in a Morning, who is indeed as careful as he can, to watch diligently, and spy out the Filth in his Way, not that he is curious to observe the Colour and Complexion of the Ordure, or take its Dimensions, much less to be paddling in, or tasting it: but only with a Design to come out as cleanly as he may.   (60)

This extinct critic taught one to identify the waste products of the human mind so as to avoid rather than immerse oneself in them. The third kind of critic, the only surviving type and the true modern critic in the narrator's sense, on the contrary sets himself the task 'to travel thro' this vast World of Writings: to pursue and hunt those Monstrous Faults bred within them: to drag out the lurking Errors like *Cacus* from his Den; to multiply them like *Hydra*'s Heads; and rake them together like *Augea*'s Dung' (61–2). The modern critic collects what is monstrous, rejected, excrescent. Wanting to preserve writings of indifferent quality, or simply displacing quality as the criterion for including books in a library, as Wotton suggested, is here travestied as the desire to amass and paddle in as much excrement as possible. More than one of the titles invented for the books of the imaginary libraries Robert Crawford discusses in Chapter 1 hinted that the library gone wrong is one in which waste is preserved. Swift's relish for filth is evident in his elaboration of the image of the critic 'paddling' in ordure. It is one instance of the tendency of the physical to displace the spiritual in the *Tale*, even though

Swift's reifications are apparently admitted to the text with the purpose of travestying materialistic accounts of the world.[32]

The *Tale*'s modern critic has a fellow in a poem Swift published thirty years later. In *The Lady's Dressing Room*, Swift exposes the folly of idealizing the human physical form with what appears to be a relish for the gross.[33] Discovering the contents of his physically idealized lover's chamber pot on a clandestine foray into her dressing room breaks Celia's spell over Strephon, and demoralizes him. The poem gleefully tells us that order is sprung from confusion, and that gaudy tulips rise from dung. While the ostensible moral is that the inseparability of beauty and corruption should induce us to prefer good sense over any physical qualities, many readers have found that the issue of the poem is its protagonist's and author's simultaneous attraction to and revulsion from corporeal femininity, figured through excrement. Can one read back from Strephon to the *Tale*'s modern critic, and to Wotton's promiscuously stocked library? *The Lady's Dressing Room* recognizes that the ideal is bound to the corrupt. But Swift refuses the notion that ideal knowledge is bound to the corruption of modern critical learning. Notionally, *The Lady's Dressing Room* only presents idealized or dese-crated feminine corporeality to reject them both. The *Tale* is concerned to preserve idealized learning from its corruption. Where the two texts are compar-able is in Swift's frequently noted attraction to that which he seems to be writing against—the physical, the excremental, the gross.[34]

One member of Swift's first audience, Lady Mary Wortley Montagu, under-stood Swift's preoccupation with corrupted female bodies as an attempt to regu-late female behaviour. She wrote a poem answering Swift's in which she suggests that his poem was motivated by revenge for being rejected by a female sex worker for his impotence. She is unconcerned at the threat of the poem exposing her dressing room, as she says it will furnish her with toilet paper.[35] Montagu understood Swift's poem as a form of vengeful discipline or regulation that identifies femininity as at least tainted by and at worst entirely constituted by excrement, things better rejected. Her poem is a refusal to conform, performed through the appropriation of the low register. Twenty years after writing her poem, Montagu found another, even more combative, way to respond to Swift, one that again turns his identification of femininity and excrement back upon him, and which also connects excrement and libraries:

---

[32] John Traugott, 'A Tale of a Tub', in *Modern Essays on Eighteenth-Century Literature*, ed. Leopold Damrosch Jr (Oxford: Oxford University Press, 1988), 33.

[33] Jonathan Swift, *The Lady's Dressing Room* (London: J. Roberts, 1732).

[34] For a discussion of the poem's reception and an interpretation suggesting the poem looks into the creative process itself, see Daniel Cook, *Reading Swift's Poetry* (Cambridge: Cambridge University Press, 2020), 246–60.

[35] Mary Wortley Montagu, *The Dean's Provocation for Writing the Lady's Dressing Room* (London: T. Cooper, 1734).

She made a ribald joke of her grudge against Pope, Swift, and Bolingbroke. She told [Francis] Hutchinson they were rascals, and 'shew'd him her Commode, with false back of books': their works. This arrangement, she said, gave her 'the satisfaction of shitting on them every day'.... One can imagine her cackling over this sudden self-association with her fictional whore, Betty, in 'The Reasons that Induced Dr Swift'[.][36]

In turning her commode into a bizarre literary conflict zone, Montagu employs against Swift the same trope of author become book that is at the core of the 'Battel'. I will close this chapter with a discussion of some early steps towards the feminization of the library, recognizing a continuing desire to regulate female comportment in operation in the project for a ladies' library.

When in Dublin and later as Dean of St Patrick's Cathedral, Swift was near two significant libraries, one at Trinity College Dublin, the other founded by Narcissus Marsh in 1703, just around the corner from St Patrick's. As Dean, from 1718 Swift sat on the board of Marsh's library.[37] Although both, eventually, 'public' libraries, these were relatively inaccessible places, and I am unaware of any indication that they were used by women.[38] Emma Clery has demonstrated the non-linear but progressive feminization of eighteenth-century literary culture, partly by distinguishing the feminine virtues distributed by commercial societies from the ideals of a more masculine civic humanism.[39] Bringing books and learning out of masculinized spaces and into a wider and explicitly female world was one aim of the essayistic and periodical literature of the first half of the eighteenth century. Mr Spectator wished to bring 'Philosophy out of Closets and Libraries, Schools and Colleges, to dwell in Clubs and Assemblies, at Tea-Tables and in Coffee-Houses'.[40] If the tea-table is the only venue on that list that strongly suggests mixed-gender company, David Hume's description of the role of the essay writer is more definitive. The essayist is an ambassador from the learned to the conversable world, where women are sovereign. Men of sense, Hume says, respect women's judgements on books in domains appropriate for conversation, the

---

[36] Isobel Grundy, *Lady Mary Wortley Montagu: Comet of the Enlightenment* (Oxford: Oxford University Press, 2001), 566–7.

[37] Bullard, 'What Swift Did in Libraries', 70. Bullard goes on to note Swift's involvement with prominent private book collectors such as Edward Harley and Richard Mead.

[38] Marsh's Library was made permanent and public by law in 1707, despite Swift criticizing part of the Bill. See Muriel McCarthy, 'Introduction', in *The Making of Marsh's Library: Learning, Politics and Religion in Ireland, 1650–1750*, ed. Muriel McCarthy and Ann Simmons (Dublin and Portland, OR: Four Courts Press, 2004), 13, 26. The resolution of the Irish commons to fund TCD's library dedicates money 'for creating a Publick Library' in the College. See Brendan Grimes, 'The Library Buildings up to 1970', in *Essays on the History of Trinity College Library*, ed. Vincent Kinane and Anne Walsh (Dublin and Portland, OR: Four Courts Press, 2000), 73.

[39] Emma J. Clery, *The Feminization Debate in Eighteenth-Century England: Literature, Commerce, and Luxury* (Basingstoke: Palgrave Macmillan, 2004), *passim* and, for example, 5–9.

[40] *The Spectator*, ed. Donald F. Bond, 5 vols (Oxford: Clarendon Press, 1965), I, 44, No. 10, Monday 12 March 1711.

'Delicacy of their Taste' being above 'all the dull Labours of Pedants and Commentators'.[41] By 1742, then, women were recognized as possessing a distinct literary domain over which they were adequate or even the best judges. Addison and Hume in their own ways contribute to the feminization of specific literary spaces and canons, giving women access to and responsibility for literature. Another project of the periodical press of Addison's time, for a ladies' library, used an anthology of improving literature designed for women as a way of emphasizing the responsibilities of the female condition.

Swift was friendly with the group of men behind the 1714 publication of an anthology of texts for women called *The Ladies Library*. Nancy Kendrick has summarized the history of calls in early periodical literature to establish such a library.[42] In *Tatler* No. 248 in 1710, the year of the reissue of the *Tale*, Richard Steele had suggested the assembly of a 'Female Library'. Addison developed the idea in *The Spectator*, reporting an encounter with a Lady and her library, and asking readers for suggestions of improving reading for women (No. 37). Later, Addison moved from consideration of a 'ladies library' in the sense of a collection of books to pondering a 'ladies library' in the (considerably downsized) sense of an anthology of extracts from books. This use of the word 'library' to mean a collection of extracts had begun to be used at the end of the seventeenth century. Now Addison suggested he would search out passages relevant to women in 'the best Authors ancient and modern' (*Spectator* No. 92), who normally wrote for men. He chides Steele for not having produced the 'Catalogue of a Lady's Library' as promised (No. 528). Steele had read George Berkeley's *Treatise Concerning the Principles of Human Knowledge* (1710), and sought out his acquaintance when Berkeley arrived in London in 1713.[43] Berkeley wrote for Steele's *Guardian* and was also contracted to produce 'a Common place or Collection' of those improving passages for ladies.[44] This three-volume anthology was published as *The Ladies Library* and was said to be 'Written by a Lady' and 'Published by Mr STEELE' under Tonson's imprint in 1714.[45] The first volume has a dedication and preface signed by Steele, the latter of which notes the involvement of a clergyman in the preparation of the text, and that it is 'collected out of the several Writings of our greatest Divines, and [is] dispos'd under proper Heads, in order to

---

[41] Hume, *Essays*, 533–5, citation from 536.

[42] Nancy Kendrick, 'Berkeley's Bermuda Project and *The Ladies Library*', in *Berkeley Revisited: Moral, Social and Political Philosophy*, ed. Sébastien Charles (Oxford: Voltaire Foundation, 2015), *Oxford University Studies in the Enlightenment (formerly SVEC)*, 2015.9: 244–5.

[43] For the evidence of Berkeley's involvement see Stephen Parks, 'George Berkeley, Sir Richard Steele and *The Ladies Library*', *The Scriblerian* 13.1 (Autumn 1980): 1–2, and E. J. Furlong and David Berman, 'George Berkeley and *The Ladies Library*', *Berkeley Newsletter* 4 (December 1980): 4–13.

[44] *The Correspondence of George Berkeley*, ed. Marc A. Hight (Cambridge: Cambridge University Press, 2013), letter 39, Berkeley to Percival, 23 February 1713, 81–2.

[45] The other example of Berkeley's literary transvestism is his *Maxims Concerning Patriotism. By a Lady* (Dublin: [s.n.,] 1750). Some have speculated that the attribution indicates the participation of Berkeley's wife, Anne (née Forster), in the work.

fix in the Mind general Rules for Conduct in all the Circumstances of the Life of Woman'.[46] The heads of each volume respectively concern virtues and vices (chastity, pride), the various stations occupied by women (wife, mother, daughter), and religious observances or attitudes (prayer, zeal). Each volume has an index that always adds a second level of description so as not to open the slightest gap between information and instruction. Addressing women, the anthology blends the qualities of ancient and modern books. It is in some sense exemplary, establishing patterns for conduct that women can follow in their practice; and it is a manual, selected, organized and indexed to maximize the efficiency of its presentation, to permit access to passages without the labour of reading the whole work, let alone all the works from which it was selected.

The Ladies Library weaves its excerpts into continuous prose. It excerpts only modern texts, the first volume containing passages from Lucas's *Enquiry after Happiness*, Fénelon's *Education of a Daughter* in Hickes's translation, Jeremy Taylor's *Holy Living*, Halifax's *Advice to a Daughter*, *The Whole Duty of Man*, Fleetwood's *Relative Duties of Parents and Children*, *The Ladies Calling*, La Bruyère's *Characters*, John Scott's *Christian Life*, Tillotson's *Sermons*, Allestree's *The Art of Contentment*, *The Government of the Tongue*, and (extensively) Mary Astell's *A Serious Proposal*.[47] There are passages as yet unaccounted for in the anthology that it is presumed are written by Berkeley himself. One of these, occurring within a citation of Fleetwood's *Relative Duties*, indicates the severity of the regime of social regulation of which the anthology forms a part. In a passage on the necessity of fortitude in married life there is an insertion that describes obedience in marriage as 'a Command, the Breach of which is a Sin, and the Punishment of all Sin, Death eternal'.[48] Improvement of women through reading might be a means of recognizing partial autonomy, but that autonomy is severely limited by the naturalized subordination to men. Leah Price has shown how practices of anthologization were implicated in the transition from 'a culture in which serious critics appreciated timeless truths while frivolous ladies devoured stories' to one in which 'women relished ornamental digressions and men demanded the narrative point'.[49] This earlier anthology for women readers had more fundamental regulation of social conduct in mind. The relationship between the novel, the library, and femininity in the later eighteenth and nineteenth centuries will be discussed by Fiona Stafford in the following chapter.

---

[46] *The Ladies Library*, 3 vols (London: Jacob Tonson, 1714), I, sig. A6r–v.

[47] Earlier work on the sources of the anthology was carried out by George A. Aitken, 'Steele's *Ladies' Library*', *The Athenaeum: Journal of English and Foreign Literature, Science, the Fine Arts, Music and the Drama* 2958 (Saturday, 5 July 1884): 16–17, and Greg Hollingshead, 'Sources for the *Ladies' Library*', *Berkeley Newsletter* 11 (1989–90): 1–9.

[48] *Ladies Library*, I, 145–6.

[49] Leah Price, *The Anthology and the Rise of the Novel: From Richardson to George Eliot* (Cambridge: Cambridge University Press, 2000), 7.

The anthology possesses characteristics of modern books: layers of paratextual matter; a pseudonymous editor/author; heads and indexes that presort material into a more accessible format for a previously excluded class of reader. The book also exhibits the tendency to plagiarism attributed to moderns: it selects and republishes the work of other unacknowledged authors. As well as the edition of the *Tale* now used as its copy text, 1710 also saw the passage of the first copyright act, or Act for the Encouragement of Learning.[50] Royston Meredith, the owner of the copyright in Jeremy Taylor, was quick to spot the anthologist's use of his property and noted that 'the whole Three Volumes are intirely a Collection out of Books'.[51] It was also a commercially successful and widely distributed book. The English Short Title Catalogue lists editions in 1722, 1732, 1739, 1751, and 1752. In America it was the 'women's conduct book most widely circulated during the first half of the eighteenth century', was read by many (male) undergraduates at Harvard, and Franklin recommended to his wife that his daughter read it repeatedly.[52] By method of construction and presentation, commercial success, geographic distribution, and demographic of readership the *Ladies Library* shows, in a very different way from the *Tale*, the complicity of the ancient manner of thinking with modern technologies of book production, distribution, libraries, and storage. Though the *Ladies Library* has nothing to compare with Swift's monstrous feminization of Criticism, and aims to admit more women to more parts of learning, it does so in order to subject female behaviour to strict regulation. In some ways such a regulated *Library* can be seen as countering the unseemly freedoms enjoyed by those women who came to be ridiculed for their addiction to the circulating libraries that developed in the eighteenth and nineteenth centuries.

[50] For the passage of the act and its implications for literary property see Mark Rose, *Authors and Owners: The Invention of Copyright* (Cambridge, MA: Harvard University Press, 1993), 42–8.

[51] [Royston Meredith,] *Mr Steele Detected: Or, the Poor and Oppressed Orphan's Letters to the Great and Arbitrary Mr Steele; Complaining of the Great Injustice Done, to the Publick in General, and to Himself in Particular, by the Ladies Library* (London: John Morphew, 1714), 5–6, 18.

[52] Kevin J. Hayes, *A Colonial Woman's Bookshelf* (Knoxville, TN: University of Tennessee Press, 1996), 65–6.

4

What Are Books for? Darcy's Library, Crabbe's *The Library*, and Shillito's *The Country Book-Club*

Fiona Stafford

Throughout the long eighteenth century, new books were appearing in libraries and libraries in new books. One of the best-known literary references to libraries occurs in the eighth chapter of *Pride and Prejudice*, when Elizabeth Bennet is spending a long evening at Netherfield Hall, while her poorly sister Jane languishes upstairs. Alarmed at the thought of playing cards in uncongenial company, Elizabeth opts for a book and, after an unprovoked verbal sally from Caroline Bingley, is rescued by Bingley himself:

> Elizabeth thanked him from her heart, and then walked towards a table where a few books were lying. He immediately offered to fetch her others; all that his library afforded.
>
> 'And I wish my collection were larger for your benefit and my own credit; but I am an idle fellow, and though I have not many, I have more than I ever look into.'
>
> Elizabeth assured him that she could suit herself perfectly with those in the room.
>
> 'I am astonished,' said Miss Bingley, 'that my father should have left so small a collection of books. – What a delightful library you have at Pemberley, Mr. Darcy!'
>
> 'It ought to be good,' he replied; 'it has been the work of many generations.'
>
> 'And then you have added so much to it yourself, you are always buying books.'
>
> 'I cannot comprehend the neglect of a family library in such days as these.'[1]

In a few lines of well-observed dialogue, Jane Austen conveys the social complexities surrounding the acquisition and upkeep of a private library. In Regency society, possession of books was indicative of class and character: the contrast

---

[1] Jane Austen, *Pride and Prejudice*, ed. R. W. Chapman, 3rd rev. ed. (Oxford: Oxford University Press, 1965), 37–8.

between Bingley's careless attitude and that of his friend Darcy is pointed. The library at Pemberley is a 'family library', accumulated through 'many generations': in other words, Darcy belongs to an old, landed family, whose wealth and status is long established. His sense of responsibility is inherited and entails the mainten-ance of tradition. Upkeep of the library is part of his family duty, the library itself a symbol of stability and steadily accumulating wisdom. Bingley, on the other hand, has only been left a few books from his newly moneyed father and has so far done little to extend his stock—for which he apologizes to Elizabeth, whose choice is limited accordingly and whose opinion of him likely to be lowered as a result. Not that Bingley is remotely embarrassed by his deficiency as he cheerfully observes, 'I am an idle fellow, and though I have not many, I have more than I ever look into.'

Jane Austen, an avid reader and writer, was a shrewd observer of contemporary attitudes to reading, books, and libraries. When *Pride and Prejudice* was published in 1813, the gentleman's library was as much a status symbol as well-managed parkland. A fine book collection was an essential part of the estate and a clear sign of good taste, breeding, and, above all, wealth. Libraries filled with valuable books had been a prominent feature of country houses since the seventeenth century, while many new Georgian mansions boasted splendid rooms lined with magnifi-cent oak shelving to accommodate rows of leather-bound treasures. Books, like dinner services, cutlery, carriages, and servants, wore their owner's distinctive livery and were arrayed in neatly matching polished rows.

During the 1790s, when Austen was writing 'First Impressions', the original version of *Pride and Prejudice*, book buying suddenly became a matter of high fashion, especially among the wealthy Whig circles. Prominent public figures such as Earl Spencer and the Duke of Devonshire attracted international attention by lavishing their largesse on books—a phenomenon that inspired the Earl's private librarian, Thomas Frognall Dibdin, to add his own contribution to the collection in 1809 in the form of a 'bibliographical romance' entitled *Bibliomania; or Book Madness*. Diagnosis of 'this fatal disease' was not very difficult: symptoms included a thirst for 'black letter' printing, uncut pages, hand-coloured illustra-tions, and fine bindings.[2]

The obsession with book buying continued to grip Britain in the early nine-teenth century, partly fuelled by the sudden availability of treasures from the deposed French aristocracy, partly in imitation of British royal tastes. Anxieties about safe investments made books an attractive, long-term commodity, while the fashion for luxury volumes grew ever more extravagant. Key events raised public

[2] Mark Purcell, *The Country House Library* (New Haven and London: Yale University Press, 2017), 160–3; M. Beros, 'Bibliomania: Thomas Frognall Dibdin and Early Nineteenth-Century Book-Collecting', *TXT* 1 (2014): 140–5; Thomas Frognall Dibdin, *Bibliomania: or Book-Madness: Containing Some Account of the History, Symptom, and Cure of the Fatal Disease* (London, 1809). Dibdin's later *Bibliophobia* (London, 1832) charted the demise of the intense pursuit following the collapse of the book trade in 1826.

interest in book collecting to unprecedented heights. The sensational sale of the 3rd Duke of Roxburghe's fabulous library in June 1812 led to the foundation of the exclusive Roxburghe Club, which is still flourishing, its membership limited to forty bibliophiles. At the high-profile, well-reported, and much-discussed auction, rare books commanded dazzling figures. The greatest treasure in the collection, Christopher Valdarfer's Venetian edition of the *Decameron* of Boccaccio, printed in 1471 and resplendent in gold and green morocco, sold for the 'gigantic sum' of £2260.[3] In *Pride and Prejudice*, Bingley's income of £5000 a year is regarded by his acquaintances as very substantial, which gives an indication of the kind of money being invested in rare books—and how this might have struck a contemporary.

The sensational sale of the Duke of Roxburghe's collection took place in the very year that Jane Austen was completing the revisions to 'First Impressions' and turning it into *Pride and Prejudice*. Whether conceived in the 1790s or during the 1812 period of revision, Caroline Bingley's interest in the 'delightful library' at Pemberley and Mr Darcy's predilection for 'buying books' has much more to do with her sense of fashion and eye to what her brother's friend may be worth than with any personal taste for reading. The point is underlined a day or two later, when another evening at Netherfield offers Caroline a second chance to impress Mr Darcy:

> At length, quite exhausted by the attempt to be amused with her own book, which she had only chosen because it was the second volume of his, she gave a great yawn and said, 'How pleasant it is to spend an evening in this way! I declare after all there is no enjoyment like reading! How much sooner one tires of any thing than of a book! When I have a house of my own, I shall be miserable if I have not an excellent library.'
>
> No one made any reply. She then yawned again, threw aside her book, and cast her eyes round the room in quest of some amusement.[4]

This is the very passage quoted by the Bank of England on the new £10 note, honouring Jane Austen's bicentenary in 2017. Although it would be hard to find a more fitting character for a banknote than Caroline Bingley, the quotation chosen—'there is no enjoyment like reading'—was not quite the straightforward tribute that the Bank intended. The novel from which the words were taken is nevertheless preoccupied with the very different ways in which people value books, as well as with the benefits of books and reading to society at large.

The Roxburghe auction amazed, but did not necessarily delight, the nation. On 18 June 1812, the day after the sale, *The Times* denounced the huge sums commanded by the rare books as a 'lamentably erroneous way of indicating the love of learning'.[5]

---

[3] Purcell, *The Country House Library*, 162.   [4] Austen, *Pride and Prejudice*, 54.
[5] *The Times*, 18 June 1812, cited in Purcell, *The Country House Library*, 162.

Bibliomaniacs had already attracted disapproval from men of letters such as Isaac D'Israeli, who had remarked that amassing 'an enormous heap of books' was a habit 'infecting weak minds', but the publicity surrounding the auction made book collecting headline news.[6] The enormous bids brought into sharp focus the uncomfortable truth that Austen presents so playfully in her novel: admiration of libraries and their contents is not at all the same as valuing reading and education. Books did offer a way of acquiring knowledge and wisdom, but they were also the weapons of polite society—enabling skilled users to show off, outdo rivals, or puff themselves with pride. Whether Mr Darcy's determined pursuit of reading suggests a certain self-consciousness about contemporary book collecting is left to his own readers to consider.

As Austen demonstrates in her novels, books provided a surprising range of social functions. A book might be a means to attract attention or a screen to hide behind, a refuge from social hubbub or a cue for conversation, a way to fend off unwelcome encounters or to further a flirtation. Social anxiety could be masked or exposed through the careful deployment of a polished volume. Books and libraries were also the doors to education and mental travelling for those excluded by class or gender from the privileges of wealthy young men. In *Mansfield Park*, the arrival of little Fanny Price in the spacious home of her affluent cousins offers opportunities for extensive mental travelling through their well-stocked library. With such a range of social significance, libraries became theatres, and books the props for Austen's comedy. If Caroline Bingley attempted to secure the object of her marital ambitions with a matching volume, her rival Elizabeth Bennet escaped an unwanted proposal in a scene set in her father's library.

Austen's exuberant treatment of books and libraries reflects the wider questions of her age. If Darcy's concern for the family library at Pemberley 'in such days as these' carries Burkean overtones in a period rocked by revolution and prolonged warfare, Mr Bennet's offers a retreat from paternal responsibility in a family of 'silly' and very noisy women.[7] It is a very grand kind of garden shed, conveniently placed at the heart of the house. At the same time, the novel reveals that his daughters, though lacking a governess or formal schooling, have been encouraged to read. The younger girls, Kitty and Lydia, may show little inclination to benefit from this opportunity, but the elder sisters, Jane and Elizabeth, have acquired a very good education. Mary, the middle daughter and 'only plain one in the family', is determined to learn—or at least to be seen as clever.[8] Austen herself, unable to enjoy the advanced education taken for granted by women in later centuries, still benefitted from her family's book collection, the grand library at her brother's house in Kent, a local circulating library, and, perhaps most important of all,

---

[6] Isaac D'Israeli, *Curiosities of Literature*, 5 vols (London, 1807), cited in Beros, 'Bibliomania', 143.
[7] Austen, *Pride and Prejudice*, 38, 29, 71.   [8] Austen, *Pride and Prejudice*, 25.

enlightened parents and brothers, who encouraged her to read.[9] Once the Austens moved to Bath, the scope for reading widened, as well as Jane's opportunities for observing other people's behaviour among books and libraries.

Access to a library in this period was largely dependent on the accidents of birth—on money, class, gender, and parental attitudes. Books were, however, becoming more widely available than in earlier decades. The circulating library that so delighted the Austen family when it opened in the tiny Hampshire village of Steventon in 1798 was part of the great expansion of reading and book borrowing in the later eighteenth century. The transformative social effects of cheaper publishing and the wider distribution of books were explored by Richard Altick in 1957 in *The English Common Reader*. His work laid the foundations for scholars such as Isabel Rivers, Jon Klancher, John Brewer, William St Clair, Peter Garside, and Abigail Williams, whose various contributions have done much to establish a detailed picture of British print culture and consumption in this period.[10]

In a recent study of the astonishing proliferation of Georgian books and different kinds of provincial libraries, Ina Ferris has emphasized the importance of 'private subscription libraries, literary clubs, reading societies', commenting that the 'lines between them cannot be firmly drawn'.[11] Everyone, it seems, was suddenly an avid reader. But whether access to books was necessarily evidence of increasing social equality remains a matter of debate. Judging by the representations of reading, library visiting, and book collecting *within* the pages of the period, these ideal agents of enlightenment often proved to be objects of dispute. Far from being regarded as unequivocal benefits to the world, libraries and book clubs seem to have been inherently contentious—whether on account of controversial issues within books, or because of their physical form, value, and accessibility. Mr Bennet's blessed haven or Jonathan Swift's battlefield? The long eighteenth-century library offered polarized opportunities—and a space to allow numerous, contrasting perspectives to cross and, perhaps, cohere.

*   *   *

[9] For Austen's reading, see Olivia Murphy, *Jane Austen the Reader: The Artist as Critic* (New York: Palgrave Macmillan, 2013); Antony Mandal, *Jane Austen and the Popular Novel* (Basingstoke: Palgrave Macmillan, 2007).

[10] Richard Altick, *The English Common Reader: A Social History of the Mass Reading Public 1800–1900* (Chicago: University of Chicago Press, 1957); Isabel Rivers, *Books and Their Readers in Eighteenth-Century England* (Leicester: Leicester University Press, 1982), Vol 2, (London: Continuum, 2001); Jon Klancher, *The Making of English Reading Audiences* (Madison: University of Wisconsin Press, 1987); John Brewer, *The Pleasures of the Imagination* (New York: Farrar, Straus and Giroux, 1997); William St Clair, *The Reading Nation in the Romantic Period* (Cambridge: Cambridge University Press, 2004); Peter Garside, James Raven, and Rainer Schöwerling (eds.), *The English Novel 1770–1829: A Bibliographical Survey of Prose Fiction Published in the British Isles*, 2 vols (Oxford: Oxford University Press, 2000); Abigail Williams, *The Social Life of Books: Reading Together in the Eighteenth-Century Home* (London: Yale University Press, 2017).

[11] Ina Ferris, *Book-men, Book Clubs, and the Romantic Literary Sphere* (London: Palgrave Macmillan, 2015), 103. See also Williams, *The Social Life of Books*, 110–22.

Among the many books Jane Austen included in her fictional libraries were those by George Crabbe. When staying in London in 1813 after the publication of *Pride and Prejudice* and already hard at work on *Mansfield Park*, she looked out eagerly for this favourite contemporary poet.[12] Crabbe's latest collection of poetic *Tales* had been published in 1812 and would soon be enjoyed by her new heroine, Fanny Price, at Mansfield Park, seat of Sir Thomas Bertram, whose bookcases are shown a certain disrespect over the course of the narrative. Fanny's interest in Crabbe's *Tales* is a little internal joke, since the heroine's name derives from Crabbe's earlier poem, *The Parish Register*, published in 1807. It appeared in a volume that startled the literary world by breaking a silence of twenty years.[13] Crabbe's collection included hitherto unpublished poems, while also giving many older, half-forgotten works a new lease of life. Among them was *The Library*, which originally appeared in 1781, but which had since been so heavily revised that, in her definitive scholarly edition, Norma Dalrymple-Champneys decided to include both texts, 'Conflation of the two being impracticable owing to the extensive differences'.[14] The revised version of *The Library* included greater emphasis on religion, with the section on theological books repositioned ahead of philosophy, as appropriate to the work of a poet who was also a priest. A poem that might have risked seeming a throwback to an earlier era also managed to catch something of the new age because 'The Library' was now a much more fashionable topic than it had been in 1781. The poem's reappearance in 1807 was perfectly timed for the new wave of bibliomania, while also demonstrating that many of the book-related questions aired by Austen had been attracting interest for several decades. Although there is no reference to Darcy owning a copy of Crabbe, his collection at Pemberley must be a repository of books, books about books, and books about books about books.

The title of Crabbe's poem implicitly raised the question of what kind of library 'The Library' might be—whether a particular individual's collection or a generic ideal? He was explicitly exploring the very purpose of books. The poem begins with a conventional, later eighteenth-century image of 'the sad Soul, by care and grief opprest' seeking comfort in vain, before proposing a universal remedy for depression:

> But what strange art, what magic can dispose
> The troubled mind to change its native woes?
> Or lead us willing from ourselves, to see

---

[12] To Cassandra Austen, 15 September 1813, *Jane Austen Letters*, ed. Deirdre Le Faye, 3rd ed. (Oxford and New York: Oxford University Press, 1995), 218.

[13] Neil Powell, *George Crabbe: An English Life 1754–1832* (London: 2004), 162–8.

[14] George Crabbe, *The Complete Poetical Works*, ed. Norma Dalrymple-Champneys and Arthur Pollard, 3 vols (Oxford: Clarendon Press, 1988), I, 648. All references to Crabbe's poetry are to this edition.

Others more wretched, more undone than we?
This BOOKS can do; – nor this alone; they give
New views to life, and teach us how to live;
They soothe the griev'd, the stubborn they chastise,
Fools they admonish, and confirm the wise:
Their aid they yield to all; they never shun
The man of sorrow, nor the wretch undone:
Unlike the hard, the selfish, and the proud,
They fly not sullen from the suppliant crowd;
Nor tell to various people various things,
But shew to subjects what they shew to kings.[15]

Books, according to the opening paean, can offer solace to all, irrespective of class or character: a strong justification for their social efficacy. By the time of the poem's republication in 1807, the idea of something equally beneficial to 'subjects and kings' had taken on a rather different resonance from the moment of its first appearance, because its new readers were only too conscious of the French Revolution, the fate of the French royal family, the recurrent mental illness of the British king, and arguments for the rights of his subjects. Anything that might be comforting to all was indeed worth considering in these circumstances—and especially for those, like Crabbe, afflicted by mental-health problems and social insecurity. The invitation to enter the 'sacred Dome' of the library (which lost its reverent adjective in 1807) is presented as a reliable means to psychological recovery—a place of comfort to the afflicted and moral guidance to the stubborn, foolish, and wise alike.[16]

If the introduction presents the Library as an unfailing resource for moral and mental well-being open to all comers, however, *The Library* offered its author a more practical stepping stone into success and society. It did rescue him from 'labouring in despair', but not in quite the way the opening lines suggested. In 1780, Crabbe had abandoned his job as a surgeon's apprentice in rural Suffolk to try his luck as a writer in London. Although he had had a few poems published, his initial attempts to establish himself in the metropolis went badly awry and, short of cash and connections, he was becoming desperate. As a last-ditch attempt to fend off poverty and disappointment, Crabbe approached Edmund Burke, who read his poems, picked out *The Library*, offered advice on revisions, and then took it to Robert Dodsley with a strong recommendation for publication.[17] Burke's influence on the London literary world meant that *The Library* not only was published to a warm reception but also led to the appearance of a second poem, *The Village*, which secured Crabbe's reputation. Rereading his own poem two

---

[15] George Crabbe, *The Library* (1781), ll. 37–50.   [16] Crabbe, *The Library* (1781), l. 52.
[17] Crabbe, *Complete Poetical Works*, I, 645–7; Powell, *George Crabbe*, 69–72.

decades later for the new, revised edition of 1807, the poet was able to reflect on how *The Library* had delivered him from despair through means very different from those proposed in the poem's opening lines. Such retrospective insight was nevertheless in keeping with the original poem, whose conventional assurances open the way to a Johnsonian satire on books and reading, before finally arriving at a more worldly solution to despair. Burke's support had included an introduction to the Duke of Rutland, who became Crabbe's patron and the subject of a fulsome address towards the end of *The Library*.[18]

The idealized view of books set out at the start is repeatedly challenged over the course of the poem. Instead of speaking alike to 'subjects' and 'kings', the very form of contemporary books underlined the different social standing and disposable income of their implied readers:

> Lo! all in silence, all in order stand,
> And mighty Folio's first, a lordly band;
> Then Quarto's their well-order'd ranks maintain,
> And light Octavo's fill a spacious plain;
> See yonder, rang'd in more frequented rows,
> An humbler band of duodecimo's;
> While undistinguish'd trifles swell the scene,
> The last new Play, and fritter'd Magazine[19]

Lest anyone miss the point of this anthropomorphic parade, Crabbe hammers it home in the next well-ordered sequence:

> Thus 'tis in life, where first the proud, the great,
> In leagu'd assembly keep their cumbrous state;
> Heavy and huge, they fill the world with dread,
> Are much admir'd, and are but little read;
> The Commons next, a middle rank are found;
> Professions fruitful pour their offspring round;
> Wits, Bards, and Idlers fill a tatter'd row;
> And the vile Vulgar lie disdain'd below.[20]

This was in many ways a brave passage for an impoverished poet who was relying on wealthier readers for survival. The parallel between books and men creates uneasy shifts between folios and 'the proud, the great' who are dreaded but 'little read'. Whether 'the great' refers to men of influence in society or to the great authors whose works receive the most lavish editions and command the highest

---

[18] Crabbe, *The Library* (1781), ll. 586–9. Crabbe became the Duke's domestic chaplain in May 1782.
[19] Crabbe, *The Library* (1781), ll. 132–9.   [20] Crabbe, *The Library* (1781), ll. 140–7.

prices is not explicit. Crabbe may have been evoking great folio volumes of dynastic or county history—the grandest books for the grandest families? Whatever the precise target, his satire is plain enough. Big books were for big men—because they cost so much. The passage had even greater resonance in 1807, an age of both bibliomania and the increasing democratization of reading. A small, inexpensive book might reach many more readers, but whether such cheap, accessible volumes could ever really compete with vast, gold-tooled leather tomes remained an open question.

As he satirized the social hierarchy inherent in books, Crabbe was also claiming his own literary inheritance by evoking Joseph Addison's humorous observations on literary rank and precedence in *The Spectator*:

> I have observed that the Author of a *Folio*, in all Companies and Conversations, sets himself above the author of a *Quarto*; the Author of a *Quarto* above the Author of an *Octavo*; and so on, by gradual Descent and Subordination, to an Author in *Twenty-Fours*. This Distinction is so well observed, that in an Assembly of the Learned, I have seen the *Folio* Writer place himself in an Elbow-Chair, when the Author of a *Duo-decimo* has, out of just Deference to his superior Quality, seated himself upon a Squabb. In a word, Authors are usually ranged in Company after the same manner as their Works are upon a Shelf.[21]

In the eighteenth-century library, as in life, size mattered. Jane Austen, who read both Addison and Crabbe attentively, as well as books of many sizes and shapes, may well have recalled their observations on folios in her mischievous creation of Mr Collins. Among the many errors committed by the pseudo-sagacious clergy-man cousin is his determined pursuit of Mr Bennet, 'who was most anxious to get rid of him', into the private sanctuary of the Longbourn library. With unerring instinct for the most expensive object and most irritating conduct, Mr Collins reinforces his faux pas, 'nominally engaged with one of the largest folios in the collection, but really talking to Mr Bennet'.[22]

Addison's remarks on literary pride were published in a daily journal, which gave particular relish to the lines on the lower ranks and the, as yet unsettled, question of which authors came at the very bottom of the pack—the pamphleteer, or 'the Author of Single Sheets and that Fraternity who publishes their Labours on certain Days'.[23] Evidently amused by his lowly spot, Addison was even more diverted by the way his status rose simply as a consequence of his essays being

---

[21] *The Spectator*, No 529, 6 Nov. 1712, *The Spectator*, ed. Donald Bond, 5 vols (Oxford: Clarendon Press, 1965), IV, 386. Addison's influence is noted by Dalrymple-Champneys; Crabbe, *Complete Poetical Works*, I, 652.

[22] Austen, *Pride and Prejudice*, 71.   [23] *Spectator*, IV, 386.

collected into a series of bound volumes: 'After which I naturally jumped over the Heads not only of all Pamphleteers, but of every *Octavo* writer in Great Britain, that had written but one Book.'[24] Victory in the literary Olympics of the day was determined not by the increasing skills of the writer-contestants, but by the shrewd decisions of their publishers. As an unknown poet rather than an established prose writer, Crabbe may have been less amused by the essay than most of Addison's many admirers. And yet, with its broad, diverse readership of men and women, *The Spectator* was offering a new kind of *literary* lineage which promised to become an alternative to the old patriarchal dynasties and systems of patronage. For those who had not been born great and were most unlikely to have greatness thrust upon them, there might still be a chance of achieving greatness through writing books. But was poetry the best way forward?

Crabbe's fictional library revealed the competing claims of not only differently sized books but also different genres. As the poem moves from imaginary shelf to shelf, considering books of History, Medicine, Law, Politics, Theology, Natural History, Philosophy, Romance, and Drama, the absence of its own kind becomes more and more noticeable. Rather than commanding a sizeable section of polished verse, the poetry publications in Crabbe's library are squeezed into a dismissive couplet:

> Abstracts, Abridgements, please the fickle times,
> Pamphlets and Plays, and Politics and Rhymes.[25]

Whether this is witty Popean zeugma, false modesty, or a genuinely pessimistic assessment of the place of contemporary poetry is left for the reader to judge, but if the catalogue of literary kinds raises expectations of a final triumphant parade of great poets, *The Library* refuses such satisfaction. Instead, the grand finale ushers in the 'Genius of the place', who offers only a muted defence of the 'Muse's Song, the Poet's Pen', being more concerned with exposing false visions: 'Ambition's lofty views, the Pomp of State, / The Pride of Wealth, the Splendour of the Great.'[26]

Satire on the wealthy and powerful was a bold strategy for a young, unknown poet in 1781, but by 1807 the traditional moral conclusion, which remained unaltered, had acquired a stronger political edge. The understated defence of poetry, on the other hand, came to seem even more restrained in a decade primed by Wordsworth's stirring claims in the Preface to *Lyrical Ballads*.[27] By the time he

---

[24] *Spectator*, IV, 387.   [25] Crabbe, *The Library* (1781), ll. 97–8.
[26] Crabbe, *The Library*, (1781) ll. 600–1.
[27] Wordsworth added the preface to the second, expanded edition of *Lyrical Ballads* in 1800 and expanded it in 1802, inserting an extensive answer to the question 'What is a Poet?'; William Wordsworth and S. T. Coleridge, *Lyrical Ballads*, ed. Fiona Stafford (Oxford: Oxford University Press, 2013), 103–7.

prepared his poem for republication, however, Crabbe's own life experience had caused him to doubt whether the worldly visions of 'Ambition' and 'splendour' were really any 'less happy than' those of the Poet.[28] For readers of 1807 the contrast between the outlook conveyed by Crabbe's *The Library* and that of Wordsworth, whose entirely new collection of *Poems, in Two Volumes* appeared in the same year, could hardly have been starker.

The Library concludes by revisiting the opening hopes of finding moral support in books and refuses affirmation. The promises of soothing balms and mental wealth turn out to be idle dreams, as genre after genre is addressed and found wanting. Even the 'lasting mansions of the dead', where works that have survived their moment to be revered by posterity are housed, offer little comfort:

> Crown'd with eternal fame, they sit sublime,
> And laugh at all the little strife of time.[29]

Although this *is* upholding the conventional view that the best authors transcend their time, Crabbe's phrasing carries the suggestion that the literary greats are somehow looking down and laughing at the rest of us. As this apostrophe to the Immortals is followed immediately by the satire on the pride of folios, it is hard to find much reassurance in the notion of literary greatness. The highly ambivalent description of great books as 'the tombs of those who cannot die' underlines the potential emptiness of traditional ideals of literary immortality and, in doing so, poses the urgent modern question—what are books for? What *is* the real purpose of writing?

If the ideal writer were not, after all, aiming at a lasting monument, perhaps he wrote primarily for his contemporaries? But here, any hopes of contemporary fame are checked by the threatening presence of the 'Critic Army rang'd around' (521). The lot of the modern writer could hardly be less enviable, judging by Crabbe's summary:

> What vent'rous race are ours! what mighty foes
> Lie waiting all around them to oppose!
> What treacherous friends betray them to the fight!
> What dangers threaten them! yet still they write:
> A hapless tribe! to every evil born,
> Whom villains hate, and fools affect to scorn;
> Strangers they come, amid a world of woe,
> And taste the largest portion ere they go.[30]

---

[28] Crabbe, *The Library*, (1781) l. 603.   [29] Crabbe, *The Library*, (1781) ll. 114–15.
[30] Crabbe, *The Library*, (1781) ll. 534–41.

The slipping personal pronouns, 'ours' / 'them' / 'they', confuse the distinction between the Critic and the Poet, which is not inappropriate in a poem caustic about so many kinds of book. Crabbe's voice and the implicit inclusion of himself in 'what vent'r ous race is ours' seem rather forlorn, as if his daring consists not so much of vying with critics as in the very suggestion that he might think of joining the ranks of the poets.

The military metaphors, familiar from the mock-heroic traditions of earlier decades, summon up prose as readily as poetry: as so often in this poem, Swift's *Battel of the Books* is clearly opening from a nearby shelf. Where Swift had presented the mock-heroic Battle in St James's Library with remarkable wit and energy, belying any thought of his own inferiority to the Ancients through this highly imaginative tour de force, Crabbe's evocations are less confident or sustained. When Crabbe introduces the repulsive modern Spider, he makes it representative of contemporary medical books. Rather than develop the allegory with Swiftian energy, however, Crabbe lets his Arachne retreat from view before any admirable Bee has appeared to flatten her lair. Crabbe's poem is rather more pessimistic than Swift's prose, since his condemnation of modern medical treatises is a further repudiation of the ideal of literary immortality: bad medical advice, once in print, 'relentless kills through future times'.[31] Such books were much better consigned to obscurity and buried in dust.

Although Crabbe's extended critique reflects his personal rejection of a medical career in favour of poetry and the Church, his choice is hardly corroborated by the ambivalent attitudes towards volumes of poetry or theology. Religious works are shown to be just as 'controversial' as any others—'Endless disputes around the world they cause'—their authors characterized by 'Peace in their looks, and vengeance in their pen'.[32] Readers of 1807 knew only too well that Crabbe's debut in the 1780s had been followed by a silence of over twenty years, but even in the original poem of 1781 the closing compliments to his patron make the persistent criticism of wealth and power ring rather hollow.

Crabbe's delivery from early poverty and obscurity by the success of his poem offered a compelling reason for writing. Whatever ideals Wordsworth might have put forward in the Preface to *Lyrical Ballads*, for many budding authors writing remained a means of survival, a way of earning fame and money. This hard truth also gave Crabbe's broad-brush rejection of other writers and critics a rather different dimension from the lofty, moral justifications of Augustan satire. Folios and great men might be 'Heavy', 'huge', and 'proud', but they were also the safest bastion against oblivion, irrespective of Prince Posterity.

If the form and tone of Crabbe's *The Library* reflect the period in which he began his career as a writer and its subject suited the moment of republication, the

---

[31] Crabbe, *The Library*, (1781) l. 249.   [32] Crabbe, *The Library*, (1781) ll. 360, 365.

poem itself has a singular quality. Though echoing Pope, Swift, Addison, and Johnson, and anticipating Dibdin and Austen, *The Library* is perhaps representative only of Crabbe's own, peculiarly self-excoriating, take on the world. Less well known, but telling in comparison, is another mock-heroic poem on books and their readers from the same decade by another East Anglian poet. Charles Shillito's *The Country Book-Club* was published in 1788, also with support from patrons. This slim pamphlet, financed largely by subscribers in Essex, took readers into a very different kind of library, housed not beneath a stately Dome but, rather, the rafters of a village pub, where the regulars convene to 'taste the sweets of liter'ture – and *wine*'.[33] Shillito's poem also satirizes the various motives for acquiring books, but rather than presenting a solitary voice surrounded by a multitude of dead authors and vast volumes, much of its gentle humour derives from the characters of the local, and not entirely literary-minded, members of the Country Book-Club. In the warm and welcoming atmosphere of the inn, we are introduced to the village Surgeon, the Vicar, the Squire, the Draper, the Bookseller, the Curate, and the Innkeeper himself.

Although the Book-Club procures books for members to share, the subsequent discussions are a demonstration not of social equality so much as social distinction. While the Squire arrives in a painted chariot, adopts 'city speech' and 'keeps aloof, to shew he's better bred', he is no intellectual match for the Draper, a 'self-taught scholar' and 'though of mean degree, / The hamlet boasts few men more wise than he'.[34] Leaving behind his 'servile shop-board and the shears' for the evening, the Draper quells the others through his 'shrewd remark and quick reply'.[35] In true eighteenth-century fashion, the Book-Club is at once a refuge from daily trials and a place to take up arms. Like Crabbe, Shillito includes an evocation of the *Battel of the Books*, underlining the allusion with wordplay as the members launch into their literary disputes:

> Now books are made their *missile* force to try;
> Swift as artill'ry balls. Huge volumes fly.
> *Congreve*, and *Bunyan*, *Chesterfield* and *Carr*,
> Light troops and heavy, wage promiscuous war.
> E'en airy *Yorick* falls like pond'rous lead,
> And cracks his joke on some rich peasant's head.
> At length the potent juice obscures each brain,
> And Chaos holds his universal reign.[36]

Swift's famous *Battel* is reinforced by echoes of *The Rape of the Lock* and *The Dunciad*, while Sterne's witty parson Yorick is recruited to demonstrate the

---

[33] Charles Shillito, *The Country Book-Club. A Poem* (London, 1788), 15.
[34] Shillito, *The Country Book-Club*, 19–20.   [35] Shillito, *The Country Book-Club*, 20.
[36] Shillito, *The Country Book Club*, 38.

limitations of some of those assembled. But the battle ends without serious casualties, as this mock-mock heroic allows the disputants to sink under the influence of alcohol. The Latin tag on the title page, '*concordia discors*', like the accompanying Rowlandson vignette, sets a tone of overall geniality, accommodating enough for the wide range of personalities and social classes that make up the Country Book-Club.

The contested question of the true purpose of books is neatly dismissed in Shillito's summary of the Club's activities:

> Thus, meeting to dispute, to fight, to plead,
> To smoke, to drink – do any thing but read,
> The club – with stagg'ring steps, yet light of heart,
> Their taste for learning shewn, and *punch* – depart.[37]

Rather than serious satire, Shillito's *The Country Book-Club* is a comic, affectionate mock poem, which celebrates as well as satirizing reading. The elderly bookseller is allowed a kinder and more sustained portrait than the prickly Draper or self-satisfied Squire, suggesting that Goldsmith is the true presiding presence in this unnamed, though far from deserted, village rather than the harder-hitting satirists of earlier decades. Shillito's comedy, like the Rowlandson cartoon on the title page, is aimed at gently puncturing the pomposity of the more serious writers of his day and bringing any elevated claim for the purpose of poetry down to earth. What he reveals is a social dimension of books rather different from Addison's or Crabbe's rankings of folios down to twenty-fours. The members of his Country Book-Club are proud of their books and conscious of their differences in rank and opinion; and yet they turn out to have essential things in common, in their shared interest in local gossip and ghost stories, their support for a local author, their related opposition to hostile London critics, and, even more heartily felt, their united admiration for the beautiful young barmaid. Isabel's entry with a tray of drinks draws attention to an aspect of the Club both unifying and excluding—its all-male membership. This is quite a different kind of country village library from the one to which Jane, Cassandra, and Mrs Austen subscribed.

Shillito's *The Country Book-Club* offers a variety of reasons for valuing books—from intellectual improvement and entertainment to professional advancement or income. What emerges most strongly from his poem, however, is the essentially social dimension of books, whether conducive to argument or agreement or simply providing an excuse for getting together for a drink. As Abigail Williams has suggested in *The Social Life of Books*, valuing a book in this period was often not a reflection of the content but of the very varied circumstances in which they

---

[37] Shillito, *The Country Book-Club*, 39.

were enjoyed.[38] And this takes us back to the scene in *Pride and Prejudice*, where the inadequacy of Bingley's library is also a sign of his kindness, inclusiveness, and lack of pretension. What Elizabeth (and therefore her readers) value at this point in the novel is not Bingley's brain or education, but his solicitous attention to a young woman, who has been embarrassed and bullied by the other members of his household. Darcy may appear superior in his book buying and extensive reading, but Bingley demonstrates an instinctive compassion and courtesy that are ultimately much more important. Like Crabbe, Shillito, Wordsworth, and many others in this period, Austen raises questions about the true purpose of books and libraries. Why do they exist and what are they for? Were authors writing for themselves, whether for personal satisfaction, income, immediate fame, or immortality, or were their labours entirely for the benefit of others? Wordsworth made stirring claims for poetry as the 'rock of defence of human nature', but for many of his contemporaries the value of books and libraries lay in their capacity to bring people together to enjoy each other's company or a jolly good row—which might bring these fictional readers of two centuries ago closer to many book club members of today.[39]

[38] Abigail Williams, *The Social Life of Books: Reading Together in the Eighteenth-Century Home* (London: Yale University Press, 2017), 36–63.

[39] William Wordsworth, Preface to *Lyrical Ballads*, *Lyrical Ballads*, ed. Fiona Stafford (Oxford: Oxford University Press, 2013), 106.

5

Libraries and the Formation of Character in Nineteenth-Century Novels

J. Louise McCray

Twenty-first-century writings about libraries often dwell with unease upon the place of the individual amongst the bookshelves. Matthew Battles's *Library: An Unquiet History*, for example, records how easily the user of the modern research library moves from empowering dreams of self-realization to a sense that their particular life has been overwhelmed, consumed, or possessed by the collection.[1] This chapter traces that tension through a variety of nineteenth-century fictional libraries that lay claim to the personal identities of the characters that encounter them—some of them literally harbouring the long-lost names of protagonists in their bookshelves. This intimate relationship between library and character formation is used persistently by novel-writers to trouble the concept of self-definition. For these authors, libraries become a way of exploring what checks or circumscribes autonomous individuality.

My discussion centres on four nineteenth-century novels featuring characters that come to be known or defined through libraries: William Godwin's *Fleetwood* (1805), Walter Scott's *The Antiquary* (1816), George Eliot's *Middlemarch* (1872), and Mary Augusta Ward's *Robert Elsmere* (1888). These works represent several different ways of imagining the encounter between library and individual. *Fleetwood* involves a process of character formation: the individual is generated and shaped by the library. *The Antiquary* involves a process of discovery: the subject is detected and legitimated through the library. If in *Middlemarch* the library becomes a zone of incarceration, then in *Robert Elsmere*, it is the site of a process of incarnation: individual character is materialized in the library. These alternative ways of figuring library-character relations correspond to specific accounts of what constrains, delimits, or directs personal identity. Godwin is primarily concerned with the experience of educational environment; Scott, with the licence of historical testimony; Eliot, with the limitations of a bookish life; and Ward, with the magnetism of collective intellectual movement. As this chapter develops, I shall draw on other writings as supplements or counterpoints,

---

[1] Matthew Battles, *Library: An Unquiet History* (London: Heinemann, 2003), 3–21.

indicating something of wider nineteenth-century contexts in which these concerns emerged.

Ultimately, what unites these novels is the way that each account of character formation through the library simultaneously advertises the submission of the individual to forces beyond the self. For each character there is a sense that they find their life in the library only to lose control over it, and their stories consequently raise questions about what is particularly personal about personal identity. In the later eighteenth century, during a period when novel-reading in particular increased markedly, the growing teaching of Rhetoric and Belles-Lettres in Scottish and American universities, English Dissenting academies, and elsewhere is but one indication of the way prominent thinkers, including Adam Smith, Hugh Blair, and Lord Kames, took a pronounced interest in the regulation of personal reading, not least among the impressionable young whose characters might be formed by it.[2] Indeed, the Romantic era is increasingly recognized as a time of marked 'media consciousness', in which printed pages and other media took hold of the literary imagination as never before.[3] The nineteenth century in Britain saw this interest intensify in an era when the definition of individuality came under singular pressure from philosophers, scientists, and cultural critics.[4] Rather than examining these phenomena directly, my argument indicates one manner in which they converged. In various ways, libraries in nineteenth-century fiction gave voice to one of the most mysterious experiences of being a person: that the individual never has the privilege of naming themselves, but instead is persistently identified and known from without.

The nineteenth century was, of course, a pivotal time in library history. John Sutherland in a recent survey of 'Literature and the Library in the Nineteenth Century' rightly emphasizes the substantial proliferation of institutional libraries, particularly after the 1850 Public Libraries Act.[5] From at least 1818 the use in English of the new word 'librarianship' hints at the increasing professionalization of libraries, and in 1819, in the fifth book of his *Tales of the Hall*, George Crabbe (whose work is discussed by Fiona Stafford in Chapter 4 of the present volume) uses the word 'librarian' for what may be the first time in English poetry. A poem of 1838 by the English philanthropist John Kenyon features the heavenly ministrations of 'librarian Spirits' among 'celestial shelves', indicating that an idealistic

---

[2] See, e.g., Robert Crawford, ed., *The Scottish Invention of English Literature* (Cambridge: Cambridge University Press, 1997); Felicity James, 'Romantic Readers', in *The Oxford Handbook to British Romanticism*, ed. David Duff (Oxford: Oxford University Press, 2018), 478–94.

[3] See, e.g., Ina Ferris and Paul Keen, 'Introduction: Towards a Bookish Literary History', in *Bookish Histories*, ed. Ferris and Keen (Basingstoke: Palgrave Macmillan, 2009), 1–15; Andrew Piper, *Dreaming in Books: The Making of the Bibliographic Imagination in the Romantic Age* (Chicago: Chicago University Press, 2009).

[4] See, e.g., J. W. Burrow, *The Crisis of Reason: European Thought, 1848–1914* (New Haven: Yale University Press, 2000), 147–69.

[5] John Sutherland, 'Literature and the Library in the Nineteenth Century', in *The Meaning of the Library*, ed. Alice Crawford (Princeton: Princeton University Press, 2015), 124–50.

view of libraries' place in culture and society was developing.[6] By 1853, according to *Norton's Literary Gazette*, 'all librarians' in the United Kingdom, including Sir Anthony Panizzi of the British Museum reading room, were talking about a forthcoming librarians' convention to be held in New York which would, among other things, unite high ideals and practical vision to help create 'a nation of readers'.[7] Victorian writers and social reformers often saw such libraries as shaping individual character as well as the nation as a whole. Samuel Smiles's bestselling *Self-Help; with Illustrations of Character and Conduct* (1859) indicated that a 'library' that was sufficiently 'select' might shape personal advancement, though Smiles warned too that it was possible to 'exaggerate the importance of literary culture', and noted that 'We are apt to imagine that because we possess many libraries, institutes, and museums, we are making great progress.'[8] John Ruskin was more unequivocally enthusiastic, seeking to provoke readers of his *Sesame and Lilies* (1865) by asking, 'How much do you think we spend altogether on our libraries, public or private, as compared with what we spend on our horses?' Interested in the regulation of reading and its relation to the 'formation' of 'character' in women as well as men, Ruskin hoped that 'it will not be long before royal or national libraries will be founded in every considerable city, with a royal series of books in them; the same series in every one of them, chosen books, the best in every kind'.[9]

Institutionally, Ruskin's missionary zeal (if not his commendation of the 'royal') was matched by the establishment of the American Library Association in Philadelphia in 1876, which prompted the first, fully 'transatlantic' International Conference of Librarians in London the following year.[10] Attended by numerous British and American librarians including the influential editor, librarian, and poet Richard Garnett of the British Museum, and by Melvil Dewey, this London meeting instigated in 1877 the UK's own Library Association, whose Annual Conference in 1880 marked the start of efforts to establish in Britain professional examinations in librarianship.[11] Held from 1885 onwards, these examinations led in 1902 to the teaching of librarianship courses under the auspices of the London School of Economics, and, eventually, in 1917, to the establishment of the 'pioneer' School of Librarianship at University College London.[12]

---

[6] John Kenyon, *Poems: For the Most Part Occasional* (London: Edward Moxon, 1838), 102.

[7] Gabriella Magrath, 'Library Conventions of 1853, 1876, and 1877', *Journal of Library History, Philosophy and Comparative Librarianship* 8.2 (April 1973): 54, 56.

[8] Samuel Smiles, *Self-Help; with Illustrations of Character and Conduct* (London: John Murray, 1859), 281, 272.

[9] John Ruskin, *Sesame and Lilies* (1865; repr. New York: Silver, Burdett and Co., 1900), 50, 94, 68.

[10] For more on these conferences, see Magrath, 'Library Conventions'.

[11] See Gerald Bramley, *A History of Library Education* (New York: Archon Books and Clive Bingley, 1969).

[12] William Arthur Munford, *A History of the Library Association* (London: Library Association, 1976), 175.

As John Sutherland, Chris Baggs, and others have shown, all this legislative and professionalizing activity not only spurred the growth of municipal and other institutional book collections but also helped ensure that public libraries featured in nineteenth-century creative writing—most notably, perhaps, in the fiction of George Gissing.[13] However, the present chapter's concentration on English novelists' portrayal of fictional libraries deliberately attends to significant texts which Sutherland and Baggs do not cover, and the fictional libraries upon which I focus are all private household collections. Treated more fully than public libraries in the fiction of the time, these sorts of libraries were frequently romanticized, and sometimes fetishized, throughout nineteenth-century literature. Especially treasured was the library of the gentleman-scholar in the writings of Victorian 'bookmen' such as T. F. Dibdin and Andrew Lang; usually such private, gentlemanly libraries were contrasted, implicitly or explicitly, with the less exclusive varieties of public or rate-aided libraries that were developing in Britain and attracting much debate.[14] The novelists whose work I explore tapped into this intimate image of the private library in order to evoke issues surrounding identity, genealogy, and ownership in a way that perhaps would not quite be matched by, say, a club library, a cathedral library, or the reading room of the British Museum. Nonetheless, throughout this century of growing interest in the personal and professional control of libraries, book collections of all kinds—public and institutional as well as private—threw into sharp relief the 'always already' aspect of social life, the pre-existing web of possibilities from which individual character could never be completely wrested free. Indeed, it may be that fictional portrayals of the interaction between the library and the shaping of character both anticipated and spurred more public, professional, and institutional interest in the provision of libraries which might, at their best, enhance what Smiles called 'character and conduct'.

Godwin's *Fleetwood; or, the New Man of Feeling* is the tale of a person conscripted by a reading space. Fleetwood, the only son of a wealthy nobleman, is forged in and through his personal reading closet during childhood; this is the site where, always solitary, he retreats with select books from the main library of his father's house, indulging his imagination at whim. '[H]ere it had ever since been my custom to retire with some favourite author, when I wished to feel my mind in its most happy state,' he records, indicating his use of this book space as a means to private emotional gratification.[15] The danger that the room represents is

---

[13] Sutherland, 'Literature and the Library in the Nineteenth Century'; Chris Baggs, 'The Public Library in Fiction: George Gissing's *Spellbound*', *Library History* 20.2 (July 2004): 137–46.

[14] See Penny Fielding, 'Reading Rooms: M. R. James and the Library of Modernity', *Modern Fiction Studies* 46.3 (2000): 749–71.

[15] William Godwin, *Fleetwood: or, The New Man of Feeling*, in *Collected Novels and Memoirs of William Godwin*, ed. Pamela Clemit, vol 5 (London: Pickering, 1992), 194. All further page references in this chapter are supplied in the body of the text.

later articulated by Ruffigny, a family friend, who warns Fleetwood against mental self-indulgence in a speech about the proper use of libraries. 'I pass some hours of every day . . . in this apartment,' Ruffigny observes, as he shows Fleetwood his own book collection,

> but my life is principally in the open air. . . . The furniture of these shelves constitutes an elaborate and invaluable commentary; but the objects beyond those windows, and the circles and communities of my contemporaries, are the text to which that commentary relates.   (69)

When they seal off individual character from the outside world, he insinuates, libraries pervert book-reading from its proper end, which is the integration of truth, justice, and goodness into community life. They assume a masturbatory function, establishing patterns of mind that begin and end in self-service.

This advice is too late to change Fleetwood's intellectual temperament, however, and simply pinpoints the flaws of his childhood environment. Undisciplined and insulated reading habits have so channelled his character that he is unable to accommodate the feelings and desires of others; he has forfeited healthy social existence. This problem is dramatically displayed when his library closet is unwittingly appropriated by his new wife, a move he receives as a sign that she is careless about the things most meaningful to him. He attempts to read in the main library, but it is not as private as his old closet, not as convenient, not as steeped in memory—and he grows bitter (194–6). His jealous reaction, foreshadowing an eventual breakdown of marriage and of mind, reveals the extent to which the intellectual cocoon of his youth has malformed his character and incubated a social monster.

In *Fleetwood*, then, book spaces become emblematic of the sinister power of educational environments over individuals. This feature encapsulates the logic of all Godwin's novels, each of which is based upon 'confessions' of narrator-protagonists designed to reveal the intellectual fibre underlying their actions. To some extent these works participate in a wider trope of literary dysfunction, some of whose origins might be traced to the dangerous influence of the library in *Don Quixote*: the hero's desultory reading in *Waverley* (1814), for instance, shapes his 'wavering and unsettled' character, and Catherine Morland's private absorption in Gothic novels results in social illiteracy and embarrassment in *Northanger Abbey* (1817).[16] But Godwin's examples are much darker than those of Austen or Scott, for the effects of his characters' bad reading are less easily accommodated or corrected by subsequent social experience—in fact, as his characters are shaped by their reading they come to unsettle the very definition of functional society.

---

[16] Walter Scott, *Waverley; Or, 'Tis Sixty Years Since* (London: Penguin, 1985), 48, 73; Jane Austen, *Northanger Abbey*, ed. Marilyn Butler (London: Penguin, 2003), 8.

Fleetwood was specifically intended to flesh out Godwin's view of the disastrous intellectual consequences of aristocracy, as articulated in his infamous treatise *Political Justice* (1793). His convictions about the primacy of the life of the mind and its distortion by inherited social structures owed much to the educational ethos of eighteenth-century religious Dissent, and were shared by many other reform-minded novelists at the turn of the century, including Elizabeth Inchbald, Mary Wollstonecraft, and Mary Hays.[17]

Libraries evoke competing associations of reformation and corruption with especial force in Hays's *Memoirs of Emma Courtney* (1796), which turns the critical spotlight upon women's education. The eponymous heroine is barred in early life from access to her father's glass-fronted bookcase; instead, the foundations of her mind are laid haphazardly by the 'sensational' literature that she finds in a commercial circulating library. Emma's character is subsequently driven by disordered feeling; although the glass case is eventually opened to her under her father's jurisdiction, it is too late—its books only provide her with an agonizing recognition of a person she can never be. The library glass functions simultaneously as window and barrier, symbolizing the circumstances by which Emma finds the world of masculine learning always tantalizing yet unattainable—a dynamic revisited a century later by Margaret Oliphant's 'The Library Window' (1896). Both Hays and Godwin instil library experience into well-worn negative character types—the feeble-minded woman, the selfish aristocrat—in order to propose the necessity of educational reform for the rectification of social ills.

Throughout the century cultural commentators including S. T. Coleridge (whose *Biographia Literaria* saw reading as vital to character formation), J. S. Mill, Thomas Carlyle (who was instrumental in founding the London Library in 1841), and John Ruskin drew from this association between libraries and the genesis of character. Its ambivalence even infiltrated the government-commissioned *Report from the Select Committee on Public Libraries* (1849), which set out to document a national need for free-entry, rate-supported libraries, especially amongst the poorer members of society. At its most interesting, this report, which led to the most important piece of Victorian library legislation, the Public Libraries Act of 1850, explores fundamental questions about how desirable character is formed, with stories about the transformation of individual readers used to make arguments about the potential for local and national development through libraries. For some contributors, the key to such social progress was a particular kind of library access; for others, it involved a certain kind of book; for others again, it meant a specific type of reading culture or environment. Alongside the reformist fiction discussed above, the *Public Libraries* report probes deep

---

[17] See J. Louise McCray, '"Peril in the means of its diffusion": William Godwin on Truth and Social Media', *Journal of the History of Ideas* 81.1 (January 2020): 67–84; J. Louise McCray, 'Novel-Reading, Ethics, and William Godwin in the 1830s', *Studies in Romanticism* 59.2 (2020): 209–30.

issues of aetiology through its association of libraries and character. Where does individual character come from, and how much control does anyone have over its development?

Such questions were articulated through striking metaphors. An important pattern of gustatory imagery presented readers as eaters, books as meals, libraries as ordinaries. The prevalence of such images in all kinds of literature had a long history: in his *Essays* Francis Bacon had written during the Renaissance about how 'Some *Bookes* are to be Tasted, Others to be Swallowed, and Some Few to be Chewed and Digested'.[18] Enjoying renewed currency from the 1790s onwards, this imagery of physical ingestion reflects a sense that *what* and *how* you read becomes part of you—it makes up the self. It contains a moral charge deployed to recommend particular kinds of reading practices (for example, those that 'digest' materials rather than 'gobble them down' hastily) and particular kinds of reading matter (for example, novels described as non-nutritious food, philosophy or theology as wholesome sustenance).[19] So Emma Courtney contrasts the 'intellectual feast' of her father's library with the sensational novels she 'devoured – little careful in the selection', a picture of indiscriminate binge eating.[20] Repeated images of ingestion encapsulate the first version of the relationship between library and character. Godwin and his contemporaries often depict characters who are formed by their hungry interactions with the library; this imagined process reveals anxieties about the power of educational environment to feed, constitute, and conscript individuals.

Walter Scott's fictional libraries became a means of recasting such explorations of the sources of identity as a process of detection and legitimation. In *The Antiquary* Jonathan Oldbuck's extensive library—a sprawling collection of books, manuscripts, and objects—orchestrates the network of meaning by which William Lovel's real name and noble lineage come to be identified and cleared from disgrace. This personal history is discovered and interpreted through a variety of media—textual records, material trinkets, oral tales—and the process is shadowed throughout by the printer's motto of Oldbuck's fifteenth-century ancestor, *Kunst Macht Gunst* ('Skill Wins Favour'). Intriguingly, however, the favour that Lovel seeks is won in the end not primarily by his own ability but by the skills of others in piecing together his family history. Scott uses the antiquary's library as a synecdoche for the arduous necessity of correctly discerning legitimacy from imposture; in doing so he raises fundamental concerns about how this character-forming process of discernment happens and who has authority over it.

---

[18] Francis Bacon, *Essays* (London: Oxford University Press, 1966), 204–5 ('Of Studies').

[19] For wider context see Denise Gigante, *Taste: A Literary History* (New Haven: Yale University Press, 2005).

[20] Mary Hays, *Memoirs of Emma Courtney*, ed. Marilyn Brooks (Peterborough: Broadview Press, 2000), 53.

Nourished by materials from Oldbuck's library, Lovel's story is in part the story of historiography; the quest for his identity is bound up with questions about the mediation and interpretation of the past. The antiquary's library represents the eclectic alliance of means by which history is built into present-day social life: the documentary evidence of texts and objects; the testimonies of community storytellers; the dreams, speculations, and educated guesses of agents implicated by its meaning. When Scott introduces Oldbuck's library, he describes a lumber room of curiosities and fragments obscured by dust, a metonymic view of the past and its knowability. Lovel has to peer through a 'thick atmosphere' in order to discern

> book-shelves, greatly too limited in space for the number of volumes placed upon them,...amid a chaos of maps, engravings, scraps of parchment, bundles of papers, pieces of armour, swords, dirks, helmets, and Highland targets.

This library, an exaggerated version of the comfortable gentleman's traditional bookroom whose contents frequently extended to take in artefacts beyond mere leather-bound volumes, is the clutter of lost worlds, a 'wreck of ancient books and utensils', in which the 'prostrate folio' lies alongside shards of Roman pottery.[21] Its features are also modelled in its owner, whose speech is a patchwork of quotations from myriad sources, a disconcerting blend of pedantic scrutiny and wild, illimitable ramble.

In some respects, the plot of *The Antiquary* connects this historiographical process figured in the library to the cohesion and resolution of present-day individual character. Lovel, discovered to be the heir of Glenallen, represents a new generation of gentry whose genealogical story combines birthright with moral integrity—and to some extent England with Scotland. Yet the antiquarian library and its owner also imbue this narrative with ambiguity. The reader is explicitly encouraged to compare Oldbuck's endeavours with those of Don Quixote; although he can be an acute critic and investigator, Oldbuck is often a dupe. Early on, for example, a mistake he makes about a coin has rendered him a laughing stock to local peasants. This error foreshadows other misperceptions. Readers are introduced to his library through the bemused perspective of Lovel; Scott's narrative technique echoes Cervantes's use of the priest and the barber to explore Don Quixote's ill-fated library. The ardency of Scott's bibliophile, rummaging through alleyway stalls for black-letter ballads and first editions, is gently undercut by the detachment of the non-collector, whose ironic filter throws into relief the arbitrariness of antiquarian pursuits.[22] Oldbuck's library encapsulates a

---

[21] Walter Scott, *The Antiquary*, ed. David Hewitt (Edinburgh: Edinburgh University Press, 1995), 21–2.

[22] Scott, *The Antiquary*, 23–5.

murky relationship between history and fantasy that is never fully clarified, but reinforces Ian Duncan's description of *The Antiquary* as a novel insistent upon its own fictionality, exploiting 'the logic of a Humean "moderate scepticism" at the service of things as they are'.[23] The library-fuelled search for Lovel's personal identity brings activities of detection and creation into an equivocal yet intimate relationship.

The most striking aspect of this identity search is that the man in question has little to do with it. Oldbuck's detective work enlists Lovel in a dramatic story of community redemption, but he himself is either silent or absent for most of the novel. Here Scott was partly drawing on a legacy of Gothic fiction: as Deidre Lynch has highlighted, earlier novelists including Ann Radcliffe had put scenes of reading to a sort of necromantic use, with libraries in particular becoming sites where protagonists and readers alike were haunted by family histories and unexpectedly recruited into their chronicles.[24] Scott appropriates this trope of bibliographical–genealogical ambush, using the antiquary's library to inscribe his rather passive protagonist into a story of familial and national identity. *The Antiquary* depicts a subject who is discovered, named, and legitimated by others— who submits to the interpretive lens of the library. This process uncovers an ambivalent celebration of the way past stories come to form present-day character and identities.

The tension between discovery and invention that Scott deploys in *The Antiquary* becomes a feature of libraries in many later nineteenth-century novels. Frequently in the mid-century *Bildungsroman*, for example, childhood encounters with domestic book collections are used both to signal the innate superiority of protagonists' inner lives and to describe their circumstantial genesis. The eponymous hero of *David Copperfield* (1850) reads 'as if for life' amongst his late father's library of fiction and travel writing, sustaining his 'hope of something beyond that place and time' by feeding his imagination. In *The Mill on the Floss* (1860), young Maggie Tulliver's intense relationship with the household books marks her out as unusually rich in thought and feeling, and her horror when they are later auctioned to pay family debt makes a sharp contrast to her brother Tom, who values them on the same terms as the furniture.[25] These bookish scenes speak of the protagonists' imaginative sensitivity, emotional empathy, and spiritual yearnings, all of which are conspicuously lacking in the communities that surround them.

---

[23] Ian Duncan, 'Walter Scott and the Historical Novel', in *The Oxford History of the Novel in English*, vol 2 (Oxford: Oxford University Press, 2015), 322. Scott would later revisit this dynamic in his *Reliquiae Trotcosienses; or, The Gabions of the Late Jonathan Oldbuck Esq. of Monkbarns* (1830), which, as the title indicates, drew a playful comparison between his fictional antiquary and his own activities as collector and historical romancer.

[24] Deidre Lynch, 'Gothic Libraries and National Subjects', *Studies in Romanticism* 40.1 (2001): 29–48.

[25] Charles Dickens, *David Copperfield* (London: Vintage, 2017), 56–7; George Eliot, *The Mill on the Floss*, ed. Gordon Haight (Oxford: Oxford University Press, 2015), 223.

They thus frame the process by which individuals strive to realize their place amongst inhospitable surroundings. These characters are shaped by their access to personal libraries.

Many satirical writings seized the opportunity to subvert this association between libraries and interior depth, deploying libraries instead to delineate or expose the fabrication of character. In W. M. Thackeray's *Vanity Fair* (1848), the library at Queen's Crawley advertises its owners' ignorance and colludes in social fraud: the crafty governess Becky Sharp drops into conversation a name found in a library book of heraldry, leading her employers to believe she has noble ancestry. As Leah Price indicates, Thackeray delights in the material surfaces of print media, repeatedly flaunting the object status of books by recording their uses as missiles, screens, and wrapping paper.[26] This preoccupation with surfaces sustains the sense that nothing in this tale has inner integrity: personal identity itself is a farce—hence the subtitle 'A Novel Without a Hero'. A later example of this countercurrent is *The Importance of Being Earnest* (1895), a play which trades upon the foundling trope so common in early-century novels such as *The Antiquary*. Wilde's final library scene—in which imposture and genuine article become one—brilliantly conflates the themes of bibliographic integrity and performance that Scott, amongst others, had deployed eight decades earlier.

Other nineteenth-century characters, however, are best described as incarnated in the library. Elements of this are visible in the so-called 'bibliophilic essays' of the 1820s by writers including William Hazlitt, Charles Lamb, and Leigh Hunt. These describe libraries in vividly intimate terms, deliberately blurring boundaries between persons and books.[27] In Hazlitt's 'On Reading Old Books' (1821), the essayist's 'scanty library' actually makes up his self through its involvement in processes of mind and body, collating it and protecting it from fragmentation. Books 'bind together the different scattered divisions of our personal identity', Hazlitt declares, casting the book owner as a sort of meta-book, bound and rebound over time.[28] Hunt's 'My Books' (1823) traces authorial life towards its final end of bibliographic incarnation, expressing his own aspiration to 'remain visible in this shape'—note Hunt's use of the verb *remain*, rather than *become*; his essay has already confounded the speaker's affective, intellectual, and physical being with his personal library.[29] All these writers imbue the material forms and

---

[26] Leah Price, *How To Do Things With Books In Victorian Britain* (Princeton: Princeton University Press, 2012), e.g. 76, 131, 273 n. 7.

[27] See Ina Ferris, 'Bibliophilic Romance: Bibliophilia and the Book-Object', and Deidre Lynch, '"Wedded to Books": Bibliomania and the Romantic Essayists', both in the Romantic Libraries issue of *Romantic Circles Praxis Series* (University of Maryland, Feb. 2004), https://www.rc.umd.edu/praxis/libraries/index.html, accessed 19 Feb. 2019; Ina Ferris, 'Book Fancy: Bibliomania and the Literary Word', *Keats-Shelley Journal* 58 (2009): 33–52.

[28] William Hazlitt, 'On Reading Old Books', *The Complete Works of William Hazlitt*, ed. P. P. Howe, 21 vols (London: J. M. Dent & Sons, 1931), vol. 12, 221.

[29] Leigh Hunt, 'My Books', in *Essays and Sketches*, ed. R. Brimley Johnson (London: Oxford University Press, 1906), 95.

spatial contexts of their books with deep meaning, prescribing appropriate bindings, typographies, and storage spaces by describing them as extensions of metaphysical realities. They celebrate private, *Fleetwood*esque closet libraries because—in contrast to the reading rooms of public libraries or the grand libraries of aristocratic dwellings—those are small enough to manifest the idiosyncrasies of individuals. These essayists discover themselves substantiated, their characters formed in their libraries as they write about them, foreshadowing the self-realization of Walter Benjamin's essay 'Unpacking my Library' (1931) over a century later.

This incarnational process is deployed for rather different purposes of characterization in Eliot's *Middlemarch* (1872), in which Mr Casaubon provides one of the most famous intersections of library and character in fiction. Casaubon's narrow, gloomy bookroom does more than simply reflect or complement an ugly truth about its owner—it bodies forth a mental architecture, exteriorizing the prolixity and obscurity of his inner world. Casaubon's library is not so much character-forming as character-deforming. Eliot draws attention to this through her persistent use of spatial language to describe the disappointing process by which Dorothea comes to know something of Casaubon's mind after their marriage. She is dismayed to discover she is 'exploring an enclosed basin'; that 'the large vistas and wide fresh air which she had dreamed of finding in her husband's mind were replaced by anterooms and winding passages which seemed to lead nowhither'. Casaubon's barrenness of thought and feeling is repeatedly materialized, epistemology of character made inseparable from 'the dark bookshelves [of] the long library' at Lowick.[30]

This library's most disturbing function is its corporealization of linguistic redundancy: it is a place that harbours empty forms, defunct signs, unmet expectations. The ever-accumulating collection of notes for Casaubon's never-to-be-written magnum opus forges an alliance between proliferation of text and failure to communicate. The volumes are depicted not primarily as bearers of intellectual content but as mute objects taking up space, weighing down shelves and minds. These associations even transfer to the bookcase in Dorothea's boudoir, the contents of which begin to seem to her like simulacra, 'immovable imitations of books' (271). In *Middlemarch* verbal communication also conspicuously fails in the library, the absence or frustration of the couple's spoken words leaving a vacuum for unvoiced feelings. Silence becomes a necessity for Casaubon—any exposure of his emptiness must be expelled or locked away like the critical pamphlet from Brasenose that lies buried in a library drawer. It is significant from this perspective that Casaubon dies outside his library, a sort of revenge of the real upon his 'small hungry shivering self' (277).

---

[30] George Eliot, *Middlemarch*, ed. David Carroll (Oxford: Oxford University Press, 1998), 193, 72. All further page references in this chapter are supplied in the body of the text.

Eliot uses her novel to explore how new vistas may emerge from such dead ends. 'Every limit is a beginning as well as an ending,' its finale declares. In Dorothea's case, this lesson assumes the dimensions of the library once again. A short while after Casaubon's death,

> the shutters were all opened at Lowick Manor, and the morning gazed calmly into the library, shining on the rows of note-books as it shines on the weary waste planted with huge stones, the mute memorial of a forgotten faith.   (530)

Still silent in this description, the library's volumes now assume a memorial function, allowing the living to negotiate relations between the past and the present. Dorothea holds an imaginary conversation with her husband, rearranges his notes into sequence, and then inscribes a note of defiance onto the posthumous instructions left to her. Eventually an even more radical 'beginning' takes place here, as the library becomes the site of Dorothea's romantic union with Will Ladislaw. When Will's presence is announced, Dorothea identifies the library as the particular place in which Casaubon's 'prohibition seemed to dwell', and then renounces its hold over her by finally forcing her feelings into words (793).

This use of the library to body forth endings and beginnings becomes the epicentre of M. A. Ward's controversial *Robert Elsmere* (1888). Ward's libraries do not just guide but transubstantiate the evolving intellectual lives of individuals, which in turn mark the tide of intellectual history proper. At the centre of her plot is the renowned Murewell Hall library of Roger Wendover, infamous sceptic and man of letters. As Daniel Cook has pointed out, there is a sort of symbiosis between this library and its owner, including a physical correspondence between books 'full of paper marks' and their scholar, whose labours have 'left marks upon him physically'.[31] When Robert and Langham enter Wendover's library during his absence, they can trace his life and character in its shelves: his books are 'a chart of his own intellectual history', which moves from the Anglican theology of the Tractarian movement to the scepticism of eighteenth-century philosophy, to the historicism of modern German philology (209). This library obviously represents 'the forces of an epoch' (210), naturalized by the suggestion that its books have 'drifted thither one by one, carried there by the tide of English letters' (207). But it also manifests something tangibly personal:

> The room seemed instinct with a harsh commanding presence. The history of a mind and soul was written upon the face of it; every shelf, as it were, was an

---

[31] Mrs Humphry [Mary Augusta] Ward, *Robert Elsmere*, ed. Miriam Elizabeth Burstein (Brighton: Victorian Secrets, 2013), 209–10; all further page references in this chapter are supplied in the body of the text. Daniel Cook, 'Bodies of Scholarship: Witnessing the Library in Late-Victorian Fiction,' *Victorian Literature and Culture* 39:1 (2011), 107–25.

autobiographical fragment, an 'Apologia pro Vita Mea.' [Langham] drew away from the books at last with the uneasy feeling of one who surprises a confidence, and looked for Robert.   (210)

The Murewell Hall library has a prosthetic function: it both represents the absent Wendover and constitutes him. At the same time, Wendover's bookish life crystallizes the cutting edge of European opinion, a phenomenon that transcends the individual. A character and a moment of history are simultaneously 'instinct' here, intimately real; this is why, as Cook notes, the Oxford scholar Langham is both fascinated and compelled to look away.[32]

Ward's account of this library displays her affinity to the idealist philosophies of Hegel, Fichte, and others, as popularized and developed in Britain by writers including Thomas Carlyle and T. H. Green (to whom *Robert Elsmere* is dedicated). In particular, Carlyle's 1840 lecture on 'The Hero as Man of Letters' speaks directly of books as vestments, a concept central to his earlier mercurial fiction *Sartor Resartus* (1836). 'The thing we called "bits of paper with traces of black ink," is the *purest* embodiment a Thought of man can have,' he contends; the library for Carlyle is the 'true University'—a temple of books where great writers are prophets or priests whose lives and works constitute 'a "continuous revelation" of the Godlike in the Terrestrial and Common'.[33] Carlyle's missionary vision is endorsed in *Robert Elsmere* as the protagonist adopts the saying of his mentor Henry Grey: '*The decisive events of the world take place in the intellect. It is the mission of books that they help one to remember it*' (211). This view of agency also drives Ward's plot, according to which Robert's embroilment in Wendover's library instigates his recruitment into the evolution of mind that it embodies. He abandons orthodox belief in the divinity of Jesus and in miracles, pursuing instead 'new ways of worship' that will keep the spirit of Christianity alive for the modern mind (413). The library here is a womb, and Robert's experience is portrayed as a necessary, albeit painful, character-forming rebirth.

Libraries in *Robert Elsmere* speak of death as well as life, however. The sceptical scholars Wendover and Langham both use books to shut themselves off from social ties and defy legitimate relational claims, symbolized by the architectural separation of Wendover's library from the rest of the Hall, to which it is connected by a passage that narrows the closer one gets to its entrance. The Squire is a sort of 'spiritual medusa' (270), whose clinical and socially withdrawn intellectual pursuits have frozen his sympathy. While in some ways reminiscent of Casaubon, his character also evokes Carlyle's description of the constitutional sceptic in *Heroes*

---

[32] Cook, 'Bodies of Scholarship', 114, 116.
[33] Thomas Carlyle, *On Heroes, Hero-worship and the Heroic in History*, ed. George Wherry (Cambridge: Cambridge University Press, 1911), 168 (emphasis in original), 165, 166.

and Hero-Worship, who is 'spiritually a paralytic man', a person whose obsession with critical tools has stagnated the soul's natural course towards belief.[34] In this context it is fitting that eventually he is haunted by the immaterial dimension he denies, and that he dies amongst the barren upper chambers of the library, which contain only books and no furniture. These rooms contrast sharply with Robert's small library at the rectory, the location of which was specifically chosen for its accessibility to visitors, and in which books mingle freely with tools, sports equipment, and specimens of local wildlife.

This library comparison is used to make a case for the humanitarian-focussed theological liberalism that Robert comes to espouse. Ward depicts the intellectual movement that the Hall library embodies as an inevitable force, but draws a dark picture of the havoc it wreaks when divorced from relational sympathy. Serving to redress Wendover's impotence, as the novel nears its conclusion, yet another library is introduced: that of the New Brotherhood of Christ, Robert's unorthodox religious society which takes root amongst the working class of East London. Robert's plan for their building includes, in line with the ideals of Victorian library reformers and legislators, 'a library and reading-room open to both sexes, well stored with books, and made beautiful by pictures' (569), alongside a lecture room, naturalist's club, and gymnasium. Here a new kind of intellectual life will be manifested, one that reinterprets the 'testimonies' of the past and puts them to contemporary use amongst the poor, attempting to mould the character of each reader by uniting mind and body, male and female, individual and community. *Robert Elsmere* finishes with an account of this idealistic library under construction, 'becoming a most fascinating place, under the management of a librarian chosen from the neighbourhood' (576). Its germination signals a social and intellectual sea change, redressing Wendover's failure of social paternity.

In *Robert Elsmere*, then, a continuous and powerful interplay of library and character is deployed in order to dramatize a world in which individuals are inseparable from underlying historical forces of mind. There is an interesting reversion to that gustatory language used by Godwin and other early nineteenth-century reformers: 'Wait', warns the sombre Newcombe, 'till you have watched that man's books eating the very heart out of a poor creature' (178). In this image, the reader of Wendover's library is absorbed into a larger bookish world—one that holds the threat of unbelief—rather than incorporating books into their individual life. This figure exposes a dialectic in Ward's novel between the library as incarnation of self—its ultimate manifestation—and the library as a stomach that absorbs or digests readers into itself, amounting almost to a dissolution of personal identity. Robert's nature, in fact, is described explicitly as a

---

[34] Carlyle, *Heroes*, 177.

sort of promising blank, 'mobile, impressionable, defenceless' (331). His wife, Catherine, whose orthodox Christian beliefs and anti-intellectual stance preclude her from sharing in Robert's 'conversion', is depicted by contrast as rigid and ironlike. She never enters Wendover's library or that of the Brotherhood. Her exclusion from the library reflects that she cannot participate in its evolutionary movement; she can only feel herself 'caught and nipped in the great inexorable wheel of things' (555).

Catherine's experience of this 'inexorable wheel' indicates the two-edged nature of Ward's fictional libraries, which both celebrate the transcendent imperatives to which human lives are subject and register the agony that they entail for individuals. In *Robert Elsmere*, the modern world's firmer grasp upon religious truth necessitates the demolition of beliefs that are cherished by particular people. A parallel of sorts can be drawn with *Fleetwood*, in which the power of libraries to germinate habit and disposition is also allied to ambivalent consequences. Godwin channelled it into a call for the emancipation of society through educational reform, yet his novel also raises the spectre of determinism by adopting the perspective of an individual character who can only retrospectively recognize and mourn his relationship to the library in the form of a confession. While in some ways anticipating the constricting library of Casaubon in *Middlemarch*, Oldbuck's library in *The Antiquary* assumes, like that of *Fleetwood*, an equivocal relation to the individual: on the one hand, its role in the detection of Lovel's story celebrates the various means by which the past allows present identities to cohere. Yet on the other hand, this quest for meaning is never fully distinguished from quixotic folly or wish fulfilment, and the reader is left wondering about the agency of Lovel, whose character remains a sort of blank, like Robert Elsmere, to be filled in by outside forces.

In sum, I have tried in this chapter to highlight fictional libraries that, by initiating various tensions in the construction of characters, encourage readers to question the authority sources of personal identity. J. W. Burrow places such a movement at the centre of nineteenth-century intellectual history, describing how 'the absolute claim of individual autonomy' that animated liberal philosophy repeatedly confronts the limits of its domain; his account characterizes the period as one in which 'the self' is chronically elusive.[35] This is the dynamic that the novelists considered here have dramatized through their depictions of characters that emerge from, or through, or in, the library. Their libraries promise to make sense of the subjects allied to them, but always somehow swallow them up; they offer meaning whilst they threaten self-integrity. It is a pattern that qualifies the recent literary history of James Eli Adams, in which a distinguishing feature of the later nineteenth-century novel is its new attention

---

[35] Burrow, *Crisis of Reason*, 147–8.

to 'a host of forces…that constrain human self-determination' and 'strain the faith in personal autonomy that was so crucial to Victorian liberalism, and was epitomised in the ideal of the self-made man'.[36] This attention was already at the heart of early-century novels by Godwin and Scott, and figurations of the library constitute a significant aspect of it.

[36] James Eli Adams, *A History of Victorian Literature* (Chichester: Wiley-Blackwell, 2012), 211–12.

6

Margaret Oliphant's
'The Library Window'

Elisabeth Jay

Margaret Oliphant published her late short story 'The Library Window' in *Blackwood's Edinburgh Magazine* in January 1896. The date is significant. She had vowed to abandon novel-writing the previous year, after the death of her remaining adult son,[1] and penning the intimate reflections she had been preparing for her autobiography now distressed her: the last desolate fragment of her autobiography written in the spring of 1895 read, 'And now here I am all alone. I cannot write any more.'[2] Bereft of her children, and with many of her closest friends now dead, Oliphant increasingly lived in an imaginative space between memories of her past and musings about the afterlife, or between 'the Seen and the Unseen', as she characterized her tales of the supernatural. These stories of liminality, which had begun in 1879 with *A Beleaguered City*, had appeared only intermittently over the years: Oliphant sought to explain their very particular genesis and nature to her publisher—'Stories of this description are not like any others. I can produce them only when they come to me.'[3] In January 1897 Oliphant published the very last of these distinctive tales in which she sought to map out her vision of the afterlife and the continuing journeys of those close to her.[4] Though set in a recognizable, this-worldly location, 'The Library Window' belongs to this group of Oliphant's later writings increasingly haunted by the ghosts of her past.

The *fin de siècle* was in any case a time ripe for retrospection. Queen Victoria's diamond jubilee was approaching and Oliphant, who counted Windsor's other famous widow among her devoted readers, was swift to jump on this particular bandwagon, updating her 1880 life of the Queen, and publishing further essays

---

[1] Letter of 7 Dec. 1894, in *The Autobiography and Letters of Mrs M.O.W. Oliphant*, ed. Mrs Harry Coghill (Edinburgh and London: Blackwood, 1899), 417; repr. in *The Selected Works of Margaret Oliphant: The Pickering Master Series*, ed. E. Jay and J. Shattock, 25 vols (London; Pickering & Chatto, 2011–17), vi, 281.

[2] *The Autobiography of Margaret Oliphant. The Complete Text*, ed. E. Jay. (Oxford: Oxford University Press, 1990), 154; *Selected Works*, vi, 107.

[3] Letter of 13 Nov. 1884 in *Autobiography and Letters*, ed. Coghill, 321. *Selected Works*, vi, 219.

[4] 'The Land of Suspense', *Blackwood's Magazine* 161 (January 1897): 131–57.

summarizing the reign.[5] Her other major money-earning venture at this time involved further revisiting of her past. She had been commissioned to produce *The Annals of a Publishing House, William Blackwood & Sons, Their Magazine and Friends*, and this history of the publishing firm with which her name was most associated offered her the chance both for the thumbnail biographical sketches in which she had long excelled and for a type of refracted autobiographical commentary on her professional life and times.

As she delved further into the Blackwood archives, Oliphant was repeatedly struck by the very masculine nature of their enterprise. A decade before, she had noted how the coterie the Blackwoods had gathered around them in 1829, when they moved into their premises at No. 45, George Street, Edinburgh, had favoured 'the manly pen' of the Empire's soldiers and sailors: 'She has her ladies too, but, shall we own it? Perhaps loves them less.'[6] The New Year's Eve scene with flickering firelight momentarily illuminating 'the pictured brethren on the walls' renders the firm's inner sanctum a little similar to the interior of the library that the female narrator conjures up in the short story 'The Library Window'.

A brief summary of the story is necessary at this point if the subsequent discussion is to prove intelligible. It is a tale of a young girl's summer spent in a thinly disguised St Andrews, here named St Rule's in allusion to the early twelfth-century tower of the church which preceded St Andrews Cathedral. The story, we eventually discover, is retrospectively related by the girl, who is now a mother and widow. As a girl she had been sent by her parents to stay with her elderly aunt Mary in the hope that this experience would render her less 'fantastic and fanciful and dreamy, and all the other words with which a girl who may happen to like poetry, and to be fond of thinking, is often made uncomfortable'.[7] Her tolerant, elderly aunt allows the girl to take possession of a deeply recessed window on the first floor looking out onto the college library opposite and a little further down the street. Here she sits, surrounded by books and a sewing basket, but able to absorb snippets of the conversation from her aunt's visitors, who include an elderly gentleman of a scientific bent called Mr Pitmilly and a Lady Carnbee, whose diamond ring capable of stinging to the heart and her general witchlike demeanour are strongly reminiscent of Sleeping Beauty's wicked godmother.

A conversation about the furthermost window of the library opposite triggers the girl's interest. Its opaque appearance is variously explained by its being simply very dirty; or a window bricked up during the years of the window tax; or a painted *trompe l'oeil*; or one of the ornamental blank window spaces recently

---

[5] For a detailed account of the various subsequent, revised, and enlarged versions of the 1880 life of Queen Victoria, see *Selected Works*, vii, 199–202. ''Tis Sixty Years Since', *Blackwood's Magazine* 161 (May 1897): 599–624.

[6] 'In Maga's Library: The Old Saloon', *Blackwood's Magazine* 141 (January 1887): 126–53; 127.

[7] 'The Library Window', *Blackwood's Magazine* 159 (January 1896): 1–30. *Selected Works*, xii, 265–99.

made fashionable by 'the great new buildings on the Earthen Mound in Edinburgh', structures erected in the 1830s and 1840s.[8] Although the window remains opaque in daylight, on a series of twilit evenings the girl gradually makes out more and more of a library room behind the window, seeing a desk, a large picture in a frame, and finally a young, beardless scholar who sits continually writing. Anxious to put a stop to the girl's growing obsession with the window, Aunt Mary and Lady Carnbee, who both share the girl's gift of second sight, persuade her to accompany them to a party in the Library Hall. The girl grudges attending 'A mere party, a conversazione (when all the College was away, too, and nobody to make conversation!)';[9] and it is indeed disappointing, for there the girl is told that the window she sees had been installed as a blank architectural decoration, hidden in any case by a bookcase. Returning home much distressed, on this evening she sees the scholar respond to her by opening the library window and smiling at her. Although one or two pieces of ambiguous evidence support her claim, she is treated as a hysteric. Nevertheless, her aunt confesses that women of their blood who share second sight have each had a similar experience, possibly inspired by a family legend about a flighty young woman who had lured the scholar from the library using Lady Carnbee's diamond ring as a token, only for the scholar to be killed by the young woman's brothers. Hoping to verify her own experience, three nights later the girl narrator steals out to the street after midnight, but sees nothing. The following day she is removed from St Rule's by her mother, never to return. In a brief coda, the narrator tells us she had once more glimpsed the scholar when she returned from abroad as a widow with young children. In due course she had inherited Lady Carnbee's ring but, still fearful of it, has chosen to bury it in a house she owns but does not live in.

Like all the best tales of the supernatural this story has a certain indeterminacy: resisting a collapse into simple allegory or *roman-à-clef*, it leaves us with unsettling disjunctures and unanswered questions. For one thing, the narrative time frame is never entirely resolved. The first-person narrator's opening paragraph moves from past tense recall of a particular place and time to a present tense, very personal, impression of summer nights in St Rule's, despite the narrator's later assertion that she has never revisited the town. This trope, which recurs later in the tale,[10] has the effect of merging the young girl of that particular summer with her older persona, just as the prose style of the piece incorporates both the short sentences and apparently transparent emotional responses of the young girl and the more reflective commentary of the older figure looking back on her younger self. This blending of subjective and objective is familiar to readers of Oliphant's

---

[8] After the 1843 Disruption in the Church of Scotland Oliphant's parents had joined the emergent Free Church of Scotland, which quickly commissioned a theological college (New College) and a new Assembly Hall in Edinburgh. In 1893 Oliphant had published the biography of New College's first principal, Thomas Chalmers.

[9] 'Library Window', *Selected Works*, xii, 289.   [10] 'Library Window', *Selected Works*, xii, 276–7.

autobiography, where her commentary on scenes from her past life often seems to spring from a desire to forestall the reader's criticism. In this tale the mature reflections of the narrator operate to temper the impassioned narrative of the young girl and to provide an air of legitimacy to her account. This uncanny collapsing of time past and time present in turn echoes the story's insistence on an ancient legend being re-enacted.

The plot itself raises questions and inconsistencies. What do the scholar, the window, the library, and the token signify? Why did the experience or gift that Aunt Mary and Lady Carnbee share with the girl leave them as spinsters, while the girl marries, even if only to be widowed early? What are we to make of the very deliberate situating of fairy tale devices and rituals in a contemporary setting which pays due attention to verifiable spatial and chronological detail?

For those remaining of Oliphant's closest circle—her two adopted nieces, and two daughters of John Tulloch, who had been Principal of St Mary's College, St Andrews between 1855 and 1885[11]—the references to St Andrews and to the library that is known today as the King James Library would have formed an easily decipherable code. Indeed, it is possible that the story was initially conceived as a family Christmas ghost tale for this group. Each of the main characters' names in the story is taken from estates and villages surrounding St Andrews. Aunt Mary's surname is Balcarres, the name of a local big house 10 miles south of St Andrews; Lady Carnbee's name is taken from that of a village 8 miles south of St Andrews, and Mr Pitmilly, who likes to be known as Pitmilly, Morton, references a farm of that name on the Pitmilly estate, 5 miles south-east of St Andrews. There is a reference to the year (1861–2) when the New Town Hall was being built, necessitating the 'assemblies' being held in the library: it was from about this date that Oliphant and her young family had started to take summer vacations in St Andrews, and by the 1880s she habitually holidayed there, often alone.[12]

Speaking of the broad High Street, which could seem quiet to visitors, the narrator reflects, 'There are even exceptional moments when it is noisy: the time of the fair, and on Saturday nights sometimes, and when there are excursion trains.'[13] Visiting over the time of the August Lammas Fair, from 1863 Oliphant and her party would have been able to take a passenger train from Edinburgh, a service dramatically interrupted by the Tay Bridge disaster of 1879. When the line reopened in 1887, twelve trains ran daily from Edinburgh, and there was an upsurge of excursion trains from Dundee.

So this is the story not of 'A Library Window' but of 'The Library Window'. What was it about the King James Library that held especial significance for

---

[11] He is buried beneath a large memorial at the centre of the Eastern Cemetery in St Andrews. His wife, Jane Anne Sophia (1826–87) is buried with him.

[12] Margaret Oliphant, A Memoir of the Life of John Tulloch (Edinburgh and London, William Blackwood & Sons, 1888), 437.

[13] 'Library Window', Selected Works, xii, 269.

Oliphant? It was apparently not the special collections. Before her one disappoint-ing visit, the tale's narrator says, 'I never visited the old College Library, but I had seen such places before, and I could well imagine it to myself.'[14] The following vignette in one of her early *Blackwood's* articles suggests that Oliphant had probably availed herself of a ticket to the British Museum reading room soon after she and her husband set up home in London in 1852:

> There she is – behold her! – in the library of the British Museum, with her poke bonnet, her india-rubber overshoes; perhaps – most likely – some sandwiches in that pocket...There she sits all the dull November day, the London fog peering in at her through the big windows; nobody blowing a trumpet to clear the way as she goes home through the dingy streets of Bloomsbury...putting up with an omnibus, and possibly carrying her notes in her little bag or basket.[15]

When Oliphant returned from her European wanderings in the mid-1860s to base herself in Windsor so that her boys might receive an Eton education, she found herself in need of a major lending library. Despite its expensive fee and its predominantly male ethos, the London Library, founded in 1841 at the urging of Thomas Carlyle, could provide her with the books she needed whether at home or when, as increasingly often, she was travelling. John Blackwood, her publisher, sponsored her when she applied for membership in 1868, and she was still using its facilities when she moved back to London in 1896.[16]

It seems likely therefore to have been a personal response to the King James Library which provoked the tale. This library, built close to a site associated with teaching since the university's foundation in 1411, was in effect the heart of the university enterprise. For centuries it would have been, like most libraries, whether private, domestic, or institutional, a distinctively male space.[17] Aunt Mary makes the point early in the tale that the Old Library does not even employ women servants to do the cleaning,[18] and to an extent Oliphant's story forms part of that stream of feminist protest which would culminate in Virginia Woolf's *A Room of One's Own* (1929). Indeed, when I first wrote about this story a quarter of a

---

[14] 'Library Window', *Selected Works*, xii, 275.

[15] 'Modern Light Literature – History', *Blackwood's Magazine* 78 (October 1855), 437–51; 437.

[16] As shown by this note in her diary for 1896: 'Go to London Library to look up National Biography on Charles Lamb.' *Autobiography of Margaret Oliphant*, ed. Jay, 160.

[17] For a discussion of the way in which even the reading rooms of the British Museum, which had admitted women since the Museum's inception in 1753, isolated and marginalized female readers, see Ruth Hoberman, 'Women in the British Museum Reading Room During the Late-Nineteenth and Early-Twentieth Centuries: From Quasi- to Counterpublic', *Feminist Studies* 28:3 (Autumn, 2002): 489–512.

[18] In practice this situation was to change very swiftly: the first woman to be listed as a staff member was Mary Davidson Cornfoot, Assistant Librarian from 1899 to 1900 onwards, joined by Jessie A. Paterson from 1905–6. I am very grateful to Rachel Hart, Senior Archivist, Special Collections, St Andrews University Library, for this and subsequent information about the library's records.

century ago, I saw in the beardless scholar at the window the mirror reflection created by a girl who yearns for quiet solitude in which to write, but who has been so indoctrinated by the cultural rules of her upbringing that she can only conceive of the scholar as male.[19]

Yet it would have been curious for Oliphant to launch a protest at women's exclusion from this university library in the mid-1890s for three reasons. The first is that as a close friend of the Tullochs she would surely have been aware that women had long been able to gain some form of access to the books in this library. Its records show that professors had been borrowing volumes for named women, not necessarily limited to family members, since the early 1780s, and a woman is first named in her own right as a borrower in 1835. By the 1890s, with the explicit permission of the University Senate and for an annually renewable payment of ten shillings and sixpence, women could borrow books in their own right for the purposes of 'literary research', a privilege of which Oliphant may well have availed herself during her annual holidays.

Second, she would certainly have been aware of St Andrews's leading and early role in furthering women's education in the UK. From 1892 women had been admitted as full students to the university, and in 1896 the first university-owned residence in the United Kingdom for women students was opened by St Andrews.[20] Oliphant, who had visited her elder adopted niece since her 1893 marriage to William Valentine, a Dundee jute merchant, would also have been aware of the university's outreach work in Dundee, where Tulloch and his colleagues lectured to mixed audiences. Valentine was himself a Governor of University College and a member of University Council.

The third reason why it is unlikely that this tale is a straightforward protest against women's exclusion from libraries is Oliphant's strong personal reservations about the increasingly vociferous demands for girls to receive the same educational opportunities as their brothers. In an earlier novel Oliphant as narrator had expressed the opinion that current advice to spend as much on a girl's as a boy's education was fine for those with ample means, but even then should preferably be preceded by a signed agreement that the girl would agree not to marry a poor curate.[21]

In 'The Library Window' the male scholar's constant writing never comes to anything, and the family legend has it that when he ventured beyond the library into the real world of passions and relationships this brought about his instant

---

[19] Elisabeth Jay, *Mrs Oliphant: 'A Fiction to Herself': A Literary Life* (Oxford: Clarendon Press, 1995), 263–6.

[20] Susan Sellers, '"Mischievous to the public interest": The Lady Literate in Arts Diploma and the Admission of Women to the University of St Andrews, 1876–1914,' in *Launch-site for English Studies: Three Centuries of Literary Studies at the University of St Andrews*, ed. Robert Crawford (St Andrews: Verse, 1997), 107–23.

[21] *The Marriage of Elinor*, 3vols (London: Macmillan, 1892), iii, 708.

death (in this regard, he is a kind of male Lady of Shalott). The tale's sustained contrast between the window recess where the girl's creative imagination is fed and the library window through which the unproductive solitude of the scholar's labours can be seen strongly suggests that more may be achieved through observing the domestic and social rituals of daily life than in libraries. Just such a theme had sparked Oliphant's interest in writing her autobiography. Comparing herself with George Eliot, Oliphant admitted, 'I always avoid considering what my own mind is worth', before wondering, 'Should I have done better if I had been kept, like her, in a mental greenhouse and taken care of?'[22]

By the time she penned these words it had also become clear to Oliphant that, despite their early scholarly promise, neither of her sons had amounted to much in adult life: indeed, her unsociable younger son's only employment had been as an intermittent assistant in the Queen's Library at Windsor Castle, cataloguing books on genealogy.

For Oliphant, however, the King James Library was indelibly associated with another scholar, Principal Tulloch, whose memoir his family had commissioned her to write. Something of Oliphant's impatience with the self-indulgent and non-productive life of scholarship comes across in her picture of Tulloch's last summer in St Andrews:

> His very step, large, soft and stately as he crossed the little quadrangle – perhaps to sit in the sun under the mossed apple-trees of the old garden, perhaps to take a meditative turn along the Walk, not without some leisurely observation in the midst of his thoughts of the growth of the trees he had planted, perhaps to go up to the College library and consult some authority there – had in it something of the leisure of the long summer holiday, disturbed by no compulsory work and leaving room for those gentle studies of predilection which are more recreative than any amusement.[23]

She found Tulloch's repeated mental breakdowns and monumental self-pity, all apparently triggered by a Latin false quantity when making a public speech, both risible and bitterly reprehensible, for she attributed the death of her 10-year-old daughter in Rome to having made the journey there with Tulloch's wife and children to meet him from the first of his many rest cures.[24]

Moreover, it is not as if the girl narrator is deprived of the stimuli a library might offer. Just as Oliphant as a young girl had done her writing, instead of needlework, 'at the corner of the family table', while also taking 'her share in conversation, going on all the same with my story, the little groups of imaginary

---

[22] *Autobiography of Margaret Oliphant*, ed. Jay, 14–15; *Selected Works*, vi, 16.
[23] Oliphant, *Memoir of the Life of John Tulloch*, 437.
[24] *Autobiography of Margaret Oliphant*, ed. Jay, 106–9; *Selected Works*, vi, 69–70.

persons, these other talks evolving themselves quite undisturbed', so this girl sits in the window recess between her neglected sewing basket and her books, constructing whole stories for herself from the interplay between her books and overheard snatches of conversation. Even when Oliphant was in sole control of her own household, she read and wrote in a study which was little more than an annex to the main drawing room, where, as she said, 'all the feminine life of the house' went on.[25] A family photograph of these rooms shows books and pictures in profusion.[26] Oliphant had come to an appreciation of the visual arts late, courtesy of her artist husband who had aspired to become known for the large historical and biblical representations popular in mid-century. She too approached pictorial art as a series of framed scenes or narratives. 'The Library Window' shares with her autobiography the impression of being talked through an album of family pictures where the people, their surroundings—whether a landscape, or a closely observed interior, or the lighting—each receive attention in turn, but all are used as a means of recreating the precise emotional significance of the scene. This affords the narrator the double status of a character represented within the picture and a guide who enjoys the benefit of hindsight.

As evidenced by the photograph of her study and drawing room, the books in Oliphant's house lay scattered on tabletops as well as stacked in bookshelves, and when the girl narrator of 'The Library Window' conjures up for herself the scholar's working room, she imagines 'a little pile of books on the floor...– not ranged regularly in order, but put down one above the other, with all their angles going different ways'.[27] For the girl's imaginings, and the story of 'The Library Window' itself, are not created *ex nihilo* but partly inspired by a library of books accumulated over the course of a lifetime of reading and reviewing. Oliphant found the absence of library cataloguing serendipitous:

There is no more delightful eccentricity in a library than the way in which books will occasionally group themselves in defiance of every rule of appropriateness or harmony. It is wrong, we know, and contrary to every rule, but we confess it gives us great gratification now and then to find our books arranged according to the good old rule and simple plan of common size, or shape, or binding, so that stately Gibbon shall for once in a way find himself standing side by side (and much good would it do him) with Mr Pickwick; and Dr Johnson, in his most solemn mood lean upon the cultured impertinence of Mr Andrew Lang.[28]

[25] *Autobiography of Margaret Oliphant*, ed. Jay, 30; *Selected Works*, vi, 28.
[26] See Jay, *Mrs Oliphant:'A Fiction to Herself'*, image facing 149.
[27] 'Library Window', *Selected Works*, xii, 278.
[28] 'In Maga's Library: The Old Saloon', *Blackwood's Magazine* 141 (January 1887): 145.

We know that George Eliot's private library contained some 10,000 books and Trollope's 8,000.[29] We have no account of Oliphant's personal library, which is particularly unfortunate in that, unlike Eliot's library which was merged with that of her partner G. H. Lewes, Oliphant's collection would have shown us something of the working library of a single professional woman. Nevertheless, 'The Library Window' offers quiet proof of how such personal libraries affected nineteenth-century literature. The story includes an overt reference to Samuel Richardson's *Pamela*, but there are also more discreetly placed allusions. On the day when the scholar appears to her, the girl's imagination is totally absorbed in an escapist adventure story which takes her far from 'St Rule's, and the High Street, and the College Library' so that she feels herself 'really in a South American forest, almost throttled by the flowery creepers, and treading softly lest I should put my foot on a scorpion or a dangerous snake'.[30] The scene comes from G. A. Henty's first children's book, *Out on the Pampas*, in which one of the young settlers who has accompanied his parents to Argentina does indeed almost tread upon a pretty but venomous snake—just the kind of story Oliphant might have read to her own 12- and 9-year-old boys when the book first came out in 1868. The scholar's first appearance occurs 'about Midsummer Day – the day of St John, which was once so much thought of as a festival, but now means nothing at all in Scotland'.[31] For a Walter Scott aficionado like Oliphant, the traditional associations with midsummer dreams of future lovers would have been enriched by memories of Scott's 1799 ballad 'The Eve of St John', in which the Lady of Smaylho'me learns that the lover she has entertained three nights in a row must have been a ghostly presence, since her husband slew and buried him on the first of these nights. This poem may also have lain behind the token ring which still has power to sting. At their final meeting the Lady's ghostly lover brands her wrist 'with an awful sign' so that, like Lady Carnbee, henceforth the Lady of Smaylho'me will wear coverings on her hand.

The girl-narrator is puzzled by her aunt Mary's repeated assertion that 'yon ring is the token', and outraged by the accusation that she, like her legendary predecessor, is dreaming of 'some man that is not worth it'.[32] Yet the tale repeatedly returns to the sting that the girl receives from Lady Carnbee's diamond ring. Worn by a woman who shares the girl's second sight, the ring proves itself a double-edged gift. The inherited gift of second sight, or the poetic imagination necessary for conjuring up fiction, had similarly proved double-edged for Oliphant herself. In old age she suffered from a wound to her hand made by the constant use of her

[29] See William Baker, 'The Libraries of George Eliot and George Henry Lewes', ELS Monograph Series 24 (Victoria, BC: University of Victoria, 1981), and John Sutherland, 'Literature and the Library in the Nineteenth Century', in *The Meaning of the Library: a Cultural History*, ed. Alice Crawford (Princeton and Oxford: Princeton University Press, 2015), 124–50.

[30] 'Library Window', *Selected Works*, xii, 280.   [31] 'Library Window', *Selected Works*, xii, 279.

[32] 'Library Window', *Selected Works*, xii, 297, 299, 283.

pen over so many years: 'a hole in her right forefinger' which would not heal.[33] Was this story intended as Oliphant's farewell to fiction and to the personal library where her tales had been conceived and fed by her reading? By the time she wrote 'The Library Window' she was planning to abandon her home in Windsor for lodgings in London, so that her personal library would have to be broken up. The story's narrator claims that the ring is now 'locked up in an old sandal-wood box in the lumber-room in the little old country-house which belongs to me, but where I never live. If any one would steal it, it would be a relief to my mind.'[34] Perhaps, try as she would, her imagination was a gift that could not be stilled or extinguished.

The ring was also the token initially intended to unite the world of the male scholar with that of the young woman. Interestingly, R. H. Hutton, the only contemporary critic to write at any length on this story, assumed unquestioningly that the scholar was the main character in a tale of revenge which he takes by driving women to melancholy madness. Hutton complained that it seemed to trivialize the afterlife if the spirits of the dead were 'chiefly engaged...in completing some little transaction of reparation or revenge, in which they had been interested in this life'. The tale's coda, however, remains ambivalent about the scholar and his intentions. The widowed narrator claims that if the face she has occasionally seen in crowds has been that of the scholar, then he no longer harbours revenge in his heart. On the other hand, the occasion she best recalls occurred when she was returning home from abroad, recently widowed, 'very sad, with my little children'. His appearance cheered her: 'I landed almost cheerfully, thinking here was someone who would help me. But he disappeared.'[35]

This moment is strikingly similar to a personal recollection of Oliphant's: encumbered with a two-month-old baby and three other children, she anticipated help in landing at Marseilles from that 'great scholar' Dr Kennedy of Shrewsbury, a casual travelling acquaintance she had made as she returned from Italy after her husband's death; but at the vital moment he disappeared.[36] During the first few months of her widowhood she was to receive a series of rebuffs from men she had trusted in, such as her oldest brother and her publisher, John Blackwood. Principal Tulloch, the scholar from St Andrews, was merely one in a long train of men who, Oliphant believed, had let her down. Perhaps the device of generalizing his significance by placing him amongst crowds elsewhere was a gesture to appease the Tulloch family, who had been none too pleased with her biography of their late father. Nevertheless, the final sentence of this teasing tale, 'The Library Window', returns us firmly not to any library but the King James Library at St Andrews:

---

[33] Letter of 6 October 1896 in *Autobiography and Letters*, ed. Coghill, 288; *Selected Works*, vi, 427.
[34] 'Library Window', *Selected Works*, xii, 299.   [35] 'Library Window', *Selected Works*, xii, 299.
[36] *Autobiography of Margaret Oliphant*, ed. Jay, 87; *Selected Works*, vi.

Yet I never knew what Aunt Mary meant when she said, 'Yon ring was the token,' nor what it could have to do with that strange window in the old College Library of St Rule's.[37]

The tale's coded references to Oliphant's own history did nothing to prevent its lasting popularity. Given more general currency in the posthumous collection *Stories of the Seen and the Unseen* (1902), its notable contribution to the ghost story genre secured it an afterlife, in contrast with so many of Oliphant's novels which fell out of print soon after her favourite three-decker format expired in the late 1890s. The tale was selected by Dorothy L. Sayers for inclusion in *Great Short Stories of Detection, Mystery and Horror* (1928),[38] and secured a mid-twentieth-century French translation.[39] Meanwhile it was published by Hutchinson in *Fifty Years of Ghost Stories* (1936), and survived to make it into the same publisher's *Walk in Dread: Tales from 'A Century of Ghost Stories'* (1970). The development in the later decades of the twentieth century of an interest in women's writing began to see Oliphant's star rise again, and with it the popularity of 'The Library Window'.[40] The growth of an interest in national literatures also helped: in Douglas Gifford's anthology of short Scottish stories it served to illustrate the duality inherent in the Scottish temperament, which he saw as running through their tales of the supernatural.[41] In 2019 Broadview Press chose the story for one of its critical editions.[42]

The inclusion of 'The Library Window' in the Sayers anthology, together with the following comment by that twentieth-century master of ghostly tales M. R. James, speaks to Oliphant's influence on the genre:

Rhoda Broughton, Mrs. Riddell, Mrs. Henry Wood, Mrs. Oliphant – all these have some sufficiently absorbing stories to their credit...The religious ghost story, as it may be called, was never done better than by Mrs. Oliphant in 'The Open Door' and 'A Beleaguered City'; though there is a competitor, and a strong one, in Le Fanu's 'Mysterious Lodger'.[43]

---

[37] 'Library Window', *Selected Works*, xii, 299.

[38] Published in America as *Second Omnibus of Crime*, ed. Dorothy L. Sayers (New York: Coward-McCann, 1932).

[39] 'La Fenêtre de la Bibliothèque', trans. Marguerite Faguer, in *Les Oeuvres Libres*, (Nouvelle série 128) (Paris: Librairie Arthème Fayard, 1957).

[40] Three publishers produced collections of her supernatural tales: *Margaret Oliphant: Selected Short Stories of the Supernatural*, ed. Margaret K. Gray (Edinburgh: Scottish Academic Press, 1985), 210–48; *A Beleaguered City and Other Stories*, ed. Merryn Williams (Oxford: Oxford University Press, 1988), 287–331; *A beleaguered city: and other tales of the seen and the unseen*, ed. Jenni Calder (Edinburgh: Canongate, 2000), 363–402.

[41] *Scottish Short Stories 1800–1900*, ed. Douglas Gifford (London: Calder & Boyars, 1971), 252–94.

[42] Margaret Oliphant, *The Library Window: A Story of the Seen and the Unseen*, ed. Annmarie S. Drury (Peterborough, ON: Broadview Press, 2019).

[43] M. R. James, 'Some Remarks on Ghost Stories', *The Bookman* (December 1929): 169–172, in *Collected Ghost Stories*, ed. Darryl Jones (Oxford University Press, 2011), 414.

Whether Oliphant might have been sufficiently interested in the work of an Etonian, whose schooldays had overlapped with her younger son, to read M. R. James's first ghost story when it appeared in 1895 is not known.[44] The fact that James, three years younger than her valetudinarian son, had become a fellow of King's College, Cambridge, in 1887, and was director of the Fitzwilliam by 1893 was unlikely to have endeared him to Oliphant. She had once dreamt of such successes for her sons, but as 'The Library Window' suggests, by the late 1890s she harboured particular reasons for feeling academic scholarship overrated compared with the possibilities of combining observation of the real life going on around her with the resources to be found in a personal library.

---

[44] 'Lost Hearts', *Pall Mall Magazine* VII, no. 32 (1895), repr. in *Ghost Stories of an Antiquary* (1904).

7

M. R. James's Libraries

Darryl Jones

Widely recognized during his own lifetime as the pre-eminent anglophone codi-cologist, M. R. James spent much of his life in libraries. His scholarly output, over a period of some forty years, was prodigious, and at the heart of it is the series of descriptive catalogues he produced of the manuscript holdings of various libraries and collections.[1] There are thirty-six of these catalogues in all, including cata-logues of the collections of sixteen Cambridge colleges (there were twenty-one colleges at the time of James's death in 1936, so he did almost all of them), and those of other institutions with which he was associated—Eton College, and the Fitzwilliam Museum, plus the manuscript collections of the J. P. Morgan Library, the John Rylands Library, Lambeth Palace (there were five volumes of this), Westminster Abbey, Aberdeen University Library, and a number of other smaller collections. In 1926, he embarked on his most ambitious project, a catalogue of the entire medieval manuscript collection of Cambridge University Library—an endeavour so vast that it remained unfinished on his death, and was never published.[2] His biographer Richard William Pfaff puts it well when he suggests that, in his cataloguing endeavours, James was trying to reconstruct 'a *bibliothèque imaginaire* of the whole of medieval England', which he carried in his mind.[3]

In an obituary notice, the librarian and scholar Stephen Gaselee wrote of James: 'there has never been before, and probably there will never be again, a single man with the same accomplishment and combination of memory, palaeography, mediaeval learning, and artistic knowledge.... I consider him in *volume* of learn-ing the greatest scholar it has been my good fortune to know.'[4] Modern codicol-ogists have tended to view James as a brilliant but eccentric cataloguer: vastly knowledgeable and with a phenomenal work ethic, but also with a tendency to

---

[1] For comprehensive bibliographies of M. R. James's work, see S. G. Lubbock, *A Memoir of Montague Rhodes James* (Cambridge: Cambridge University Press, 1939), 49–87; Richard William Pfaff, *Montague Rhodes James* (London: Scolar Press, 1980), 427–38.

[2] See Pfaff, *Montague Rhodes James*, 325–30; Jayne Ringrose, 'The Legacy of M. R. James in Cambridge University Library', in *The Legacy of M. R. James: Papers from the 1995 Cambridge Symposium*, ed. Lynda Dennison (Donington: Shaun Tyas, 2001), 23–36.

[3] Pfaff, *Montague Rhodes James*, 58.

[4] Stephen Gaselee, 'Montague Rhodes James, 1862–1936', *Proceedings of the British Academy* 22 (1936): 433. Gaselee was Pepys Librarian and Fellow of Magdalene College, Cambridge, and Librarian and Keeper of Papers at the Foreign Office.

limit himself only to describing those elements of manuscripts in which he was personally interested.[5] In approaching the business of cataloguing, James himself acknowledged that he had very little to work with in terms of established practice: 'I have had to learn my job as I went on: my catalogues were on a scale that had not been tried before.'[6] As well as the catalogues, James produced an enormous body of scholarly literature—monographs, critical editions, articles—on a wide variety of libraries and their contents.

He also, of course, wrote ghost stories. Still credited today with being among the best in the genre, James's tales employ a lucid and frequently conversational narrative style (often a product of the occasions of their composition and telling, as Christmas entertainments for friends and Cambridge colleagues), and specialize in suggesting rather than depicting supernatural events. His ghosts are glimpsed figures, black shadows, strange smells, inchoate masses, or things 'ill-defined and impalpable' which manifest themselves in the anxiety, disturbance, and often illness of his protagonists.[7] His technique of placing his characters in realistic, everyday contexts (the contexts, that is, in which his own life was lived), and then, 'into this calm environment let[ting] the ominous thing put out its head, unobtrusively at first, then more insistently, until it holds the stage', can be seen as moving the ghost story on from its Gothic nineteenth-century predecessors and redefining it for the twentieth century.[8]

James's stories are a kind of imaginative surplus or by-product of his formal scholarship, to which they are intimately connected. His first catalogue appeared in 1895, the same year that his first ghost story appeared in print. This was 'Canon Alberic's Scrap-book', 'a tale of haunted biblioclasty', in the words of Patrick J. Murphy, 'that recoils at the plundering of medieval manuscripts—even as it plunders James's dearest scholarly interests as a rich vein of imaginative material'.[9] Unsurprisingly, then, libraries feature in many of the stories, and in virtually all of those in the first two volumes, *Ghost Stories of an Antiquary* (1904) and *More Ghost Stories of an Antiquary* (1911), which were both published while James was still at King's College, Cambridge. James was a great scholar and a great institutionalist (Director of the Fitzwilliam, Provost of King's, Vice-Chancellor of Cambridge, Provost of Eton, Order of Merit), and yet the stories seem to reveal disturbances below the smooth surface of an extraordinarily

---

[5] See Dennison, 'Introduction', in *The Legacy of M. R. James*, 1–10.

[6] M. R. James, *Eton and King's: Recollections, Mostly Trivial, 1875–1925* (1926; Ashcroft, BC: Ash-Tree Press, 2005), 131.

[7] M. R. James, 'Casting the Runes', in *Collected Ghost Stories*, ed. Darryl Jones (Oxford: Oxford University Press, 2011), 250.

[8] M. R. James, 'Introduction' to *Ghosts and Marvels*, ed. V. H. Collins (Oxford: Oxford University Press, 1924), in *Collected Ghost Stories*, 407.

[9] Patrick J. Murphy, *Medieval Studies and the Ghost Stories of M. R. James* (University Park, PA: Pennsylvania State University Press, 2017), 2. 'Canon Alberic's Scrap-Book', originally entitled 'A Curious Story', was first published in *The National Review* 25 (March 1895): 132–41.

successful intellectual and public career. The critic Peter Davidson has rightly commented on James's 'remarkably bleak' sensibility, which views the world as 'a supernatural minefield'.[10]

In this chapter, I shall be looking at the ways in which James's stories represent libraries, in particular, as sites of mystery, anxiety, and terror—as fundamentally *occult* spaces. 'The occult is *rejected knowledge*': James Webb's definition is one which is widely accepted and used by most modern scholars of the occult.[11] The dialectic, the creative tension, between institutional scholarship and unlicensed occult research, between manuscript cataloguer and ghost story writer, makes James such a powerful and effective writer of supernatural fiction. As Stephen Gaselee and many others testified, he simply knew more than anyone else, and the demonic and supernatural were a large part of what he knew.

In the next section, I will offer an overview of some of James's stories, looking at the ways in which codicological or bibliographical research is figured in his work as a dangerous activity, a playing with forces which typically unleash literal demons. The final section of the chapter will offer an extended reading of James's most librarianly story, 'The Tractate Middoth', whose meaning grows out of an intimate understanding of the cataloguing system, and even the very floor plan, of Cambridge University Library, the library for whose manuscript collection James dreamed of creating a total catalogue.

The Demon in the Library

Sir Shane Leslie, the Irish diplomat and Home Ruler, who knew James well (he was a student at King's, and the pair corresponded right up until James's death), thought of him as 'a kind of *magus* to whom all the secrets of a manuscript were revealed at a single glance, who never forgot anything, and who had an extra-natural insight into ghostly worlds'.[12] The word *magus* often accompanied descriptions of James: L. J. Lloyd closes a 1947 critical essay by adapting the last line of 'An Episode of Cathedral History', 'IBI CUBAVIT LAMIA', as 'IBI CUBAVIT MAGUS'.[13]

---

[10] Peter Davidson, *The Idea of North* (London: Reaktion, 2016), 163.

[11] James Webb, *The Occult Underground* (La Salle, IL: Open Court, 1974), 191. For modern scholarship, see, for example, Wouter J. Hanegraaff, *Esotericism and the Academy: Rejected Knowledge in Western Culture* (Cambridge: Cambridge University Press, 2012); Christopher Partridge, ed., *The Occult World* (London and New York: Routledge, 2016).

[12] Pfaff, *Montague Rhodes James*, 424. This is Pfaff's paraphrase of Leslie's attitude to James.

[13] L. J. Lloyd, 'The Ghost Stories of Montague Rhodes James', *Book Handbook* 4 (1947): 53. 'IBI CUBAVIT LAMIA' is from the Vulgate version of Isaiah 34:14, which the King James Version translates as 'The screech owl shall rest there', and the Revised Standard Version as 'There shall the night hag alight'. See James, *Collected Ghost Stories*, 267, 452. James uses the same passage from Isaiah in 'Canon Alberic's Scrap-Book': *Collected Ghost Stories*, 13.

James was acutely aware of the intimate historical connections between books, manuscripts, and writing, on the one hand, and magic, the arcane, and the occult on the other, and thus of the sense in which all libraries are, fundamentally, supernatural spaces. As the historian of magic Owen Davies writes, in its deep origins 'the very act of writing itself was imbued with occult or hidden power'.[14] The word *grimoire*, a magical book, is a derivation of 'grammar'. In 1921, James set about the task of imaginatively reconstructing and cataloguing the library of the Elizabethan magus John Dee. James was interested in Dee as simultaneously a magician and a bibliophile. For Dee, the former activity was dependent on the latter to such an extent that he proposed a cataloguing project of his own, the creation of a kind of British Library of Magic. 'Dee was not merely an alchemist and a spiritualist,' James thought, 'but a really learned man, and one who had done his best...to stimulate interest in the rescuing of MSS. from the dissolved monastic libraries and to induce the sovereign to establish a central national collection of them.' When Dee left England in 1583 for a journey to Bohemia and Poland, his neighbours in Mortlake broke into his house, stole his scientific instruments, and plundered his library. 'The cause of the raid was no doubt Dee's dealings with spirits, which not unnaturally earned him the reputation of being a sorcerer,' James comments.[15] Dee's library contained an extensive selection of magical and alchemical works by Roger Bacon, Albertus Magnus, Ramon Lull, and others.

The classical scholar Sir Roger Mynors, who was a pupil at Eton when James returned there in 1918, recalled 'the feeling when you met him he was slightly larger than life *and* could if necessary conjure a demon out of a brass bottle or tell you the names of the soldiers at the foot of the Cross'.[16] Devils and demons of various kinds played an important role in James's imaginary: the lamia and the magus naturally had much to do with one another. It is not always strictly accurate to refer to his tales as 'ghost stories': many of them are in fact tales of occult demonology. In his library researches, James encountered demons on an almost daily basis.

In James's first published story, 'Canon Alberic's Scrap-book' (1895), a demon is conjured—not from a bottle but, seemingly, from a book, which Dennistoun, a curator at the Fitzwilliam Museum (of which James was the Director from 1893 to 1908), discovers during a visit to Saint-Bertrand-de-Comminges in the Pyrenees (which James himself visited in the spring of 1892). At the same time as James was writing 'Canon Alberic', he was cataloguing the manuscript collection of the Fitzwilliam. His published catalogue (also from 1895) contains dozens of

---

[14] Owen Davies, *Grimoires: A History of Magic Books* (Oxford: Oxford University Press, 2009), 2.
[15] M. R. James, *List of the Manuscripts Formerly Owned by John Dee, with Preface and Identifications* (Oxford: Oxford University Press, 1921), 3, 4.
[16] Pfaff, *Montague Rhodes James*, 426.

descriptions of the various devils and demons he encountered in the Fitzwilliam collection. In the Death of Judas, for example, in MS 20 24a.27, 'A black devil flying down from R[ight] draws his (nude) soul out of his stomach'.[17] An illustration from the *Legenda Aurea* in MS 22 p. 24. 55 has 'Black clouds. Devils on earth. Men in eaves mourning: hell-hounds running about hills. Lurid sky'; while another at MS 22 p. 194. 153 has 'Egeus prostrate with staff; a devil strangles him behind'.[18] Often, these devils are described as being 'shaggy' or 'hairy'.[19] In a manner characteristic of James, Canon Alberic's demon is covered in 'coarse black hairs'.[20]

In James's story, the seventeenth-century Canon Alberic de Mauléon 'had doubtless plundered the Chapter library of St. Bertrand to form this priceless scrap-book'.[21] Canon Alberic's scrapbook itself is a compendium of codicological wonders, including 'a fragment of the copy of Papias "On the Words of Our Lord," which was known to have existed as late as the twelfth century at Nîmes'.[22] This particular manuscript long obsessed James. In 1888, several years before writing 'Canon Alberic', he went on an archaeological dig to Cyprus, where he visited the monastery of the Cypriot Saint Mnason, which he found 'in a frightful state'.[23] This was a particular disappointment, as his friend Lionel Ford wrote that he pictured him 'in a monastery, uprooting a Papias from a bundle of dull old manuscripts'.[24] This was something the pair had evidently discussed, as Papias took on an almost talismanic significance for James as the supreme prize for the manuscript-hunter. When he first got wind of the possibility of going to Cyprus, he had confided to his parents that 'if a copy of Papias turns up I shall be all the better pleased'.[25] In his 1919 monograph on codicology, *The Wanderings and Homes of Manuscripts*, James returned to this particular manuscript, writing: 'It is almost a relief that catalogues [of ancient English libraries] do not tell us of supremely desirable things such as Papias on the Oracles of the Lord or the complete Histories and Annals of Tacitus.'[26]

Also included in the scrapbook is an illustration of King Solomon commanding a demon. This is an illustration from the apocryphal *Testament of Solomon*, a work which James knew very well, and wrote about many times—beginning, rather amazingly, with 'Occult Sciences', a paper he delivered in Eton in February 1881, when he was 18 years old, and which was written under the

---

[17] M. R. James, *A Descriptive Catalogue of Manuscripts in the Fitzwilliam Museum* (Cambridge: Cambridge University Press, 1895), 38.

[18] James, *A Descriptive Catalogue of Manuscripts in the Fitzwilliam Museum*, 46, 50.

[19] See, for example, James, *A Descriptive Catalogue of Manuscripts in the Fitzwilliam Museum*, 113, 120, 153.

[20] James, 'Canon Alberic's Scrap-book', in *Collected Ghost Stories*, 11.

[21] James, 'Canon Alberic's Scrap-book', 8.   [22] James, 'Canon Alberic's Scrap-book', 7.

[23] M. R. James, letter to family, 17 January 1888, CUL MS. Add. 7480 D6/293.

[24] Lionel Ford, letter to M. R. James, 27 December 1887, CUL MS. Add. 7481 F74.

[25] M. R. James, letter to family, 13 November 1887, CUL MS. Add. 7480 D6/291.

[26] M. R. James, *The Wanderings and Homes of Manuscripts* (London: SPCK, 1919), 79.

influence of Collin de Plancy's encyclopedia of demonology, *Dictionnaire Infernal*. This 'appalling book' (in James's own phrase) was first published in 1818, and is full of memorably detailed illustrations of a great number of demons. James had first encountered it in July 1879, when he was 16 years old.[27] *The Testament of Solomon* is a classic of demonology, in which King Solomon commands a variety of demons, beginning with Ornias, and including Beelzebul [*sic*] himself, and makes them do his bidding, which includes building the Temple in Jerusalem. The definitive English translation of *The Testament of Solomon* was published by the Oxford theologian and orientalist F. C. Conybeare in the *Jewish Quarterly Review* in 1898, though James also provided a loose translation/paraphrase in *Old Testament Legends* (1913). In the 1920s, James corresponded with the great historian of magic Lynn Thorndike, helping him with some of the details for his chapter on Solomonic magic in Volume II of his eight-volume *History of Magic and Experimental Science*.[28] John Dee's library, as reconstructed by James, contained at least one book of Solomonic magic, the alchemical *De philosophia Salomanis*.[29]

Like Solomon, Alberic summons a demon, who offers him wealth and foresight: 'Answers of the 12th of December 1694. It was asked: Shall I find it? Thou shalt. Shall I become rich? Thou wilt. Shall I live an object of envy? Thou wilt. Shall I die in my bed? Thou wilt.'[30] The illustration from *The Testament of Solomon* offers a memorable account of the demon's appearance: 'Imagine one of the awful bird-catching spiders of South America translated into human form...and you will have some faint conception of the terror inspired by this appalling effigy. One remark is universally made by those to whom I have shown the picture: "It was drawn from the life."'[31] Helen Grant has plausibly identified this demon as Ornias, the major recurring demon from *The Testament of Solomon*.[32] The story comes to a climax when the demon manifests itself behind Dennistoun's head as he reads the scrapbook. The scrapbook goes to the Fitzwilliam Museum (here called the Wentworth Collection), all except the illustration, which is photographed and then burnt.

---

[27] Michael Cox, *M. R. James: An Informal Portrait* (Oxford: Oxford University Press, 1983), 43. The paper has been published as James, 'Occult Sciences', subscribers' supplement to *The Ghosts and Scholars M. R. James Newsletter* 5 (February 2004). For James on *The Testament of Solomon*, see also, for example, 'The Testament of Solomon', *The Guardian* (Church Newspaper), March 15 1899, 367; 'Solomon and the Demons', in *Old Testament Legends: Being Stories out of Some of the Less-Known Apocryphal Books of the Old Testament* (London: Longmans, Green & Co. 1913), 107–19; *The Lost Apocrypha of the Old Testament: Their Titles and Fragments* (London: SPCK, 1920), 51–3; 'The Testament of Solomon', *Journal of Theological Studies* 24 (1923): 467–8.

[28] Lynn Thorndike, *A History of Magic and Experimental Science*, Vol. 2 (New York: Columbia University Press, 1923), 281 n.5.

[29] James, *John Dee*, Fr. 166, p. 32.   [30] James, 'Canon Alberic's Scrap-book', 8.

[31] James, 'Canon Alberic's Scrap-book', 9.

[32] Helen Grant, 'The Nature of the Beast: The Demonology of "Canon Alberic's Scrapbook"', in *Warnings to the Curious: A Sheaf of Criticism on M.R. James*, ed. S.T. Joshi and Rosemary Pardoe (New York: Hippocampus Press, 2007), 227–37.

As a young man in the early 1880s, James read 'Barrett's *Magus* and other classics of wizardry, which made a deep impression on me'.[33] Drawing freely on the works of Cornelius Agrippa, Francis Barrett's occult opus *The Magus* (1801) was, in the words of Owen Davies, 'the first major English discourse on spirit conjuration since the seventeenth century', and a book which its author believed would help to bring about an English 'magical renaissance'.[34] The book is full of portraits of demons—Apollyon, Belial, Theutis, Asmodeus, 'The Incubus', Ophis, 'The Spirit Antichrist', Astaroth, Abaddon, Mammon—reproduced in hand-tinted colour plates and, as James might have said, 'drawn from the life'.[35]

Some of the principles of Barrett's treatise seem to underlie another of the earliest stories, 'Lost Hearts' (written in 1892–3, published in 1895, but set in 1811). This is the tale of another participant in Barrett's English 'magical renaissance', the Regency occultist Mr Abney, whose 'library contained all the then available books bearing on the Mysteries, the Orphic poems, the worship of Mithras, and the Neo-Platonists'.[36] Mr Abney has committed the serial murder of children in pursuit of his occult investigations because 'It is recorded of Simon Magus that he was able to fly in the air, to become invisible, or to assume any form he pleased, by the agency of the soul of a boy whom, to use the libellous phrase employed by the author of the *Clementine Recognitions*, he had "murdered".'[37] This is the passage to which Mr Abney alludes here, in Alexander Roberts and James Donaldson's contemporaneous (1886) translation of the *Clementine Recognitions*: 'Now when Niceta and I asked him how these things could be effected by magic art, and what was the nature of that thing, Simon began thus to explain it to us as his associates. "I have," said he, "made the soul of a boy, unsullied and violently slain, and invoked by unutterable adjurations, to assist me, and by it all is done that I command."'[38] At the close of 'Lost Hearts', Mr Abney is murdered in his library, his chest torn open by the vengeful ghosts of his victims.

'Casting the Runes' (1911), perhaps James's most celebrated story, enacts a clash between two forms of scholarship, as Karswell, the rogue independent scholar and occultist, and Dunning, the representative of institutional knowledge, disagree over the meaning and reality of the supernatural. Dunning is a peer reviewer for a learned journal, who at the beginning of the story rejects Karswell's submitted article; in a manner which might appeal to many academics, Karswell responds to rejection by setting a demon on his hostile reviewer. Theirs is an encounter which is played out in the British Library, where Karswell slips a

[33] James, *Eton and King's*, 129.   [34] Davies, *Grimoires*, 135.

[35] Francis Barrett, *The Magus, or Celestial Intelligencer; Being a Complete System of Occult Philosophy* (1801; York Beach, ME: Samuel Weiser, 2000). This is a full-size facsimile of the 1801 first edition, and reproduces the colour plates between pages 104 and 105.

[36] James, 'Lost Hearts', in *Collected Ghost Stories*, 15.   [37] James, 'Lost Hearts', 22.

[38] Alexander Roberts and James Donaldson, eds. *The Anti-Nicene Fathers: The Writings of the Fathers Down to A.D. 325*, vol. 8 (Peabody, MA: Hendrickson, 1995), 100.

demon-summoning runic parchment into Dunning's notes on MS Harley 3586, which he is studying in 'the Select Manuscript Room of the British Museum'.[39] Harley 3586 is a deliberate choice on James's part—the manuscript of the story in the British Library shows James initially writing 'Harley 30' and changing his mind.[40] ('Casting the Runes' is the only James manuscript in the British Library's possession; they acquired it deliberately because it uses the Manuscript Room as an important location.)[41] MS Harley 3586 contains two monastic registers from the fourteenth century, and two letters from the seventeenth century, one from the antiquarian Thomas Blount, and one from the Balliol scholar Thomas Goad.

Three years after the publication of 'Casting the Runes', James published an edition of the Welsh clergyman Walter Map's twelfth-century compendium *De Nugis Curialium*, which he went on to translate in 1923 as *Courtiers' Trifles*. In their 1983 parallel text of James's editions, C. N. L. Brooke and R. A. B. Mynors (that is, Roger Mynors, who believed James could conjure a demon from a bottle) point out that one of the works which James consulted in preparing his 1914 edition was the Wormsley Priory cartulary, which contains some documents relating to Walter Map (Wormsley is in Herefordshire, on the Welsh border).[42] This has led Patrick J. Murphy to suggest that Dunning is actually in the British Museum conducting research on Walter Map.[43] I might take this a step further, and suggest that Dunning and James are conducting *the same research*, the one which leads to the summoning of a demon.

In 'Mr. Humphreys and his Inheritance' (1911), the last story in *More Ghost Stories*, the titular protagonist inherits a country house which contains a library and a maze, each of which is an emblem of the other. At the centre of the maze is a globe, covered in occult illustrations and symbols: 'Around the place of the head the words *princeps tenebrarum* [the prince of darkness] could be deciphered.... Near the last, a man in long robes and high cap, standing in a circle and addressing two shaggy demons who hovered outside, was described as *Hostanes magus*.'[44] ('Shaggy', we remember, was James's favourite adjective for the demons of illustrated manuscripts; his stories habitually exhibit a terror of hairy monsters.)[45] Hostanes was the legendary mage of the Persian emperor Xerxes I, and was credited by Pliny the Elder with being the inventor of *written* magic, by which

---

[39] James, 'Casting the Runes', in *Collected Ghost Stories*, 153.

[40] James, Manuscript version of 'Casting the Runes', British Library MS Egerton 3141.

[41] Andrew Dunning, 'The medieval cartulary behind a ghost story', *British Library Medieval Manuscripts Blog*, 27 August 2017: 'The British Museum's curators were so delighted by James' story that, in November 1936, they purchased the autograph manuscript of the tale in his memory'; https:// blogs.bl.uk/digitisedmanuscripts/2017/08/the-medieval-cartulary-behind-a-ghost-story.html, accessed 5 May 2019.

[42] Walter Map, *De Nugis Curialium/Courtiers' Trifles*, ed. and trans. M. R. James; rev. C. N. L. Brooke and R. A. B. Mynors (Oxford: Clarendon Press, 1983), ii.

[43] Murphy, *Medieval Studies and the Ghost Stories of M. R. James*, 73.

[44] James, 'Mr. Humphreys and his Inheritance', in *Collected Ghost Stories*, 213.

[45] See Jones, 'Introduction' to *Collected Ghost Stories*, xxvii–xxix, for James's hairy monsters.

means he introduced sorcery to the Greek world and 'scattered, as it were, the seeds of the hideous craft along the way, infecting the world with it'.[46] Hostanes was, according to the *Octavius* of the Latin Christian apologist Marcus Minucius Felix, 'The foremost of those Magi both in eloquence and art.... The same Hostanes also has told us of earthly demons, wandering spirits, and enemies of mankind.'[47] These demons, according to Minucius Felix, were the source of the Magi's power: 'whatever miraculous feats they perform, they do so through demons'.[48] Like Simon Magus, Hostanes had a reputation for black magic, propounding, in Lynn Thorndike's words, 'such remedies as drinking human blood or utilizing in magic compounds and ceremonies parts of the corpses of men who have been violently slain'.[49]

Immediately on arriving at his new home, Mr Humphreys makes a resolution:

> He had all the predisposition to take interest in an old library, and there was every opportunity for him here to make systematic acquaintance with one, for he had learned from Cooper that there was no catalogue save the very superficial one made for purposes of probate. The drawing up of a *catalogue raisonné* would be a delicious occupation for winter. There were probably treasures to be found, too: even manuscripts, if Cooper might be trusted.[50]

In parallel to cataloguing the library, Mr Humphreys also maps the maze. As he sits in the library, poring over this map, he notices a hole at the centre of it:

> But surely this was a very odd hole. It seemed to go not only through the paper, but through the table on which it lay. Yes, and through the floor below that, down, and still down, even into infinite depths.... Oh yes, far, far down there was a movement, and the movement was upwards – towards the surface. Nearer and nearer it came, and it was of blackish-grey colour with more than one dark hole. It took shape as a face – a human face – a *burnt* human face: and with the odious writhings of a wasp creeping out of a rotten apple there clambered forth an appearance of a form, waving black arms prepared to clasp the head that was bending over them.[51]

---

[46] Thorndike, *A History of Magic and Experimental Science*, Vol. 1, 22, 58–9; Davies, *Grimoires*, 7.

[47] James, *Collected Ghost Stories*, 447. Hostanes was something of a favourite figure for James: see Martin Hughes, 'A Maze of Secrets in a Story by M. R. James', in *Warnings to the Curious*, ed. Joshi and Pardoe, 258–78; Rosemary Pardoe, 'Hostanes Magus', in *The Black Pilgrimage & Other Explorations: Essays on Supernatural Fiction* (King's Norton: Shadow Publishing, 2018), 43–9.

[48] Thorndike, *A History of Magic and Experimental Science*, Vol. 1, 465.

[49] Thorndike, *A History of Magic and Experimental Science*, Vol. 1, 61.

[50] James, 'Mr. Humphreys and his Inheritance', 208.

[51] James, 'Mr. Humphreys and his Inheritance', 218–19.

As they would be a generation later for the other great librarian-fabulist, Jorge Luis Borges, for James the library and the labyrinth were emblems not only for one another, but for the universe. Furthermore, the catalogue, attempting to impose order and meaning on multiplicity, was for James a *grimoire*, a book of demons.

'The Tractate Middoth'

'Ah, libraries are fine places,' Mrs Simpson says in 'The Tractate Middoth', 'but for all that, books have played me a sad turn, or rather *a* book has.'[52] The story draws heavily for its effect and meaning both on the physical layout of Cambridge University Library and on its cataloguing system. 'I've got the idea there's something wrong in the atmosphere of the library' (133), one of the librarians says; fully to understand why requires rather specialist historical knowledge.

'The Tractate Middoth' was written in 1911, the same year as both 'Casting the Runes' and 'Mr. Humphreys', as part of the burst of creativity leading up to the publication of *More Ghost Stories of an Antiquary*. As the story opens, we enter Cambridge University Library: 'Towards the end of an autumn afternoon an elderly man with a thin face and grey Piccadilly weepers pushed open the swing door to the vestibule of a certain famous library' (129). The story recounts the battle of wits between John Eldred and his cousin Mary Simpson, both of whom are attempting to track down the will of their elderly and malicious relative, Dr Rant, which is hidden inside a book somewhere in the library.

One of the first issues the story raises is of library access: who should be allowed into libraries? 'The library', Penny Fielding writes, 'is both a space and a system.'[53] As both space and system, the library was contested in the early twentieth century: was it a private collection, belonging to closed institutions, or a public space like a museum or an exhibition? As a graduate of Cambridge University, Mr Eldred has access to the library, and borrowing rights, whereas Mrs Simpson does not: while she might theoretically have been a member of one of the two women's colleges established by 1911, Girton and Newnham, she could not have been a graduate of Cambridge until as late as 1948. (James, it should be noted, opposed women's university education in all its forms, along with every other progressive idea or movement he encountered.)[54] Mrs Simpson therefore enlists the help of Mr Garrett, an assistant librarian, in her quest. Garrett occupies a role and position which is liminal to and interstitial within the various hierarchies of the library. He has access and movement, though not status and position: he fetches books for a

---

[52] James, 'The Tractate Middoth', in *Collected Ghost Stories*, 134. All further references to this story in this chapter will be incorporated into the main body of the text.

[53] Penny Fielding, 'Reading Rooms: M. R. James and the Library of Modernity', *Modern Fiction Studies* 46.3 (2000): 756.

[54] See Jones, 'Introduction' to *Collected Ghost Stories*, xv–xvi.

living, and 'lodge[s] in rooms not far from the station' (131). But, unlike the Library's various doormen and desk attendants, he is not one of James's comic working-class stereotypes ('Roberts, do you recollect the name of Heldred?' 139). He is not exactly a scholar, but nor is he a woman or a servant.

'The Tractate Middoth' sets a cryptographic challenge. It focusses on deciphering the meaning of a very specific code, the number (or numbers) '11334'. These numbers are the only clue Dr Rant gives his niece Mary as to the whereabouts of the codicil to his will which bequeaths his property to her rather than to Eldred. James had a deep interest in occulted meanings, in steganography, codes, ciphers, and secret languages, and was very familiar with 'the old books on secret writing. The "*Steganographia*" of Joachim Trithemius... Selenius's "*Cryptographia*" and Bacon's "*de Augmentis Scientiarum*," and some more.'[55] The German Benedictine abbot and bibliophile Trithemius's *Steganographia* (*Secret Writing*, c.1499) was long believed to be a *grimoire* which 'posited the existence of an occult code which would enable communication with spirits and angels', and its author was suspected of having 'commerce with demons'.[56] In his story 'The Treasure of Abbot Thomas' (1904), James presents a fictionalized version of Trithemius in the person of the cryptographic Abbot Thomas van Eschenhausen, who summons a demon to guard his treasure.

Garrett deciphers the code as a library class mark, '11.3.34'. What, or where, is '11.3.34'?[57] The current Cambridge University Library building opened in 1934; in 1911, when the story was written and set, the Library was housed in the Cockerell Building, opened in 1842, and now the home of Gonville and Caius Library. The '11' of '11.3.34' indicates its subject heading, which is Religion. Classes 1–34 in the Cockerell Building library were dedicated to religious books: 11, the story tells us, is specifically the 'Hebrew class' (129).

'The Tractate Middoth' draws on the redesigning of the physical space of the Cockerell Building in 1864 by the Cambridge librarian Henry Bradshaw.[58] A generation older than James, Henry Bradshaw was, like him, a product of Temple Grove School, Eton, and King's College, Cambridge. He was appointed Assistant Librarian at Cambridge in 1856, Superintendent of Manuscripts in 1859, during which time he completely reformed the university's manuscript department, and then University Librarian from 1867 to his death in 1886. Bradshaw's practice as a cataloguer, particularly of incunabula, was revolutionary, focussing on all aspects of the catalogued book, from illustration to bindings

---

[55] James, 'The Treasure of Abbot Thomas', in *Collected Ghost Stories*, 103.

[56] Davies, *Grimoires*, 47; Thorndike, *A History of Magic and Experimental Science*, Vol. 4, 525.

[57] I am very grateful to Liam Sims of the Rare Books Department of Cambridge University Library for helping me decipher the mystery of 11.3.34.

[58] See Henry Bradshaw, 'List of Library Classes showing in which Room each Class stands' (1864) for a reproduction of Bradshaw's original design; https://exhibitions.lib.cam.ac.uk/royal/artifacts/finding-your-books/.

to provenance.[59] James encountered Bradshaw as an undergraduate—Pfaff suggests that Bradshaw had 'the most lasting impact on MRJ's working method and approaches' of anyone he encountered as a student.[60] One of James's 1895 catalogues, of the manuscript collection of King's, paid tribute to Bradshaw for the 'brilliance and thoroughness of his work'.[61] In his autobiography, *Eton and King's* (1926), James paints a worshipful picture of Bradshaw: 'You felt there was nothing little about him, and the reverence and love he inspired needed no explanation.'[62] Shane Leslie speculated that James may have built his scholarly ambitions around Bradshaw: 'Both aimed at being librarians and no more.'[63]

The catalogue entry for 11.3.34 reads: 'Talmud: Tractate Middoth, with the commentary of Nachmanides, Amsterdam, 1707' (129). Characteristically for James, this is a combination of genuine and invented scholarship. The Middot ('measurement') is the tenth Mishnahic tractate of the order of Kodashim ('Holy Things'), the Fifth Order of the Mishna (laws), dealing with the religious ceremony of the Temple of Jerusalem. The Middot itself describes the measurements of the Second Temple of Jerusalem. Nachmanides (Moses Ben Nahman, 1194–1270) was indeed a celebrated commentator on the Talmud, although this actual work is fictional.[64] Furthermore, there is indeed a book in Cambridge University Library with the class mark 11.3.34, and it was indeed published in Amsterdam, though a century or so later than the Tractate Middoth, and it is a treatise on the persecution of Christians by the emperor Decius rather than a Talmudic commentary: Taco Hajo van den Honert, *Disputatio de Christianorum Vexatione Deciana* (Amsterdam, 1838).[65]

What is located at 11.3.34, then, is the book at the centre of the story's labyrinth—which is the library itself. In 'Mr. Humphreys and his Inheritance', Mr Humphreys either locates the centre of the maze with ease, or not at all, becoming hopelessly lost. Similarly, in 'The Tractate Middoth', Mr Garrett can sometimes locate the book immediately at class mark 11.3.34, while at other times it is impossible to find. Tiles outside Mr Humphreys's maze contain an inscription, 'PENETRANS AD INTERIORA MORTIS' ('Penetrating to the Inner Places of Death').[66] Class 11 is 'the "class" or cubicle (opening upon the central alley of a

[59] See Brett W. Walwyn, 'M. R. James and Changing Methods of Incunable Description', in *The Legacy of M. R. James*, ed. Lynda Dennison, 213.

[60] Pfaff, *Montague Rhodes James*, 48.

[61] M. R. James, *A Descriptive Catalogue of the Manuscripts other than Oriental in the Library of King's College, Cambridge* (Cambridge: Cambridge University Press, 1895), xiv.

[62] James, *Eton and King's*, 74.

[63] Leslie, 'Montague Rhodes James', in Joshi and Pardoe, eds., *Warnings to the Curious*, 32.

[64] See James, *Collected Ghost Stories*, 440 n. 129.

[65] The Cambridge University Library catalogue record for this book, including the class mark 11.3.34, can be found at https://idiscover.lib.cam.ac.uk/primo-explore/fulldisplay?docid=44CAM_ALMA21480032410003606&context=L&vid=44CAM_PROD&search_scope=SCOP_CAM_ALL&tab=cam_lib_coll&lang=en_US.

[66] James, 'Mr. Humphreys and his Inheritance', 220.

spacious gallery) in which the Hebrew books were placed' (132), a section of the library in which 'the light isn't very good' (130), and which has 'a musty smell... an unnaturally strong smell of dust' (133). Eldred, whose name is an uneasy concatenation of 'eldritch' and 'dread', refuses to enter the library any further than the vestibule, certainly will not go and get the book himself, and cannot bear to hear Garrett give a detailed account of what he finds at 11.3.34.

What does he find there? At the centre of Cambridge University Library, Mr Garrett encounters a terrifying supernatural creature who is simultaneously a dry and dusty scholar—at first glance, a clergyman reading at the table—and another version of Canon Alberic's spider-demon:

> He turned around and let me see his face – which I hadn't seen before. I tell you again, I'm not mistaken. Though for one reason or another I didn't take in the lower part of his face, I did see the upper part; and it was perfectly dry, and the eyes were very deep-sunk; and over them, from the eye-brows to the cheek-bone, there were cobwebs – thick. (133)

As often with James, explanations are left uncertain, inconclusive—but this seems to be the ghost (or the decomposing corpse) of Dr Rant himself, who was interred after his death, 'sitting at a table, in his ordinary clothes, in a brick room that he'd made underground in a field near his house. Of course the country people say he's been seen about there in his old black cloak' (135). It is implied that Dr Rant's will is a form of satanic contract: 'I don't think you'll find the witnesses in a hurry', he tells Mary (136).

At the climax of the story, in the process of tearing the sheet containing the will from the flyleaf of the *Tractate Middoth*, Eldred is attacked and killed by a demon, which manifests out of the book itself: 'two arms enclosing a mass of blackness came before Eldred's face and covered his head and neck' (142). On closer inspection, Garrett finds 'a thick black mass of cobwebs; and, as he stirred it gingerly with his stick, several large spiders ran out of it into the grass' (144). (Canon Alberic's demon, we recall, resembled 'one of the awful bird-catching spiders of South America translated into human form'.)[67] The medical examination of Mr Eldred's corpse finds 'black dust' smeared over his face and in his mouth (142). Biblioclasty, the damaging of books, the wrong kind of acquisitive scholarship undertaken by the wrong people for the wrong reasons, has deadly consequences in James's fiction. But the moral economy of 'The Tractate Middoth' is far from clear-cut, and may not in fact exist at all. Eldred is a man of 'mean sharp ways' (135) who connives to disinherit his cousin, but his death is not a straightforward case of supernatural moral retribution. The story's malign

---

[67] James, 'Canon Alberic', 9.

supernatural force attacks whoever gets close to 11.3.34, and an encounter with it leaves Garrett bedridden for several days.

As with Papias, or the *Clementine Recognitions*, or MS Harley 3586, Cambridge University Library 11.3.34 sees James transforming the raw material of his scholarly research into something altogether horrifying, as though he were simultaneously Dunning, the respectable institutional scholar, and Karswell, the rogue occultist and purveyor of rejected knowledge. Libraries, their catalogues, and their contents, were codes to be deciphered, or labyrinths to be penetrated and mapped—but certainly not by everybody. In the wrong hands—and often even in the right ones—scholarship could be a dangerous endeavour. The title of his final collection of stories, published in 1925, is surely meant to be summative: *A Warning to the Curious.*[68] For M. R. James, scholarship was to be approached with extreme caution, as libraries could be terrifying places, labyrinths full of demons and monsters.

---

[68] M. R. James, *A Warning to the Curious and Other Ghost Stories* (London: Edward Arnold, 1925).

8

The Body in the Library

Christie and Sayers

Nicola Humble

The stylized, affectless crimes and rationalist explanations of 'Golden Age' crime fiction might seem the antithesis of the supernatural logic of M. R. James's demonic psychodramas, but a number of Golden Age texts could join many of James's stories in the recently defined subgenre of 'bibliomystery': texts in which books and their institutions (libraries, bookshops, publishers) play a major role in the establishing of a mystery or its solution.[1] The world of the ancient universities which is so central a part of James's imaginative and scholarly universe is also a focus for a surprising number of crime novels published on both sides of the Atlantic in the years between the world wars, with the enclosed world of the college forming a variation on the gathering in a country house.[2] In manor house and university alike, the library is a frequent locus, variously denoting social status and intellectuality, while also figuring the ratiocinative processes of detective and reader. What follows will consider the representation of libraries in interwar clue-puzzle crime fiction, focussing on two classic works in which the physical space and the idea of the library—and the bodies within it—function in very different ways.

The phrase 'the body in the library' is repeated nine times in the first chapter of Agatha Christie's novel of the same name. It rings with incredulity as it is reiterated by servants, mistress, master, neighbours, friends, suspects, and police. When Miss

---

[1] See Otto Penzler, *Bibliomysteries: An Annotated Bibliography of the First Editions of Mystery Fiction Set in the World of Books, 1849–2000* (New York: Mysterious Press, 2014). 'Golden Age' is a convenient classification for texts in what Stephen Knight calls the 'clue-puzzle' tradition published between the wars; Julian Symons, *Bloody Murder* (London: Penguin, 1972; 1992), chs 7 and 8. It was traditionally understood to refer to British authors, but recent criticism has stressed the extent to which a parallel tradition of puzzle-based crime fiction existed in America before the development of the 'hard-boiled' form which defined itself in opposition to it. See Stephen Knight, *Crime Fiction 1800–2000* (London: Palgrave Macmillan, 2004), xiv, 93–8, and Martin Priestman, *Detective Fiction and Literature* (London: Macmillan, 1990), 151–60.

[2] Examples include Victor Whitechurch, *Murder at the College* (1932), T. H. White, *Darkness at Pemberley* (1932), Dermot Morrah, *Mummy Case Mystery* (1933), J. C. Masterman, *An Oxford Tragedy* (1933), R. E. Swartwout, *The Boat Race Murder* (1933), Q. Patrick, *Murder at Cambridge* (1932), Adam Broome, *The Oxford Murders* (1929) and *The Cambridge Murders* (1936), Michael Innes, *Death at the President's Lodging* (1936), F. J. Whaley, *Trouble in College* (1936), Douglas G. Browne, *The May Week Murders* (1937), and Glyn Daniel, *The Cambridge Murders* (1945).

Marple (already in this 1942 novel no stranger to dead bodies) is informed of the corpse and its location by the lady of the house, she 'thought her friend had gone mad'.[3] The strong implication is that bodies and libraries do not go together. The reader's first view of the body in question reveals a scene that belongs on the cover of a pulp novel (precisely not the sort of text to be found in most polite libraries):

> The library was a room very typical of its owners. It was large and shabby and untidy. It had big sagging arm-chairs, and pipes and books and estate papers laid out on the big table. There were one or two good old family portraits on the walls, and some bad Victorian water-colours, and some would-be-funny hunting scenes. There was a big vase of Michaelmas daisies in the corner. The whole room was dim and mellow and casual. It spoke of long occupation and familiar use and of links with tradition.
>
>   And across the old bearskin hearthrug there was sprawled something new and crude and melodramatic.
>
>   The flamboyant figure of a girl. A girl with unnaturally fair hair dressed up off her face in elaborate curls and rings. Her thin body was dressed in a backless evening-dress of white spangled satin. The face was heavily made-up, the powder standing out grotesquely on its blue swollen surface, the mascara of the lashes lying thickly on the distorted cheeks, the scarlet of the lips looking like a gash. The finger-nails were enamelled in a deep blood-red and so were the toenails in their cheap silver sandal shoes. It was a cheap, tawdry, flamboyant figure – most incongruous in the solid old-fashioned comfort of Colonel Bantry's library.   (10–11)

The assumptions underlying the constantly repeated incredulity about the juxta-position of the body and the library are tricky to pinpoint. Why should the location of the corpse—rather than the presence of a corpse at all—be so very surprising? Perhaps it is a matter of the sort of body: female, platinum blonde, overly made-up... a body with apparently little to do with libraries when living? Yet several characters assert the opposite—that the body in the library is 'impos-sible' in 'real life' precisely because it is such a cliché of crime fiction: 'You've been dreaming, Dolly, that's what it is,' says Colonel Bantry when his wife wakes him up with the news of the maid's discovery of the body. 'It's that detective story you were reading – The Clue of the Broken Match. You know – Lord Edgbaston finds a beautiful blonde dead on the library hearthrug. Bodies are always being found in libraries in books. I've never known a case in real life.' (3).

This metafictive insistence on the scenario as a fundamental element of crime fiction is to an extent borne out by a trawl through the archives of the crime novel. Corpses are found in libraries in a number of earlier texts: the trope is a notable

---

[3] Agatha Christie, *The Body in the Library* (London: HarperCollins, 1942; 2016), 7.

feature in the late nineteenth-century works of New Yorker Anna Katharine Green, an important figure in the development of the crime novel in the direction of the domestic plots of the Golden Age, and specified in Christie's autobiography as an early influence on her own work.[4] Curious libraries are the scenes of mysterious crimes in Green's *The Leavenworth Case* (1878) and *The Filigree Ball* (1903) (the sketch map of the library's location in the former is the first such element in a detective novel).[5] In the interwar years, the scenario is particularly popular in the subgenre of locked-room mysteries, with examples including Henry Leverage's *Whispering Wires* (1918), Edward Gellibrand's *The End of a Cigarette* (1924), Walter S. Masterman's *The Wrong Letter* (1926), G. D. H and Margaret Cole's *The Blatchington Tangle* (1926), Arthur Applin's *The Actress* (1927), Herman Landon's *Mystery Mansion* (1928), Wyndham Martyn's *The Death Fear* (1929), Henry C. Beck's *Death by Clue* (1933), and Scobie Mackenzie's *Three Dead, One Hurt* (1934). American Charles Dutton, author of *Murder in a Library* (1931) particularly specialized in this situation, which he also used in *The Underwood Mystery* (1921), *The Shadow on the Glass* (1923), and *The Crooked Cross* (1926).[6] The repeated use of the trope in what are mostly minor examples of the form certainly justifies Christie's treatment of it as already hackneyed by 1942. Given this, we might ask what the purpose is of its reuse: is there anything more to be done with the body in the library? I would suggest that it is precisely for its worn-out nature that Christie deploys it.[7] As a trope it figures an ironic, self-referential approach which comes to particularly characterize the Golden Age crime novel, part of the distancing, artificial effect with which it renders violence safely anodyne. Further, Christie uses the library as a synecdoche for the country house itself, and for the social values of the fiction which she builds on it. The interior geography of the country house imagined by interwar crime fiction is highly conventionalized: a Cluedo-esque matter of expansive entrance halls and drawing rooms, billiard rooms, boot rooms and—particularly—libraries. The country house is the only sort of domestic dwelling large enough to reason-ably contain a library, and much status is carried in the possession of a 'library' rather than a 'study', though the terms are often applied interchangeably to the same room. Colonel Bantry's 'library' is just such an anomalous space, referred to

---

[4] Agatha Christie, *An Autobiography* (London: William Collins, 1977), 216. 'Many of the later "whodunit" techniques are first found in a coherent sequence in Green' (Knight, *Crime Fiction 1800–2000*, 53).

[5] On the paradigm of the library in Green's fiction, see Michael Cook, *Narratives of Enclosure in Detective Fiction: The Locked Room Mystery* (Palgrave Macmillan, 2011), 43–61.

[6] For further details of these and other obscure locked-room mysteries, see Robert Adey, *Locked Room Murders and Other Impossible Crimes: A Comprehensive Bibliography* (Minneapolis: Crossover Press, 1991).

[7] In the wake of Christie's deployment, the trope is often used in clue-puzzle texts for parodic effect: see, for example, Michael Innes, *Appleby and Honeybath* (1983), William Brittain, 'The Man Who read John Dickson Carr' (1965), and Julian Symons's 'Take that Body Out of the Library!', *Suspense*, July 1960.

variously by both terms and often used as a sitting room. Its status as 'library' has less to do with its function as a repository of books, and more to do with matters of class and gender. The room is a library more than it is a study mainly because the former is a grander designation and the Bantrys are members of the landed country gentry; the room, with its comfortable shabby armchairs, its 'good old family portraits', and its large table strewn with the devices of leisure and work (pipes and estate papers) as well as books, speaks, we are told, of 'long occupation and familiar use and of links with tradition': it establishes their rank and the continuity of their social place and their occupation of the house and control of its estates. The books that we might see as the central focus of a library are notably de-emphasized: within the logic of the particular sort of conservatism espoused by Christie, the library of inherited books affords her gentry characters cultural capital while freeing them from the suspicious intellectuality of actually reading.[8] It is also a specifically masculine room—not the Bantrys' library, but the Colonel's. The discovery of a young woman's body in that room implies a sexual connection between her and the room's owner—an association much enjoyed by the local gossips. The trope of the body in the library speaks of some of the historically specific concerns of 'Golden Age' crime fiction, in which more domestic models of the masculine function as palliation for the trauma of the First World War; in this context the eruption of violence into the room specifically designated as peaceful masculine sanctum perhaps figures mid-war anxieties about both peace and masculinity.

We might read this and other descriptions of libraries in crime fiction in terms of what Gaston Bachelard calls the poetics of space: it is notable that the room is depicted almost entirely in terms of horizontal surfaces—the big table with its clutter, the hearthrug with its blonde—but not the vertical forms of shelves which are surely what crucially make a library a library.[9] The libraries of crime fiction are very often actively read by the detectives who are the reader's proxy. Many, like Colonel Bantry's, are significant for their physical form or their furnishings: in Margery Allingham's *Police at the Funeral* (1931), the domestic library of the deceased Master of Ignatius College is significant mainly for a 'high-backed yellow brocade chair' in which it is insisted no one else may ever sit, its looming Gothic presence signifying the patriarchal authority which the wastrel members of his extended family will fail to achieve.[10] Others understand the library primarily in terms of the geography of its bookcases and the logic of its book collections. In A. A. Milne's 1922 *Red House Mystery*, a locked-room puzzle with a Wodehousian

---

[8] For more on the studied anti-intellectuality of Christie's fiction see Alison Light, *Forever England: Femininity, Literature and Conservatism Between the Wars* (London: Routledge, 1991), 75–8; and Nicola Humble, *The Feminine Middlebrow Novel 1920s to 1950s* (Oxford: Oxford University Press, 2001; 2004), 21–2.

[9] Gaston Bachelard, *The Poetics of Space* (Boston: Beacon Press, 1994).

[10] Margery Allingham, *The Police at the Funeral* (London: Vintage Books, 1931; 2007), 141–2.

tone (notably singled out for disdainful attack in Raymond Chandler's iconic essay 'The Simple Art of Murder'), the self-appointed amateur detectives investigate the library of their host, who has seemingly disappeared after killing his long-lost brother:[11]

> There was indeed a 'frightful lot' of books. The four walls of the library were plastered with them from floor to ceiling, save only where the door and the two windows insisted on living their own life, even though an illiterate one. To Bill it seemed the most hopeless room of any in which to look for a secret opening.[12]

But find the secret passage they do, as Antony, who 'could never resist another person's bookshelves', 'reads' the arrangements of the books to locate the very dullest (collections of sermons the owner inherited from his clergyman father) in order to find those hiding the entrance. In Victor Whitechurch's *Murder at the College* (1932), two 'libraries'—in this case the term signifies collections of books rather than rooms—are 'read' by the detective: announcing that '[o]ne often judges a man by his library', his discovery that the victim had 'a whole row of detective novels' alongside the more conventional 'standard works, poetry, belles lettres, architecture' leads to the solution of the crime in the former's own amateur detections.[13] The novel begins with a reading of the bookshelves of the academic who will eventually be revealed as the murderer: the striking feature of the description is that the only books depicted are those written by himself.

For Dorothy L. Sayers's Oxford-University-set *Gaudy Night* (1936), libraries are also highly readable spaces, much inflected with the politics of gender and class. At the start of the novel detective writer Harriet Vane, the love interest of Sayers's serial detective Lord Peter Wimsey, receives a poison pen letter while back at her Oxford college for a gaudy—a reunion. For the rest of the 500-page novel, she investigates the increasingly violent actions of its author in the all-female college, while simultaneously mulling over Lord Peter's repeated proposals of marriage and her own ideas about the appropriate life course for an intellectual woman. She observes closely the lives of the dons of Shrewsbury College, considering their mental state as she tries to rule them in or out as suspects. The crudely sexual nature of the letters and pictures scrawled on walls leads her—a product of a culture widely aware of Freud—to blame a repression at the heart of the broadly celibate collegiate life, a misreading produced by her own anxieties and which is explained away when Lord Peter finally arrives on the scene towards the end of the novel (and reveals the culprit to be one of the college servants rather than a don).

---

[11] Raymond Chandler, 'The Simple Art of Murder', 1944, in Howard Haycraft, ed., *The Art of the Mystery Story* (New York: Carroll & Graf, 1983), 226–9.

[12] A. A. Milne, *The Red House Mystery*, 1922 (OTB e-book publishing, 2015), loc.1077.

[13] Victor Whitechurch, *Murder at the College*, 1932 (Kindle ed., 2013), loc. 572; 528.

Running counter to her suspicions is an intensely lyrical account of Oxford as both physical space and avocation, which is centred particularly on the joys of scholarship (and which culminates in a wheeling bird's-eye vista of the city from the roof of the Radcliffe Camera library). Academic life is understood to consist mostly of research. Students are unformed, negligible figures, given to sunbathing in the quad and fighting about boyfriends rather than taking advantage of their academic opportunities, or they are obsessives, making themselves ill with over-work. There is little focus on the activity of teaching—the dons who care about their students are cast as neurotic, over-involved schoolteacher types. More psychologically healthy, as far as Harriet and the novel are concerned, is the sweepstake the SCR run about Finals results, in the course of which they discuss the chances of their 'horses' in bracingly uncaring tones. The true purpose of the academic life for the novel is not teaching but scholarship, and many libraries feature centrally in this endeavour. A marker of the college's increasing success in establishing itself in the until-recently male enclave of Oxford is that it has now outgrown its original library and has just finished building a new one. The decoration and shelving of this library in preparation for its opening by the Vice Chancellor (and the poison pen's inevitable despoliation of it the night before the opening) occupy several chapters of the novel. It is notable that the original buildings of the college, when it consisted of 'the one funny old house with ten students [who] were chaperoned to lectures in a donkey carriage', are what has been knocked down to accommodate the New Library (always capitalized): full intellectual membership of the University coming at the price of letting go of the college's ramshackle, hard-fought beginnings.[14] The role of the library in estab-lishing this status brings to mind Virginia Woolf's comparison, in *A Room of One's Own*, of the intellectual atmosphere of a male and a female Oxbridge college (mainly represented by the quality of the meals served in each), the book begin-ning with her account of being turned away from the library of the male college, her gender of apparently more weight than her status as honoured guest.

After hearing many details about it being set up, we finally see Shrewsbury's new library only after it has been attacked:

> The New Library was a handsome, lofty room, with six bays on the South side, lit by as many windows running nearly from the floor to the ceiling. On the North side, the wall was windowless, and shelved to a height of ten feet. Above this was a space of blank wall, along which it would be possible, at some future time, to run an extra gallery when the books should become too many for the existent shelving. This blank space had been adorned by Miss Burrows and her party with a series of engravings, such as every academic community possesses, representing

¹⁴ Dorothy L. Sayers, *Gaudy Night* (London: Hodder & Stoughton, 1935; 1987), 45.

the Parthenon, the Colosseum, Trajan's Column and other topographical and classical subjects.

All the books in the room had been dragged out and flung on the floor, by the simple expedient of removing the shelves bodily. The pictures had been thrown down. And the blank wall space thus exposed had been adorned with a frieze of drawings, roughly executed in brown paint, and with inscriptions in letters a foot high, all of the most unseemly sort. A pair of library steps and a pot of paint with a wide brush in it stood triumphantly in the middle of the wreckage, to show how the transformation had been accomplished.

'That's torn it', said Harriet.   (109–10)

The library is first characterized as imposing, vertical architectural space—lofty, high-windowed, with bays; the empty space above the shelves, with its potential to be expanded into a gallery, currently decorated by random classical images, is more important than the books, whose identity and means of organization is unspecified. The books are chiefly depicted in terms of mess and fuss: flung *en masse* to the floor with their shelves; the source of librarian Miss Burrows's dusty exhaustion. On being awakened with the news, her response is less horror at the attack than at the task of re-shelving: 'How loathsome! And do you mean to say all those books have got to be done *again*?' (113). Considered in terms of Bachelard's phenomenological topoanalysis, where the axis of verticality 'oppose[s] the rationality of the roof to the irrationality of the cellar' (18), the library's bookcases, in their ordered upward aspiration, represent reason, but the books themselves, thrown to the ground, paradoxically figure, if not the dark subterranean imaginings of the cellar, the everyday besmirchment of the quotidian and the bodily. Saved from the attack, because they have yet to be put in place, are the library's greatest treasures, contents of the display cases which greet the Vice Chancellor when a hurried day's work has all restored: 'the Chaucer Folio, the Shakespeare First Quarto, the three Kelmscott Morrises, the autographed copy of *The Man of Property*, and the embroidered glove belonging to the Countess of Shrewsbury' (115). A mixture of the valuable, the meretricious, and the bathetically irrelevant, this list of collegiate library possessions speaks to the still precarious nature of the women's colleges in implied comparison to the immense wealth of the men's (and there may be a sly joke in the Galsworthy reference—the novel's theme of a man who considers his wife property connecting to Harriet's anxiety about marriage).

Libraries figure in many other ways in the novel: the proofs of the life work of one of the dons are torn and mutilated when left on a library table; a modern novel has its pages torn out in a similar scenario; two dons get into a fight when the notes of one of their students are defaced in yet another library-based attack. The 'Poltergeist', as the poison pen writer comes to be known, attacks mainly through the instruments of learning: 'breaking ink-bottles, flinging papers into the fire, smashing lamps...and throwing books through the windowpanes' (185).

Libraries are therefore a logical focus for her aggression, but it turns out that they also lie at the heart of her motives. The attacks had begun when a new fellow, Miss de Vine, came in to residence. When Lord Peter finally takes over from Harriet as chief investigator, his artless questions in the Senior Common Room about the moral absolutes of scholarship lead to her revelation of an incident from her past, when, as the head of 'a provincial college', she was involved in the examination of professorial theses for a Chair of History at York University. A man sent in 'a very interesting historical paper', but she 'happened to know that the whole contention was untrue, because a letter that absolutely contradicted it was actually in existence in a certain very obscure library in a foreign town' (328). 'Internal evidence' showed that the man must have been to the library, and he is forced to confess that not only had he seen the letter, and suppressed the knowledge because it contradicted his thesis, but he had also stolen it from the library. Luckily, he is not so alienated from academic values as to have destroyed the letter. The anecdote leads to a lengthy discussion of academic moral principles, but is later revealed to be the motive for the crimes: the guilty man had lost his career and killed himself a few years later (his is the only actual 'body' produced by the text's many libraries). The poison pen writer is his wife, Annie, now working as a college scout in order to support herself and their two daughters. Her diatribe after the revelation of her guilt challenges all of the abstract intellectual virtues at the heart of the academic life of the college:

> But couldn't you leave my man alone? He told a lie about somebody else who was dead and dust hundreds of years ago. Nobody was the worse for that. Was a dirty bit of paper more important than all our lives and happiness? ... You'd destroy your own husbands, if you had any, for an old book or bit of writing .... (426)

The 'dirtiness' of the bit of paper is important: Annie's role as a scout involves her mainly in cleaning; for her the dustiness of books (connecting also to the 'dust' of the long-dead letter writer) is their chief feature. In an earlier conversation with Harriet about the New Library she has declared that 'it seems a shame to keep up this big place just for women to study books in. I can't see what girls want with books. Books won't teach them to be good wives' (116): books, for her, are antithetical to femininity, an attitude that connects her to the trope of the Nazi 'Kinder, Kirche, Küche' running as an ominous undercurrent throughout the text, with a fellow student of Harriet's running a eugenics campaign, and the head porter and a decorator agreeing (immediately before Annie's statement, lest we miss the point) that '[w]ot this country wants ... is a 'Itler', to '[k]eep the girls at 'ome' (114).

It is not just books and libraries which are figured as dirty, but also librarians: the perennially dusty Miss Burrows, and Miss Gubbins, a fellow old student at the gaudy, about whom Harriet gossips with their tutor, decrying her boringness: Miss

Gubbins is 'a very conscientious person,' said Miss Lydgate, 'but she has an unfortunate knack of making any subject sound dull. It's a great pity, because she is exceptionally sound and dependable. However, that doesn't greatly matter in her present appointment; she holds a librarianship somewhere' (17). Harriet finds particularly distasteful Miss Gubbins's 'untidy hair, . . . ill-kept skin and [the] large white safety-pin securing her hood to her dress' (19), while the Dean wishes 'she'd wash her neck' (21). Running in tension with the abstract ideas of the importance of the intellectual life in *Gaudy Night*—the great value residing simply in 'settlement of a disputed reading' (214) in a text—there is also an intense sense of books as material objects: as made things, with manuscripts and proofs and friable pages and bindings that eventually rot, and leave their physical traces on the hands of the bodies that handle them as well as on the minds of those who read them. These books, always in process, signal the text's unwritten counter-text—all that is not said in its many appeals to the cerebral—that living, breathing bodies matter as much as abstract ideas: that Annie might have a point. Both bodily and ghostly, as figured in her naming as a poltergeist, she represents the Gothic return of the elements repressed by the hyper-rationalism of academic life.

The theme of the body in the library is further represented by a number of descriptions of the physical experience of the library reader. Growing bored of her hectic life in literary London, Harriet finds her professional writing increasingly trivial, and indulges her fantasies of a research career with desultory work on a study of Sheridan Le Fanu. She researches, not in the college library, but in the Bodleian; despite the fact that it is not the ideal source for her materials, it is a convincing cover for her discreet investigations into the crime, because 'Oxford is willing enough to believe that the Bodleian is the hub of the scholar's universe':

> She was able to find enough references among the Periodical Publications to justify an optimistic answer to kindly enquiries about her progress; and if, in fact, she snoozed a good deal in the arms of Duke Humphrey by day, to make up for those hours of the night spent in snooping about the corridors, she was probably not the only person in Oxford to find the atmosphere of old leather and central heating favourable to slumber.   (122)

Library reading is represented as a matter not of the purely cerebral but of material, *physical* sensations and pleasures, of warmth, the smell of ancient books, and the clubbish environment of the Duke Humphrey's, most ancient of the Bodleian's reading rooms. In thinking about the bodily dimension of reading here, I follow Michel de Certeau in his chapter on 'Reading as Poaching' in volume I of *The Practice of Everyday Life*, where he suggests that:

> We should try to rediscover the movements of this reading within the body itself, which seems to stay docile and silent but mimes the reading in its own way: from

the nooks of all sorts of 'reading rooms' (including lavatories) emerge subconscious gestures, grumblings, tics, stretchings, rustlings, unexpected noises, in short a wild orchestration of the body.[15]

His interest is in the gradual historical erasure of the physical (for instance, moving the lips, reading aloud) as a component of the reading experience from the early modern period onward. He does not expand on the implications of his recognition that, despite our usual modelling of the experience as one only of the mind, bodies, as they lounge, fidget, eat, and even defecate, are still intimately involved in the act of reading. I have suggested elsewhere that thinking about reading bodies, and particularly their posture, is a helpful way of mapping the shifting, slippery distinctions between different forms of reading that lie at the heart of the 'Battle of the Brows' that dominated interwar literary thinking.[16] Here, I am also interested in the library as a site of *not*-reading: as a place where the physical form of the reading act (holding a book in a library chair, surrounded by other books and readers) takes the place of the process of intellectual engagement. Later, fleeing back to Oxford from the travails of her London life, Harriet indulges in the quiet pleasures of the university empty in the Easter vacation:

> [I]n Radcliffe Square the Camera slept like a cat in the sunshine, disturbed only be the occasional visit of a slow-footed don.... Mornings in Bodley, drowsing among the worn browns and tarnished gilding of Duke Humphrey, snuffing the faint, musty odour of slowly perishing leather, hearing only the discreet tippet-tap of Agag-feet along the padded floor ... then back [after afternoons rowing on the river], with mind relaxed and body stretched and vigorous, to make toast by the fire; and then, at night, the lit lamp and the drawn curtain, with the flutter of the turned page and soft scrape of pen on paper the only sounds to break the utter silence between quarter and quarter chime.   (213)

Among the many sensory pleasures offered by the donnish life seems to be a freedom from conventional temporal ordering: the days in the library, the zone of *public* reading, are times of self-indulgent slumber—even the library itself sleeps in the sun—while the nights are times for solitary reading and writing, free of the pressures of social expectations. This idea of the library as a place of relaxation—think also of Colonel Bantry's 'big sagging arm-chairs'—points us to the issue, constantly debated in the inter-war years, of leisure reading. 'The reading habit', Q. D. Leavis remarked, 'is now often a form of the drug habit', while W. H. Auden,

---

[15] Michel de Certeau, *The Practice of Everyday Life*, vol. 1, trans. Steve Randall (Berkeley: University of California Press, 1984), 175.

[16] Nicola Humble, 'Sitting Forward or Sitting Back: Highbrow v. Middlebrow Reading', for a special issue of the journal *Modernist Cultures* on the topic of the Middlebrow and Modernism (Edinburgh University Press, April 2011).

in an article praising detective fiction, begins with an assertion that 'for me, as for any others, the reading of detective stories is an addiction like tobacco or alcohol'.[17] George Orwell, in 'Bookshop Memories', recounts his experience running a bookshop-cum-lending library in which the readers consumed popular literature—and particularly crime fiction—by the acreage.[18] In the context of this contemporary anxiety about leisured reading, the evocation of the library as a place of slumber connects to concerns about the intellectual status of detective fiction which belong to both Harriet and to Dorothy L. Sayers herself.

Harriet's anxieties about the worthiness of her career as a celebrated writer of detective fiction echoes Sayers's own. *Gaudy Night* represents a stylistic hiatus in her work, following a number of personal crises, in which she attempts to reposition the detective novel as a more serious literary form. Harriet herself, told by Wimsey that 'You haven't yet... written the book you could write if you tried' (291), begins to abandon her usual method of 'jig-saw' narratives in favour of psychological realism. The sense of fiction as opposed to 'literature' as extraneous to the purposes of the libraries 'proper' is echoed also in Harriet's consciously farcical thought—inspired by the large number of crime-fiction-reading undergraduates who are keen to meet her—that '[a] School of Detective Fiction would... have a fair chance of producing a good crop of Firsts' (159). This metafictive concern about the significance and intellectual worthiness of (crime) fiction extends to the issue of libraries. Shrewsbury College in fact has three libraries—the Old Library, the New Library, and the Fiction Library—the latter seeming mainly to serve the purpose of providing reading matter for those who cannot sleep. The Fiction Library gestures towards the one type of library which is notably missing from both of the novels considered here: the lending libraries which dominated the readerly landscape in the interwar years.[19] This absence is significant because it is in these libraries only that one would have found the material texts of these novels themselves. The lending library, like virtually every aspect of interwar British culture, was significantly stratified on class grounds. There were the exclusive London libraries such as Mudie's and the Times Book Club, which were patronized by the gentry and upper middle classes; the private but widely accessible lending libraries—such as the Boots Booklovers' Library and the W. H. Smith's Circulating Library—which, with branches in every town, attracted a loyal middle-class readership; and the cheap 'tuppenny' libraries run from local newsagents, of which Q. D. Leavis commented disdainfully that 'it is

---

[17] W. H. Auden, 'The Guilty Vicarage', 1948, in Robin W. Winks, ed., *Detective Fiction: A Collection of Critical Essays* (London: Prentice-Hall, 1980), 15.

[18] Q. D. Leavis, *Fiction and the Reading Public*, 1932 (London: Chatto & Windus, 1978), 7; George Orwell, 'Bookshop Memories', 1936, *The Collected Essays, Journalism and Letters*, ed. Sonia Orwell and Ian Angus, vol. 1, *An Age Like This, 1920–1940* (Harmondsworth: Penguin, 1971).

[19] See Nickianne Moody, 'The Boots Booklovers' Libraries', *Antiquarian Book Monthly* (Nov 1996): 36–8, and Humble, *The Feminine Middlebrow Novel*, 36–43.

common to find a stock of worn and greasy novels' read by 'a clientele drawn from the poorest class'—figuring a profound anxiety about the trace of the hands of other readers, which is also suggested by the existence of special classes of membership in the Boots libraries which guaranteed access to books in their newest, most pristine form.[20] Although the private lending library makes an appearance in a number of interwar British novels, such as Elizabeth Bowen's *The Death of the Heart* (1938), E. M. Delafield's *Provincial Lady* series (1930 onwards), and Denis Mackail's *Greenery Street* (1925), it is rarely a focal point for crime fiction, despite the pronounced self-referentiality of the genre. In this we see a distinction between British and American Golden Age texts, as it is almost exclusively in the latter that the lending library—both private and public—appears. In Charles Dutton's 1931 *Murder in a Library*, the library in question, where a spinster librarian is murdered, is a municipal one; in his *Streaked with Crimson* (1929), a local librarian solves a murder mystery, while Lawrence G. Blochman's *Death Walks in Marble Halls* (1942) is set in the New York Public Library. While images of private and scholarly libraries offer numerous figurations of the concerns of the interwar crime puzzle-clue for writers of both nations, it is only in American texts that the possibilities of the library as a democratic institution begin to be imagined.

---

[20] Leavis, *Fiction and the Reading Public*, 7.

9

On the Shelf? Women, Librarians, and Agency in Twentieth-Century Fiction

Alice Crawford

For Jo March in *Little Women* (1868–9) a small library is 'a region of bliss'. Access to a larger, formal one in a grand New England house makes her clap her hands and prance, 'as she always did when especially delighted'. Yet Jo, whose creator Louisa M. Alcott had stern views on proper reading matter for the young, never becomes a librarian.[1] Probably the first female professional librarian in fiction is another, rather different New Englander, Miss Catching in Henry James's *The Bostonians* (1886). In Harvard University Library Miss Catching is 'working on the catalogue'. To the male protagonist, Ransom, she explains its 'mysteries', which 'consisted of a myriad little cards, disposed alphabetically in immense chests of drawers'. Ransom, 'deeply interested' in his library tour, 'considered with attention the young lady's fair ringlets and refined, anxious expression, saying to himself that this was in the highest degree a New England type'. He is told that Miss Catching is 'wrapped up in the [feminist] cause', and he worries that if she realized his own opposition to that cause, then 'she should not know under what letter to range it'.[2] Though Miss Catching may be mocked for her professional orderliness, in a novel that is very alert to the politics of gender, James, attuned to social change, brings into fiction—for a moment at least—a New Woman librarian.

Her American location is appropriate. In 1877, the Philadelphian librarian Lloyd B. Smith had drawn the attention of a library conference in London 'to the employment of ladies in libraries in America'.[3] That same year, Harvard University's chief librarian, Justin Winsor, founder and president of the new American Library Association, had told the same London conference that at Harvard 'they take lady assistants into the library', and the audience had applauded when Winsor pointed out that there was present at their conference that very day 'a representative of the American lady librarians (loud cheers), one

[1] Louisa M. Alcott, *Little Women* (1868–9; repr. Boston: Little, Brown, 1934), 40, 55; for Alcott on library reading see Emily Hamilton-Honey, 'Guardians of Morality: Librarians and American Girls' Series Fiction, 1890–1950', *Library Trends* 60.4 (Spring 2012): 771–2.
[2] Henry James, *The Bostonians* (London: Macmillan, 1886), 240, 241.
[3] 'Librarians in Congress', *Times*, 6 October 1877, 10.

who had been librarian of Wellesley College, eight miles from Boston, where the president is a lady, all the professors are ladies, and 400 ladies are the students'.[4] In America, and especially in the Boston area, women were taking advantage of the new professional opportunities librarianship offered. It was in Boston that Melvil Dewey had set up his company, the Library Bureau, beginning the *Library Journal* while serving as secretary to the American Library Association which he had co-founded. Boston-born Lucy Toulmin Smith, who became librarian of Manchester College, Oxford, told the 1899 International Congress of Women that 'America with its 5,000 libraries offered plentiful provision for women, by whom they were chiefly served'.[5] English librarian Minnie Stewart Rhodes James, after working for Dewey's Library Bureau in London, emigrated to Boston in 1897, becoming active in the American Library Association and working as librarian at Boston's Library Bureau.

Though in the early twentieth century fiction on both sides of the Atlantic began to attend in more detail to women who worked in libraries, published studies of the topic tend to be short magazine pieces (often addressed to librarians by librarians), or library-school students' dissertations, or bibliographies, among which the most notable by far is Grant Burns's alphabetically arranged bibliography *Librarians in Fiction*, which lists an impressive 343 occurrences of librarians in anglophone novels, short stories, and plays.[6] The present chapter suggests that this field would bear more detailed investigation from the point of view of literary and cultural criticism and history. Moving between American and British fiction, and with a particular but not exclusive focus on middlebrow fiction, its focus is on how novelists and short-story writers present the figure of the librarian. Though I shall make the point that one of the most convincing depictions of a female library worker is authored by a man, and that female novelists do not write only about libraries whose librarians are women, I am interested principally in how, often wryly, female writers of twentieth-century fiction present the struggles of women for agency within the increasingly professionalized field of librarianship. A few of the texts discussed here are well known, but almost no reader will be familiar with them all, so, in addition to quotation, I offer some brief account of each of their plots. Progressing chronologically to afford a sense of literary history, the chapter provides examples from across a range of genres that offer

---

[4] 'Librarians in Congress', 10.   [5] 'International Congress of Women', *Times*, 5 July 1899, 10.
[6] See, for example, Christopher Brown-Syed and Charles Barnard Sands, 'Some Portrayals of Librarians in Fiction – A Discussion', *Education Libraries*, 21.1–2 (1997): 17–24; Jon Noble, 'From Tom Pinch to Highliber Zavora: The Librarian in Fiction', *Orana*, 37.3 (November 2001): 23–8; noteworthy library students' dissertations include several written by Master of Library and Information Science students at Kent State University and now available online: Margaret A. Elliott, *The Librarian's Stereotyped Image in Romance Novels, 1980–1995: Has the Image Changed?* (1996); Barbara Kitchen, *Librarian's Image in Children's Fiction* (2000). Also available online is Virginia Vesper's 1994 report for Middle Tennessee State University, *The Image of the Librarian in Murder Mysteries in the Twentieth Century* (1994). Grant Burns, *Librarians in Fiction: A Critical Bibliography* (Jefferson, NC: McFarland, 1998).

entertainment and amusement as well as imaginative insight to twenty-first-century readers who care about libraries in literature.

Katharine Ruth Ellis's 1909 novel *The Wide Awake Girls in Winsted* is surely the only children's book with an opening chapter entitled 'Starting a Library'.[7] College girl Catherine Smith, home for the summer holidays, collaborates with her female chums to establish a library in small-town Winsted, and install her intellectually precocious, but socially awkward friend Algernon Swinburne as its librarian. Algernon, whose mother has clearly done him no favours in naming him after the famous poet, seems to the girls to be perfect for the job, as he knows 'an amazing amount' and is 'a veritable walking library'. They are convinced, too, that the job will relieve him of his crippling shyness and that it would be 'fine' for the town 'if all that knowledge of his could be used . . . '.[8]

The girls' confidence proves well placed, and the library is duly set up, becoming a valued community hub responsive to its users' needs. Algernon blossoms in the role of librarian, especially after Catherine explains to him how he would be better liked if he talked a lot less. Taking her advice, he 'squares his shoulders' and becomes a reformed character. By the end of chapter 2 his friends agree that 'he walks better already' and that the library has been the making of him.[9]

Though in 1909 a reviewer in the *Journal of Education* compared *The Wide Awake Girls in Winsted* favourably with the work of Louisa M. Alcott, and considered it 'an exceedingly interesting and genuinely valuable book for girls to read', nowadays the book infuriates with its insistence that, although it is the group of college girls who take the initiative in setting up the library, and who do most of the preliminary work, it is their nice but ineffectual beta-male friend who becomes the librarian.[10] The association of librarians with ineffectual masculinity has precedents in earlier American writing: Herman Melville's 'grub-worm of a poor devil', the 'sub-sub-librarian' mentioned at the start of *Moby Dick* clearly belongs, as the author puts it, to a 'hopeless, sallow tribe'.[11] In *The Wide Awake Girls* Catherine, not Algernon, conceives the plan and prevails on her doctor parents to use their influence to acquire the library building and to square the arrangements with the town council. It is she and her girlfriends who clear out the cobweb-infested building where the books are to be housed, and who afterwards sit hand-sewing the curtains for the windows. Algernon is absent, turning up only later to install his prized stationery items on his desk. For modern readers, the storyline in which all the female characters seem to have agency, but who use it simply to put a *man* in a professional librarian post, is frustrating.

[7] Katharine Ruth Ellis, *The Wide Awake Girls in Winsted* (Boston: Little, Brown & Co., 1909).
[8] Ellis, *The Wide Awake Girls*, 12, 10, 12.   [9] Ellis, *The Wide Awake Girls*, 22.
[10] 'The Wide-Awake Girls of [*sic*] Winsted', *Journal of Education*, 70.16 (28 October 1909): 441.
[11] Herman Melville, *Moby Dick, or, The Whale* (1851; repr. London: Constable, 1922, 2 vols), I, xii.

A writer of her time, Ellis sidesteps a prickly issue. Her girls are bright, opinionated young women who talk enthusiastically about their college experiences ('Dexter', Chicago, and Wellesley are all mentioned), yet the question of their own possible later careers is never satisfactorily addressed. Helping out at the library one day, Catherine finds herself explaining a Greek myth from Nathaniel Hawthorne's *Tanglewood Tales* to a child who approaches her, and does so with such skill that Algernon suggests she should become a professional storyteller. Though Catherine seizes on the idea with delight, the twenty-first-century reader observes her settling for what was, even in 1909, an insipid and much too ladylike non-career.

We cannot help but be surprised that, in a novel written when more and more American women were beginning to qualify for professional careers, the spirited Catherine is not allowed to contemplate professional librarianship as an option. L. M. Montgomery had permitted her Anne of Green Gables to qualify as a professional teacher in 1908, and in *The Wide Awake Girls* Catherine's own mother is a professional doctor. Women had been working in American public libraries since the 1850s and the number of library schools where they could acquire professional qualifications was increasing. Dewey had opened the first of these at Columbia College in 1887, transferring it to New York State University in Albany in 1889. The initial student intake had been of seventeen women and three men, and by 1899 Dewey was telling the International Library Conference that, to his thinking, 'a great librarian must have a clear head, a strong hand, and, above all, a great heart. And when I look into the future, I am inclined to think that most of the men who will achieve this greatness will be women.'[12]

However tantalizing it may be to wonder if Catherine's 'Dexter' College might reference the real-world Drexel Institute of Art, Science and Industry, where one of the earliest library schools opened in 1891, and to picture her returning there after a summer playing at libraries to tackle a real library qualification, we are left with a text in which this future is not imagined. In 1909 it is still too early for Catherine Smith to be seen using her increasing awareness of agency to have a go at becoming one of Melvil Dewey's great women librarians. And even if she had done so, early twentieth-century fiction writers, particularly those writing in North American versions of the sentimental small-town 'Kailyard' genre associated with J. M. Barrie, might not have been supportive. Miss Watkins, the 'very strict', irritable, new librarian of 'the little New England town' in one of the stories in Josephine Dodge Daskam's *Whom the Gods Destroyed* (1902), wants everything 'properly systematised', and is presented as much less sympathetic than the ailing small boy who acts as 'little librarian' there and who dies of scarlet fever.[13] The

---

[12] Melvil Dewey, 'The Ideal Librarian', quoted in full, *The Library Journal* 24.1 (1899):14.
[13] Josephine Dodge Daskam, *Whom the Gods Destroyed* (New York: Charles Scribner's Sons, 1902), 161, 175, 182.

long-winded American novelist Winston Churchill is more sympathetic towards his character Lucretia Penniman, whom he presents in his historical novel *Coniston* (1906) as 'one of the first to sound the clarion call for the intellectual independence of American women' and as the person 'who started the Brampton Social Library, and filled it with such books as both sexes might read for profit. Never was there a stricter index than hers.'[14] Yet even here there is a critical dig in that last sentence, and the climate of early twentieth-century fiction, even in the America of Melvil Dewey, took some time to welcome professional female librarians.

Dorothy Canfield's short story 'Hillsboro's Good Luck' features a librarian who *does* go to library school and exerts her agency with vigour.[15] Appearing first in *Atlantic Monthly* in 1908 but republished in Canfield's collection *Hillsboro People* (1915), it tells how philanthropist Josiah Camden (a shade of Andrew Carnegie?) endows the remote Hillsboro community with an out-of-the-box, modern library building and stock, crushing out of existence the home-made library that the townspeople have loved and fostered since time immemorial. The endowment includes the new professional librarian Miss Martin, freshly qualified from Dewey's library school in Albany. Full of 'missionary fervour', she begins at once to 'practice all the latest devices for automatically turning a benighted community into the latest thing in culture'.[16] Miss Martin's new regime sweeps aside the voluntary staffing rota under which the ladies of Hillsboro proudly took turns to look after the library for a day. Gone are the happy fund-raising evenings on which people came together to stage 'entertainment for buying new books'.[17] Gone, too, is the homely shelving system which saw each year's new book acquisitions placed together, regardless of subject, located by the name of the fund-raising entertainment which had bought them.

Efforts have repeatedly been made to revaluate Canfield's fiction as that of a novelist significant among modern realist women writers, who operated across a perceived border between 'middlebrow' and 'highbrow' fiction. Those efforts often tend, however, to examine in particular what her work meant to her better-known friend and contemporary, Willa Cather, who has come to be regarded as 'on the modernist bright side' rather than on the 'darkened side of literary history'.[18] It may be Canfield's commitment to middlebrow realist fiction that attracts her to depicting the details of the daily life of a professional female librarian, but it should not be assumed that her attitude towards this figure is uncomplicated. As Jaime

[14] Winston Churchill, *Coniston* (1906; New York: Macmillan, 1907), 8.
[15] Dorothy Canfield, 'Hillsboro's Good Luck', in *Hillsboro People*, by Dorothy Canfield (New York: Holt, 1915): 187–206. Page references in this chapter are to this edition. Originally published in *Atlantic Monthly* 102 (July 1908): 131–9.
[16] Canfield, *Hillsboro People*, 197, 198.   [17] Canfield, *Hillsboro People*, 188.
[18] Janis P. Stout, 'Dorothy Canfield, Willa Cather, and the Uncertainties of Middlebrow and Highbrow', *Studies in the Novel*, 44.1 (2012): 27, 28.

Harker argues in *America the Middlebrow*, Canfield may have been a 'tireless activist' for progressive causes, writing for a 'progressive middlebrow' audience sympathetic to the struggles of professional women.[19] Yet in this story her narrator makes it clear that, now that the new librarian 'with her fresh white shirt-waist and pretty, business-like airs' is installed in her handsome, oak-finished office, Hillsboro people are assigned the books she tells them they should have rather than the ones they actually want.[20] The old lady confined to bed with a cold, who sends to the library for some light reading to cheer her convalescence, is allocated a Henry James novel and never enters the library again. The little girls who ask for the Elsie books are given *Greek Myths for Children* instead. Squire Pritchett, who comes in to consult his favourite condensed handbook of geology to identify a stone, is dismayed to be offered, instead, a vast encyclopedia of geology in forty-seven volumes. The mismatch between the community and its new library is as ludicrous as it is cruel, and this story of library professionalization does not end happily. Unbending, 'firm of purpose', the librarian is frozen out by the people her library is supposed to serve. The insolent new janitor she appoints to replace the slow-witted old man who had done the job for years burns the library down on a drunken spree, and Miss Martin resigns grimly 'to marry the assistant to the head of the Department of Bibliography at Albany'.[21]

An unsettling tale, Canfield's 'Hillsboro's Good Luck' leaves the reader perplexed about where sympathy should lie. The new librarian *is* obtuse about her community, implacable in her fervour to impose the new rules of library science, but the Hillsboro people are troublingly malevolent in their behaviour towards her too. The girls are envious of her. 'She was a very pretty librarian indeed, and she wore her tailor suits with an air which made the village girls look uneasily into their mirrors....'[22] The farmers supplying the wood for the library stoves connive to ensure that she pays far more than the going rate, arguing meanly that 'it wasn't her money but Camden's, who had tossed them the library as a man would toss a penny to a beggar...'.[23]

So often associated with all that is civilized, good, and worth preserving in a society, the library in this story becomes instead a catalyst for moral decline. The money which has made Camden's benefaction possible is discovered to have been acquired by 'colossal and unpunished frauds', making Hillsboro's new library a compromised and dirty gift. Uncertain about how to behave towards the young librarian, people begin to fight with one another—'...neighbours and old friends were divided into cliques, calling each other, respectively, cheats and hypocrites'.[24] The community's moral compass comes adrift.

---

[19] Jaime Harker, *America the Middlebrow: Women's Novels, Progressivism, and Middlebrow Authorship Between the Wars* (Amherst: University of Massachusetts Press, 2007), 23.
[20] Canfield, *Hillsboro People*, 197.   [21] Canfield, *Hillsboro People*, 199, 205.
[22] Canfield, *Hillsboro People*, 197.   [23] Canfield, *Hillsboro People*, 202.
[24] Canfield, *Hillsboro People*, 202.

The story closes with the smouldering remains of Miss Martin's library disappearing under the soft new growth of woodbine and wild flowers. Mrs Foster sets off to dust the much-loved books in the old library, preparing them to be borrowed again. It is as though the clock has been put back, the shocking rift caused by the new library repaired. All seems set for the peaceful continuance of the old ways. The tale appears to leave its female librarian vanquished, thrust back where she belongs into the safe tradition of marriage and domesticity. Is its message that the bright young women leaving Albany with their library degrees, looking forward to professional careers, are inimical to society, a trend to be resisted? Is too much agency for women a dangerous thing?

Published before America entered World War I, Canfield's portrayal of an American female librarian is far less positive than either Edith Wharton's of the untrained librarian Charity Royall in her novel *Summer* (1917), or Sinclair Lewis's of the Chicago library-school-trained Carol Kennicott in his *Main Street* (1921), though it shares with these fictions a sense of a provincial milieu.[25] Life is difficult, too, for Marcia May, assistant librarian in a Chicago branch library, in Elizabeth Irons Folsom's 1923 short story 'Natural Selection'.[26] She falls in love with the boy next door, blue-collar worker Larison Quoid, who has served as a pacemaker in a steel mill and now works as a factory carpenter. Their attraction is mutual and passionate, but the relationship fails to survive the class difference between them. Sharply observed and economically told, this story is one of the earliest to consider the problem of class for librarians, and depicts a clash of cultures as brutal and intractable as the one which results in the burning down of Hillsboro's ill-fated library. This tale of the mid-1920s again declines to show a female librarian in a clear, triumphant trajectory towards a fulfilling career outside the home, describing her ongoing struggle for agency and her need to choose between love and class-appropriate employment. The tale uses the figure of the female librarian to make clear the difficulty and complexity of women's rise in society. There may be painful consequences for both sexes if they are permitted to rise above men.

Very different in setting and tone is Jane Oliver's 1933 epistolary novel *Business as Usual*. Helen Christina Easson Rees, who wrote as 'Jane Oliver', was the daughter of a Scottish doctor. An adventurous and well-off woman, she was a qualified pilot, and 'shared a love of flying' with her husband, John Rees, in whose memory she endowed a well-known British literary prize.[27] She was an accomplished historical novelist as well as a chronicler of her own times, and had a sense of what might interest a predominantly female readership. Co-authored with her

---

[25] Edith Wharton, *Summer: A Novel* (London: Macmillan, 1917); Sinclair Lewis, *Main Street* (New York: [s.n.,] 1920.

[26] Elizabeth I. Folsom, 'Natural Selection', in *As We Are: Stories of Here and Now*, ed. W. B. Pitkin (New York: Harcourt Brace, 1923), 47–72 (first publication).

[27] John Rees wrote under the name 'John Llewelyn Rhys'; 'Jane Oliver' [obituary], *Times*, 8 May 1970, 12.

friend Ann Stafford, who provided the illustrations, *Business as Usual* is set partly in a department store, and was one of the books chosen to be promoted by the department store Selfridge & Co. in London's Oxford Street during the run-up to Christmas in 1933. For a reviewer in *The Scotsman* in March that year it was a book that 'bubbles over with fun-making and good humour'.[28] Its heroine, Hilary Fane, is another young woman striding hopefully out into the world of work.[29] Made redundant from her post as assistant librarian at 'Corstorphine Municipal Library', Edinburgh, she decides to take a gap year in London and find an interesting job to keep her busy before returning to marry her doctor fiancé Basil. Unlike Canfield's Miss Martin, Hilary has from the beginning the agency and confidence not of a library school degree, but of her class and of her time at Oxford University. The job she eventually takes is in the busy lending library of Everyman's Stores in Oxford Street, and she shares the ups and downs of her time there with her family, to whom she writes letters home.

The novel is distinctive in that, unlike nineteenth-century and almost all earlier twentieth-century novels, it offers accurate descriptions of some of the actual tasks performed by the library staff—running the mail-order Rational Reading Service, handwriting address labels, investigating letters of complaint, conducting a staff seating survey, responding to customer enquiries. More than that, in a tellingly detailed account of professional working conditions, Jane Oliver knows how to convey the sheer weariness produced by a day in the book stacks: 'I'm derelict,' writes Hilary after her first day. 'My feet are in a bowl of Radol and my head is bloody but unbowed.'[30] Hilary's combination of humour and literary allusion (here to William Ernest Henley's once popular poem 'Invictus') marks her out as well read and smart, as well as tired and sore-footed.

This young woman, however, is really only playing at being a proper librarian. Jane Oliver regarded this novel as one of her 'light-hearted satires', and its narrative tone recalls the *de haut en bas* voice of E. M. Delafield's *Diary of a Provincial Lady* (1930).[31] The reader is conscious always that, while 'slumming it' as a library clerk and living parsimoniously in a London bedsit on £2.10.0 a week, Hilary is still the daughter of Professor and Mrs Fane of University Close, Edinburgh, and that she has the safety net of her class to rescue her if catastrophe strikes.[32] The story of life in the library is interspersed with accounts of country-house weekends, car trips with rich friends, and visits from her aunt, Lady Barnley, who descends on the library service desk to whisk her off for a restaurant tea. She does not have to spend long on the lowest rung of the library career ladder, catching the eye of the managing director Mr Grant and being speedily

---

[28] 'New Fiction', *Scotsman*, 27 March 1933, 2.
[29] Jane Oliver and Ann Stafford, *Business as Usual* (London: Collins, 1933).
[30] Oliver, *Business as Usual*, 126.
[31] Jane Oliver, 'Ann Stafford', *Times*, 29 September 1966, 14.
[32] E. M. Delafield, *Diary of a Provincial Lady* (London: Macmillan, 1930).

promoted to the more class-appropriate position of Assistant Staff Supervisor. Her wages go up, she moves to more salubrious accommodation, and is delighted to furnish her new rooms with her Aunt Bertha's gifts of expensive furniture from Everyman's. The employment of a cook/cleaner for the new premises ensures that she need not soil her hands with domestic work at the end of her library day.

While this novel appears to be addressed to a middle-class readership, it does cast a sympathetic glance from time to time at those who really do have to live on £2.10.0 a week—or less—and asks the reader to wonder (like Hilary) how they do it. Travelling to her job, she notices other classes at work, the 'men on drays', the 'little man with a cartload of cabbages', the chars or dailies 'coming from making other people's breakfasts' ('quite unresentfully', she thinks), and some even older women who 'go from one dust-bin to another with sacks ... they lift the lids and finger the muddle inside with grey, careful hands that never miss a bottle or a crust'.[33] The head librarian at Everyman's, Hilary's initial boss Miss Sparling, with her 'nasty, pointed, rattish face', who sits 'bristling behind the vase of semi-putrid Michaelmas daisies' on her desk, is clearly also a woman of slender means, but one who is offered no miraculous escape from the social stratum into which she was born.[34] She is the stereotypical spinster librarian, for whom life has been hard—who has no agency—and who instinctively visits her revenge on the world around her by trying to make sure that life for others atrophies too. Things, she tells Hilary, 'had always been done in a certain way, and therefore must always continue to be done just so'.[35]

Business as Usual is not a straightforward tale about the empowerment of female librarians in the 1930s. While Oxford graduate Hilary has seemed at the beginning to slip free from the fetters of her Edinburgh parental home, to throw off the patriarchy, and escape into the independence of a self-started London career, we leave her at the end safely engaged to the swoon-worthy Mr Grant (the miserable Basil having been ditched for his lack of sympathy with her gap-year experiment), and looking forward to the continuation of the comfortable upper-middle-class life to which she has always been accustomed. The 'business as usual' of the title will not need to be *her* business for long. The elegant line drawing by Ann Stafford which accompanies Hilary's account of her first encounter with Mr Grant shows him towering '*Very* god like' over the tiny figure of herself at her desk, hands open towards him in supplication.[36] The patriarchy is reinvoked with a few strokes of the pen. Marriage, domesticity, and the subjugation of self await her with the same inevitability as they have for Hillsboro's unfortunate Miss Martin. Again, however engaged with the actual business of library work it may be, this is a socially conservative work of middlebrow fiction. Perhaps the very social-realist conventions that lead the author to portray the work of her middle-

---

[33] Oliver, *Business as Usual*, 56.   [34] Oliver, *Business as Usual*, 53.
[35] Oliver, *Business as Usual*, 139.   [36] Oliver, *Business as Usual*, 102.

class librarian also encourage an adherence to what some middlebrow novelists may have regarded as the realities of life for many 1930s British professional women.

Philip Larkin's *A Girl in Winter* (1947) explores the quintessential struggle for agency of library assistant Katherine Lind.[37] Emphasizing the importance of non-biographical approaches to Larkin in his chapter on 'Radical Ellipsis: A Girl in Winter', the literary critic John Osborne risks downplaying the precise sense of library work that is part of what makes it so effective, though it is important to realize, too, that the experience of this female library worker is very much an imaginative creation in a work of nuanced literary fiction.[38] Written in 1945 when Larkin was working at the public library in Wellington, Shropshire, this novel is enriched by his first-hand knowledge of librarianly tasks, and by his ability to evoke the ponderous atmosphere of a war-darkened English public library. Katherine, whose surname in German means 'gentle' or 'soft', and who takes pleasure in 'the completeness with which she could cover her thoughts', is a refugee from a European country.[39] The story is the account of her working day as she accompanies her colleague Miss Green to the dentist, sees her home, retrieves Miss Green's lost handbag from Miss Veronica Parbury in the city suburbs, and returns to work, where she has a brutal argument with her spiteful library superior Mr Anstey. It ends with the visit to her flat of soldier Robin Fennel, the young Englishman who was her penfriend before the war, and with whose family she has spent some happy summer weeks many years before.

'Who is Katherine?' the novel puzzles. Deprived by the war of her national identity, she is both classless and stateless, struggling to find a place for herself in the new order, and longing to be enfolded into the safe, English middle-class world she remembers from her stay with the Fennels. She inhabits multiple roles: the meek, put-upon junior who must listen wordlessly to the bitter invective of Mr Anstey; the warm-hearted friend who accompanies her co-worker to the emergency dentist; the sensible nurse who takes the patient home and provides warm milk and painkillers after the operation; the risk-taker who uses her initiative to track down the lost handbag; the generous lover who comforts her soldier boyfriend on his embarkation leave. Crucially, she is the fiery young woman who defies her overbearing manager, angrily throwing at him her knowledge of his secret love affair and using her agency at last to speak truth to power. It is a moment which allows her, too, to break free from the carapace of her own guardedness, to be herself, and to express what she feels, even if it is simply 'how glad she was if she had hurt him!'[40]

---

[37] Philip Larkin, *A Girl in Winter* (London: Faber & Faber, 1947).
[38] John Osborne, *Radical Larkin: Seven Types of Technical Mastery* (Basingstoke: Palgrave Macmillan, 2014), ch. 1.
[39] Larkin, *A Girl in Winter*, 16.   [40] Larkin, *A Girl in Winter*, 213.

No easy definition of 'a person' is possible, the novel suggests, just as in the messy, war-broken world there is now no easy definition of class. The explosive verbal outburst between the two librarians mirrors the eruption and resettling of social strata, the upheaval of the status quo, which the war has catalysed. Mr Anstey has only been promoted to his chief librarian's post because of conscription. The 'real head', a 'very different kind of person altogether', young and with a university degree, has had to go off to fight, leaving Anstey, son of a corporation workman, to accede temporarily to his job. ('They used to live in Gas Street,' reports the gossipy Miss Green.)[41] Anstey needs to cling on to his new, elevated status, while Katherine has to fight to have her voice heard, to have her post-war self defined. Operating substantially within the conventions of social realism, yet enhanced by a poet's deployment of telling imagery, Larkin's novel closes on images of melting ice, as Katherine and Robin lie together in bed, listening to the ticking of his watch and knowing that at last, after long days of iron-hard cold, snow is falling softly outside. Their dreams are like ice floes 'moving down a lightless channel of water'.[42] Everything is fluid in this war-shattered world. The accepted order of things has been profoundly disturbed, and all people can do is be kind to one another and hope that a future of some sort exists. Katherine and Robin are 'sort of' in love; he 'sort of' proposes, and she 'sort of' accepts. Hesitantly loving each other for this night at least, they fall asleep, seeming 'to mingle in their minds'.[43] Perhaps Katherine will be enfolded into the Fennels' middle-class world (Robin's niece has been named after her, he reveals)—but perhaps not. Connections are made, a degree of agency has been acquired, but all remains tentative, provisional. However much he may have been berated by some recent readers of his correspondence and other writings for his attitudes to women, this male novelist writes with subtly searching insight into the mind of a junior female library worker, portraying her life inside as well as outside the confines of her employment.

Contrasting with the provisionality and hesitation of Larkin's novel, a new 'definiteness' is detectable in the librarians of American science fiction in the late 1940s and 1950s, though strikingly in this environment only male librarians are envisaged. An emerging breed of alpha males, they possess new agency as the heroic guardians of knowledge. 'The dropping of the atom bomb in 1945 made science fiction respectable,' said Isaac Asimov, and for some sci-fi writers in this newly sanctioned literary space the trope of the librarian begins to carry a sobering weight of social comment.[44] Written against the Cold War backdrop of

---

[41] Larkin, *A Girl in Winter*, 37.   [42] Larkin, *A Girl in Winter*, 248.
[43] Larkin, *A Girl in Winter*, 248.
[44] Isaac Asimov, *Nightfall, and Other Stories* (Garden City, NY: Doubleday, 1969): 93. For another post-war librarian in science fiction, see Martin Loran, 'An Ounce of Dissension', in *Pacific Book of Australian SF*, ed. John Baxter (Sydney: Angus & Robertson, 1968), 27–48. Asimov's own story of 'girl librarians', 'Death of a Honey-Blonde', is understandably censured by Burns, *Librarians in Fiction*, 124.

McCarthyism and the threat of intellectual censorship, Ray Bradbury's 1947 short story 'Bright Phoenix', a clear rehearsal for his 1953 novel *Fahrenheit 451*, makes explicit the librarian's potential role in frustrating humanity's free fall into intellectual nihilism.[45] Catapulted into the future of April 2022, readers meet librarian Tom, who regards his library as 'a cool cavern, or fresh, ever growing forest' which he must protect from Chief Fire Officer Jonathan Barnes, whose mission it is to burn the books. 'The books are dangerous,' says Jonathan. 'Good God, no two agree. All the damn double-talk. All the lousy babel and slaver and spit. So, we're out to simplify, clarify, hew to the line.'[46] Openly heroic, Tom stands his ground against the firemen's push to suppress this clamour of ideas in books. He is a leader of men. The firemen obey him when he tells them to move quietly. Readers in the library accept his instruction to carry on reading while the intruders move in. Calmly he takes the Fire Officer across the road to a café, where he shows that ordinary people—the café owner, the waiters, a passing friend—have all ensured that the contents of the books will not die as they will live on in their heads. Keats, Plato, Einstein, Shakespeare, Lincoln, Poe—all have been memorized in a massive act of passive resistance orchestrated by the assertive male librarian. Later, at the end of *Fahrenheit 451*, these 'human books' appear again as the determined band of intellectuals whom fireman Montag meets in the scrubland beyond the city limits, scratching a living for themselves, carrying their books in their heads and keeping ideas alive. Old-fashioned, isolated from society, stubbornly resistant to change, these 'book custodians' share the normally negative attributes of the stereotypical librarian, irrespective of gender. Yet now such librarianly qualities denote heroism, perspicacity, and a strength of purpose which may in the end be the only things which make the survival of the human mind possible. These new walking libraries are also incarnations of agency.

Operating outside the constraints of social realism, Bradbury is able to present a positive, even heroic, sense of the librarian's mission which seems denied to any of the female librarians in the fictions discussed above. His male librarian's idealism is all the clearer, though, because unconstrained by the mundane. Yet it was precisely her 'unique eye and ear for the small poignancies and comedies of everyday life' which led Philip Larkin to champion the fiction of Barbara Pym.[47] A gentler, but nevertheless persistent, heroism surrounds Pym's female librarians in *An Unsuitable Attachment* (the novel she completed in 1962), who use their agency to stir things up and show that, in a world settling into new, disturbing post-war patterns, nothing can remain the same.[48] The old order has disappeared.

[45] Ray Bradbury, 'Bright Phoenix', *The Magazine of Fantasy and Science Fiction* (May 1963), 23–9. Written 1947; Ray Bradbury, *Fahrenheit 451* (1953).

[46] Bradbury, 'Bright Phoenix', 24.

[47] Philip Larkin, 'Reputations Revisited', *Times Literary Supplement*, 21 January 1977, 66.

[48] Barbara Pym, *An Unsuitable Attachment* (London: Grafton, 1982); written in 1962 but rejected by publishers until 1982.

The genteel area of London where librarian Ianthe Broome lives has become a cheerful mix of race and class. 'So many *black* people', says Lady Selvedge as she passes through it on her way to open a bazaar. 'And do I see *yams* on that stall?'[49] Ianthe marries library assistant John Challow, a man several years younger than her, inferior to her socially, and who horrifies her relatives by not even being a qualified librarian. Her former library colleague Miss Grimes makes another 'unsuitable attachment', shocking everyone by marrying in her retirement a Polish widower she meets in a pub, and sinisterly disappearing to live in Ealing. Heroines in their way, both librarians have bravely crossed social and cultural divides. Stylistically and generically, Pym's novel may seem conservative in its depiction of a society where everything is mixed up and changed. The prim Ianthe who has never before made tea at half past six 'like the "working classes"', now finds herself opening a tin of pork luncheon meat and cooking frozen peas 'like *Americans*'.[50] Worse, she can now brazenly submit to being kissed by John Challow outside a Tube station, and finds herself in the end thrilled to be married to a man whose librarianly alpha-maleness asserts itself in his ability to put up shelves in her kitchen. Pym's picture of the library at the anthropological institute where Rupert Stonebird works, turned upside down as its staff prepare for the afternoon's garden party, is the perfect image of a world in disarray:

> at a table, among the piles of learned journals that seemed appropriate to such a library, sat two elderly women hulling strawberries and arranging them in small dishes, counting aloud so that the portions were scrupulously equal. Cut loaves and pats of butter balanced on top of the journals, while African sculptures had been pushed aside to make room for plates of cakes. Bottles of milk stood on shelves half full of books and an urn appeared to be boiling furiously and spurting steam on some valuable-looking old bindings.[51]

'I suppose it's wrong to have preconceived ideas about people', says vicar's wife Sophia Ainger towards the end.[52] Working within the conventions of social-realist fiction, Pym certainly wants to dispel any preconceived ideas her readers may have about librarians, and has fun doing so. Strong enough to subvert the old order and get what they want, her librarians make things happen. Ianthe Broome, courted by both John Challow and her boss Mervyn Cantrell, as well as more tentatively by the wavering Rupert Stonebird, easily proves Sophia wrong in her belief that 'librarians aren't really very lovable sort of people'.[53] Librarians both, and pursued by metaphors of heterogeneity to the end, Ianthe and John are toasted in Entre-Deux-Mers wine at their wedding reception, and embark on

---

[49] Pym, *An Unsuitable Attachment*, 61. [50] Pym, *An Unsuitable Attachment*, 30, 197, 30.
[51] Pym, *An Unsuitable Attachment*, 209. [52] Pym, *An Unsuitable Attachment*, 247.
[53] Pym, *An Unsuitable Attachment*, 192.

married life 'encasseroled', as one guest puts it, in each other's arms, '– the bay leaf resting on the *boeuf bourguignon*'.[54] Minutely detailed, and entertaining through a pinpoint accuracy of phrasing, *An Unsuitable Attachment* is, in Larkin's phrase, a deft social comedy of 'middle-class post-war England', but it is also one in which the female as well as the male professional librarian is granted a sense of agency and satisfaction.

Alice Ellis in Jane Smiley's *Duplicate Keys* (1984) is another librarian learning to survive in a world which is messy and mixed up, although, unlike Ianthe Broome, she encounters elements of real danger in her learning experience.[55] A complex, assiduously plotted 'librarian as detective' story whose 'structural diversity' has been examined by Jane S. Bakerman, this novel works well as both a thriller and an 'innocence to experience' account of its librarian-heroine's growing up.[56] A librarian at New York Public Library, Alice enters her friend Susan's apartment one day to find Susan's husband, Denny, and their mutual friend Craig shot dead. Suspicion falls on the surprisingly large number of friends, acquaintances, and strangers who have duplicate keys to the flat. The novel follows the police investigation and describes Alice's journey through a series of mysterious events (including a terrifying night-time chase along the window ledges of her apartment building) to the realization that it is her best friend Susan who is the perpetrator. She acquires the agency of self-knowledge and a new, clear understanding of the world around her.

At the beginning Alice appears the quintessential librarian. She regards herself in the mirror: 'Yes, she looked neat and thin. And pinched, prim, without chic, entirely thirty-one and absolutely a librarian'.[57] She is innocent, untested by life, and (like Larkin's Katherine Lind) self-contained to a degree which keeps her profoundly 'apart' from others. Her former husband likens her to a house with 'a multitude of drawers and cupboards built into the walls like a card catalogue, and no surfaces for the reception of anything'.[58] The story shows her opening up, loosening the ties of her 'tight little life' to receive painful realizations about herself and others.[59]

Like so many stories about librarians, this novel too concerns itself with issues of class and, not least, with how social class relates to personal agency. Alice and her five friends from the Midwest have drifted to New York in the seventies, hoping in the classless, bohemian way of the time to make their fortunes in the music business. Though this dream has faded, the friends have appeared to stay close until the murder reveals that betrayals and infidelities have in fact been

---

[54] Pym, *An Unsuitable Attachment*, 251.
[55] Jane Smiley, *Duplicate Keys* (London: Jonathan Cape, 1984).
[56] Jane S. Bakerman, 'Renovating the House of Fiction: Structural Diversity in Jane Smiley's *Duplicate Keys*', *Midamerica*, 15 (1988): 111–20.
[57] Smiley, *Duplicate Keys*, 106.   [58] Smiley, *Duplicate Keys*, 181.
[59] Smiley, *Duplicate Keys*, 45.

causing the disintegration of the group for some time. Unknown to Alice, several of her friends have slipped into illicit love affairs and drug-related activities. As Inspector Honeyman explains, '...a violent crime is the beginning of a train of events, and a sign that whatever balance a given social network has achieved is strained. The crime is a change, and the change is always sudden and profound, affecting every member of the network in unforeseen ways and often violently.'[60] Alice has to confront the blasting apart of her social network, and adjust to a new reality. Their 'classlessness' has led, she realizes, to a kind of moral degeneracy which has eroded, rather than enhanced, personal agency. They would have been safer to have identified themselves with the certainties and values of the middle class. 'Unlike some of the others, Alice had never spoken contemptuously of the middle class. A job, an apartment, a washing machine, some money to spend, these were goods, not evils.'[61] Her friends, she sees, have fallen off the 'precipice' that is the middle class, but she will take care to hang securely on, keeping her work at the library a solid, remunerative, and respectable constant. 'Whatever the police did, or Ray's friends did, the library would go on, employing her to catalogue and do reference.'[62]

'A mighty fortress is our library', says Susan, evoking the connotations of religious safety and strength in the Martin Luther hymn as her friend returns to work there in the days after the murder.[63] Alice agrees, looking with pleasure at its sunlit façade and imposing lion statues. Yet this identification of the library with security can be problematic, Smiley suggests, and she uses some of the conventions of crime fiction to highlight this. It is not long before Alice finds the apparent safety the library offers compromised. The police come to question her on the library steps. She remembers an incident a year before when a reader had been stabbed, and a library colleague had wrestled the attacker to the reading room floor, holding him 'pinned in a pool of the victim's blood until the guards and a policeman could get there'.[64] Another member of staff, she recalls, had been shot at from a neighbouring building as she sat working at her desk on the fourth or fifth floor—'the bullet came through the window and went through her hair'.[65] Now, instead of finding safety in the labyrinth of book stacks, she finds them fearful and menacing, thinking she is being followed as she walks around them, glimpsing 'a flash of fabric, the heel of a shoe disappearing', listening for footsteps, inching terrified along the darkened aisles towards the elevator.[66] The library becomes a place of perilous risk, and Smiley hints that this may be bound up with threats to intellectual coherence. The very arrangement of the books is

[60] Smiley, *Duplicate Keys*, 221.   [61] Smiley, *Duplicate Keys*, 45.
[62] Smiley, *Duplicate Keys*, 45.
[63] Smiley, *Duplicate Keys*, 66; 'A Mighty Fortress is our God' (German: 'Ein feste Burg ist unser Gott'), by Martin Luther, *c.*1529.
[64] Smiley, *Duplicate Keys*, 90.   [65] Smiley, *Duplicate Keys*, 160.
[66] Smiley, *Duplicate Keys*, 159.

dangerously random, Alice realizes—three different cataloguing systems are in use, so that the works by a single author are scattered over seven floors, the oldest books simply shelved by size and date of acquisition rather than by subject or author. No longer a symbol of order and meaningful pattern, the library now denotes chaos, its books 'shelved in the wrong spots for years' or 'treated carelessly by clerks and librarians who were long gone'.[67] Published just a year after the first English translation of Umberto Eco's *The Name of the Rose*, Smiley's contemporary library detective story, like Eco's historical novel, plays with conceptions of coherence and incoherence made manifest in the arrangement of a library.

In the end Alice emerges to a new understanding of what the library means. Tired of 'living [her] life like a librarian', of behaving 'in that pale librarianly way', she adjusts at last to the idea that the best friend she has loved is a murderer, that others she thought she knew well have had subterranean lives she knew nothing about.[68] There can ultimately be no escape from danger, she realizes, in either libraries or life itself. Jeopardy lurks on the edges of even the safest existence. Travelling to the Rikers Island jail to meet her friend Noah, who is being released, she sees that 'the neighborhood [is] middle class, nearly up to the bridge'.[69] We leave her in the final pages, released by this new understanding from her 'tight little life', walking in the Botanic Gardens, and kissing her new botanist friend Henry 'lightly on the cheek'.[70] An early conversation has established that both are cataloguers.

> '...Did you catalogue all day?'
> 'How did you know?'
> 'It was Monday. I catalogued today, too.'
> 'I do little poetry magazines.'
> 'I do plants from mainland China.'[71]

After the cataclysmic upheavals of the plot, the novel ends softly and life-affirmingly with the peaceful conjunction of two cataloguers. The poetry and plants they organize may offer a new and gentler order. Ultimately in *Duplicate Keys*, neither Alice nor Henry is required to compromise their individual professional agency.

By the 1990s female novelists may have grown less concerned to foreground the need for agency of female librarians, but issues of agency are still discernible in their treatment of libraries and those who staff them. In A. S. Byatt's *Possession* (1990), the most library-imbued novel of the twentieth century's last decade, the unnamed male librarian has the agency of being the framer and facilitator of all

---

[67] Smiley, *Duplicate Keys*, 158.
[68] Smiley, *Duplicate Keys*, 207, 212.
[69] Smiley, *Duplicate Keys*, 294.
[70] Smiley, *Duplicate Keys*, 306.
[71] Smiley, *Duplicate Keys*, 76.

the ensuing action.[72] Appearing only in the novel's first paragraph, he removes from the safe, dusts, and hands to Roland Michell the copy of Vico's *Principi di Scienza Nuova* which has belonged to Henry Randolph Ash, and in which Roland is about to find two drafts of an unknown, field-changing letter from Ash to Christabel LaMotte. He observes that the 'book-bills and letters' interleaved with the book's pages do not seem to have been touched before, tiptoes to the phone to obtain his superior's permission for the material to be used, and returns to say that 'The Librarian would be glad to know of any important discoveries Mr Michell might make'.[73] His role thereafter is simply to stand by in blissful ignorance as Roland slips the pages into his Oxford Selected Ash and takes them out of the library. 'When he left, with his green and tomato boxes heaped on his Selected Ash, they nodded affably from behind the issue desk. They were used to him. There were notices about mutilation of volumes, about theft, with which he quite failed to associate himself.'[74]

Inspired by Eco's *The Name of the Rose* and by the Margery Allingham detective mysteries Byatt read in her youth, *Possession* escalates from these modest moments of librarianly involvement into an extravagantly detailed literary quest which follows scholars Roland Michell and Maud Bailey as they try to uncover a possible love affair between Victorian poet Henry Randolph Ash and Christina Rossetti-like writer Christabel LaMotte. A tale about 'possession' in several senses, it asks many complex questions about who owns what. Some are enquiries familiar to professional librarians: who owns the documents the scholars pursue? Who owns the copyright? Other questions have more wide-ranging repercussions. Are those who study the documents 'possessed' by the subjects who wrote them? Do the scholars 'possess' the people they study? Do the various lovers in some way 'possess' one another?

Byatt's novel may indeed have something quietly humorous to say about the very slightness and marginality of the librarian's role. We are amused by the ease with which the letters are removed from the library's possession, by the passivity of the duped library staff, and by the failure of the librarian's duty of care. As in Smiley's *Duplicate Keys*, here is a library which is *not* a safe place, where security is breached, and a dusty nineteenth-century letter is suddenly released dangerously into the modern world to be fought over in a series of tense, scholarly battles. Ironically, we realize, this failure of librarianly care has actually facilitated the research. The gloriously complex literary quest only blossoms *because* Roland sneaks the letters out beneath the librarian's nose and exposes them to further investigation. Freeing them from the deadening clutch of the librarian (they are 'exhumed from Locked Safe no.5') has been crucial.[75] As Jane Smiley's librarian also discovered, libraries can sometimes be too safe to be healthy.

---

[72] A. S. Byatt, *Possession* (London: Chatto & Windus, 1990).   [73] Byatt, *Possession*, 5.
[74] Byatt, *Possession*, 11.   [75] Byatt, *Possession*, 3.

Like Smiley's novel, Byatt's postmodern narrative of scholarly detection and intrigue partakes of some aspects of crime fiction, that twentieth-century genre most famous for its fascination with bodies in libraries. Apparently infinitely adaptable, with its essential focus on the motivation of actions, crime fiction may be the genre that, more than any other, offers scope for the investigation of agency, whether in the complex literary fictions of Byatt and Eco or in more straightforwardly conventional middlebrow articulations. Though she operates much more traditionally in the popular crime fiction genre, at least in her sense of zest and fun, the contemporary American author Jo Dereske continues the excited engagement of Byatt's exploration of the library world. However, in *Miss Zukas and the Library Murders* (1994), Dereske, instead of focussing on academic researchers, places her librarian firmly in the foreground of the action. For all that she has taught in the University of Washington's Creative Writing pro-gramme and discussed crime fiction at the Library of Congress, Dereske unashamedly packages her product as simple 'light reading'.[76] As the twenty-first-century *Library Journal* puts it, extolling *Miss Zukas and the Library Murders*, 'no biblio-mystery collection is complete without a tale of an indefatig-able librarian-turned-sleuth'.[77]

Plucky, OCD-ish, 36-year-old assistant librarian Helma Zukas is a woman feistily aware of her own hard-won and effective sense of agency, and in this first of twelve light-hearted 'Miss Zukas' novels Dereske raises the bar for the popular 'librarian as detective' genre. Neat, calm, hypernaturally attentive to detail, Helma teams up with her harum-scarum artist friend Ruth to unravel the clues and find who is responsible for the decidedly untidy body in her library. A double murderer, kidnapper, and dealer in dodgy art, her boss, nasty Albert Upman, director of Washington State's Bellevue Public Library, turns out to be a librarian guilty of distinctly greater failures of library care than the hapless librarian of *Possession*. Worse, he does not even have a *bona fide* library qualification.

The delicious oddness of Helma's quirks make this novel sing. We enjoy knowing that she hangs her clothes by category and colour: '...first her short-sleeved blouses, beginning with a white sleeveless top and ending with a navy blue silk, then her long-sleeved blouses and turtlenecks, followed by skirts, pants and dresses'; that she favours coordinated clothing—'...the blue of her skirt exactly mirrored the tail feathers of the Brazilian enameled bird pin on her burgundy sweater'; that she wears a hairnet in bed, manicures her fingernails and toenails on bath days and squeegees her ears with Q-tips on shower days; that she washes her dishes by hand in Ivory dish soap; that she dislikes using elevators, knows the

---

[76] Jo Dereske, *Miss Zukas and the Library Murders* (New York: Avon Books, 1994); Dereske is one of a panel of writers who contributed to the Judith Austin Memorial Lecture at the Library of Congress, 24 April 2006: https://www.loc.gov/item/webcast-3888/.

[77] Nancy Pearl, 'Murder by the Book: Biblio-Mysteries', *Library Journal*, 1 September 2004: 207.

exact number of milligrams of caffeine in a cup of tea or coffee, specifies a box, not a bag, for the transport of her single Sunday croissant, places a tissue over the receiver of a public payphone before speaking, and declines grapes because she does not eat purple food.[78]

A former librarian herself, Dereske is clearly having fun with the librarian stereotype, and uses her experience of the profession to enrich the detail of the plot—it is an inconsistency in the library director's stock-weeding process which triggers the countdown to the first murder. While creating the stereotype, however, Dereske playfully subverts it, allowing Helma to break free from the librarianly mould and escape into distinctly unlibrarianly adventures. She deciphers the code on a scrap of paper left inside a book the murder victim was using, deals with an intruder in her apartment, rescues her friend in the middle of the night from a rendezvous with a man who is later found dead in the boot of a car, is drugged and kidnapped at sea, escapes from a locked room, and finally extricates herself and Ruth from the clutches of the deranged, gun-wielding Mr Upman. Her prize is the admiration and growing affection of the handsome police chief Wayne Gallant who comes to the rescue, the nominative determinism of his name one of the book's many quiet jokes.

In 1994, Miss Helma Zukas is a librarian who can stand up for herself. Treasuring her own sense of agency, she declines to be patronised. 'I hope you don't feel deductive reasoning skills are restricted to the police', she tells Chief Gallant crisply.[79] Clearly the deductive reasoning skills of a professional librarian are just as good. She takes exception to being likened to a male detective. Called 'a regular Sherlock Holmes' by the sneering Mr Upman, she responds coolly, 'There are numerous female sleuths you could compare me to. It's not necessary to always refer to men.'[80] At last, in this final decade of the twentieth century, Jo Dereske offers us a female librarian who knows that she is the equal of any male member of the profession:

> Sometimes Helma suspected that Mr Upman owed his library job to being a man. In a field dominated by women, a disproportionate number of library directors were men. 'Library boards prefer male directors,' she remembered Miss McKinney saying in library school, as if the female students might as well absorb that little fact right along with the Dewey decimal system and the Anglo-American Cataloguing Rules.[81]

Where in 1909 the Wide Awake Girls in Winsted submissively *placed* a man in a library post, Helma Zukas in 1994 has had the agency and intelligence to *remove* an undeserving man from his.

---

[78] Dereske, *Miss Zukas and the Library Murders*, 71, 7.
[79] Dereske, *Miss Zukas and the Library Murders*, 87.
[80] Dereske, *Miss Zukas and the Library Murders*, 197.
[81] Dereske, *Miss Zukas and the Library Murders*, 25.

10

The Act of Borrowing; or, Some Libraries in American Literature

Kristen Treen

As he pieced together his *Autobiography* over the latter half of the eighteenth century, Benjamin Franklin revealed that the story of his life, like that of the nation he had helped to found, was a story of reading. Like the haphazard composition of his memoirs—interrupted intermittently by diplomatic assignments, the upheaval of revolutionary war, and the momentous project of American Independence—the readerly habits of Franklin's youth were far from orthodox. He enjoyed neither the leisurely perusal of the aristocrat nor the methodical researches of the man of letters. Scholars have generally plumbed Franklin's reading material to gauge his peculiarly American politics of self-invention.[1] But they tend to overlook the fact that this Founding Father was an inveterate borrower of books, and proud of it. The *Autobiography*'s account of the first quarter of Franklin's life suggests that the precariousness of his borrowing habits was as important to his formative development as the content of the books that came into his hands.

A hint of pride can be detected, for instance, in the opening tale of his English Protestant forebears, forced by a climate of religious persecution under Queen Mary to secure their English Bible to the underside of a joint-stool, snatching illicit moments of worship as and when they could:

> When my Great Great Grandfather read in it to his Family, he turn'd up the Joint Stool upon his Knees, turning over the Leaves then under the Tapes. One of the Children stood at the Door to give Notice if he saw the Apparitor coming, who was an Officer of the Spiritual Court. In that Case the Stool was turn'd down again upon its feet, when the Bible remain'd conceal'd under it as before.[2]

---

[1] See, for example, Alan Craig Houston, *Benjamin Franklin and the Politics of Improvement* (New Haven, CT: Yale University Press, 2008), 1–21; Michael Warner, *The Letters of the Republic: Publication and the Public Sphere in Eighteenth-Century America* (Cambridge, MA: Harvard University Press, 1990), 74–96.

[2] Benjamin Franklin, *Benjamin Franklin's Autobiography*, ed. Joyce E. Chaplin (New York; London: W.W. Norton, 2012), 12–13.

Franklin's own illicit moments of reading were not quite as hazardous, but they were just as hasty and twice as daring. For as Franklin acquired books piecemeal, his mode of reading prompted him to try new and unusual ways of living. Where his ancestors were forced to suppress their beliefs, Franklin experimented overtly with acts of self-invention. This picking and choosing led him to defy the patriarchal rule of his father's library: he denounced shelves of devout religious tracts in favour of a secular approach to morality. 'My Father's little Library consisted chiefly of Books in polemic Divinity,' Franklin complained, 'most of which I read, and have since often regretted, that at a time when I had such a Thirst for Knowledge, more proper Books had not fallen in my Way.'[3] There were plenty to come. Cutting ties with his homeland, Franklin replaced his childhood edition of *The Pilgrim's Progress* with Burton's Historical Collections, before consuming a series of texts that changed his beliefs with each passing page. He 'meets' a book by Thomas Tryon which inspires him to take up a vegetable diet; Daniel Defoe's 'Essay on Projects' instils an obsession with invention; and a stray issue of *The Spectator* teaches him composition—after writing out its passages verbatim, Franklin revels in a new-found power to refine his own output into its 'best Order'.[4] He ditches Sunday worship for a course of literary instruction.

Franklin's bookishness is the source of his self-improvement, but the indiscriminate nature of his borrowing is undoubtedly pragmatic. Young Ben never simply imitates, or does what he's told: the secular ethics born of reading indiscriminately prompt him to adapt exempla to what he finds humanly possible. Moreover, the passage of other people's books through his hands contributes a materialist element to what, by now, we might recognize as Franklin's distinctly American moral philosophy. Apprenticed at his brother's printing shop, 'I now had Access to better Books,' Franklin writes: 'An Acquaintance with the Apprentices of Booksellers enabled me sometimes to borrow a small one, which I was careful to return soon and clean.'[5] As a reader of books yet to be sold, Franklin proves himself a responsible borrower who respects systems of commercial circulation; tellingly, he also sees the potential in working a collectively beneficial endeavour from the pristine page of private property.

Franklin's account of his readerly credentials makes it seem inevitable he should have founded one of the North American colonies' first Library Companies. This social venture took off when the members of his club, all artisan craftsmen, decided to pool their books into a 'common Library'.[6] Inviting the people of Philadelphia to take out subscriptions, and founding 'the Mother of all the North American Subscription Libraries', Franklin presented fellow colonists with the tools for their self-improvement, and looked on as his secular philosophy spread. 'These Libraries have improv'd the general Conversation of the

---

[3] Franklin, *Autobiography*, 17.   [4] Franklin, *Autobiography*, 17–20.
[5] Franklin, *Autobiography*, 18.   [6] Franklin, *Autobiography*, 67.

Americans,' he wrote, 'made the common Tradesmen and Farmers as intelligent as most Gentlemen from other Countries, and perhaps have contributed in some degree to the Stand so generally made throughout the Colonies in Defence of their Privileges.'[7] According to this Founding Father's interpretation of the nation's origins, America was read into existence by an expanding community of curious borrowers and the labours of diligent readers.

Franklin's subversive acts of borrowing provide my starting point for a more sustained consideration of this activity as performed by figures occupying the institutional libraries of American literature (and I emphasize institutions here, as opposed to explicitly commercial circulating libraries which were often run out of bookstores and small businesses).[8] Taking an interest in acts of borrowing, rather than the mechanisms of lending that dominate histories of United States library development, complicates the notion of the American library as a democratic institution. During the nineteenth and early twentieth centuries, writers and artists critiqued the limits of America's changing democratic practices through the borrower's evolving art, and this figure's imaginative uses, manipulations, and circumventions of the library's various systems of organization. Many of the borrowers in the reading rooms of America's literary libraries—social, domestic, reference, and free—were members of the entitled white upper classes: male readers and writers privileged enough to procure their own collections and access the hallowed halls of learning, and in many cases prominent enough to influence those institutions' long-term development. What these literary and often liberal voices draw attention to, however, alongside the voices of the women, African Americans, and working-class labourers who manage to penetrate the walls of public and private collections, are the contradictions which came to characterize the conception of the 'American library' by the beginning of the twentieth century. While libraries should—Franklin hoped—embody and engender the democratic practices of the young Republic, the new rhetoric of lending which accompanied the rise of taxation-funded 'free' libraries from the mid-nineteenth century onwards revealed a darker side to the ostensible utopianism of this public-facing project.

It wasn't that the ideal of the library as democratic site ever disappeared from view. Rather, the evolving relationship of libraries to their borrowers reflected the shifts 'democracy' underwent during this period as the conception of liberal individualism changed, often at the hands of the genteel classes who oversaw American libraries. At the dedication of the Boston Public Library's new McKim Building in 1888, popular poet Oliver Wendell Holmes, Sr., had marked the

---

[7] Franklin, *Autobiography*, 66–7.
[8] Haynes McMullen, *American Libraries Before 1876* (Westport, CT, and London: Greenwood Press, 2000), 138.

imminent expansion of the country's first free, state-funded municipal library as the dawning of a new era in the dissemination of knowledge:

> Let in the light! in diamond mines
> Their gems invite the hand that delves;
> So learning's treasured jewels shine
> Ranged on the alcove's ordered shelves...
>
> Behind the ever open gate
> No pikes shall fence a crumbling throne,
> No lackeys cringe, no courtiers wait, —
> This palace is the people's own![9]

Holmes imagines an institution where unfettered freedom of access to 'learning's treasured jewels' reflects this library's equal dedication to serving individuals across society's wide spectrum. His version of the Boston Public Library matches the borrower's mobility amongst 'the alcove's ordered shelves' with the social mobility, the promise of classlessness ('no lackeys cringe, no courtiers wait') that comes to those who read. Yet as the end of the century drew near, it became abundantly clear that the liberty offered patrons by the Boston Public Library's fellow institutions came with a caveat. Contemplation of open shelf policies across regional branches in the 1890s raised the same anxieties expressed by concerned progressives at the founding of the American Library Association in 1876. Amid the ongoing upheaval of economic disparity, workers' protests, racial violence, political corruption, and social schism, came a call for mass education within reason, the carefully controlled democratization of knowledge to be overseen by reformers amongst the cultural elite.

As libraries became monuments to a new reform movement, reading habits of the individual borrower, intent on self-improvement, were displaced by librarians' theories of responsible lending.[10] New organization technologies, free reading rooms, and limited borrowing rights would transform the self-made man into the dutiful American citizen. Careful librarianship, as sociologist Charles Zueblin observed in 1902, would educate the masses and determine the kinds of books that would pass into borrowers' hands. 'The tendency in public libraries to-day', he wrote, 'is to make all the books in the branch libraries accessible to the public, but

---

[9] Oliver Wendell Holmes, Sr., 'For the Dedication of the New City Library, Boston', in *The Writings of Oliver Wendell Holmes*, 13 vols (Boston, MA, and New York: Houghton Mifflin, 1891), XIII, 181–2, (ll. 17–32).

[10] On elite utopianism and social upheaval during the 1880s and 1890s, see, for example, Alan Trachtenberg, *The Incorporation of America: Culture and Society in the Gilded Age* (New York: Hill & Wang, 1982; repr. 2007); in relation to libraries, more particularly, see Thomas Augst, 'Faith in Reading: Public Libraries, Liberalism, and the Civil Religion', in *Institutions of Reading: The Social Life of Libraries in the United States*, ed. Thomas Augst and Kenneth Carpenter (Amherst, MA, and Boston, MA: University of Massachusetts Press, 2007), 148–83.

to limit access in the main library to the open shelves. This is done not only for the protection of the books, but for the protection of the readers. It is undesirable to limit people to a card catalogue which is generally a hopeless mystery, but it may be just as bewildering to give them access to an unlimited number of books.' Nevertheless, Zueblin warned, '[t]he public must have impartial service, even if limitations have to be put upon the borrowing of books by the people'.[11] The writers I mention below were well aware of the limitations besetting the 'borrowing of books by the people'. These writers were ready to critique each new iteration of the American library and the influences exerted over patrons. What's more, their imaginative engagements with what they variously found to be exclusive, dusty, backward-looking institutions reflect on the navigational skills, structural manipulations, and deviant reading practices necessary to attaining a true liberty of access to knowledge—or imagining it into being within the pages of the literary text.

Franklin's borrowing habits had challenged the influence of British authority over the emerging American subject. With every new book had come the possibility of performance, experimentation with new identities that undercut moral absolutism and replaced English demands for colonial loyalty, based on obedient imitation, with an American identity shaped by individual invention and the labours of trial and error. Franklin's juvenile borrowings, like the careful framing of his *Autobiography*, posed a challenge to the English canon, and he fully believed that the kinds of private thinking and collective debate promoted by the Library Company of Philadelphia had done the same. By the dawn of the nineteenth century, however, the question of British influences over the new Republic's literary output had become a cause for concern, and some authors found themselves worrying over the state of American literature within the library's looming precincts.

This shouldn't be surprising if we acknowledge the composition of some early collections. As scholars of colonial subscription libraries have demonstrated, librarians throughout the late eighteenth and early nineteenth centuries had relied heavily on imports of British and European texts as they scrambled to expand their permanent collections. In pursuing what Michael Baenen describes as 'high cultural aspirations' synonymous with the founding of institutional libraries in early nineteenth-century America, librarians were also wont to spend windfalls and bequests on 'serious books of enduring worth'. For various New England institutions, Baenen argues, this meant ensuring a good supply of tomes by standard authors, '[keeping] up with the progress of British scholarship', and purchasing valuable antiquarian titles available on the British and American

---

[11] Charles Zueblin, *American Municipal Progress* (New York: Macmillan, 1902; repr. 1916), 230–1.

markets.[12] Even as the printing of specifically American texts began in presses of the kind where Franklin started out, the ambitious social elite who oversaw early libraries' funding looked across the Atlantic for works they felt would rouse contemporary readers to what Emerson later called 'high intellectual action'. Early American libraries were saturated with British product.

While American writers acknowledged the necessity of engaging with a longer British and European tradition, which might educate Americans in what Emerson helpfully termed the 'best thoughts and facts', the institutionalization of the British canon within library walls led to uneasy questions about the nature and purpose of American literary output.[13] For some American writers, this made the institutional library the ideal metaphor with which to reimagine their transatlantic relationship with British literary authority, and to explore the kinds of borrowing necessary to stake America's claim to a serious literary heritage. For Emerson, writing in the late 1840s, the cultural value of the classical British and European traditions was clear: "Tis ... an economy of time to read old and famed books,' he wrote in 'Society and Solitude' (published 1870); '[n]othing can be preserved which is not good; and I know before-hand that Pindar, Martial, Terence, Galen, Kepler, Galileo, Bacon, Erasmus, More, will be superior to the average intellect. In contemporaries, it is not so easy to distinguish betwixt notoriety and fame.'[14]

As Emerson pointedly claimed, though, serious engagement with these authors was *not* to be found in the library, or facilitated by systems of organization designed to expand one's readerly horizons. 'I visit occasionally the Cambridge Library, and I can seldom go there without renewing the conviction that the best of it all is already within the four walls of my study at home. The inspection of the catalogue brings me continually back to the few standard writers who are on every private shelf... The crowds and centuries of books are only commentary and elucidation, echoes and weakeners of these few great voices of time.'[15] If his claim seems short-sighted to modern readers, it also plays strategically into the philosophy of self-reliance with which Emerson had begun to explore the dimensions of American individualism. In shunning the clamour of polite society—manifested, in this case, in the library's crude commotion of 'commentary and elucidation'— for the solitude of his own private collection, the man of self-reliance might participate in a mode of reading at once valuable to his own 'nature', and, by

[12] Michael A. Baenen, 'A Great and Natural Enemy of Democracy? Politics and Culture in the Antebellum Portsmouth Athenæum', in *Institutions of Reading*, 92–3. On eighteenth-century American book imports, see also Kyle B. Roberts and Mark Towsey, eds., *Before the Public Library: Reading, Community, and Identity in the Atlantic World* (Leiden and Boston, MA: Brill, 2008); James Raven, *London Booksellers and American Customers: Transatlantic Literary Community and the Charleston Library Society, 1748–1811* (Columbia, SC: University of South Carolina Press, 2002).
[13] Ralph Waldo Emerson, *The Complete Works of Ralph Waldo Emerson: Society and Solitude*, ed. Edward Waldo Emerson, 12 vols (Boston, MA, and New York: Houghton Mifflin, 1904), VII, 197.
[14] Emerson, *Complete Works*, 196.   [15] Emerson, *Complete Works*, 194–5.

following his internal logic, valuable to humankind more broadly. 'The best rule of reading', Emerson declared,

> will be a method from Nature, and not a mechanical one of hours and pages. It holds each student to a pursuit of his native aim, instead of a desultory miscellany. Let him read what is proper to him, and not waste his memory on a crowd of mediocrities. As whole nations have derived their culture from a single book, — ... so, perhaps, the human mind would be a gainer if all the secondary writers were lost, — say, in England, all but Shakespeare, Milton, and Bacon ... With the pilot of his own genius, let the student read one, or let him read many, he will read advantageously.[16]

In replacing the library catalogue with 'native aim', Emerson sacrifices popular preference and taxonomic order for individual intuition, which doubles as cultural, or indeed *national*, discernment. The source of that elision can be found in Emerson's notion of the 'native aim' and its close affiliation with 'Nature': the influence of an individual's surroundings upon the sensibility is a worthier guide than the jostle of the library catalogue, and leads, Emerson implies, to a form of assimilation befitting the character of their national scene. Library patronage is not conducive to the qualities of self-reliance that Emerson believes central to the American psyche. Indeed, in circumventing the library—that structure so iconically associated with the rise of the classical civilizations he references—Emerson leaves the individual's 'native' powers of assimilation free to discern which 'single book' this new Republic might derive its culture from. His model of reading suggests his own collected *Essays* might be just the book for the job.

Like Franklin's nose for a borrowing opportunity, Emerson's notion of an inherent, environmentally dependent genius taps into the Scottish common sense philosophy of the association of ideas, which had shaped transatlantic debates about the nature of cognitive order and individual taste during the eighteenth and early nineteenth centuries.[17] Proposing that one idea followed another through one's train of thought according to a principle of relation—or 'sympathy'—between them, this philosophy argued that such relations were formed by an individual's past experiences; thus ideas and observable phenomena stimulated sequences of thought and sensation in the subject. Empirical experience, that is, structured memory itself along the lines of a natural sequential order guaranteeing the relevance of each thought's place within memory's organized whole. For philosophers from David Hume to Archibald Alison, the order one's empirical experiences impressed upon the mind also helped explain the origins of

---

[16] Emerson, *Complete Works*, 195.
[17] William Charvat, *The Origins of American Critical Thought, 1810–1835* (Philadelphia: University of Pennsylvania Press, 1936).

taste and, more particularly, the psychological workings of collective taste.[18] This theory proved central to intellectual debates about the unique nature of American taste for the first three or more decades of the nineteenth century. In the present context, and bearing Emerson's comments in mind, the library's taxonomic organizational structure might readily be aligned with the mind's orderly edifice, its thoughts catalogued according to principles of 'natural' connectivity—those sympathies, coincidences, associations which serve to connect our ideas during the course of our lived experience. Tellingly, American writers of this period consciously used moments of readerly digression and imaginative transgression to figure the workings of an American sensibility confronted with a largely British literary inheritance. The workings of the American mind, they appear to suggest, deviate from established Old World models of organization and taste.

Perhaps the most overt of these transgressive moments takes place in Washington Irving's *The Sketch-Book of Geoffrey Crayon, Gent.* (1819). Having crossed the Atlantic with an antiquarian's craving for the tangible stuff of British literary culture (Shakespeare's local tavern, the last literary remains of King James I of Scotland), Irving's narrator finds himself in the British Library's reading room, in a scene which 'reminded me of an old Arabian tale, of a philosopher shut up in an enchanted library, in the bosom of a mountain, which opened only once a year'. The exotic air of enchantment soon dissipates, however, as the American observer catches Britain's eminent 'book-makers' 'in the very act of manufacturing books'. The treasures of the English literary tradition become the scraps upon which contemporary authors feed: 'I was, in fact, in the reading-room of the great British Library,' Crayon notes in disbelief, 'an immense collection of volumes of all ages and languages, many of which are now forgotten, and most of which are seldom read: one of these sequestered pools of obsolete literature to which modern authors repair, and draw buckets full of classic lore, or "pure English, undefiled", wherewith to swell their own scanty rills of thought.'[19] Even in enshrining the gems of the English literary canon, Irving observes, the most impressive libraries advance their imperial programmes of preservation to the detriment of literary creation past and present: in the shadow of the library, literary integrity is sure to decay.

Of course, Crayon conducts many borrowings himself in the course of his critique, even though, as a non-member, he isn't permitted to call books up from the British Library's collection. Yet his sketch deploys quotations from sources including Shakespeare, Spenser, and the King James Bible. The conditions of his commentary, however, distinguish his literary gleanings from those of the scholars

---

[18] On the uses of the association of ideas in eighteenth- and early nineteenth-century literature and philosophy see Teresa Barnett, *Sacred Relics: Pieces of the Past in Nineteenth-Century America* (Chicago, IL: University of Chicago Press, 2013).

[19] Washington Irving, *The Sketch-Book of Geoffrey Crayon, Gent.*, ed. Susan Manning (Oxford: Oxford University Press, 2009), 70.

around him because Crayon happens to fall asleep in the midst of this fraudulent bustle. His dream transforms the solemn scene of polite pilfering into a burlesque portrait of scavenging where would-be authors clothe themselves in ill-fitting costumes of literary yesteryears, exposing themselves for the 'vulgar' thieves they are: 'no one pretended to clothe himself from any particular suit,' he observes, 'but took a sleeve from one, a cape from another, a skirt from a third, thus decking himself out piecemeal, while some of his original rags would peep out from among his borrowed finery.'[20] Crayon's dream becomes more fantastical as the portraits of offended authors lining the reading room's walls come to life and wreak revenge on the poorly dressed pilferers below.

At its simplest, Crayon's dream deepens Irving's criticism of an increasingly lazy British literary tradition, dependent on stealing rather than thoughtful allusion or imaginative invention.[21] This is an indictment, too, of the musty, exclusive antiquarian libraries, which, in venerating ancient texts, establish a culture of writing dependent solely on an overbearing sense of tradition that can only result in shoddy work and a nostalgic readership. As he falls asleep, though, Crayon enters into a reverie in which allusion and the American inheritance of English tradition produce a very different sort of literary engagement. Against the calculated plagiarisms of the English writers, this American's wandering mind ambles beyond the systems of catalogue and collection to create a fiction of the library that animates tradition to disrupt stagnant modes of literary production. As Crayon's fancy puts paid to English claims of literary heft and authenticity (Spenser's 'pure English, undefiled'), his allusion-heavy account of the dream exemplifies a creative submergence in literary tradition which champions the rich polyvocality of the transatlantic text.

There's a playful irreverence to this Yank's nap amongst the stacks too, which Irving emphasizes as Crayon awakens with an 'immoderate fit of laughter'. 'Nothing of the dream had been real', Crayon writes, 'but my burst of laughter, a sound never before heard in that grave sanctuary, and so abhorrent to the ears of wisdom, as to electrify the fraternity.'[22] Crayon is swiftly ejected by a stern librarian, who grows sterner still on learning that this interloper has no library card. But the laughter resounds at the end of the sketch: the only 'real' part of this fiction, Crayon's laughter into the library's sacred silence, is transgressive, spontaneous, vitally alive. Reminiscent of Franklin's haphazard readings, for all its fun, it seems an apt precursor to the 'native' genius that 'pilots' Emerson's American reader. Crayon's laugh, though, is a little more certain about ways in which the liberal, democratic subject might navigate the library's historical hulk. Breaking

[20] Irving, *Sketch-Book*, 72.
[21] For an extended reading of this scene, see Richard V. McLamore, 'The Dutchman in the Attic: Claiming an Inheritance in *The Sketch-Book of Geoffrey Crayon*', *American Literature* 72.1 (March 2000): 31–57.
[22] Irving, *Sketch-Book*, 74.

the most famous of the library's rules, Crayon's laugh represents the American borrower's pragmatic challenge to the mouldering and exclusive institution of English letters.

The American borrower's pragmatism was to take many shapes as the nineteenth century progressed, but it is important to reiterate the dangers that readers and writer alike associated with the library's potential miscellaneousness. Another unflattering iteration of this institution's acolytes occurs at the outset of Herman Melville's *Moby-Dick* (1851), in the form of the 'painstaking burrower and grubworm of a poor devil of a Sub-Sub' Librarian, whose toils result in Melville's encyclopaedic gesture towards the nature of the 'Leviathan'.[23] A burrower rather than borrower—and example of the library's potentially overwhelming effects—the reviled Sub-Sub would appear to exemplify bookwormery at its lowest: sent into the world to gather word of the whale, this unpractised junior-junior librarian 'appears to have gone through the long Vaticans and street-stalls of the earth, picking up whatever random allusions to whales he could anyways find in any book whatsoever, sacred or profane'. The resulting list of 'higgledy-piggledy whale statements' cannot, Melville warns us, be taken for 'veritable gospel cetology'.[24] Providing only 'a glancing, bird's eye view of what has been promiscuously said, thought, fancied, and sung of Leviathan, by many nations and generations, including our own', the Sub-Sub's intellectual toil amounts not to a transcendent notion of the *essence* of the whale but what Peter Riley has called 'the most superficial or manual of literary beginnings'; 'the "authentic" mindful work' of capturing the whale, he suggests, 'starts . . . with the work of the author'.[25]

While Riley has explored the sense of endearment that the narrator appears to feel for this abject figure, the Sub-Sub's miscellaneous approach remains at issue.[26] His global roving might remind us of canny Geoffrey Crayon, but there's something about his method—or lack of it—that doesn't quite gel. This librarian's randomness—like the promiscuity of thought which emerges from an international gathering of texts—neither a whale nor an author makes. Ishmael's knowing greeting, as Riley observes, signals the appearance of an imperturbable authorial presence, our guide through the 'Vaticans and street-stalls of the earth.' By implication the 'hopeless, sallow' Sub-Sub is reduced by his efforts; rendered indistinct by his wanderings, he is not so much a selective, order-imposing subject as a menial spread thin and diminished *by* his allotted subject.

The Sub-Sub would certainly have offended Emerson's sensibilities: for Emerson the best of American readers will follow 'a method from Nature, not a mechanical one of hours and pages'.[27] But if the digressive American reader

[23] Herman Melville, *Moby-Dick; or, The Whale* (New York; London: Harper Brothers, 1851), x.
[24] Melville, *Moby-Dick*, x.
[25] Melville, *Moby-Dick*; Peter Riley, *Against Vocation: Whitman, Melville, Crane, and the Labors of American Poetry* (Oxford: Oxford University Press, 2019), 82.
[26] Riley, *Against Vocation*, 83.   [27] Emerson, *Complete Works*, 97–8.

were to be guided by the 'pilot of his own genius', and *not* fall prey to miscellaneousness—the forms of thoughtless hawking that Irving stumbled upon in the British Museum's reading room—what shape would intelligent borrowing take?[28] What sort of organizational structures might support it? Emerson provides room to range, for all his prescriptiveness, by outlining 'three practical rules' for navigating a market ever growing ('1. Never read any book that is not a year old. 2. Never read any but famed books. 3. Never read any but what you like').[29] His more oblique evocations of the 'wise ear of Time' and 'winnow [ing] winds of opinion' which lead to endorsement, reprinting, and preservation are the self-reliant reader's way of acknowledging society's collective part in distinguishing works of value, those books which contain 'the best thoughts and facts'.[30] If 'Nature is much our friend in this matter', then nature, here, constitutes a collective genius of the ages, and 'native navigation' the sense to seek the kind of knowledge not found 'in the street and the train'.[31] If the shelves of Cambridge Library seem only to amplify the motley clamourings of the mid-century publishing scene, Emerson would remind us that the American's native aims, however collective in their composition, are best pursued beyond the distractions of the contemporary public sphere, affirmed and reaffirmed by the careful cumulation of 'every private shelf'. The frugal solitude of the home library is where discerning readers are born and raised.[32]

The reality of collecting and borrowing from domestic libraries was a much more sociable affair than Emerson admitted—and, for the literate classes in antebellum America, it would have been the most common route to reading in the decades before public libraries came to prominence. As Ronald and Mary Zboray have observed, since 'the tax-supported public library was nearly non-existent, social and circulating libraries relatively rare, and Sunday school libraries exceedingly limited [in the antebellum US], book borrowers had to depend upon holdings of family members, friends, and neighbors as much if not more than those of institutions'.[33] That the way to a well-stocked library was wealth didn't necessarily inhibit voracious readers of limited means. In fact, the selectivity that, as the Zborays have found, characterized the book-buying habits of a range of New Englanders between 1830 and 1861 would enable concurrent modes of individual improvement and communal circulation—bibliophilic habits which spoke to varying ruminations on liberal individualism that emerged at mid-century. The habits of borrowers from personal libraries resulted in literary meditations on intersubjective encounters with the minds and thoughts of library keepers, familiar reading fellows, and, very occasionally, the unknown strangers

---

[28] Emerson, *Complete Works*, 98.   [29] Emerson, *Complete Works*, 99.
[30] Emerson, *Complete Works*, 98–9.   [31] Emerson, *Complete Works*, 98–9.
[32] Emerson, *Complete Works*, 97.
[33] Ronald. J. Zboray and Mary Saracino Zboray, 'Home Libraries and the Institutionalization of Everyday Practices Among Antebellum New Englanders', *American Studies* 42.3 (Fall 2001): 65.

who may have left their mark on a well-thumbed volume. In their concern with the communal and even dialogic ways in which domestic libraries brought individual minds together, various writers revealed the role such collections played in imagining the 'native aim' of distinctly American borrowers and the nature of their relationship with the literate nation. Such figurations found heightened significance as the country was sundered by Civil War.

As the seat of sentimental ideas of sympathy and communal understanding—feelings widely held to uphold the national 'household' too—the bourgeois homestead, American sentimentalists argued, should foster familial exchange, sustain friendships, and expand its benevolent influence into the community at large.[34] Personal libraries offered a compelling model for visualizing and exploring the constitutive bonds of which local communities were, ideally, to be made. For this reason, covetous keepers of personal collections and intensely solitary students of ancient tomes don't tend to fare well in literary terms—especially if the crazed figures that inhabit Edgar Allan Poe's works are anything to go by. While the desolate narrator of 'The Raven' (1845) is haunted by an avian vision that seems to have been sparked by long hours of desperate, lonely reading—'vainly had I sought to borrow / From my books surcease of sorrow — sorrow for the lost Lenore'—it is in Roderick Usher's deranged shadow of a library that Poe's narrator begins to grasp the psychological disorder of his ailing friend: 'Many books and musical instruments lay scattered about, but failed to give any vitality to the scene. I felt that I breathed an atmosphere of sorrow.'[35] As Poe makes clear, Usher's collection is definitely *not* a library, yet those 'books which, for years, had formed no small portion of [his] mental existence' fuel a 'wild ritual' of reading which leads to obsession and the ultimate, physical obliteration of the Usher mansion.[36] A collection finds meaning in the organizing presence of its collector; Usher's cluttered assemblage dominates his own mind, and bespeaks the dangerous ways in which the acquisitive psyche can become all-consuming. In the shadow of Usher's primal passion, the fall of the house of Usher, and its implications for the national household, speak for themselves.

Beyond the Gothic library, however, those writers concerned with reform saw lending from domestic collections as a social salve. Had Roderick Usher sought guidance from the likes of Catharine Beecher and Harriet Beecher Stowe, he may well have been advised to start a personal lending library, for his moral health. To writers occupied with works of reform—the kind that started at home—personal libraries, when shared, could be levelling forces, bringing benefits to amateur

---

[34] On sentimental philosophies of domesticity see, for example, Lori Merish, *Sentimental Materialism: Gender, Commodity Culture, and Nineteenth-Century American Literature* (Durham, NC: Duke University Press, 2000).

[35] Edgar Allan Poe, 'The Raven', *American Review* (February 1845): 143; 'The Fall of the House of Usher', *Burton's Gentleman's Magazine* (September 1839): 146.

[36] 'The Fall of the House of Usher', 149.

'librarians' and borrowers alike. Despairing of wealthy households whose 'elegant books increase in their closed bookcases, [and] fine pictures and prints remain shut in portfolios, to be only occasionally opened by a privileged few', Beecher and Stowe used the pages of their *American Woman's Home* (1869) to criticize elite exclusivity and argue for the social benefits of transforming personal wealth into a communal resource.[37] To seek to 'elevate destitute neighbors to... culture and enjoyment' shouldn't amount to a contrived performance of benevolent intentions, but a Christian act comprising '*humility* and *meekness*', which sacrificed the desire for 'wealth, honor, and position' in the name of class-defying lowliness.[38] Such aims may sit awkwardly with the mutually shaping relationship between liberal individualism and property ownership that had become so central to conceptions of the white American's constitutional rights. But bound-up in the *right* kinds of purchase, collection, and lending—as Beecher and Stowe's approach to domestic economy would suggest—was the potential for improvement via care, frugality, and even thriftiness. Similar qualities prompted prudent shaping of personal libraries, serving also to steer the thoughts and interests of like-minded borrowers. In fact, cultivating one's domestic library could help explain the complex workings of the gregarious American's extremely busy mind, as Oliver Wendell Holmes, Sr., Boston's polymathic poet-doctor suggested in 1872: 'I suppose I have as many bound volumes of notions of one kind and another in my head as you have in your Representatives' library up there at the State House,' he wrote in one of his popular conversational essays:

> I have to tumble them over and over, and open them in a hundred places, and sometimes cut the leaves here and there, to find what I think about this and that. And a good many people who flatter themselves that they are talking wisdom to me, are only helping me to get at the shelf and the book and the page where I shall find my own opinion about the matter in question.[39]

If, in America's increasingly busy urban boarding houses, one might begin to lose track of one's own miscellaneous thoughts, social interactions might act as a kind of index for one's inner library, bringing order to one's precarious miscellany of notions.

In the wake of a war which had brought about the beginnings of radical cultural change, the workings of home libraries might even facilitate incorporation of marginalized groups into a social world that would, some writers argued, be all the better for it. For the indomitable Jo March of Louisa May Alcott's *Little*

---

[37] Catharine Beecher and Harriet Beecher Stowe, *The American Woman's Home; or, The Principles of Domestic Science* (New York; J.B. Ford, 1869), 438.
[38] Beecher and Stowe, *The American Woman's Home*, 439.
[39] Oliver Wendell Holmes, Sr., *The Poet at the Breakfast-Table* (Boston, MA: Houghton Mifflin, 1900), 1.

Women (1868–9), libraries of wealthy relatives and wealthier neighbours not only help focus a hazy yet urgent 'ambition . . . to do something very splendid' but stage scenes in which an awkward, avowedly 'unfeminine' demeanour is refined and even socialized—although, in Jo's case, socialization doesn't necessarily amount to the flattening of what Alcott calls her 'queer performances'. The time Jo illicitly spends in Aunt March's library—'[t]he dim, dusty room with the busts staring down from the tall book-cases, the cosy chairs, the globes'—gives her unprecedented access to 'a wilderness of books, in which she could wander where she liked', and Jo ranges widely, 'devour[ing] poetry, romance, history, travels, and pictures like a regular book-worm'.[40] This unrestricted 'region of bliss' may be implicitly transgressive, not least because of the unmitigated freedom it gives Jo to *be* miscellaneous (there is no household librarian here to bestow or withhold, or suggest reads appropriate for a little woman).[41] Access to this freedom, however, comes with a duty to old Aunt March, a childless spinster whom the Marches displease when they refuse to give Jo up to her charge. Aunt March eventually decides to take Jo on as her 'companion,' amidst rumours that she has written the March family out of her will. For Jo, though, the wonders of the library—so often interrupted by Aunt March's 'shrill voice' and many needs—are tempered not by the prospect of a bequest, but by the fondness she develops for 'the peppery old lady' and the sense of responsibility that comes with putting her literary wanderings on hold.[42] 'The training she received at Aunt March's was just what she needed,' the narrator observes, 'and the thought that she was doing something to support herself made her happy.'[43]

But not all eager readers had benefactors to borrow from, or even the resources with which to cultivate their literate lives, and depictions of social progress commonly associated with literary libraries—personal and public—tend to omit African Americans, indigenous peoples, and other aspiring readers of colour. Significantly, the self-emancipated hero of *Uncle Tom's Cabin* (1852), George Harris, can only set up his 'study'—'an open writing-desk, pens, paper, and over it a shelf of well-selected books'—in Canada, where he can be free from laws which would enslave him, and those that would prohibit his literacy. George's 'zeal for self-improvement' marks his place amidst the ranks of self-reliant American citizens that Emerson imagined and Stowe, Alcott, Holmes, and others championed; in reminding us that George had to 'steal the much coveted arts of reading and writing' during his enslavement, though, Stowe unmasks the hypocrisy of that enduring myth of American identity and the racist system that upholds it.[44] Forced to steal his reading materials and with them his freedom, George, among

[40] Louisa May Alcott, *Little Women; or, Meg, Jo, Beth and Amy* (Boston, MA: Roberts Brothers, 1868), 59–60.
[41] Alcott, *Little Women*, 60.   [42] Alcott, *Little Women*, 59.   [43] Alcott, *Little Women*, 60.
[44] Harriet Beecher Stowe, *Uncle Tom's Cabin; or, Life Among the Lowly* (London: John Cassel, 1852), 374.

many other enslaved men, women, and children intent on literacy, is a transgressive American borrower through and through; the irony is that, in order to practise 'self-cultivation' and experience the individual refinement and social selfhood that the domestic library's liberal education makes possible, he must leave America altogether.

Frederick Douglass, one of the country's most energetic critics of slavery, and foremost African-American orators, would have agreed: permitted entry to the Bibliothèque nationale de France during a trip to Paris, Douglass encountered himself anew. As he attempted to navigate 'this wilderness of books, gathered from all the world and printed in all languages', he found orientation in self-reliance: 'I was tempted to ask if any word of mine was to be found there [within the library],' he wrote; 'In a few minutes...there was laid before me a book of my bondage and my freedom.' Gazing upon his own narrative of self-emancipation within an institution dedicated to culture and access to knowledge, Douglass could align himself, too, with 'hundreds of readers...ranged around the vast reading-room, engaged in reading and writing'. A proven member of this vast, literate collective, Douglass felt what he would not readily be permitted to feel on American soil: 'I need not say,' he noted, pointedly, 'there I felt the freedom of France and myself a man among men.'[45]

Douglass visited Paris over twenty years after Abraham Lincoln proclaimed emancipation, in 1886, and his commentary betrays the fact that black acts of borrowing remained constrained and contested in the US in spite of the momentous progress the public libraries movement had made during that time. This period saw the rise of the public library on a grand scale. The era of corporate ownership and big business, coupled with reformers' renewed intent on reimagining national power and cultural cohesion on an ever-increasing scale, would, as Alan Trachtenberg has argued, leave 'barely any realm of American life... untouched'. The 'incorporation of America', he writes, affected 'politics, education, family life, literature, and the arts'. With this change came 'subtle shifts' in 'ideas regarding the identity of the individual, the relation between public and private realms, and the character of the nation'.[46] As philanthropic magnates including Andrew Carnegie followed in the footsteps of earlier businessmen like John Jacob Astor and poured wealth into building imposing public libraries, vast reading rooms suggested new figurations of national endeavour and citizenly behaviour, not all of which were as radical or inclusive as their proponents liked to claim. Public libraries, as Carnegie understood them, could be powerful influences in the battle for betterment of the 'masses': 'I choose free libraries as the best

---

[45] Frederick Douglass, 'My Foreign Travels', *Frederick Douglass Papers, Series One: Speeches, Debates, and Interviews*, vol. 5: 1881–1895, ed. John W. Blassingame (New Haven, CT: Yale University Press, 1992), 301.

[46] Alan Trachtenberg, *The Incorporation of America* (New York: Hill & Wang, 1982; repr. 2007), 5.

agencies for improving the masses of the people,' he noted, 'because they give nothing for nothing. They only help those who help themselves.... They reach the aspiring, and open to these the chief treasures of the world — those steeped up in books. A taste for reading drives out lower tastes.'[47] Carnegie's bootstrap ideology was widely shared among wealthy north-eastern elites seeking solutions to economic disparity and subsequent worker unrest, not to mention the plethora of physical ills and intellectual afflictions that, as they understood it, continued to keep the lower classes low. And, to a degree, the incorporation of library culture during the Gilded Age sustained the aspiration for a self-improving, self-motivating populace that Franklin and Emerson had both held dear. 'As Carnegie... succinctly summarized,' writes Thomas Augst, 'the "agency" of the public library was moral uplift... not a system of welfare that would "pauperise" steel workers by robbing them of their initiative and independence.' These public libraries, he notes, were 'the nineteenth century's most impressive symbols of what Astor terms the "general good of society," of liberal capitalism's capacity to create "civilization"'.[48]

In many cases the aspirational aims of these magnates bore fruit. The best, most progressive of the free and public libraries fashioned citizens from borrowers of all ranks and races through lending practices which fostered personal responsibility and covenants based on trust. These values would be prized in the ever-expanding urban settings which replaced distinct, localized communities and birthed new constructions of collectivity. For one New Yorker writing in 1872, the 'workings of the Boston [Public] Library' were 'admirable in all their details': that institution's success, they suggested, was founded in the powers the library bestowed on its patrons through its open-shelf policy. 'There, 100,000 volumes are open to the public from ten to thirteen hours a day, according to the season, and nearly one-fourth of these books are subject to the order of anybody who wishes to take them home; the sole condition being that the applicant shall give the names of two citizens as references.'[49] Such dependence on a system of civic recognition might well breed exclusion, but the experiences of Sappho Clark, the African-American heroine of Pauline Hopkins's *Contending Forces* (1900), speak to the Library's constitutive role in imagining a fair, racially diverse expression of civil society. Initially hesitant to enter 'a place of public resort for fear of insult', this abused southerner finds that, 'in the free air of New England's freest city', she might '[drink] great draughts of freedom's subtle elixir': '[t]o this woman, denied association with the vast sources of information, which are heirlooms to the

[47] Andrew Carnegie, 'Why Mr Carnegie Founds Free Libraries'. In *Campaigning for a Public Library: Suggested Material for Newspaper Use and for General Circulation* (Madison, WI: Wisconsin Free Library Commission, 1906), 7.
[48] Thomas Augst, 'Introduction: American Libraries and Agencies of Culture', *American Studies* 42.3 (Fall 2001): 11–12.
[49] 'Free Public Libraries', *New York Times*, 14 January 1872, 4.

lowliest inhabitant of Boston, the noble piles, which represented the halls of learning, and the massive grandeur of the library, free to all, seemed to invite her to a full participation in their intellectual joys.' In the wake of her sexual assault—unrecognized and unpunished by white southern society—Boston's library is a balm; touching an inner sense of self oppressed by racism and lynch law, it draws out 'her beauty-loving nature' while initiating her into a nourishing, intellectual society, broadly construed: 'The hidden springs of spirituality were satisfied and at rest, claiming kinship with the great minds of the past, whose never-dying works breathed perennial life in the atmosphere of the quiet halls.'[50] In the library, Clark begins to find faith in freedom and experiences a selfhood, personal and civic, long denied African Americans in the South.

But not all public libraries were as approachable as Boston's. As Augst recognizes, public libraries were also instruments of social control wielded by the few, and the rules with which trustees and librarians regulated public contact with their holdings seemed, to many, to invert the seemingly democratic approach to self-improvement touted by magnanimous donors. 'As informal functions of the domestic library were delegated to public libraries,' Augst reminds us, 'an entire habit of culture was overshadowed, if not eclipsed, by forces of centralization and professionalization—by formal protocols of cultural authority that became embedded in bureaucratic institutions.'[51] The gregarious consciousness—sociable yet independent—cultivated by the patrons of household libraries would undergo reform, and even alienating atomization, in attempting to access the jealously guarded collections of urban public libraries. Looking back to the familiar libraries of the nineteenth century from the wonders of the twenty-first, Edward Bellamy's accidental time traveller, Julian West, in *Looking Backward, 2000-1887* (1889), captures the worst of the early iterations of America's public libraries from the 'temptation of the luxurious leather chairs' and 'book-lined alcoves' that welcome the readers of his future:

> I cannot sufficiently celebrate the glorious liberty that reigns in the public libraries of the twentieth century as compared with the intolerable management of those of the nineteenth century, in which the books were jealously railed away from the people, and obtainable only at an expenditure of time and red tape calculated to discourage any ordinary taste for literature.[52]

Closed-shelf policies, erratic opening hours, and complex, selective registration procedures contributed to the unwelcoming unnavigability for which certain

---

[50] Pauline Hopkins, *Contending Forces: A Romance Illustrative of Negro Life North and South* (New York: Oxford University Press, 1988), 115–16.

[51] Augst, 'American Libraries', 9.

[52] Edward Bellamy, *Looking Backward, 2000–1887* (Boston; New York: Houghton Mifflin, 1889), 221.

institutions were infamous. The same *New York Times* correspondent who celebrated Boston's Public Library found fault with the Astor Library's inaccessibility.
The Astor Library,

> as we have often had occasion to complain, comes far short of being what its
> founder probably designed it to be, and is practically a failure as either a free or
> public library in any just sense of the terms. Popular it certainly is not, and, so
> greatly is it lacking in most of the essentials of a public library, that its stores
> might almost as well be under lock and key, for any access the masses of the
> people can get thereto.[53]

Perhaps it was the Astor's early designation as a reference library that hampered
its transition to a people's palace; either way, we might speculate on Washington
Irving's response to the poor reputation of this stuffy literary institution, considering he had, until his death, acted as president of its board of trustees. We might
also wonder what he would have made of one of its most unwholesome literary
patrons: the parochial and unscrupulous Confederate veteran Basil Ransom.
Discerning cultural critic that he was, Henry James was well aware that the
contempt for social softness had grown exponentially among a segment of the
cultural elite desperate to instil a new sense of collective purpose and civic duty in
a country still nursing sectional wounds opened by the Civil War. Published
serially between 1885 and 1886—around the same time that Frederick Douglass
reflected on his freedom in the Bibliothèque nationale—*The Bostonians* played up
that critique by satirizing arguments for social welfare, women's rights, and racial
equality in ways which nettled the New England community of former abolition-
ists and the next generation of aspiring reformers. Yet, as Basil's final, violent
triumph over his cousin Olive Chancellor and her community of women's rights
advocates suggests, James also saw the shape of conservative reform to come—a
reactionary response that prioritized white nativism over alternative forms of
liberal, sympathetically charged union.

Ensconced in the Astor's reading room, Basil is the antithesis of the citizen-
patron, an anti-borrower extraordinaire whose 'stiff' opinions occasion an even
stiffer engagement with the Astor's antique collections and an inflexibility of
imagination fit to make the pragmatic Geoffrey Crayon wince.[54] A fan of Alexis
de Tocqueville, whom he avidly reads within the library's restrictive walls, Basil is
a conservative of the strictest order, a sceptic of democratic freedoms overseen by
federal forces rather than state legislation, who reveals the sting of Confederate
defeat in the process. In his famously critical treatise on the American experiment,
Democracy in America (1835–40), de Tocqueville had issued an urgent warning

---

[53] 'Free Public Libraries', 4.
[54] Henry James, *The Bostonians* (London: Macmillan, 1886), 188.

about the kinds of 'despotism' a democracy might spawn: as the individual's pursuit of life, liberty, and happiness continued apace, he argued, moral ties of social responsibility were wont to loosen.

> The first thing that strikes the observation is an innumerable multitude of men, all equal and alike, incessantly endeavouring to procure the petty and paltry pleasures with which they glut their lives. Each of them, living apart, is a stranger to the fate of all the rest... As for the rest of his fellow citizens, he is close to them, but he does not see them; he touches them, but does not feel them; he exists only in himself and for himself alone; and if his kindred still remain to him, he may be said at any rate to have lost his country.

Such selfishness grants the federal government 'immense and tutelary power': in the name of the people, it 'chooses to be the sole agent and only arbiter of [their] happiness; it provides for their securities, foresees and supplies their necessities, facilitates their pleasures, manages their principal concerns [and] directs their industry'.[55] In effect, the federal government doesn't exist *for* its people, it exists *through* them, in the most sinister of ways.

Basil Ransom is a devotee of de Tocqueville's theories, and his efforts in the Astor fuel his long-held 'desire for public life'. Ironically, this feeling replicates the same despotic power play that de Tocqueville decries: 'To cause one's ideas to be embodied in national conduct appeared to [Basil] the highest form of human enjoyment.'[56] Basil sits at a momentous intersection of American politics— between moderate progressivism and socio-Darwinist conservatism—that would define its debates about social welfare and rights of citizenship for decades to come. And although the location where he nurtures his plans for social trans- formation might place him within the camp of progressive reform, his choice of library betrays the limits of his devotion to any real form of social uplift—as does the dubious essay on the 'rights of minorities' that he composes during the 'spare hours and chance holidays' he spends toiling there.[57] For while Basil imagines that abandoning his law office to make the Astor his centre of operations will make his 'solitary studies' a little more 'public', his relationship to the reading room's other occupants only replicates the disconnected state of society de Tocqueville describes: 'he is close to them, but he does not see them; he touches them, but he does not feel them; he exists only in himself and for himself alone.'[58] Even as Basil enacts the intellectual toil and curiosity he would see in the members of his imaginary democracy, his reliance on the Astor's old, guarded tomes and its institutional exclusivity evidences the kind of control he would exert over the

---

[55] Alexis de Tocqueville, *Democracy in America*, 2 vols (New York: J. & H. G. Langley, 1841), II, 338.
[56] James, *The Bostonians*, 188.   [57] James, *The Bostonians*, 188–9.
[58] James, *The Bostonians*, 188.

consumption of the reading masses. It also permits James a wry comment—for all the reservations he expresses, in this novel and elsewhere, about the direction of the post-war democratic project—on the un-American qualities of Basil's bitter, Confederate kind of self-reliance.

Indeed, Basil's ideas ultimately fail to circulate. Replacing despotism with other forms of paternalistic or tyrannical government, the southerner with a Federal grudge appears, to the reform-minded periodical editors reading his dubious 'paper on the rights of minorities', almost comically outdated—by 'about three hundred years'.[59] Only *almost* comically though. 'The disagreeable editor was right about his being out of date, only he had got the time wrong. He had come centuries too soon; he was not too old, but too new.'[60] The narrator's aside is troubling—is this a moment of free indirect discourse? An endorsement of the Confederate's defeated yet dangerous thinking? Or a moment of prophecy and prescience on James's part? If Basil Ransom soon recognizes that his doctrines 'would probably not contribute any more to his prosperity in Mississippi than in New York' and struggles to think of any 'country where they would be a particular advantage to him', his conquest of wide-eyed Verena Tarrant at the novel's end suggests there is something that America's next generation might find alluring about Basil's insidious political philosophy, whether they wanted to or not.[61] Verena may have access to Harvard's University Library and the tomes it makes readily available through its new card catalogues, which are organized by female professionals. But progress is only as good as the establishments which uphold it, and James's rendering of the Astor suggests a fundamental need for institutional renovation.

America's libraries—literary and literal—wouldn't always suffer from their associations with cultural elitism and the dubious characters that defended its various manifestations. Susan Allen Toth and John Coughlan's *Reading Rooms* (1991), a jubilant collection of literary reflections on the wonders of the country's public libraries, attests to the imaginative power libraries would continue to exert well into the twentieth century and beyond.[62] But by the dawn of the twentieth century, the American public library had become a fitting means of exploring the captivating, ever-evolving concept of American democracy and its vexed relationship with structures of institutional authority. For those cultural leaders who funded, filled, and organized the nation's network of public libraries, and buttressed the legacies they enshrined, the growing masses of literate, independent, and inquisitive American readers continued to inspire anxieties about the forms of education and betterment appropriate to that chimerical beast, the 'American citizen'.

---

[59] James, *The Bostonians*, 189.   [60] James, *The Bostonians*, 189.
[61] James, *The Bostonians*, 188.
[62] Susan Allen Toth and John Coughlan, ed., *Reading Rooms* (New York: Doubleday, 1991).

Some even turned to literary libraries, hoping to strike upon the right arrangement for the job. Emerson's cherished conception of readerly economy, for example—the 'conviction that the best of it all is already within the four walls of my study at home'—would strike a chord in the 1900s, as the ongoing explosion of printed matter and literate readers, coupled with the proliferation of public libraries, threatened to bewilder and even bedevil an American workforce that was growing with the country's commercial and bureaucratic industries. President of Harvard University Dr Charles William Eliot based his 'Five-Foot Shelf of Books' (also termed 'The Harvard Classics') upon Emerson's chief premises, aiming to enable 'the busy man or woman' to skip the time-consuming process of scouring 'the modern public library['s] hundreds of thousands of books' by offering immediate access to 'the cream of the world's writings'—all from the comfort of their own homes. Eliot's bid for large-scale cultural cultivation combines elite aspirations to social reform with the self-improvement salesman's enticing rhetoric of quick fixes. Offering customers 'a liberal education in 15 minutes [of reading] a day', Eliot's adverts assured potential customers that '[t]hrough the Harvard Classics people have found out that the classics are not dull, but intensely stirring, not beautiful old antiques, but stimulating to modern thought with vital application to everyday life'. Eliot's project championed accessibility and sought to democratize the knowledge to which, his ads implied, public libraries impeded rather than facilitated access. It also made buyers out of potential borrowers, and brought the library-as-institution into the domestic sphere in a way that, for all his complaints about indiscriminate readerships, Emerson may well have baulked at. Can 'native genius' thrive on prescription alone? Might a 'method from Nature' be taught in a matter of feet and minutes? Emerson advises us to 'Never read any but what you like', whereas Eliot's shelf is filled with 'books that made *him* happy and wise'.[63] There is little time to snooze in this rendition of the American library, and still less to dream.

And that is precisely what the most inventive borrowers imagined by American writers strive to do: to dream, and imagine themselves anew. The urgency of Eliot's library to *prove* its relevance 'to everyday life' is telling, as is its attempt to solve the problem of ranging borrowers by recasting them as receptive readers, ready to be moulded. The best borrowers of American literature, though, tend to thrive on the personal adaptability they find in the midst of institutional rigidity. Spurring new forms of social participation, intellectual improvement, and personal resilience, some of these figures also find ways of undermining the myth of white superiority and condescending paternalism for which library and archive are so often bywords. These acts may seem isolated, or limited in their repercussions; but as literary history demonstrates, they have the potential to resonate. In

---

[63] 'In this busy age there is only time for the best books', *Popular Science Monthly* (January 1928), 87. [Italics my own.]

forging the words and signature of a white colleague to procure access to Memphis's segregated library, the young Richard Wright could have little idea of the power he would find in books: 'It was not a matter of believing or disbelieving what I read, but of feeling something new,' he wrote of the experience in his memoir, 'of being affected by something that made the look of the world different.... I now felt that I knew what the white men were feeling. Merely because I had read a book that had spoken of how they lived and thought, I identified myself with that book.'[64] That moment of identification provided the impetus for Wright's own endeavours as a literary author. It also resulted, decades later, in a children's book about the incident—*Richard Wright and the Library Card* (1997)—an account which stands testament to the creative capacities of those borrowers who find themselves willing and able to navigate the imposing halls of America's manifold libraries.[65]

[64] Richard Wright, *Black Boy: A Record of Childhood and Youth* (New York: Harper, 1945), 218.
[65] William Miller and Gregory Christie, *Richard Wright and the Library Card* (New York: Lee & Low Books, 1997).

11

'Modified Bliss'

Libraries in Modern Poetry

Robyn Marsack

Not least of the small, incidental pleasures
Of having the school library to look after
Has been to learn that there is in existence
A library classification system called Bliss,

And a variation of it called Modified Bliss.[1]

James Keery

Like Casaubon's library in *Middlemarch*, many of the libraries of nineteenth-century literature are the private book collections of privileged gentlemen, but there emerges in the later part of that century a new note in poetry which celebrates the flourishing of public libraries. One of the earliest of these poems is J. G. Whittier's 'The Library', which heralds the 1875 opening of Haverhill Public Library in Massachusetts. Like some other celebrants of public libraries, Whittier displays almost messianic enthusiasm for libraries as places where, as he puts it with exclamatory excitement, 'Life thrills along the alcove hall' and 'The lords of thought await our call!' Prefiguring such later and wordier encomia as Amy Lowell's 'Boston Athenaeum Poem', Whittier sings the public library as a place of intense bookish delight. Regarded in isolation, his poem, like Lowell's, might seem eccentric; but such works help inaugurate a subgenre of 'library poems', running to several hundred in number, which celebrate libraries as institutions that are open to a broad and diverse public and where, from the early twentieth century onwards, increasing numbers of female as well as male readers discover if not sheer unalloyed delight, then at least what Irish-born poet James Keery in the late twentieth century termed (with a nod towards librettist W. S. Gilbert's 'modified rapture' in *The Mikado*) 'Modified Bliss'.

Contrasting with older literary accounts of individuals' libraries or of academic libraries such as those depicted by M. R. James which were set aside as the province

---

[1] I would like to dedicate this chapter to librarian-anthologists Lizzie MacGregor and Hamish Whyte. The epigraph comes from James Keery, 'Modified Bliss', in *That Stranger, The Blues* (Manchester: Carcanet, 1996).

of academic males, modern library poems often reflect and reflect on the dizzying inclusiveness of the library as conceived by patrons concerned with public benefit. If mill owner and philanthropist Ezekiel James Madison Hale, whose largesse helped found Haverhill Public Library, was one such patron, then by far the best-known endower of libraries in the English-speaking world was the Scots American Andrew Carnegie. While the first five Carnegie libraries had closed stacks, from which books had to be requested and delivered (with all the assumptions of knowledge and confidence that system implied), the Pittsburgh neighbourhood library in Lawrenceville, established in 1898, was built with open stacks for self-service; moreover, it had a room specifically set aside for children. Here are the key ingredients often found in a modern library poem: freedom to enter and to choose—under, of course, the eye of the librarian.

Readers and librarians form the cast of these modern poems about libraries. The buildings themselves may be described by poets: from Les Murray's account of the baroque splendours of the St Gallen Library to J. V. Cunningham's sly view of the statuary of the finely landscaped Huntington, but more often the scene is the familiar twentieth-century public library with its steps, doors, stairway—entering and leaving libraries are moments as important as sitting in them—its long tables and shaded lamps.[2] Such public buildings, let alone the humbler 'school library' evoked by James Keery, are very far from the dark labyrinths and mazes that populate modern fantasy fiction, where knowledge tends to be both secret and dangerous. These libraries in poetry may be grand, but their similarities to churches reside in the reverence and silence required of readers rather than in a sense of the numinous like that conjured by the architecture of libraries in modern fantasy literature. As in some fantasy narratives, however, the organization of knowledge is a matter of fascination, from the poet Veronica Forrest-Thomson's severe yet playful 'Catalog' to James Robertson's affectionate description of Edinburgh Central Library's card index.[3] Walter Benjamin, in his famous essay 'Unpacking My Library', suggests that 'if there is a counterpart to the confusion of a library, it is the order of its catalogue.'[4] When Seamus Heaney gave a speech at the Scottish Poetry Library, he lingered lovingly on the vocabulary of libraries: 'holdings' involved a 'sense of treasure being kept', while 'stack' implied 'promise, richness, golden reliability of

[2] Les Murray, 'Three Interiors', in *Collected Poems* (Manchester: Carcanet, 1991); J.V. Cunningham, 'I, too, have been to the Huntington', in *Collected Poems and Epigrams* (London: Faber & Faber, 1971).

[3] Veronica Forrest-Thomson, 'Catalog', in *Collected Poems and Translations* (Lewes: Allardyce, Barnett Publishers, 1990); James Robertson, 'To the Card Catalogues of the City Library', in *Edinburgh: An Intimate City*, ed. Bashabi Fraser and Elaine Greig (Edinburgh: Department of Recreation, Edinburgh City Council, 2000).

[4] Walter Benjamin, 'Unpacking My Library', in *Illuminations*, trans. Harry Zohn (London: Fontana/Collins, 1973), 60.

the corn'.[5] It is abundance—both confusing and glorious—that is the impetus for so many modern library poems.

'There, in the unlovely stacks, / the books sleep cramped as sailors', writes Mary Jo Salter, taking a more wearied view in 'Reading Room'. Hers is in the Williston Memorial Library, Mount Holyoke College (another Carnegie library, this one built in 1905 to resemble Westminster Hall), watched over by carved figureheads, lamps dangling from their hands; here 'thousands of periodicals / unfurl their thin, long-winded sails'.[6] Her neat play there on 'long-winded' encompasses verbosity and the sails unfurling over decades under the breath of readers, together with a suggestion that the periodicals are 'winded', having run out of their own breath, unopened for years. Mainly, in this archaic space, the poet is struck by the sheer mass of books compared to the span of our lives: 'So little time to learn what's worth / our time!'

Overwhelmingly, the library is the site of memory, both cultural and personal. As such, it can be idealized, and hymned as a site of abiding cultural capital, if not quite of unbounded bliss. The American poet Karl Shapiro, trained as a librarian, declares simply: 'At the centre of all human culture stands the library. At the centre of civilization stands the library.'[7] (Shapiro won the Pulitzer Prize for poetry with his 1944 collection *V-letters and other poems*, based on the censors' microfilms of letters written by serving American soldiers; he felt himself honoured more by the fact that copies of his book were placed in all US Navy ship libraries.) Though not all poets present the issue as directly as Shapiro, in many poems the library is a kind of shorthand for, or compacted site of, 'civilization', and the theme of coming across the works of ancient poets on the shelves characterizes a small subsection of library poems. Iain Crichton Smith writes of doing that 'In Paisley Library', and in his memories of student days at Aberdeen University simply declares: 'No library I haven't loved. / My food is books.' Yet if Smith finds bliss there, he is aware that the ideal library may be compromised in its engagement with modern commercial pressures. He asks, presciently: 'How reconcile / the market to the library, the till / to strict Lucretius?'[8] Expanding the food simile in a recent poem, Alberto Ríos reminds us of the changed configuration of libraries, with their sofas and coffee machines (a way of reconciling the library to the market?):

---

[5] Quoted in Robyn Marsack, 'Remembering Seamus Heaney (1939–2013)', *Poetry Reader* (Scottish Poetry Library) 14 (Winter 2014), 4.

[6] Mary Jo Salter, 'Reading Room', in *A Phone Call to the Future: New and Selected Poems* (New York: Knopf, 2008).

[7] Karl Shapiro, 'The Poetry Wreck', in *Creative Glut: Selected Essays*, ed. Robert Phillips (Chicago: Ivan R. Dee, 2004), 253.

[8] Iain Crichton Smith, 'Aberdeen University 1945–1949', in *New Collected Poems*, ed. Matthew McGuire (Manchester: Carcanet, 2011).

> The doughnut scent of it all, *knowledge*,
> The aroma of coffee being made
>
> In all those books, something for everyone,
> The deli offerings of civilization itself.[9]

What kind of 'civilization' is represented on the shelves increasingly concerns recent poets as they engage not just as writers but also as readers with library environments of 'modified bliss'.

The present chapter focuses on libraries' readers and what they are looking for or how they behave; on who is allowed in and who is kept out; and on the librarians, who make the decisions. Sometimes, however, people using libraries are not there to read at all, as Charles Reznikoff recognized. The Cooper Union Reading Room was set up in New York in 1859, 'to be open from 8 a.m. to 10 p.m., free to all persons, male and female, of good moral character'. Its first Annual Report boasted that it was 'fitted with every comfort and convenience as regards light, warmth and ventilation'. Reznikoff, writing a century later, describes it:

> Men and women with open books before them –
> and never turn a page: come
> merely for warmth
> not light.[10]

More often, poems are inhabited by ardent readers. 'So Many Books, So Little Time' is the title of a poem by Haki R. Madhubuti, and thinking about what people seek in and desire of a library, he finishes:

> readers & writers looking for a retreat,
> looking for departure & home,
> looking for open heart surgery without the knife.[11]

The last line sums up the powerful emotional connection that occurs in libraries, where the hush conceals the intensity of the individual reading experience. Those contradictory impulses, departure and returning home, are the key to the swathe of poems in which the library is the site of often pleasurable personal memory, especially recollection of childhood and adolescence. This is a rich seam for poets to mine, opened here by Gerald Stern's 'Stepping out of Poetry':

---

[9] Alberto Ríos, 'Don't Go into the Library', 2017, https://poets.org/poem/dont-go-library (accessed 18 March 2019).
[10] Charles Reznikoff, 'XXIII Cooper Union Library', in *The Poems of Charles Reznikoff: 1918–1975*, ed. Seamus Cooney (Boston: David R. Godine, 2005).
[11] Haki R. Madhubuti, 'So Many Books, So Little Time', in *HeartLove: Wedding and Love Poems* (Chicago: Third World Press, 1998).

> What would you give for your dream
> to be as clear and simple as it was then
> in the dark afternoons, at the old scarred tables?[12]

Modern poems about libraries bring back not only the building but the person the writers were in that setting, with an indiscriminate appetite for books, finding their place or their way out of a place: the library as retreat or launching pad. Randall Jarrell was writing his poems about young readers in the 1950s, out of a sophisticated and also heartfelt debate with himself over the values of art and imagination. He vacillates between contrary representations of the library—as a place of near-blissful delight but also of 'gloom'—and his poems are suffused with nostalgia and melancholy.

> I rarely feel happier than when I am in a library – very rarely feel more soothed and calm and secure; and there, in the soft gloom of the stacks, I feel very much in my element – a book among books, almost.[13]

In 'A Girl in a Library' Jarrell speaks as the university teacher he was, looking at a student dozing over a book, 'an object among dreams', tenderly patronizing her: 'with what yawns the unwilling / Flesh puts on its spirit, O my sister!' He summons the ghost of Tatyana—that great reader—from Pushkin's poem *Eugene Onegin* to comment on the 19-year-old American girl, whom he imagines, too, in her 'pink strapless formal', the 'Spring Queen' of legend playing out her destiny far from the books that may be of no use to her.[14]

Jarrell cannot quite decide if this reader's books are useless. He is a writer very much attuned to children's experience, and in 'Children Selecting Books in a Library' his sympathies are with the young readers whose lives are 'full of sorcerers and ogres', and who have not yet escaped from 'the capricious infinite'. The poem ends with the possibility the books offer: of exchange—another person's 'sorrow' traded for 'our own'—and of 'the great / CHANGE, dear to all things not to themselves endeared', a marvellously aphoristic line.[15] The capital letters give the word unexpected prominence, harking back to an eighteenth-century style of personification ('dear Change'), almost as if the poet were trying to convince himself; or perhaps they are an indication of the sudden illumination of the reader. Surely, as a brilliant translator of Rilke, Jarrell is thinking of that poet's famous

---

[12] Gerald Stern, 'Stepping Out of Poetry', in *This Time: New and Selected Poems* (New York: W.W. Norton, 1998).

[13] Jarrell quoted by Dennis O'Driscoll, 'The library of adventure', in *Librarians, Poets and Scholars*, ed. Felix M. Larkin (Dublin: Four Courts Press, 2007), 309.

[14] Randall Jarrell, 'A Girl in a Library', in his *The Complete Poems* (London: Faber & Faber, 1971), 15.

[15] Randall Jarrell, 'Children Selecting Books in a Library', *The Complete Poems*, 106.

admonition: 'You must change your life!'[16] But this qualified optimism has disappeared in the finality of his judgement in 'The Carnegie Library, Juvenile Division', where the title itself, formally correct, implies a childish, immature comprehension:

> We found in you the knowledge for a life
> But not the will to use it in our lives
> That were always, somehow, so different from the books'.
> We learn from you to understand, but not to change.[17]

That melancholy conclusion is not echoed by many writers. Remembering a later decade in 'Maple Valley Branch Library, 1967', Rita Dove presents the voracious adolescent reader on the cusp of change, with a lyric immediacy very different from Jarrell's high rhetoric. She slips

> into the Adult Section to see
> what vast *tristesse* was born of rush-hour traffic,
> décolletés, and the plague of too much money.[18]

Here, again, we are aware of a library that cannot keep itself wholly apart from the commercial pressures of the adult world. Though we cannot tell if she is reading Françoise Sagan, and maybe Scott Fitzgerald, or perhaps even John Updike, Dove's adolescent reader reads big books and small, *Gone with the Wind* and haiku, history books and art books; there is a huge relish in description of these reading days, which sometimes provided 'all the world on a single page'. And she carries all the books she can out into her own world, past some graffiti with its unlooked-for encouragement:

> I CAN EAT AN ELEPHANT
> IF I TAKE SMALL BITES.
> *Yes*, I said, to no one in particular: *That's*
> *what I'm gonna do!*

This message of release and possibility seems to have particular force for girls of the second half of the century. Lesbia Harford, poet, novelist, and political activist who graduated from the University of Melbourne with a law degree in 1916, has

---

[16] Rainer Maria Rilke, 'Archaic Torso of Apollo', trans. Vernon Watkins, in *Modern European Poetry*, ed. Willis Barnstone (New York: Bantam Books, 1966), 122.

[17] Randall Jarrell, 'The Carnegie Library, Juvenile Division', *The Complete Poems*, 98.

[18] Rita Dove, 'Maple Valley Branch Library, 1967', in *On the Bus with Rosa Parks* (New York: Norton, 1999).

her reader 'In the Public Library' sadly reflecting 'that her soul had been / Slain by her woman's body'; the books might be available but give her no consolation:

> Woman was made to worship man, they preached,
> Not God, to serve earth's purpose, not to roam
> The heavens of thought...[19]

That world, on the democratic shelves of the public library, had indeed changed by the 1990s. 'She desires the keys / to the National Library', Kathleen Jamie declares of her liberating figure 'The Queen of Sheba', suggesting that access to books can only empower the girls of Scotland.[20] At around the same time, in her poem 'Biography', Jackie Kay (who would later become Scotland's 'Makar' or official national poet) presents a scene of shamed yet resolute emancipation:

> *My father caught me at it one day.*
> *Radclyffe Hall dropped out from inside Bunty.*
> *Page 106 was enough for him: he frog-marched me*
> *down to the library where Cow Lick stammered,*
> *'I thought it was for you,'*
> *and my father disturbed the silence:*
> *'What is the matter with you?' in between tight teeth.*[21]

Finding the book, then taking it home: this is the passage that allows for personal change. 'Because of Libraries We Can Say These Things' is the title of Naomi Shihab Nye's poem describing a girl's revelatory discovery—'What the town has not given her / the book will provide'—and it is domesticated: 'She will have two families. / They will eat at different hours.' The world inside and outside the book will be experienced in parallel, and the solitary reading figure—so often a cultural sign of the misfit—will be invisibly accompanied. She will sit outside on the step, but

> she will not be alone.
> She will have a book to open
> and open and open.
> Her life starts here.[22]

[19] Lesbia Harford, 'In the Public Library', at *internetPoem.com* website, https://internetpoem.com/lesbia-harford/in-the-public-library-poem/.

[20] Kathleen Jamie, 'The Queen of Sheba', in *The Queen of Sheba* (Newcastle: Bloodaxe, 1994).

[21] Jackie Kay, 'The Year of the Letter: Biography', in *Darling: New and Selected Poems* (Tarset: Bloodaxe, 2007).

[22] Naomi Shihab Nye, 'Because of Libraries We Can Say These Things', in *Fuel* (Rochester, NY: BOA Editions, 1998).

This almost blissful feeling that books can kick-start a life is also strong in Dorianne Laux's poem 'Books', in which a girl leaving high school has stolen a book from the library to take with her.[23] She has chosen *A Tree Grows in Brooklyn*, Betty Smith's classic novel of an aspirational girl and her immigrant family in the early twentieth century: 'This is all you need as you take your first step / toward the street ... Into whoever you're going to be.' Compare the elation of these American girls with the scene in Scottish poet Liz Lochhead's 'The Choosing', where the speaker is riding home on the bus and catches sight of the girl with whom she used to compete for primary-school prizes. Mary is pregnant, sitting with her attentive husband,

> And I am coming from the library
> with my arms full of books.
> I think of those prizes that were ours for the taking
> and wonder when the choices got made
> we don't remember making.[24]

The library stands for one kind of life: rather than 'civilization' it represents opportunity, a departure from the expectation for girls. This class and/or gendered consciousness of the library is powerfully evoked by William McIlvanney, son of an ex-miner:

> In the library the first time
> I stood in a pool of awe.
> Wonder for taking, acres of promise.
> The lady with the specs
> And the hair-tuft on her cheek
> Asking me if I had washed my hands.
> The holy ritual of the water – what was this?
> Superstitious as a Goth, I grabbed and ran.[25]

He writes of this temporary rout as the 'seed of an anger perennially mine', of 'the hope I lugged to that place', and yet 'forgives', he says, 'the determined absence of himself he was to find' in the pages and pages he turned there, the spaces and margins that were blank, and in which only the graffiti spoke of 'him and his pals'.

---

[23] Dorianne Laux, 'Books', in *Smoke* (New York: BOA Editions, 2000).

[24] Liz Lochhead, 'The Choosing', in *A Choosing* (Edinburgh: Polygon, 2011).

[25] William McIlvanney, 'In the Library', in *Long Overdue: A Library Reader*, ed. Alan Taylor (London and Edinburgh: Library Association/Mainstream Publishing, 1993).

Tom Leonard also remembers the clean hands rule, in his introduction to *Radical Renfrew*, the poetry anthology he compiled as a result of being appointed Writer in Residence at Paisley Central Library.

> The place where a democratic freedom of encounter with Literature has occurred is in the free public libraries. It is not that they haven't operated censorship, but the public libraries have remained the one place where anyone can build his or her own relation with the literary world. It was in the public library in Pollok that I built mine. The five-to-seven department, just a green tin cupboard with about eight shelves, and the books facing out the way. You had to wrap your books in newspaper, and you had to show your hands. Then the day when I could use the Junior Department for the 7-14s, a whole wall under the window. Real books at last, that wouldn't be finished as soon as you got home.[26]

In 'View of the Library of Congress from Paul Laurence Dunbar High School', Thomas Sayers Ellis explores the experience of marginality from the perspective of a student at an all-black public high school, encouraged in his writing by a white substitute teacher.[27] He hands the student an obituary of the poet Robert Hayden, the first African-American writer to be Consultant in Poetry to the Library of Congress (1976–8). No one among the boy's friends or their mothers knows of the Library, although their relatives work in some famous Washington locations. In the poem he describes throwing rocks at these places with his friends, and how they 'always fell short'. That physical distance, then, is compounded by the notion that the institutions and all they represented were virtually a stone's throw away, yet never reached. At the same time, his own school is named after Paul Laurence Dunbar (1872–1906), an African-American poet who wrote in standard English and in dialect (the latter in itself controversial: was he betraying or representing his people?), and was the lyricist of an immensely successful Broadway musical, *In Dahomey*. The sense of achievement, and that of barriers, is equally strong, and mediated through the talismanic library. When the boy looks it up ('open to all taxpayers and citizens'), he realizes that his Aunt Doris had worked there for years, the one who had bought him coveted blood-red loafers.

> I was beginning to think
> Like a poet, so in my mind
> Hayden's dying and my loafers
> Were connected, but years apart,
> As was Dunbar to other institutions –
> Ones I could see, ones I could not.

---

[26] Tom Leonard, ed., *Radical Renfrew* (Edinburgh: Polygon, 1990), xxxi–xxxii.
[27] Thomas Sayers Ellis, excerpts from 'View of the Library of Congress from Paul Laurence Dunbar High School', from *The Maverick Room* (Minneapolis: Graywolf Press, 2005).

Wanda Coleman, born in Watts, the suburb of Los Angeles torn by race riots in 1965, had discovered her library all right, but felt that black readers were not welcome in it. As in McIlvanney's poem, the librarian is remembered as the gatekeeper: her 'gray eyes policed me thru the stacks like dobermans':

> she watched me come and go, take books and bring books
> she monitored the titles and after a while decided
> she'd misjudged her little colored girl
> and for a time she tried to apologize in her way. to engage
> in small talk. i never answered back. once, she set
> special books aside to gain my trust respect smile
> i left them untouched[28]

The simple phrase 'her little colored girl' encapsulates a whole way of thinking: the tone is perfect, as if overheard in conversation: 'I've got an interesting little colored girl coming in ...'. Coleman also recalled in interview the segregation of books by gender in those days:

> When I went to the library (Ascot and Downtown branches), I could read 'Cheryl Crane, Nurse,' books by the Brontë sisters, and Nancy Drew mysteries — yes, those horrible things! But I wasn't allowed to read Sir Arthur Conan Doyle or H.P. Lovecraft — the boys' books.[29]

It is very satisfying to learn that the Ascot branch is now named after this independent reader.

The theme of division or displacement is taken up by Tom Leonard in his Foreword, which considers whether the library is a place where you find yourself at home, because away from your home, or a place that does not offer you anything recognizable as home? As the twenty-first-century novelist Sophie Divry frames the paradox in her *Library of Unrequited Love*, the library represents paradise to some, powerlessness to others. Leonard says that he values his University Library card enormously, but that the Library offers a 'specialised view of the world. Its filters have excluded literature by working-class people, though there are books in plenty about "them".'

> In some ways it's here that the public libraries come into their own, and in others
> it's where they have been most frustrating. ... while the public has been out front

---

[28] Wanda Coleman, excerpts from 'Chapter 2 of the Story', from *Bathwater Wine* (Santa Rosa, CA: Black Sparrow/David R. Godine, 1998).

[29] See https://www.poetryfoundation.org/harriet/2014/12/a-wanda-coleman-branch-of-the-los-angeles-public-library- (accessed 3 May 2019).

borrowing the books, through the back there has always been that world you see over the librarian's shoulder...[30]

The world of librarians, the gatekeepers or gate-openers, is the subject of much library poetry. In a recent professional survey of the UK information workforce, just over 78 per cent are women; in the US, women accounted for 79 per cent of librarians, so it is not surprising to find this gender imbalance reflected in poetry. Very few male librarians make an appearance, though exceptions include 'the frightened male librarian' in Weldon Kees's 'The Situation Clarified' and the severe Head Librarian in Selima Hill's 'The Waterfall Man'—both figures in dark fantasies; and the marmoreal figure of 'the librarian Mangan' as depicted by Susan Howe, 'Roosting on a ladder / for several months'.[31] In 'Hannah, are you listening?' poet-librarian Hamish Whyte pays tribute to a young female library assistant full of 'sass and gall', but she is not the familiar female stereotype, memorably portrayed by George Bailey's wife in *It's a Wonderful Life*. If George had not saved Mary for matrimony and motherhood, she would have been a scared spinster librarian wearing glasses, like the one dismissively described by Raymond Chandler in *The Big Sleep*:

> She'll always be high on nerves and low on animal emotion. She'll always breathe thin air and smell snow.... she will probably turn out to be one of those acid-faced virgins that sit behind little desks in public libraries and stamp dates in books.[32]

Yet the female librarian emerges in poetry as an object of desire, as in Sean O'Brien's 'The Beautiful Librarians', a poem in which that English poet sets aside his formerly disenchanted, even sour, memories of libraries to praise the librarians of his title: young graduates who sit at the issue desk 'Like Françoise Hardy's shampooed sisters / With cardigans across their shoulders', sophisticated objects of adoration.[33] Unlike Leonard, O'Brien is not thinking of the book treasures that may be accessible only to librarians but of their staffroom, once glimpsed, where they smoked and probably talked about men. The evocation of a particular generation, already date-stamped themselves (Françoise Hardy's song in English 'All Over the World' was a chart-topper in Britain in 1965, just as O'Brien entered adolescence), has a Larkinesque note of regret. Not least at the

[30] Leonard, ed., *Radical Renfrew*, xxxiii.

[31] Weldon Kees, 'The Situation Clarified', in *The Collected Poems*, ed. Donald Justice (Lincoln: University of Nebraska Press, 1975); Selima Hill, 'The Waterfall Man', in *Violet* (Newcastle: Bloodaxe, 1997); Susan Howe, 'Roosting on a ladder...', in *The Nonconformist's Memorial* (New York: New Directions, 1993); Hamish Whyte, 'Hannah, are you listening?' in *Hannah, Are You Listening?* (Glenrothes: HappenStance, 2013).

[32] Chandler, quoted in Taylor, ed., *Long Overdue*, 113–14.

[33] Sean O'Brien, 'The Beautiful Librarians', in *The Beautiful Librarians* (London: Picador, 2015).

end of the poem, where not only the 'ice queens in their realms of gold' (a nice Keatsian allusion) are gone, but the book stock as well. Dating from the early twenty-first century, O'Brien's poem seems both erotically charged and attuned to the threats faced by many British public libraries in an era of austerity. The libraries of his youth are, like their librarians, objects of longing.

Charles Bukowski in 'hey Ezra, listen to this' is perfectly frank about his randy student memories. He fed on the 'deliberate glorious / rancor' of the critics he read in the library, although 'wasn't it strange / that all I wanted to do then was / lift the skirt of the librarian'?[34] Don Paterson in his long poem 'The Alexandrian Library' carves out space for 'the level blue gaze of the lovely librarian', who, shushing in her 'nylons' and 'starched whites', is a fantasy amalgam of librarian/nurse/psychiatrist.[35] The shushing is, of course, another library stereotype, although the silence has its value. Carol Ann Duffy begins her librarian stanza in 'The Model Village' with it, yet silence contributes to the atmosphere of 'a refuge, the volumes breathing calmly,...Outside is chaos / lives with no sense of plot'.[36] The chaos outside is figured in the boys and girls whose absence McIlvanney lamented. How to admit them into libraries and preserve order and decorum? How to protect readers who want to read, and at the same time entice potential new readers? This dilemma may be presented humorously, but it is a real conundrum, especially in these days of severe local authority cuts. Many writers have been vocal in support of libraries, testifying to their importance in their own writing lives, but campaigning poems seem to be few and far between; O'Brien's combines nostalgia with political critique, and the theme of Ian McMillan's 'Why We Need Libraries' from the 1990s is clear from the title.[37] The survey conducted in the present chapter suggests that the defence poems were, in essence, already written. All along, in hymning libraries' 'modified bliss', poets were acting as their champions.

Back in 1984, in his collection *Aye nowyir talkin*—'interpretation of conversation with youngsters', actually published by Glasgow District Libraries—John Swan heard in Gary's words the same indignation that McIlvanney felt, and shaped them into his poem 'bard':

> Ahm bard fae thi liebari
> Ah cannae get back in
> Thill no let haufa ma mates in wae mi[38]

---

[34] Charles Bukowski, 'hey Ezra, listen to this', in *War All the Time* (Santa Rosa, CA: Black Sparrow, 1984).

[35] Don Paterson, 'The Alexandrian Library', in *God's Gift to Women* (London: Faber & Faber, 1997).

[36] Carol Ann Duffy, 'The Model Village', in *Selling Manhattan* (London: Anvil, 1998).

[37] Ian McMillan, 'Why We Need Libraries', in *To Fold the Evening Star: New and Selected Poems* (Manchester: Carcanet, 2016).

[38] John Swan, 'bard', in *Aye nowyir talkin* (Glasgow: Glasgow District Libraries, 1984).

Of course it is the librarian, 'buck teef / an big rim glasses' who is the forbidding presence. We hear this from the other side in poet-librarian Lynn Davidson's 'Muirhouse Library', her tone sympathetically weary:

> I try to shush teenagers raging on 30p energy drinks and the deep sting of their parents' habits and one girl says *This is Muirhouse doll, we won't be quiet.* And they won't and every day we have to ban them and every next day they're back again ...[39]

Librarians' interactions with the public may be admonitory, but poet-librarian Andy Jackson, in his tribute to the Scottish Poetry Library, 'Enquiry Desk', instances the kind of enquiry they have to be patient with:

> Do you have the one
> with that poem they read at the funeral
> in that movie?[40]

Angela McSeveney, in 'Public Library Assistant', reminds us of their discreet witness: 'Silent I wield my datestamp over *Infertility* / And *Coping with Bereavement*'.[41] Helen Conkling pays tribute to the library where 'Silence lived [there] like a leafy depth', and the intuition of the strict, deaf librarian who noticed what she'd been reading: '"You might like this," Miss Hart said, / handing me a volume of Chekhov'.[42] The wrecking of libraries—the destruction of their 'bliss'—need not be the insidious effects of cuts, but of straight-out warfare. Libraries as a site of metaphorical battles between ancients and moderns have been eclipsed in contemporary poems by libraries as physical ruins. The librarian can be a heroine, like Iraqi Alia Muhammad Baker who saved 30,000 books and is memorialized by Philip Metres:

> How a Basra librarian
> could haul the books each night,
> load by load, into her car,
>
> the war ticking like a clock
> about to wake. Her small house
> swimming in them....[43]

---

[39] Lynn Davidson, 'Muirhouse Library: When Yellow's on the Broom', in *Islander* (Wellington and Bristol: Victoria University Press/Shearsman, 2019).

[40] Andy Jackson, 'Enquiry desk', in *Umbrellas of Edinburgh*, ed. Russell Jones and Claire Askew (Glasgow: Freight, 2016).

[41] Angela McSeveney, 'Public Library Assistant', in *Coming Out With It* (Edinburgh: Polygon, 1992).

[42] Helen Conkling, 'Mock Orange', in *Red Peony Night* (Pittsburgh: University of Pittsburgh Press, 1997).

[43] Philip Metres, 'Hearing of Alia Muhammed Baker's Stroke', https://www.splitthisrock.org/poetry-database/poem/hearing-of-alia-muhammed-bakers-stroke.

With a few exceptions, this chapter has been confined to English-language poems and has focused on work from Britain and the United States. The most famous poet-librarian of the twentieth century, however, is surely the Argentinian Jorge Luis Borges. In his 'Poema de los Dones', translated by Alastair Reid as 'Poem of the Gifts', Borges describes the 'splendid irony' of his situation: his appointment as Director of the Argentine National Library (after the fall of Perón in 1955) coincided with his finally becoming blind.[44] Because of his condition, the 'infinite tomes' are to him 'As distant as the inaccessible volumes / Which perished once in Alexandria'—the destruction of the ancient library is a touchstone for several modern poems—as distant as they were, in fact, for a blind nineteenth-century predecessor. In stately, rhymed quatrains, Borges proceeds without 'self-pity or reproach' to take the measure of his loss:

> In shadow, with a tentative stick, I try
> The hollow twilight, slow and imprecise –
> I, who had always thought of Paradise
> In form and image as a library.

Britain's most famous poet-librarian is doubtless Philip Larkin. When asked by an interviewer for names of poet-librarians other than Borges, Larkin replied—tongue-in-cheek, perhaps, but it is hard to be sure—

> Who is Jorge Luis Borges? The writer-librarian I like is Archibald MacLeish . . . he reorganized the whole Library of Congress in five years simply by saying, 'I don't understand and I don't agree,' and in wartime, too. Splendid man.[45]

Robert Crawford has pointed out that the word 'library' is in fact absent from MacLeish's *Collected Poems*.[46] Larkin's own poems on libraries are two short commissioned pieces marking anniversaries at the Brynmor Jones Library at the University of Hull, to be found in his *Collected Poems*, but they are very slight. Very different is 'Libraries: a celebration', the exuberant ode written decades later by his colleague Douglas Dunn, in which Dunn recalls his former boss Philip Larkin saying of a book written in Indonesian, 'Isn't it *wonderful*? That someone *understands* this?'[47] Again, there is an unresolved question of Larkin's tone in that '*wonderful*', but that is undoubtedly deliberate on Dunn's part. 'All

---

[44] Jorge Luis Borges, 'Poem of the Gifts' trans. Alastair Reid. In *Selected Poems* by Jorge Luis Borges, ed. Alexander Coleman (New York: Viking Books, 1999).

[45] Philip Larkin, 'An Interview with Paris Review', in *Required Writing*: (London: Faber & Faber, 1983), 60.

[46] Robert Crawford, 'The Library in Poetry', in *The Meaning of the Library*, ed. Alice Crawford (Princeton: Princeton University Press, 2015), 176–98.

[47] Douglas Dunn, 'Libraries. A Celebration', in *New Selected Poems* (London: Faber & Faber, 2003).

libraries at night are sleeping giants!' he proclaims, and ends: 'Hear this! – the wheels of my retrieval system running / On lubricants of print and permanent devotion!' Dunn's tone here, exclamatory but laced with gentle irony, might be taken as conveying his distinctive sense of 'modified bliss'.

Like the listing of books, listing the types of library reader is a trope of library poems, perhaps reflecting the form of the library catalogue. Another devoted Scottish poet-librarian, Alasdair Paterson, uses a list of forty-three similes in 'on the library' to suggest the huge range of the books inside, the way in which readers might relate to both the building and its contents—the library is for everyone, after all; there are no limiting full stops.[48] Rushing rhapsodically beyond a sense of ironic qualification, Paterson's poem ends on a note of exultation, indeed of unmodified bliss:

> it shone like a blazing hilltop victory
> it shone like the valley of last resort
> it shone like the story of you and me
>
> it shone all night

[48] Alasdair Paterson, 'on the library', in *On the Governing of Empires* (Exeter: Shearsman, 2010).

12

Borges's Libraries

Edwin Williamson

In his 'Autobiographical Essay' Jorge Luis Borges would claim that, 'If I were asked to name the chief event in my life, I should say my father's library'.[1] It was in that library that he recalled first reading *Don Quixote* and sensing that Cervantes's novel contained some mystery, some vital secret, which he had not yet the means to comprehend:

> ...I know there is something
> essential and immortal that I have buried
> somewhere in that library of the past
> in which I read the story of that knight.
> The slow leaves now recall a solemn child
> who dreams vague things he does not understand.[2]

Father's library was 'the chief event' in his life because it would be the first step on the road to becoming a writer, and the fact that it was his father who set him on this road would be crucial to the kind of writer he would become:

> From the time I was a boy, ... it was tacitly understood that I had to fulfil the literary destiny that circumstances had denied my father. This was something that was taken for granted ... I was expected to be a writer.[3]

Borges's father, Jorge Guillermo Borges, was a lawyer by profession who kept trying to make a name for himself as a writer, though he would only manage to publish a few poems and one novel, which he brought out at his own expense in 1921. Because the family lived in a rough, working-class district of Buenos Aires, Dr Borges decided to have his son 'Georgie' tutored at home until about the age of

---

[1] Jorge Luis Borges, 'An Autobiographical Essay', in *The Aleph and Other Stories 1933–1969*, ed. and trans. Norman Thomas di Giovanni in collaboration with the author (New York: E. P. Dutton, 1970), 211.

[2] 'Readers', in Jorge Luis Borges, *Selected Poems*, ed. Alexander Coleman (London: Allen Lane, The Penguin Press, 1999), 199. Further quotations from this source (abbreviated as *SP*) will be incorporated in the main text of this chapter.

[3] Borges, 'An Autobiographical Essay', 211.

11, allowing him also free access to his collection of over a thousand volumes of mostly English and French books arranged on glass-fronted shelves and kept in a room of its own. Father's library became Georgie's playground, and all the energies of a growing child were channelled into an imaginary world which soon became more real to him than the circumscribed domestic world around him. But the library was also a place of terror. Georgie was an extremely anxious child: for instance, he hated looking in mirrors because mirrors multiplied things—they would 'copy someone / and then another, and another, and another, and another...'.[4] He used to dream about peeling off his face and finding someone else's beneath it, or of taking off a mask only to discover that he was wearing another. And the books he read in Father's library often evoked similar horrors. He was frightened by Alexandre Dumas's story *The Man in the Iron Mask*, which reminded him of a poem, *Lalla Rookh* by Thomas Moore, about the Prophet of Khorassan, who kept his face veiled in order to conceal his disgusting leprosy.[5] It was as if there were no clear limits between self and world, and no stable centre within that boundless self.

One of Georgie's favourite treats was to be taken to see the tiger in Palermo Zoo. He would gaze at the beast for ages. Tigers seemed to possess a mysterious power, for they could 'only be hunted by armed men from a fort on the back of an elephant'.[6] He learned from his father about a man whose job it was to kill jaguars, which preyed on cattle, with no other weapon than a dagger. The figure of the *tigrero*, or 'tiger man', took root in the boy's imagination, for a man capable of vanquishing a tiger had to possess a degree of self-assurance which was the opposite of the myriad doubts to which Georgie himself was prey. The boy liked to imagine his father's antique Spanish dagger lying in a drawer, 'endlessly' dreaming of its tiger, 'and, grasping it, the hand comes alive because the metal comes alive, sensing in every touch the killer for whom it was wrought' ('The Dagger', *SP*, 175).

Father's library, then, was a mixed blessing: 'I felt ashamed, quite early, to be a bookish kind of person and not a man of action.'[7] This fascination of Borges's with the 'man of action' fostered an idea which long endured in his imagination: the 'man of action' was capable of clinching in combat a defining moment of true being. For example, in a story about a renegade gaucho, a lawman is so struck by the courage of the protagonist that he suddenly turns against his own men and fights alongside the outlaw; this was to be 'the night when he was finally to see his

---

[4] 'Al espejo', in *La rosa profunda*, in Jorge Luis Borges, *Obras completas* III (Buenos Aires: Emecé, 1996), 109. Unless otherwise attributed, translations from Spanish in this chapter are my own.
[5] Jean de Milleret, *Entretiens avec Jorge Luis Borges* (Paris: Pierre Belfond, 1967), 24.
[6] Borges, 'Dreamtigers', in *Selected Poems*, 75.
[7] Borges, 'An Autobiographical Essay', 211.

own face, the night when he was finally to hear his own name', because 'any life, however long and complicated it may be, actually consists of *a single moment* – the moment when a man knows forever more who he is'.[8]

This disjunction between the visceral intensity of active physical experience and the spectral 'unreality' of the library, which fostered doubts and fears and uncertainties, would assume a capital importance in Borges's thinking about literary creation. Books afforded a second-hand picture of reality, so the library would become a largely negative trope for Borges, a dystopian symbol of solipsism. The whole point was to *get out* of the library and plunge into a direct, authentic experience of the world. And so, if Georgie was to compensate for his father's failure to become a writer, if he wanted to fulfil a literary destiny, writing would have to become a form of action, the pen must become a surrogate for the dagger or the sword. But how to discover one's unique identity through writing? How could the writer imitate a man of action? As a young writer Borges would explore these questions and formulate a highly idiosyncratic poetics of his own.

* * *

Borges's favoured tendency within the emerging avant-garde was expressionism, or at least his own particular interpretation of it.[9] Originality was the overriding aim: a poet must 'throw overboard the whole of the past'—classical aesthetics, Romanticism, naturalism, symbolism, 'the whole of that vast absurd cage in which ritualists wish to imprison the marvellous bird of beauty', in order to achieve 'a naked vision of the world', a vision 'purified of ancestral stigmas'; everything must be jettisoned until 'we can each of us design our own subjective creation'.[10] Instead of being a 'passive mirror' of reality, a poem should refract experience through the 'active prism' of feeling and imagination, thereby enabling the writer to rise above contingent circumstances and 'convey naked emotion, purged of the supplementary particulars that precede it'.[11] After falling in love with a girl called Norah Lange, a budding poet whom he adopted as his protégée, he developed this early expressionism into an extreme confessional poetics.[12] In 'A Profession of Literary Faith' (1926), he likened the transaction between an author and a reader to 'a confession' based on 'one's confidence in the listener and the candor of the

---

[8] 'A Biography of Tadeo Isidoro Cruz (1829–1874)', in Jorge Luis Borges, *Collected Fictions*, trans. Andrew Hurley (New York: Viking Penguin, 1998), 213. Further quotations from this source (abbreviated as *CF*) will be incorporated in the main text of this chapter.

[9] For Borges in the Spanish and Argentine avant-gardes, see Edwin Williamson, *Borges: A Life* (New York: Viking Penguin, 2004), chs 4 and 8–10, respectively.

[10] 'Manifiesto del Ultra' ('Ultra Manifesto'), in *Jorge Luis Borges: textos recobrados, 1919-1929* (Buenos Aires: Emecé, 2001), 86–7.

[11] 'Anatomía de mi Ultra' ('Anatomy of My Ultra') [1921], in *Jorge Luis Borges: textos recobrados, 1919-1929*, 95.

[12] For Borges's relationship with Norah Lange, see Williamson, *Borges: A Life*, chs 7–10.

speaker'.[13] 'All poetry is the confession of an I, a personality, a human adventure'(*TTL*, 26); 'there are things that are poetic by merely implying a destiny' (*TTL*, 23), for 'all literature, in the end, is autobiographical' (*TTL*, 23), even though 'sometimes the autobiographical, personal substance, like a heart beating deep, disappears behind the accidents that incarnate it' (*TTL*, 25).

Still, he recognized an intrinsic problem in this romantic-expressionist poetics: 'How can we manage to illuminate the pathos of our lives? How can we interject in the hearts of others our humiliating truth?' (*TTL*, 26). The poet's very medium was an obstacle to sincerity—verse, rhyme, metaphor, language itself, tended to obscure rather than lay bare genuine feeling. His solution was that 'words have to be conquered, lived' (*TTL*, 26). By this he meant that language, though generic and impersonal, had to be imbued with the writer's particular experience of the world so that the work should bear the stamp of its maker's personality. This distinctive configuration of meaning amounted to the shaping of a unique personal destiny:

> I have now conquered my poverty, recognizing among thousands the nine or ten words that get along with my soul; I have already written more than one book in order to write, perhaps, one page. The page that justifies me, that summarizes my destiny, the page that perhaps only the attending angels will hear when Judgment Day arrives.   (*TTL*, 27)

This is Borges's first formulation of an idea that would remain with him almost to the end of his life—justification or salvation by writing. Just as the man of action might discover who he really was in a supreme moment of destiny, so too might a writer be able to discover his unique destiny in a self-defining work that would rescue him from the 'nothingness of personality'.[14]

In November 1926, however, Norah Lange fell in love with another man, the poet Oliverio Girondo, who was Borges's hated rival for the leadership of the Buenos Aires avant-garde.[15] As Borges waited for Norah to choose between her two suitors, he wrote: 'For love unsatisfied the world is a mystery, a mystery that satisfied love appears to understand.'[16] His future as a writer hung in the balance. When Norah finally rejected him, his romantic-expressionist poetics began to disintegrate. Already in 'A Profession of Literary Faith' he had recognized that language itself could be a barrier to direct communication with the reader, but he had asserted that intensity of experience and feeling would enable the poet to

[13] 'A Profession of Literary Faith', in Jorge Luis Borges, *The Total Library: Non-Fiction, 1922–1986*, ed. Eliot Weinberger (London: Allen Lane, The Penguin Press, 1999), 23–7, 25. (Published in New York as *Selected Non-Fictions*, Viking Penguin, 1999.) Further quotations from this source (abbreviated as *TTL*) will be incorporated in the main text in this chapter.

[14] See 'The Nothingness of Personality' in *The Total Library*, 3–9.

[15] For his literary and amorous rivalry with Girondo, see Williamson, *Borges: A Life*, chs 10–13.

[16] This appeared as an epigraph to Jorge Luis Borges, *El idioma de los argentinos* [1928] (Buenos Aires: Espasa Calpe/Seix Barral, 1994), 7.

'conquer' the impersonality of language and make words his own. That optimism evaporated now. In his essay 'An Investigation of the Word' (1927) he questioned the belief that poetry entailed a full confession of the self, based on the trust of the listener and the veracity of the speaker; there was 'a hemisphere of lies and of darkness' in speech which betrayed one's expressive intent; words were fickle and contingent, syntax a 'treacherous chain of events', so that language was 'nourished not by original intuitions—there are few—but by variations, happenstance, mis-chief' (*TTL*, 39). This inherent unreliability of language he called 'the general tragedy of all writing' (*TTL*, 39), for if language itself prevented the poet from communicating his feelings directly to the reader, if he could not 'conquer words' in order to mesh them with his heart, what would be the point of writing? Over the next two decades, he would scarcely write any poetry at all. Instead, he turned to prose, and would try his hand at fiction in order to find some means of expressing himself from within the prison-house of language.

In the 1930s he was racked by insomnia, nightmares, depression, and even thoughts of suicide.[17] In January 1938, after his father became terminally ill, he got a miserably paid job as an assistant in a municipal library in a poor neighbour-hood. He was surprised to find that 'there were some fifty of us doing what fifteen could easily have done', for the library's holdings were so meagre that cataloguing was hardly necessary.[18] His colleagues spent their time talking about soccer and horse racing, or telling each other smutty stories. No one showed any interest in books: one day a colleague came across a biographical note on a certain Jorge Luis Borges in an encyclopedia, and pointed out the coincidence of their names to Borges, not realizing they were one and the same person. He felt humiliated and distressed at the depths to which he had sunk. His situation was made even worse when his dying father made a very curious request. Dr Borges could not resign himself to literary failure, so he asked his son to rewrite his one published novel 'in a straightforward way, with all the fine writing and purple patches left out', and the two of them would discuss ways of improving the work.[19] Father's request brought the question of 'fulfilling a literary destiny' to a head, for how could the son save the father from failure when he had been mired in failure himself for the past ten years?

In the months following his father's death, Borges worked up an idea for a *ficción* about the implications of rewriting somebody else's novel. 'Pierre Menard, Author of the *Quixote*' is a review of the works of the eponymous French writer, recently deceased, whose most ambitious project was the rewriting of Cervantes's great masterpiece. It was not a question of copying the novel but of repeating it, of 'coming to the Quixote *through the experiences of Pierre Menard*'—that is,

---

[17] For his travails in the 1930s, see Williamson, *Borges: A Life*, chs 14–17.
[18] Borges, 'An Autobiographical Essay', 241–2.
[19] Borges, 'An Autobiographical Essay', 219–20.

rewriting it from scratch without directly consulting Cervantes's earlier version but nevertheless making his new version coincide 'word for word and line for line' with the Spaniard's text (*CF*, 91). Before his death, Menard had only managed to 'reconstruct' two chapters of Part 1 of *Don Quixote* (chapters 9 and 38) and a fragment of chapter 22. Still, had his enterprise of rewriting been successful, it would have undermined Cervantes's unique status as the author of the greatest classic in the Spanish language. After all, rewriting someone else's novel would nullify the creative personality of each writer and would effectively destroy the idea of original authorship. What's more, when Menard repeated the text of *Don Quixote* in the twentieth century, his words took on a very different meaning from Cervantes's version. Time had changed the meaning of Cervantes's text, which suggested that readers invent their own meaning as they read. Moreover, Menard's rewriting of *Don Quixote* would, strictly speaking, have been a kind of rereading of the novel, so Menard's enterprise, in effect, blurred the two roles, turning the author into a kind of reader and the reader into a kind of author.

In 'Pierre Menard' Borges presents us with a conception of writing which seems to foreshadow certain ideas later developed by French theorists, especially Roland Barthes's rejection in 'The Death of the Author' of the belief that a text communicates a message from what he called the 'Author-God', who places limits on the possible meanings of a text.[20]

It is the reader, Barthes argued, who bestows meaning on a text: every reader, one might say, is a Pierre Menard who repeats the words of the text he is reading, and changes their meaning as he adjusts them to his own subjectivity. Barthes concluded his essay with his now famous declaration, 'The birth of the reader must be paid for by the Death of the Author.'

In the case of Borges, however, the 'birth of the reader' was no cause for celebration, for in 'Pierre Menard' he had wilfully destroyed the supreme ideal of his youth—justification by writing. If a text could be 'reconstructed' by a subsequent author, and, worse still, if time changed the meaning of his words, then writing could have no reliable connection with personal experience or feeling, so it would be impossible for an author to express his true self to a trusting reader, let alone discover his unique destiny with his pen. And if creative writing was a futile exercise, what would be the point of libraries? No library could possibly satisfy the desire to achieve a true understanding of the world and one's own relation to it.

Only three months after 'Pierre Menard' appeared in *Sur*, Borges published an essay in the same literary review entitled 'The Total Library'.[21] His starting point

---

[20] Roland Barthes, 'The Death of the Author', in *Image-Music-Text*, ed. and trans. Stephen Heath (New York: Hill &Wang, 1977), 142–8.

[21] 'Pierre Menard, Author of the *Quixote*' was published in *Sur*, no. 56, May 1939; 'The Total Library' in *Sur*, no. 59, August 1939.

was the idea that, given unlimited time and a limited number of linguistic signs, those signs could be infinitely recombined to 'encompass everything possible to express in all languages' (*TTL*, 216). He then introduces the notion of a library which would contain every book ever written, or which could possibly be written. In such a library there would be millions of 'meaningless cacophonies, verbal farragoes, and babblings' (*TTL*, 216); indeed, entire generations of mankind could live and die without coming across a single intelligible page. The essay ends in tones of horror and disgust:

> One of the habits of the mind is the invention of horrible imaginings. The mind has invented Hell, it has invented predestination to Hell, it has imagined the Platonic ideas, the chimera, the sphinx, abnormal transfinite numbers... masks, mirrors, operas, the teratological Trinity: the Father, the Son, and the unresolvable Ghost, articulated into a single organism... I have tried to rescue from oblivion a subaltern horror: the vast, contradictory Library, whose vertical wildernesses of books run the incessant risk of changing into others that affirm, deny and confuse everything, like a delirious god.   (*TTL*, 216)

In 1941 he developed the central conceit of 'The Total Library' in 'The Library of Babel', in which he described the universe as an infinite library holding a finite number of books, each and every one containing only twenty-five orthographic symbols. A notable feature is the geometric uniformity of the library's structure— it consists of 'perhaps an infinite number of hexagonal galleries', all arranged in exactly the same fashion: 'Each wall of each hexagon is furnished with five bookshelves; each bookshelf holds thirty-two books identical in format; each book contains four hundred ten pages; each page, forty lines; each line approximately eighty black letters' (*CF*,113). Nevertheless, the book covers 'neither indicate nor prefigure what the pages inside will say' (*CF*,113); in fact, virtually all the books are 'formless and chaotic', given that 'for every rational line', there are 'leagues of senseless cacophony, verbal nonsense, and incoherency' (*CF*, 114). With its arch display of cod erudition, 'The Total Library' purported to be a scholarly essay, but 'The Library of Babel' was given a more narrative form, as well as a first-person narrator, both of which allowed for a degree of pathos: in view of its exact design the library could 'only be the handiwork of a god', yet Man, by contrast, was an 'imperfect librarian', who 'may be the work of chance or of malevolent demiurges' (*CF*,113).

In 'An Autobiographical Essay', Borges observed: 'My Kafkian story "The Library of Babel" was meant as a nightmare version of that municipal library' (where he was still employed at the time of writing). Much of the story's interest lies in its review of the quests undertaken by the librarians for purpose, for meaning, for some kind of salvation. There is a hint, moreover, that the narrator is a version of Borges himself: like 'all the men of the Library', he tells us, he has 'journeyed' in his younger days 'in quest of a book, perhaps the catalogue of catalogues', but his eyesight is failing, he is 'preparing to die, a few leagues from the hexagon where I was born', and it has proved impossible 'to grasp the distance that separates the human and the divine' (*CF*, 112, 113). He ends by clutching at the most fragile of straws, claiming to have found a 'solution' to the riddle of the meaningless library: given that it is infinite and the number of books is limited, then the same volumes will be repeated in the same order—which, repeated, becomes an Order of sorts. 'My solitude', he says, 'is cheered by that elegant hope' (*CF*,118).

In the combination of precision and disorientation that characterizes the Library of Babel, Borges happened to make a momentous discovery—he had come upon the trope of the labyrinth, and by giving that ancient device a metaphysical significance, he infused it with a universal pathos. The figure of the labyrinth would subsequently reappear in various guises in Borges's fiction and poetry, and would be taken in due course to be the hallmark of his peculiar imagination.

*   *   *

Just over a decade later, in 1955, Borges was appointed Director of the National Library of Argentina. It was a political appointment, a reward for his opposition to the authoritarian regime of Juan Domingo Perón, but, in truth, his elevation was scant compensation for the failure of his creative aspirations as a writer; indeed, it was a bittersweet honour, for even though he now claimed he 'had always thought of Paradise / in form and image as a library' (*SP*, 95), the fact was that he had run out of steam even as a writer of fiction (his last story, 'The End', had been published in 1953), he was close to breaking up with a much younger woman, and, to cap it all, an accident in 1954 had hopelessly damaged his already weak sight, leaving him unable to read or write.[22] His fate appeared to have been sealed: he had failed to find love, failed to engage fully with life, failed to define his true self with his pen—and here he was again, back in a library.

If in 'The Library of Babel' he had imagined the universe as a vast labyrinthine avatar of the dreadful municipal library at which he had worked for years, that horrific vision now assumed a new and even more soul-destroying form in the National Library. In 'Poem of the Gifts' he mused on 'the majesty / of God, who with such splendid irony / granted me books and blindness at one touch', handing over the 'care of this city of books' to 'sightless eyes' which could only read 'senseless paragraphs', 'infinite tomes', 'in libraries of dream':

---

[22] For his opposition to Perón and his concomitant relations with Estela Canto, see Williamson, *Borges: A Life*, chs 19–23.

> Aimlessly, endlessly, I trace the confines,
> high and profound, of this blind library.
>
> Cultures of East and West, the entire atlas,
> encyclopedias, centuries, dynasties,
> symbols, the cosmos, and cosmogonies
> are offered from the walls, all to no purpose.
>
> (*SP*, 95)

He recalls a previous Director of the National Library, Paul Groussac, who was also blind, and this precedent threatens to undermine his personal identity, for as he wanders 'through the gradual galleries' of the book-lined labyrinth, he 'often' feels with 'holy dread' that he might well be the dead Groussac, who must have 'attempted / the same uncertain steps on similar days' (*SP*, 95).

> Which of the two is setting down this poem –
> A single sightless self, a plural I?
> What can it matter, then, the name that names me,
> Given our curse is common and the same?

With his sense of self dissolving, he looks upon 'this dear world losing shape, fading away / into a pale uncertain ashy-gray / that feels like sleep, or else oblivion' (*SP*, 97).

And yet, even now, blind captive though he was in this 'city of books', the urge to create something vital in his writing had not been extinguished. In 'The Other Tiger' he describes how, as 'the fading light enhances / the complexities of the Library', he thinks of a tiger prowling in the jungle: 'in its world there are no names, nor past, nor future, / only the sureness of the present moment'; and yet, 'the tiger I am calling up in my poem is a tiger made of symbols and of shadows, / a set of literary images, / scraps remembered from encyclopedias, / and not the deadly tiger, the fateful jewel' in Sumatra or Bengal; 'the act of naming it, of guessing what is its nature and its circumstance / creates a fiction, not a living creature'; 'I know all this...yet still I keep on looking / throughout the evening for the other tiger, / the other tiger, the one not in this poem' (*SP* 117, 119).

The poignancy of this dilemma is caught in 'Borges and I', where he splits his intimate self from a much-feted public self called 'Borges', who has the habit of 'distorting and magnifying' the things they have in common:

> Some years ago I tried to get away from him: I went from suburban mythologies
> to playing games with time and infinity. But these are Borges' games now – *I will
> have to think of something else.*   (*SP*, 93; my italics)

'Borges and I' derives its force from the paranoia which underlies this account of self-alienation. 'Borges', the public man, bears down upon his fugitive 'I' like a ravenous beast closing on its prey; nevertheless, as with the search to capture the 'other tiger' in his writing, the author must press on in his quest to express his true self, the real 'I', in a work that might finally clinch his destiny. But what if that 'something else' were condemned also to be falsified by the charlatan 'Borges'? Such was the impasse that 'I don't know which of us wrote this' (*SP*, 93).

* * *

In 1964 Borges published 'Readers', the poem from which I quoted at the beginning of this chapter. The central figure is Alonso Quijano, the ageing country gentleman of La Mancha who decided to reinvent himself as a knight errant in order to restore the order of chivalry with his sword. In this poem, Borges entertains the 'conjecture' that Quijano, in fact, 'never actually left his library', and the adventures of Don Quixote were 'no more than a record of his dreaming'. 'Such, too, is my fate', observes Borges, recalling his own confinement in Father's library and his dreams of adventure in the world outside. Those boyish dreams, however, appear to him now as quixotic aspirations.

'Readers' marks the beginning of a profound re-evaluation of the poetics that had driven him to his creative impasse. Some years later, in the sonnet 'Alonso Quijano Is Dreaming' (1972), he returned to the 'conjecture' that the adventures of Don Quixote were no more than a 'dream' of Alonso Quijano. In this instance, however, it is a double dream, for not only does Quijano dream of becoming Don Quixote but Quijano himself is a dream of Cervantes. We thus have three persons with three distinct functions: first, Cervantes, the soldier who fought in the battle of Lepanto; second, the old hidalgo Alonso Quijano, reading in his library and dreaming of becoming a hero; and third, Don Quixote, the fictional hero dreamt by Quijano. Within this triad Quijano functions as a catalyst who transforms the memories of the old soldier Cervantes into the knight errant Don Quixote:

> The hidalgo was a dream of Cervantes,
> And Don Quixote a dream of the hidalgo.
> That double dream blends them both, and something
> Is happening which happened long ago.
> Quijano sleeps and dreams. A battle:
> The seas off Lepanto and the guns' rattle.[23]

We can better appreciate the development in Borges's thinking if we compare Quijano with Pierre Menard. For the nihilistic Menard, feeling and truth were impossible to convey to a reader because time changed the meaning of words; writing, therefore, was ultimately futile. However, thanks to Quijano's dream the

---

[23] 'Sueña Alonso Quijano', in *El oro de los tigres*, in Jorge Luis Borges *Obras completas* III (Buenos Aires: Emecé, 1996), 94.

Battle of Lepanto is not lost to time: 'something is happening which happened long ago'. Even though Quijano may not have set foot outside his library, his dream possesses the virtue of offering Cervantes some prospect of overcoming death, oblivion, and nothingness.

Five years later Borges wrote a third poem, 'I Am Not Even Dust', in which his identification with Alonso Quijano is so complete that he wrote it in the first person, as a covert autobiographical text in which he reflected in symbolic terms on the various stages of his evolution as a writer. The first section is analogous to the youthful phase of his career, when he dreamt of leaving the bookish 'unreality' of the library to become a 'man of action' and forge a unique destiny with his pen. It begins with Quijano's declaration, 'I do not want to be who I am' (*SP*, 397)—the old hidalgo hates his routine existence in a sleepy village in seventeenth-century Castile, and so he becomes addicted to reading books of chivalry which tell stories of Christian knights avenging their honour or meting out justice with their swords. He then asks God to send someone who might restore the noble ways of chivalry in this degenerate world. Suddenly, he declares: 'I, Quijano, / will be that champion. I will be my dream.' But no sooner does he resolve to be 'that champion' than he discovers he is as insubstantial as dust, for he is no more than someone else's dream:

> ... My face (which I have not seen)
> has never cast its image in the mirror.
> I am not even dust. I am a dream,
> woven in sleep and wakefulness
> by my brother and father, Captain Cervantes,
> who fought in the seas off Lepanto.[24]

In autobiographical terms, this section of the poem would correspond to the Pierre Menard phase in Borges's literary career, so to speak, in which an author cannot attain any lasting self-definition through his writing, and simply blurs into the reader's imagination as a kind of dream.

Alonso Quijano may be dependent on Cervantes, but it turns out that this is a mutual dependency because Cervantes, for his part, needs Quijano too. Note the curious formulation: 'my brother and father, Captain Cervantes'. Cervantes's dream may have 'fathered' Quijano, but Quijano, in turn, possesses the virtue of engendering a third party—Don Quixote—and this second dream makes them both 'brothers', inasmuch as each of them is in need of the knight of La Mancha to save them both from oblivion:

---

[24] Borges, *Selected Poems*, 397, but adapted by me to correct errors and translate Borges's meaning more accurately.

> In order that I may dream the other,
> Whose evergreen memory shall become part
> Of the days of man, I beseech you:
> My God, my dreamer, keep on dreaming me.

In this third section of the poem we find a crucial development in Borges's thinking about the role of the author and of literature itself. In the poem 'Alonso Quijano Is Dreaming', what survived the passage of time was the memory of the Battle of Lepanto, but in 'I Am Not Even Dust' it is the fictional Don Quixote of La Mancha who will remain 'evergreen' in the memory of mankind. In other words, Borges endows Quijano's dream with the power to create a literary character with such a strong identity of his own that, paradoxically, this mere figment of a double dream will be able to keep alive, and so justify, the original life experience of Cervantes, the man of action.

The library had long been for Borges the symbolic locus of an inner struggle to define and assert his sense of self against what he felt to the pressures of an overbearing and stifling family and tradition. His confinement in a library as a boy had engendered a form of madness—the quixotic idea that he must escape the library so as to imitate a man of action with his pen. That struggle had led in the end to a creative impasse, but in 'I Am Not Even Dust' the old terms are inverted—Cervantes 'dreams' of Quijano, a bookish man who goes mad in a library, but who, in turn, 'dreams' of a 'man of action', Don Quixote, who will live for evermore in the memory of humankind. And so, instead of being an obstacle to the creation of 'life' through writing, Alonso Quijano's library becomes the symbol of the creative imagination itself insofar as the mere 'dream' it engenders is capable of transforming historical experience into immortal memory.

The poem closes with a prayer: 'My God, my dreamer, keep on dreaming me'. In this reference to God, I see a further development in Borges's reflections on literary creation. The word God is spelt by Borges with a capital letter, which would suggest that he has in mind some original source for the double dream of Cervantes and Quijano which has produced Don Quixote. And it is perhaps this transcendental origin that gives the 'dream' of literature the ability to overcome nothingness and so justify the life of the author. Already in this poem we can catch a glimpse of the quasi-mystical conception of writing that Borges will explore in his final years: literary creation is essential to human existence because it points to the possibility of reaching Someone or Something ('Alguien' or 'Algo'—the capital letters are Borges's) which might save us from the nothingness into which we may be plunged by time.[25]

---

[25] For his quasi-mystical conception of writing, see Williamson, *Borges: A Life*, ch 33.

On the other hand, Borges was unable finally to overcome his agnosticism, so these concluding lines of the poem may be read in another sense. The 'God' to whom Alonso Quijano appeals is 'Captain Cervantes', his brother and father. This would mean that Quijano needed the historical experience of Miguel de Cervantes, the soldier who fought at Lepanto, as the raw material from which to create Don Quixote. Literary creation, in other words, cannot be entirely divorced from historical reality—it is human experience, in the last instance, which provides the material for the 'dream' of poetry or fiction. And the metaphor of the dream which Borges repeatedly employs in this last phase of his life has a certain precision—writing, like dreaming, is connected to everyday life, but indirectly, thanks to a process which disguises and transforms experience in ways that are still quite mysterious to us. The final lines of 'I Am Not even Dust', moreover, imply the recognition of a debt he owed his father. Just as Alonso Quijano refers to Cervantes as his 'God', so too might we see Borges acknowledging his father as a kind of creator-god, since Dr Borges's unrealized dream of 'fulfilling a literary destiny' was to determine the kind of writer his son was to become.

'I Am Not even Dust' was included in *A History of Night* (1977), and in an 'Epilogue' Borges observed that, of all the books he had published, this one was his 'most intimate', even though it abounded in 'bookish references'; but then, 'may I be permitted to repeat that the chief event of my life has been my father's library? The truth is that I have never set foot outside it, just as Alonso Quijano never emerged from his.'[26] For all that Borges had aspired to forge his own literary destiny by escaping the confines of his father's library, it was the failure of that hubristic endeavour which resulted in the kind of work that actually made his name.

---

[26] See Jorge Luis Borges, *Obras completas*, III (Buenos Aires: Emecé, 1996), 202. My translation.

13

Library and Scriptorium in Eco's
The Name of the Rose

Kylie Murray

Umberto Eco's *The Name of the Rose* shows us simultaneously a twentieth-century library and a medieval one, while presenting readers with the trope of the library as physical and ideological battle-site that has featured in earlier chapters of *Libraries in Literature*. First published in Italian in 1980, and translated into English by William Weaver in 1983, Eco's novel is famously and firmly set in the monastic culture of 1320s Italy, a period of conflict, controversy, intellectual revolution, the rise of the universities, and, with them, new knowledge. Moreover, the self-appointed guardian of this Italian abbey's books and library—as well as the most stubbornly medieval thinker of the entire novel, resistant to the intellectual renaissances of the High and Late Middle Ages—is a physically and morally blind, elderly monk named Jorge.[1] In a novel whose very title highlights the issue of naming, the name 'Jorge' is an unequivocal intertextual allusion to the twentieth-century novelist and essayist Jorge Luis Borges, whose libraries, both real and fictional, are often infinitely labyrinthine, sites of criminal activity, and spaces of subversion. Borges reflected on links between literary labyrinths, libraries, and crime in his short essay 'The Labyrinths of the Detective Story and Chesterton' and his 1978 lecture 'The Detective Story'.[2] In the former, he identifies six components for a detective story, including, appositely for Eco, 'the priority of how over who' (113), and 'a solution that is both necessary and marvellous' (114). In the latter, Borges attributes the origin of detective fiction to Edgar Allan Poe, and notes the necessity of the library to Poe's work as 'an enclosed space' (494). Such literary foundations directly underpin not only imaginative work by Borges, whose *Library of Babel* (1962) is seen as a direct source for *The Name of the Rose*, but Eco's own approach to the library of his novel. Eco leaves us in no doubt that Borges provides his most immediate source for the labyrinthine library at the heart of *The Name of the Rose*, and says in his 1983 postscript that he could not

---

[1] As neither abbot nor librarian, Jorge is not officially designated the role which he assumes.
[2] Both accessible in Eliot Weinberger (ed.), *The Total Library: Non-Fiction 1922–1986, Jorge Luis Borges*, trans. Esther Allen, Suzanne Levine, and Eliot Weinberger (London: Allen Lane, Penguin, 1999), 112–14 and 491–9 respectively. Quotation is taken from this edition of Borges's writings.

name his library's gatekeeper anything but Jorge, since 'Library plus blind man can only equal Borges, and debts must be paid'.[3]

Eco is frequently understood (and, of course, also self-identifies) as a postmodernist writer, particularly for such echoing of texts and ideas in his frequently metatextual and metaliterary 'tale of books' (6). From its first words preceding the novel's introduction, 'naturally, a manuscript', to the postscript's ending, questioning the moral value of reading, evocations concerning the repercussions of literary tradition and participation are pervasive. However, this approach is also deeply attuned to medieval culture: as Eco himself admits, 'I decided not only to narrate *about* the Middle Ages. I decided to narrate *in* the Middle Ages' (548). Furthermore, his postmodern 'Post-script' has a counterpart in the medieval literary tradition of the moral fable, so often accompanied by a concluding *moralitas* which provided an interpretive key for the reader.[4] Through his depiction of the medieval library and scriptorium as a graveyard, and as a guarding place where books, and latterly abbots, go to die, Eco repeatedly and emphatically blurs the boundaries between literariness and ethics, writing and interpreting, and, fundamentally, perception and deception. Accordingly, then, the present chapter will explore the kinds of mirrorings, reflections, and refractions that the library and scriptorium articulate, and will consider some of the implications of these.

In *The Name of the Rose* the architectural design and structural layout of the library and scriptorium convey significant cultural messages. Eco's book commences with an architectural drawing of the whole abbey complex, bringing sharply into focus the manner in which, ironically, many signifiers of meaning are non-textual in this novel that is so preoccupied with the making of books and the happenings centring on a library. Initial impressions of the abbey from Adso, Eco's young narrator, reflect the library's unusual prominence: an unrivalled 'depository of knowledge', a 'salvation of ancient learning' (40), 'spoken of with admiration in all the abbeys of Christendom' (38). By the end of the novel, however, this all changes in another example of meaning which is as shifting and uncertain as the novel's title itself. For Eco himself points out that the trope of the rose, much like his novel as a whole, involves a play on how dogmatic interpretation creates opacity rather than clarity: '[T]he rose is a symbolic figure so rich in meanings that by now it has barely any meaning left' (542).

Both library and scriptorium are housed in the 'aedificium', a building which, as its Latin etymology suggests, is on the edge: a sheer drop, an 'edifice', and, ultimately, a place of extremity, as the narrative bears out. Originally a fortress,

[3] All quotation of the novel in this chapter is taken from Umberto Eco, *The Name of the Rose*, trans. William Weaver (London: Vintage Books, 2004), giving page number in this edition.

[4] On the medieval fable tradition, see, for example, Roderick J. Lyall, 'Robert Henryson's *Morall Fabillis*: Structure and Meaning', in *A Companion to Medieval Scottish Poetry*, ed. Priscilla Bawcutt and Janet Hadley-Williams (Cambridge: D. S. Brewer, 2006), 89–104, and Edward Wheatley, *Mastering Aesop: Medieval Education, Chaucer and His Followers* (Gainesville, FL: Florida University Press, 2000).

and castle-like structure, the aedificium predates the ecclesiastical complex and is separate from it.[5] At twice the church's size, it physically and morally eclipses devotion, explicitly 'dominating the monks' (184). The aedificium's ground floor comprises a kitchen and refectory, with the scriptorium directly above, while on the top floor, above both, is the labyrinthine library. Thus the typical role of reading as devotion and endorsement of faith is thwarted: by moving towards books, the monks must simultaneously move away from sacred space and even devotional practice. Access to the library and scriptorium comes via the kitchens, a seeming incongruity, but one which, like the entire building, involves human appetites. This layout encompasses the most obviously functional culinary desires but reaches, too, into more challenging carnal ones: most memorably when Adso has a surprise sexual encounter with a local maiden in the kitchen following a nocturnal departure from the library.

In immediate anticipation of this moment, however, both perception and deception dissolve in the library through the medium of gazing at the female form depicted in manuscripts. Adso perceives images of the Virgin and the Whore of Babylon blurring into each other, and becomes conscious of how illustrations 'emerged from a pattern of interlocking labyrinths, which seemed all to refer to the tangle of rooms and corridors where I was' (258). Intoxication and even poison both infiltrate and implicate this library. To staff the scriptorium, monks highly skilled in the production of manuscripts are brought from across Europe: illuminators from Iona, Hereford, Sweden, and Spain are mentioned at work. Yet manuscript-related labours see them excused from daylight offices of prayer, thus cumulatively foregrounding yet further the disjuncture between the realms of devotion and knowledge. References to depths or bowels of the labyrinth reflect this disorientated and disrupted horizon of expectation: unsettlingly, the depths are at the top of the building. This unusual former military rather than sacred space for book-related activity bespeaks a locus of historical conflict, too: its implications of both defence and attack turn out to be pertinent to the events which unfold.

How do Eco's library and scriptorium compare with historical examples and their architectural meanings? As recent work by Richard Gameson has demonstrated, although monastic communities were irrefutably where texts were copied and new manuscripts produced, often scriptoria do not appear to occupy a defined space, even where we have surviving evidence of their outputs, or of library collections stored in book chests, book cupboards, or carrels in the Middle Ages.[6] In her study of Eco's novel, *Naming the Rose*, Theresa Coletti, too, observes

---

[5] I am indebted in this paragraph to the discussion of the aedificium's layout in relation to the abbey to Margaret Hallissy's provocative and illuminating study, 'Reading the Plans: The Architectural Drawings in Umberto Eco's *Name of the Rose*', *Critique* 42.3 (2001), 271–86.

[6] Richard Gameson, 'The Image of the Medieval Library', in *The Meaning of the Library*, ed. Alice Crawford (Princeton and Oxford: Princeton University Press, 2015), 31–71 (especially at 38–41).

that 'most monastic libraries were far more modest than [that of] the *Rose*—they did not usually involve a separate room or structure'.[7] Given that books survive with marks of provenance from actual monastic foundations with neither a documented library nor scriptorium, the identity of these monastic book hoards might have depended upon individuals rather than designated, fixed architectural spaces. I would argue that this backdrop certainly informs Eco's scriptorium and library, where both individuals and architectural structures are the guardians—and the concealers—of books and knowledge. The plot line in *The Name of the Rose* depends on the individual's control of reading and access to reading matter. However, it is also undeniable that the institution's specific architectural spaces associated with textuality come to preoccupy Eco, his characters, and his readers.

In the very structure of the two floors of the abbey's aedificium we see mirror opposites: the scriptorium is one giant room with forty large clear windows for maximum illumination, each accompanied by a desk for a monk to work at. Forty itself is a symbol of flawless order to Adso, 'a number truly perfect' (78) rooted in scriptural numerology as the ten commandments multiplied by the four cardinal virtues. All are arranged with meticulous and exquisite order for monks to produce manuscripts as a locus where text, image, colour, and light intersect: 'it seemed to me a joyous workshop of learning' (78), Adso recalls. This numerology is also mirrored in the abbot's description of the aedificium not long before his murder in a hidden wall of the library:

> 'An admirable fortress,' he said, 'whose proportions sum up the golden rule that governed the construction of the ark. Divided into three stories because three is the number of the Trinity, three were the angels who visited Abraham...'.
>
> (475)

Yet within the same architectural structure the library directly above is the scriptorium inverted: we might even call the library the literal dark side of the scriptorium within the aedificium as a whole, since it is not light that defines this space but opacity, disorder, and confusion. Vast spaces contained inside the library restrict light and perpetuate darkness:

> We passed through one of the openings. We found ourselves in another room, where there was a window that, in place of glass panes, had slabs of alabaster, with two blind walls and one aperture, like the one we had just come through. It opened into another room, which also had two blind walls. (181)

---

[7] Theresa Coletti, *Naming The Rose: Eco, Signs and Modern Theory* (Ithaca, NY: Cornell University Press, 1988), 33.

Similarly, the Franciscan Brother William of Baskerville, Adso's more learned senior colleague and fellow investigator, notes how 'at night not even the moon's rays can penetrate' this space (181). This library is not designed to facilitate learning but to conceal, and even, like the refectory, to witness things being swallowed, consumed, and lost forever—an irony which is acutely focussed when the library is finally razed to the ground along with the whole abbey complex, 'and the church, as if drawing into itself swallowed its own tower' (533). The abbey's oldest surviving monk, Alinardo of Grottaferrata, describes how 'no one goes to the library' because 'The library is a great labyrinth, a sign of the labyrinth of the world. You enter and you do not know whether you will come out' (169).

The building's architecture articulates how the heart of the library in a tangible and metaphorical sense consists of darkness and the unknown. So, for instance, Eco's readers become aware of tenets mirrored in the library's untold volumes which the monks are forbidden from reading; we sense, too, the books' bewildering organization, and the library's puzzlingly encrypted catalogue, lacking full titles, which only the librarian, Jorge, can initially decipher.[8] It is curiosity about just such a forbidden book, the sole surviving copy of Aristotle's treatise on comedy, that leads to each death in this novel.

Paradoxically, this impenetrable ideological and bibliographical fortress—with its attendant risk of being lost and never found—does incorporate order of some sort, not least because, in Richard Gameson's words, 'Libraries, medieval and modern alike, are simultaneously collections of books, spaces in which books are kept, and concepts. They are a body of knowledge and also a means of organizing it – for the way in which books are classified, and with what they are juxtaposed (not to mention how easy it is to gain access to them), can be as important as their own content in defining how they are used and perceived.'[9] We may also perceive the library's layout as unnerving, even frightening, precisely because at first glance each room seems identical to the last: in effect, it is like a hall of mirrors. Borges apparently loathed mirrors, and in *The Name of the Rose*, too, mirrors and mirrorings are problematized.[10] Eco reiterates this point by featuring actual physical as well as structural mirrors within the library. The mirror was a particularly ubiquitous medieval signifier: the 'mirror for princes tradition' was a pan-European body of advisory writing with a target audience of monarchs, rulers, and powerful aristocrats, designed to guide the reader in part by reflecting ideals.[11] Adso's encounter undercuts this staple literary hallmark image: he finds

---

[8] 'A list of titles often tells very little; only the librarian knows, from its degree of inaccessibility, what secrets, what truths or falsehoods, the volume contains' (41).

[9] Gameson, 'Image of the Medieval Library', 31.

[10] See Edwin Williamson's Chapter 12 in the present volume for further discussion of this aspect of Borges.

[11] For an overview of medieval mirror for princes literature ('speculum principis' in Latin), see Judith Ferster, *Fictions of Advice: Literature and Politics of Counsel in Late-Medieval England* (Philadelphia: University of Pennsylvania Press, 1990).

himself afraid of his own reflection in the library's mirror, revealing in microcosm a site where perception and deception converge:

> Holding the lamp in front of me, I ventured into the next rooms. A giant of threatening dimensions, a swaying and fluttering form came towards me, like a ghost.
>
> 'A devil!' I cried...

William's response is particularly revealing here: he laughs before commenting in amazement: 'Really ingenious. A mirror!' (183)

Of course, later the mirror also acts as a boundary and obstacle between our detective protagonists and the Finis Africae, the site in the library where the coveted Aristotle manuscript is concealed. Rather than revealing truth, then, the mirror deflects it: as one side of a door and a barrier which must be decoded to open and overcome its concealment of one of the most precious treasures of the library and, indeed, of Western intellectual history.

Distorted reflection and subversive mirroring are at the heart of the novel's murder mystery itself. This mystery and the crimes associated with it arise from the abbey's possession of an enormously crucial yet presumed lost text, namely the second part of Aristotle's *Poetics*, focussing not on tragedy but on comedy and laughter. Every monk who dies is in some way connected with this manuscript, and the 'detective' story culminates in Adso and William identifying the manuscript, locating its whereabouts, and understanding that the deaths assume a different significance from what they initially assumed. Jorge has acted as self-appointed gatekeeper of the most sinister kind, willing to kill anyone, including even himself, in order to prevent the dissemination of this unique surviving copy of Aristotle's work. Why is a monk so resistant to the Middle Ages' most foundational and influential philosopher?

The first clue lies with the first murder victim, Adelmo of Otranto, a young manuscript illuminator, who has been adding pictorial marginalia to a scriptural volume. Examining Adelmo's manuscript work after the murder, Adso and William, with the help of magnifying spectacles to show what is barely visible to the naked eye, find something remarkable contained in a Psalter 'in whose margins was delineated a world reversed... As if at the border of a discourse that is by definition the discourse of truth, there proceeded, closely linked to it, through wondrous allusion in aenigmate, a discourse of falsehood on a topsy-turvy universe, in which dogs flee before hare, and deer hunt the lion' (83). William understands the place of such pictorial work, and sees it as complementing sermons: 'to touch the imagination of devout throngs it is necessary to introduce exempla, not infrequently jocular, so also the discourse of images must indulge in these trivia' (86).

Venantius, the second murder victim, agrees with William by identifying the playful distortion in Adelmo's images as 'directed nevertheless to the glory of God, as an instrument of the knowledge of celestial things' (88). Yet Jorge is furiously, vehemently adamant that laughter contravenes the Benedictine rule. For Jorge laughter represents a loss of order and control, and, as such, Adelmo's depictions of nature inverted are not just untruthful but immoral:

> There are bad images that lie about the form of creation and show the world as opposite of what it should be...Little by little, the man who depicts monsters and portents of nature to reveal the things of God per speculum et in aenigmate [note the interesting mirror allusion here in 'speculum'] comes to enjoy the very nature of the monstrosities he creates and to delight in them, and as a result, he no longer sees, except through them.   (86–7)

Jorge's blindness is vividly apparent here, for in effect he is describing himself and his own actions as *The Rose* unfolds. Jorge has transformed the library into a screen and mask akin to that which Fiona Stafford's Chapter 4 in this volume describes so vividly in relation to Jane Austen: Jorge has actually denied the existence of the Aristotle manuscript which he keeps hidden, and relished the monstrosities he himself has created through calculated and meticulously executed poisons and murders. This moral irony is epitomized most vividly by his long-suppressed laughter during his own demise, when he resorts to consuming the poisoned Aristotle codex after William and Adso fathom his role as the mastermind behind the abbey's murders.

In addition to Jorge's inability to read texts due to his physical blindness, he misreads and misinterprets library-generated situations and signifiers, too, and, in further mirrorings, he causes others to misread them also. Texts of Aristotle's works were copied in monasteries throughout Christendom during this period, despite Jorge's desperation to conceal Aristotle's writing.[12] In a still further refraction, readers of *The Name of the Rose* see knowledge being debated in the scriptorium, but not the library, and through the medium of heated verbal exchange in the space set aside for writing, rather than, as we may expect, through written exchanges, or through the discourses, dialogues, and commentaries that were copied and read in manuscripts.

Misreading, or rather, the absence of reading, in the library (a phenomenon that Nicola Humble's Chapter 8 in this volume briefly discusses in the context of earlier twentieth-century crime fictions) involves not Jorge in isolation but all of

---

[12] The Middle Ages saw 'the Recovery of Aristotle' in the Latin West. See further Bernard G. Dod, 'Aristoteles latinus', in *The Cambridge History of Later Medieval Philosophy*, ed. Norman Kretzmann, Anthony Kenny, Jan Pinborg, and Eleonore Stump (Cambridge: Cambridge University Press, 1982; repr. 2008), 43–79, and in the same volume, C. H. Lor, 'The Medieval Interpretation of Aristotle', 80–98.

Eco's main characters. While *The Name of the Rose* is about solving the enigmatic events surrounding each murder, it is also mimetic of the library's labyrinthine structure, since we career down blind alleys in the path to understanding. Crucially in this regard, the novel's monkish detectives view the circumstances of the murders as corresponding to the order of the seven trumpets of the Apocalypse, namely objects falling from the sky; pools of blood; poison from water; bashing of stars; scorpions; locusts; and fire. And although these correspondences are irrefutable, William comes to realize that he has made them mean more than they do: 'What a fool – I conceived a false pattern' (502). This pattern was neither the reason nor the root cause behind the murders after all. Rather, the scriptural interpretation is something that William and we, the modern readers, have imposed on the sequence of events.

Instead, these deaths are part of Jorge's design, on account of his contempt for Aristotle as a pagan, non-Christian author who threatens scriptural learning and tradition. Perhaps modern readers can understand something of Jorge's apprehension about the new learning: with the rise of the universities came commercialization of book production, and Aristotle's work formed the backbone of the pan-European university curriculum, the *trivium* and *quadrivium*, throughout the Middle Ages.[13] However, seeing through distortion and fear has transformed Jorge from one of the abbey's most long-standing and in many ways revered monks (to whom others confess their deepest secrets and sins) into a liar and murderer who describes with chilling indifference how he plotted the murder of even his own abbot, sure he would be 'suffocated' (495). Ironically, Jorge has become an arresting exemplum of precisely that which he most fears would result from engagement with so-called subversive pagan works such as Aristotle's that deserve to remain hidden and censored in the labyrinthine library.

Eco recounts Aristotle's definition of comedy in a way which illuminates not only the structure of the story but also its signification:

> We will show how the ridiculousness of actions is born from the likening of the best to the worst and vice-versa, from arousing surprise through deceit, from the impossible, from violation of the laws of nature, from the irrelevant and inconsequent, from the debasing of characters, from the use of comical and vulgar pantomime, from disharmony, from the choice of the least worthy things. We will then show how the ridiculousness of speech is born from misunderstandings of similar words for different things, and different words for similar things... from play on words.   (500)

---

[13] On Aristotle's central role in the university curriculum, see G. Leff, 'The *Trivium*, and the Three Philosophies', in A *History of the University in Europe. Volume I: The Middle Ages*, ed. Hilde de Ridder-Symoens (Cambridge: Cambridge University Press, 1992), 307–36.

All of these tenets suffuse Eco's novel, and it contains some arresting examples of collapsing distinctions implied by 'the likening of the best to the worst and vice versa'. The monk Salvatore is depicted as brutish, particularly on account of his speaking fragments of several languages, none with fluent accuracy. Contending that he is 'not stupidus' (51), Salvatore warns Adso in broken English and Latin that require of readers a further layer of interpretation. Somewhat comically, however, Adso himself includes fragments of other languages in an uncannily similar way, including when he describes Salvatore:

> His speech was somehow like his face, put together with pieces of other people's faces, or like some special reliquaries I have seen (si licet magnis componere parva, if I may link diabolical things with the divine), fabricated from the shards of other holy objects.   (52)

There is also a material manifestation of such fragmentation when Adso attempts to recover the manuscript vestiges from the ashes of the library after it has been razed to the ground. Adso, writing in his old age, reveals that he kept these fragments all his days, persistently, obsessively attempting to decipher an overall meaning, only to conclude that there was none: a further mirroring of the novel's title and how it may yield simultaneously many meanings or, indeed, none.

In *The Name of the Rose* a more provocative collapsed distinction occurs at the very heart of the library, and in the final encounter between William and Jorge: the equivalent, we might think, of matter meeting antimatter, so different have they been in their moral code and world view throughout the narrative. However, William and Jorge come to express admiration for each other not as opposites but equals. Jorge comments on what a fine librarian William would have made, and Adso sees for himself how they are 'admiring each other, as if each had acted only to win the other's applause' (506). Once Jorge sets about erasing from existence both the Aristotle manuscript and, ultimately thereby, himself, William shows a callousness and obsessive concern with the Aristotle manuscript in language that comes straight from Jorge:

> I don't care whether he dies: damn the monster! With what he has eaten, his fate is already sealed. *But I want the book!*   (516: my italics)

Ironically, and seemingly inadvertently, then, the library of Eco's novel *does* transmit knowledge, in complex, layered ways, but does not yield it freely as we would expect. It has demanded risk, transgression, and subversion. Reverberations of laughter interspersed through the novel and, indeed, Aristotle's elusive manuscript are a key part of this. Two examples of such reverberations can be seen as pivotal in relation to the library and its goings-on. The first is a bathetic moment involving the oldest, most venerated monk in the abbey. Old Alinardo, in dialogue with Adso, while beginning to explain the hermeneutic significance of the seven trumpets of the Apocalypse, interjects comically:

> 'I heard it. All were whispering that sin has entered the abbey. Do you have any chickpeas?'
>
> The question, addressed to me, surprised me. 'No, I have no chickpeas', I said, confused.
>
> 'Next time, bring me some chickpeas. I hold them in my mouth—you see my poor toothless mouth?—until they are soft. They stimulate saliva, aqua fons vitae. Will you bring me some chickpeas tomorrow?'
>
> 'Tomorrow I will bring you some chickpeas,' I said to him. But he had dozed off. We left him and went to the refectory. (170)

The second telling example returns us to the final library scene, where all mysteries are solved: the 'how' of Borges's essay on detective novels, discussed above.[14] Although Jorge has been a menacing and murderous force, Eco gestures towards a comic way of viewing him at this point. There is no small irony in Jorge's eating of the concealed Aristotle manuscript—all-consuming as it is—and he laughs as he does eat it, then scuttles off into the dark.

> Jorge smiled, baring his bloodless gums, a yellowish slime trickled from his pale lips over the sparse white hairs on his chin[.] He laughed, he Jorge. For the first time I heard him laugh ... 'You did not expect it, William, not this conclusion, did you? This old man, by the grace of God, wins once more, does he not?' As he turns out the lamp, thrusting all into darkness once more, for the last time we heard the laughter of Jorge who said, 'Find me now! Now I am the one who sees best!' (514–15)

The library and the scriptorium have inadvertently generated and transmitted new understandings for the protagonists and for us, best articulated by William:

> Jorge feared the second book of Aristotle because it perhaps really did teach how to distort the face of every truth, so that we would not become slaves of our ghosts. Perhaps the mission of those who love mankind is to make people laugh at the truth, to make truth laugh, because the only truth lies in learning to free ourselves from insane passion for the truth. (527)

William's words push interpretive efforts back on to the readers of *The Name of the Rose*, as the novel's very title suggests. What should we make of shifting and

---

[14] See note 2 above.

uncertain significations, as epitomized by the very image of the 'rose'? The library and scriptorium are pivotal in generating significations, but not through standard engagement with their textual productions and their reading materials. Instead, it is the *denial* of access to these, and the speculation ensuing about the secrecy and concealment involved, that lead to interpretive errors, misreadings, and ultimately destruction for both the novel's characters and for readers in quest of any single, simple truth. Modern readers may conclude by pondering Borges's point about the 'priority of how over who' in a detective story, and may consider what it is that Adso has really learned through his experience and his reading (or lack thereof). Adso reveals in his later years and maturity that he attempted to preserve the library's vestiges: the burnt, only partially intelligible, fragments he could recover, to *make* them mean something, even where they clearly do not. Eco focusses acutely here on what he has gestured at throughout his most famous and compelling novel, through the medium of the library and scriptorium: a spectrum of views about the role of reading and knowledge, ranging from crucial importance at one end to, at the other, meaninglessness if texts are not accessed and transmitted in an effective, authentic way. This focus on attempts to conserve, construct, and reconstruct texts is one that draws equally on the novel's attunement to medieval library culture and to its postmodern, Borgesian awareness of the library as a potentially engulfing labyrinth that is at once the sum of a living civilization's values and, ironically, the potential enemy of civilized life.

14
Murakami's Strange Library

Chris Perkins

'All I did was go to the library to borrow some books', reads the short quotation on the back of the 2014 British translation of *The Strange Library* by the novelist known in Japan as Murakami Haruki and elsewhere as Haruki Murakami.[1] The simplicity of this quotation, along with the nostalgic presentation of the edition with its imitations of traditional library stamps, illustrations that look as if they come from antiquarian volumes, and drawings of antique reading glasses, helps domesticate the text for its target audience, making *The Strange Library* appear unthreateningly familiar. Yet the straightforward decision to borrow books leads the story's protagonist, a boy referred to simply as 'I' (in Japanese, *boku*), into a nightmarish labyrinth beneath a seemingly normal public library, and into a text whose background, genesis, and forms are themselves correspondingly labyrinthine.

This is because Murakami's *Strange Library* is not one short story but many. It first appeared in 1982 as *An Extraordinary Library Tale* (*Toshokan kitan*), serialized in a little-known Japanese magazine, *Trefle* (*Torefuru*), before being published in Murakami's 1983 short-story collection *A Perfect Day for Kangaroos* (*Kangarū biyori*).[2] Another, slightly different version, incorporating authorial alterations, and also entitled *An Extraordinary Library Tale*, forms part of a collection of Murakami's early work.[3] Next, Murakami published a picture book version of the story with illustrator Sasaki Maki. However, the addition of illustrations to the story meant for Murakami that the text itself would also have to change, this time more radically.[4] Whereas the original story was a macabre tale for adults, this new version was a picture book for children. As such the language and content of the original story were simplified extensively. The title was also changed, from *An Extraordinary Library Tale*, which contains difficult-to-read Japanese *kanji* characters, to *The Strange Library* (*Fushigi na toshokan*), a title

---

[1] Haruki Murakami, *The Strange Library*, trans. Ted Goossen (London: Harvill Secker, 2014). All Japanese names in the body of the text follow the Japanese surname/first name convention.

[2] Haruki Murakami, *Kangarū biyori* (Tokyo: Kōdansha, 1983).

[3] Haruki Murakami, *Murakami Haruki zensakuhin 1979–1989* (Tokyo: Kōdansha, 1993).

[4] Haruki Murakami, 'Atogaki', in Haruki Murakami, *Toshokan kitan* (Tokyo: Shinchōsha, 2014), 73.

which in Japanese is easier for school-age children to read. This version was published in 2005.[5]

Up to this point the evolution of Murakami's story was confined within Japan's national borders. But since Murakami is the most internationally popular of Japanese writers, it was almost inevitable that *The Strange Library* should travel abroad. Between 2014 and 2015 the story was published in the UK, US, France, Germany, Italy, South Korea, and China. But it was the children's version that travelled. New illustrations were commissioned for the UK, US, German, and Italian editions, with the French, Chinese, and Korean translations using the German pictures provided by Kat Menschik. What is surprising here is that, as a result of the international success of the story, *An Extraordinary Library Tale* was republished in Japan in 2014, now accompanied by Menschik's illustrations, which prompted yet another rewrite from Murakami.[6]

The existence of so many versions of the story, each with its own audience, context, and content, makes the work hard to analyse. Questions of genre and the relationship between images and text in the English translation have been explored, but as yet very little has been written about the context and content of the original publication in the 1980s.[7] Exploration of this involves aspects of the role of libraries in Japanese culture as well as uncovering layers of meaning hidden by the various permutations of the story as it was subsequently translated and adapted.[8] What emerges is that, in part at least, *The Strange Library* was written as a homage to Jorge Luis Borges at a point in Murakami's career when he was developing his particular literary aesthetic in the context of 1980s Japan. Images drawn from Borges of vast subterranean structures, labyrinthine corridors, and the layering of the material world, the fantastic, and non-diachronic time intersect with Murakami's ambivalent view of Japan in the 1980s to produce a terrifying fable about the dangers of embracing a postmodern, post-ethical world.

Murakami's globally read fiction of the library emerges from a particular Japanese cultural moment. In contrast to the narrative of economic stagnation and sense of malaise that came to characterize the mood of the nation from the 1990s onwards, the 1980s for Japan were a period of consumption, growth, and excitement. Japanese goods dominated world markets, standards of living rose annually, and Japan was awash with imported luxury items. In literature the

---

[5] Haruki Murakami and Maki Sasaki, *Fushigi na toshokan* (Tokyo: Kōdansha, 2005).

[6] Murakami, *Toshokan kitan*.

[7] Paul L. Thomas, 'Magical Murakami Nightmares: Investigating Genre Through *The Strange Library*', in *Haruki Murakami Challenging Authors*, ed. Matthew C. Strecher and Paul L. Thomas (Rotterdam: Sense Publishers, 2016), 47–57.

[8] The library, of course, features prominently in Murakami's 2005 novel *Kafka on the Shore*: Murakami Haruki, *Kafka on the Shore* (London: Harvill, 2005). For a discussion of function of the library in *Kafka on the Shore* complementary to the current chapter, see Ewen Jarvis, 'A Poetics of Intellectual Library Space: A Hidden Story of Natural Growth', *Double Dialogues*, 12 (2010), http://www.doubledialogues.com/article/a-poetics-of-intellectual-library-space-a-hidden-story-of-natural-growth/.

opening statement of the times was Tanaka Yasuo's 1980 novel *Somehow, Crystal* (*Nantonaku, kurisutaru*), a book about the life of a female university student and model which contained so many references to foreign consumer goods that it needed 442 explanatory footnotes. For Tanaka, who was himself a university student when he wrote his novel, it was strange that, despite Japan's material prosperity, the Japanese novel remained fixated on the question of how to live a moral life. It struck Tanaka that this question was no longer relevant to his generation; in an abundant economy the issue was not ethics, but simply how to live a pleasant life (*kibun yoku kurasu koto*).

Faced with the dearth of books about a new generation uninterested in politics or social issues, Tanaka wrote his own, and termed this generation's world view the 'crystal life'.[9] Awarded the prestigious Bungeishunju Prize in 1980, *Somehow, Crystal* seemed to mark the ascension of those Japanese New People (*shinjinrui*), a 'crystalline generation' whose values of individualism, pleasure-seeking, and mass consumption contrasted sharply with the apparently politically and socially dedicated generation that preceded them. Even the former Marxists, structuralists, and anti-capitalist thinkers of Japan's 1960s and 1970s began to embed themselves in the lives of the expanding middle class, adopting playful detachment and erasure of the self as their new philosophical position. Dense postmodern texts became bestsellers; department stores used Jean Baudrillard's work on *simulacra* in their marketing strategy.[10]

At about the same time that Tanaka Yasuo was searching for a postmodern Japanese aesthetic, Haruki Murakami was also testing literary approaches to the dizzying Japan of the late 1970s and early 1980s. Although some of this exploration was done through his early novels, Murakami also used a whole host of short stories as 'test courses' to explore what he termed 'new systems of perception' (*atarashii ninshiki shisutemu*).[11] Significantly, this period of experimentation took place as a literature which appeared to provide a method for interrogating the postmodern condition, namely Latin American magical realism, was gaining a readership in Japan.[12] Starting in 1975 with Jorges Luis Borges's *Ficciones* (1956), Japanese publishing company Shūeisha had been slowly introducing Latin American literature to Japan, but it was really in the early 1980s, with the award to Gabriel García Márquez of the 1982 Nobel Prize for Literature, that Latin American fiction really took off.[13] Furthermore, we know from various sources that Murakami was reading this literature while writing his early short stories and

---

[9]   Yasuo Tanaka, *Nantonaku, kurisutaru* (Tokyo: Kawade bunko, 2014), 230.

[10]   Akira Asada, 'A Left Within the Place of Nothingness', *New Left Review* 5 (2000): 1–26.

[11]   Yumie Yamane, 'Murakami Haruki "odoru shōjin" ron: boruhesu he no kage', *Kokubungakukō* 209 (2011), 33.

[12]   Yamane, 'Murakami Haruki', 34–6. See also Matthew C. Strecher, 'Magical Realism and the Search for Identity in the Fiction of Murakami Haruki', *Journal of Japanese Studies* 25.2 (1999), 263–98.

[13]   Yamane, 'Murakami Haruki', 34.

novels between 1979 and 1982, a period which culminated in his decision to become a professional novelist with the publication of *A Wild Sheep Chase* (*Hitsuji wo meguru bōken*).[14]

The first, 1982 version of *The Extraordinary Library Tale* was published at the start of the Japanese 'Latin American Boom', under the title *Toshokan kitan*. This Japanese title gives us a clue to the intent behind this story: *kitan* was also the word used in the 1976 translation into Japanese of a collection of fantasy stories, *Extraordinary Tales* (in Japanese *Boruhesu kaititanshū*, and in Spanish *Cuentos Breves y Extraodinarios*), a volume edited by Borges and his long-time collaborator Adolfo Bioy Casares.[15] The timing and shared use of the term *kitan* lend credence to Japanese Latin Americanist Noya Fumiaki's assertion that Murakami paid homage to Borges in producing a short *extraordinary library tale* that could be added to Borges and Casares's collection.[16] In addition, like *A Wild Sheep Chase*, this story contains a fantastical being—the Sheep Man—who, given that Borges's *Book of Imaginary Beings* (Japanese *Genjū jiten*) had been published to much acclaim in Japan in 1975, may well be Murakami's addition to the pantheon of literary beasts.[17] And finally, this is a story set in the Borgesian milieu of a labyrinthine, apparently infinite, library.

Yet it would be insensitively reductive to present Murakami's story as a playful ode to Borges and Latin American fiction. Murakami's library tale draws on Borges, but, attuned to the grain of Japanese culture, asks penetrating questions of Tanaka's all-surface, no-depth, crystalline moment. Emerging as a threatening space of confusion, trickery, and violence, where the acquisition of knowledge, if done carelessly, will take a terrible toll on the subject, Murakami's story is also inextricably linked with the history of public libraries in Japan. These have fulfilled various roles since the Western idea of the library was introduced to Japan in the 1860s. Although the role of the library at this time was to 'acquire, catalogue and make available good reading material', and despite an active Japan Library Association (JLA) forming in 1892, in reality most early libraries had closed stacks and charged fees to enter. Government funding was also limited, as the state was reluctant to allocate resources to support what it saw as the private pursuits of individuals.[18] The state's attitude to public libraries, however, changed in the 1920s, as officials became increasingly worried about the threat posed by foreign ideologies to public order, and saw public libraries as an ideal institution for the ideological guidance of the people. Although to begin with the JLA resisted this

---

[14] Yamane, 'Murakami Haruki', 35.

[15] Jorge Luis Borges and Adolfo Bioy Casares, *Boruhesu kai kitan shū* (Tokyo: Shōbunsha, 1976).

[16] Fumiaki Noya, '"Sekai no owari to hādoboirudo wandārando" ron: "boku" to "watashi" no dejabyū', *Kokubungaku* 40.4 (1995): 54.

[17] 'Genjū jiten', *Yomiuri Shimbun*, 10 March 1975, 7.

[18] Sharon Domier, 'From Reading Guidance to Thought Control: Wartime Japanese Libraries', *Library Trends* 55.3 (2007): 554.

new vision of the public library, with the passing in 1925 of the repressive Peace Preservation Law,[19] and Japan's invasion of China starting in earnest in 1931, the JLA and public library system aligned their activities with Japanese state goals by promoting books conducive to the spiritual mobilization of the nation against the looming threats of the West.[20] So, while the public library system was designed for the education of the Japanese populace, what constituted 'good' reading material was defined by the needs of the State.

With the occupation of Japan after the Second World War by the Allied forces from 1945 to 1952, the mission of the public library system was revised and expanded. In alignment with the Allied occupation's goal of bringing peace and democracy to Japan through new institutional structures, the 1950 Library Law (*Toshokanhō*) banned fees for public libraries, recognized the importance of professional librarians, and made provision for citizen participation in library management.[21] While it took some time for the concept of a fully free and open library system to take hold in Japan, beginning in the mid-1960s there was a huge expansion in public library provision as libraries, tapping into the cultural zeitgeist, marketed themselves as 'people's universities', with the mission to protect 'intellectual freedom' and 'guard the people's right to know'.[22] In 1983, the year after Murakami published his *Extraordinary Library Tale*, there were a total of 1379 public libraries in Japan, housing between them 76.6 million individual volumes.[23]

On the surface, Murakami's library is a simple instance of the post-war democratic public library. From the very beginning, however, the story gnaws away at a sense of stability in our knowledge of the surrounding environment. The library and its books are cast as a threatening presence. On entering, *boku* observes that the place is too quiet. The books suck away sound by killing off vibrations in the air. Such vibrations do not go anywhere, but just disappear. Nothing lasts for ever, not even time: 'There is a "this week" without a "next week". There was a "this week" without a "last week".'[24] Time here, then, is subjective and paradoxical. 'This week' without 'next' suggests a perception of time finishing with death; 'this week' without 'last' suggests birth. Such rumination on time provides some hint as to the allegorical nature of this text. By the end

---

[19] Richard H. Mitchell, 'Japan's Peace Preservation Law of 1925: Its Origins and Significance', *Monumenta Nipponica* 28.3 (1973): 317–45.

[20] Domier, 'From Reading', 560–1. See also Theodore F. Welch, *Libraries and Librarianship in Japan* (London: Greenwood Press, 1997), 15–17.

[21] Yoshitaka Kawasaki et al., 'The Development of Public Libraries in Japan After World War II', 62nd IFLA General Conference Proceedings, August 1996, https://archive.ifla.org/IV/ifla62/62-kawy.htm.

[22] Yoshitaka Kawasaki, 'Library History Studies in Japan and the Japan Society for the Study of Library History (JSSLH)', *Libraries & Culture* 25.1 (1990): 131.

[23] Welch, *Libraries and Librarianship*, 84.

[24] Murakami Haruki, 'Toshokan kitan' in Murakami Haruki, *Kangarō biyori* (Tokyo: Kōdansha, 1986), 199. All references to *An Extraordinary Library Tale* in this chapter are to this version, hereafter cited as 'Toshokan kitan'.

there will be death (the death of the boy's mother), and there will be birth—or at least a rebirth of *boku* back into the world.

It is not only time that is destabilized, but also language. As *boku* approaches the receptionist, a woman he has never seen before, he notices that the book she is reading is written in Japanese and a foreign language on opposite pages, and that the content—paragraph structure, diagrams—on each page is completely different. The woman's eyes work independently, taking in two different stories in two different languages simultaneously. Words and pictures are jumbled, but still the woman 'nodded along passionately'.[25] In the library we are about to enter the rules of language as we understand them do not apply, but at the same time the mishmash of images and language still have the ability to elicit pleasure. *Boku* returns his books to the woman, the first a history of submarine construction, the second the memoirs of a shepherd. Given that the boy is soon to descend into the depths of the library where he comes into contact with a strange sheep man, it appears that the content of these books will soon become the symbolic resources *boku* will use to make sense of the experience to come.

This nod to destabilization of categories and pleasure in play associated with the Japanese 1980s is coupled with a much older concern: that of authority, volition, and power. This theme emerges most strongly through the boy's interactions with the strange librarian in room 107, who is simply referred to as the old man (*rōjin*). After being sent downstairs to room 107, *boku* meets the old man and asks for books on tax collection in the Ottoman Empire. The man dutifully finds three large, dusty volumes and presents them to *boku*, telling him that the books must be read in the library reading room. When *boku* protests that the library is about to close and he must get back to his mother, the old man becomes angry and chastises him. Against his own better judgement, *boku* finds himself following the old man down beneath the library, through a labyrinth of corridors. At one point he stops and tells the old man that he is concerned that the library will close, and that the boy's mother will be worried about him if he doesn't come home soon. The old man simply dismisses the boy's concern: 'The library closing time is not a problem. If I say it is okay, then it is okay.'[26]

At face value the old man and the boy are travelling to the reading room. But an alternative reading is that the labyrinth under the library is here the mind of the boy himself.[27] Evidence for this lies in the coding of the tunnels beneath the library. Murakami is noted for his explorations of the interior worlds of his protagonists, but does not make an overt linguistic distinction between the

[25] 'Toshokan kitan', 200.   [26] 'Toshokan kitan', 205.

[27] Ewen Jarvis makes a similar point about the library in *Kafka on the Shore*, which he characterizes as 'a kind of halfway house between the conscious and subconscious, the living and the dead'. See Jarvis, 'A Poetics of Intellectual Library Space', http://www.doubledialogues.com/article/a-poetics-of-intellectual-library-space-a-hidden-story-of-natural-growth/.

everyday external world and their interior worlds.[28] Instead, the everyday external and the interior mind are presented concomitantly from the subjective position of the protagonist. The outcome is a sort of flat representational canvas, on which interior and exterior are presented as equal and interpenetrating.[29] However, throughout his work Murakami has consistently provided clues to the status of experiences by contrasting the 'light' world of the everyday and the 'dark' inner world of the unconscious mind.[30] Likewise, *boku*'s descent begins with the dim light of a single bulb and gets progressively darker until he stands in front of the reading room itself, which when opened is pitch-black (*makkura*). Faced with entering the reading room, *boku* protests but is cowed into submission by the old man, who suddenly grows in stature and scolds him for speaking out of turn. Beyond the library's reading room is a staircase, which is described as 'like an Inca well ... not a ray of light, not a chink of brightness ... as dark as if my head was completely covered with a hood'.[31] At the bottom of the stairs the boy is ushered into one further room, which will turn out to be his cell. Here he meets a small, strange man dressed as a sheep.

If we accept that the old man/librarian is leading the boy into the recesses of his mind, we can make some inferences about the librarian's role in the story. We know he is an important figure in the library, he is domineering and dismissive towards the boy, and he reacts aggressively to questions. He also speaks in the language of rules (*kisoku*): the books must be read in the reading room; doors in the labyrinth must be locked because of rules decided by 'important people' (*erai renchū*); those same important people have made thousands, even tens of thousands, more rules that must be abided by.[32] Once the boy is deposited in his cell, the librarian decrees he will only be freed if he can master the content of the three books on Ottoman Empire tax collection the boy requested. Finally, and in contrast to many of the librarians discussed elsewhere in the present volume, the librarian is male. This gendering of the librarian and, by extension, of the library is significant. The librarian can be viewed as an agent of the symbolic order, which Lacanian theorist Todd McGowan characterizes as 'the system of codes – both articulated and nonarticulated – that regulate our quotidian existence'.[33] According to Lacanians, it is the father who inducts the child into the symbolic order through the interdiction against the child's constant demand for the succour

---

[28] Strecher, 'Magical Realism', 270.

[29] See Chris Perkins, 'Flatness, Depth and Kon Satoshi's Ethics', *Journal of Japanese and Korean Cinema* 4.2 (2012): 119–33.

[30] Strecher, 'Magical Realism', 270.   [31] 'Toshokan kitan', 209.

[32] 'Toshokan kitan', 209.

[33] Todd McGowan, *Psychoanalytic Film Theory and the Rules of the Game* (London: Bloomsbury Academic, 2015), 32. The suitability of a Lacanian approach to the unconscious in Murakami has been discussed extensively. In doing so here I draw on Maria Flutsch, 'Girls and the Unconscious in Murakami Haruki's Kafka on the Shore', *Japanese Studies* 26.1 (2006): 69–79; Jonathan Dil, 'Writing as Self-Therapy: Competing Therapeutic Paradigms in Murakami Haruki's Rat Trilogy', *Japan Forum* 22.1–2 (2010): 43–64; and Strecher, 'Magical Realism'.

of the mother's body. The father lays down the law with a declarative 'no!', and the child's demands for the mother's body are replaced by a quickly repressed desire. There is a striking consonance between such psychology and the *Strange Library*, where the librarian is quite literally leading the boy away from his mother, and the boy keeps on stating how anxious she will be and how he must get back to her before she goes mad with fear.

This reading is also helpful when we think about the sheep man and the last of our cast of characters living beneath the library: a beautiful young girl whose voice box was destroyed when she was a child and who can thus only speak with her hands. On the first night of the boy's imprisonment, the sheep man promises to cook a delicious meal. However, it is not the sheep man but the beautiful girl who delivers the food. Murakami dwells upon her physical beauty as an object of desire: 'the girl that everyone sees in their dreams, and the girl that you can only see in your dreams'.[34] The fact that she cannot talk other than with her hands separates her from the symbolic order of the old man, suggesting that, in Lacanian terms, she is representative of the prelinguistic imaginary component of the boy's psyche: a fantasy image of the ideal object of desire.[35] Furthermore, an equivalence between the beautiful girl and the sheep man is also established. In a later discussion with the boy about why the sheep man does not seem to see her, the girl tells *boku*:

> 'The sheep man has the sheep man's world. I have my own world. You have your own world. Am I right?'
>
> 'Yes,' I said.
>
> 'And it doesn't follow that I don't exist just because I am not in the sheep man's world, right?'
>
> 'In other words, all those different worlds are all mixed up here. And there are some bits that cross over and other bits that don't,' I said.
>
> 'That's right,' said the beautiful girl.[36]

This equivalence is made even stronger in the 2014 Kat Menschik version of the book, in which the exchange above is coupled with an image of the girl with a set of sheep's horns.[37] Perhaps the best way to make sense of the sheep man, then, is as a projection of *boku*'s self as understood through the symbolic resources found in the memoirs of a shepherd he returned to the library at the very beginning of the story. The sheep man is also trapped, also cowed by the old man, and is sympathetic to the boy's plight. Perhaps most obviously the sheep man is a *sheep*, an animal

---

[34] 'Toshokan kitan', 218.   [35] McGowan, *Psychanalytic Film Theory*, 39.

[36] 'Toshokan kitan', 224.

[37] Murakami Haruki, *Toshokan kitan* (Tokyo: Shinchōsha, 2014), 20.

symbolic of following the leader, which chimes with the boy's description of himself as easily led.

There is one final layer to this library story that adds to the conflation of the external and interior experience of the boy: the flattening of historical time. As with his propensity to explore the inner worlds of his protagonists, throughout his novels Murakami has consistently explored the haunting of the Japanese present by memories of Japan's wartime past. Although never made explicit, *boku*'s induction into the symbolic order of the library has historical resonances which hark back to Japan's pre-war libraries and the social structure in which they were embedded. As noted earlier, and as historian Sheldon Garon puts it, pre-war Japanese public libraries were part of a mesh of institutions co-opted by the state into 'molding the minds' of ideal wartime subjects.[38] Garon points out that the process of producing wartime Japanese subjects had two sides: violence and co-option. Certainly, the pre-war Japanese state could mobilize huge numbers of police to crack down on those, such as Marxists, who dissented against the Emperor system. But the Japanese state was also adept at co-opting the missions of middle-class non-governmental organizations (such as the Japan Library Association) by promoting and supporting activities that furthered the state's aims. Moreover, subject to this double mechanism of threat and opportunity, most liberal thinkers recanted their views, pledging themselves to the national body.[39] So, while the threat of violence always hovered in the background, middle-class collaboration with the wartime state was, at face value, volitional.

Likewise, *boku* is tricked by the librarian into the world beneath the library, and it is violence against the boy (and the sheep man) that keeps him there. Yet, before the boy enters his cell the librarian carefully spells out to the sheep man that the boy has come by his own volition. The violence of the symbolic order in this story, then, underpins the outward appearance of free will and necessarily co-opts the subject. Murakami's library is thus not only a trip into *boku*'s mind but a representation of the accretion of Japanese social orders. However, rather than a diachronic process of one order replaced by another (pre-war authoritarianism erased by post-war democracy), the model presented is synchronic, with the orders interpenetrating and nestled in the protagonist's mind. Ever present, the dangers of the old order must be guarded against, and it is precisely because *boku* could not stand up to the librarian that he meets his fate. *Boku* even seems aware of this propensity but is unable to do anything about it. Just before entering the pitch-black reading room, he laments, 'why do I act like this, doing and saying things that are the opposite of what I really think?'[40]

---

[38] Sheldon Garon, *Molding Japanese Minds: The State in Everyday Life* (Princeton, NJ: Princeton University Press, 1998), 4–17.

[39] Bob T. Wakabayashi, 'Introduction', in *Modern Japanese Thought*, ed. Bob Tadashi Wakabayashi (Cambridge: Cambridge University Press, 1998), 20.

[40] 'Toshokan kitan', 208.

This historical articulation goes both ways, linking to the present of the 1980s in a move that appears directly critical of Tanaka Yasuo's crystalline generation. The critique can be found in the task *boku* must complete in order to be released from his cell. Soon after he is tricked, *boku* asks whether he will actually be set free after memorizing the books. The sheep man responds in the negative, and after some hesitation the truth comes out: 'Okay, kid. Then I'll give it to you straight. The top of your head'll be sawed off and all your brains'll get slurped right up.'[41] It turns out that brains full of knowledge are smoother and more delicious for the librarian. Yet this terrifying prospect turns out not to be so bad. In a later conversation with the sheep man, *boku* asks what it is like to have your brains sucked out.[42] The sheep man replies:

Yeah, well, it's not as bad as you might think. Apparently, it just feels like a bundle of thread inside your head is being uncoiled. At any rate there are people out there who want to give it a shot.

When *boku* asks what happens next, the sheep man replies:

You lead the rest of your life in a trance, in a dream. With no brain there is no pain. There is no frustration. You don't have to worry about time or getting your homework done. Doesn't seem so bad, does it?[43]

In this exchange, the sheep man invites *boku* to become one of Tanaka's crystalline generation. But the crystalline subject is emptied of all subjectivity; knowledge is nothing more than something to be consumed; and the nature of that knowledge does not matter as long as it is crammed inside the brain: after all the goal is to make individual brains more palatable for the symbolic order to imbibe. The description of the resultant condition recalls and articulates to the postmodern Japanese subject the pre-war Japanese state injunction to 'obliterate the self and serve authority' (*messhi hōkō*).[44] It is also difficult to ignore similarities between the task set for *boku* and the Japanese education system's reliance on knowledge-based exams, around which an entire post-war industry of crammer schools (*juku*) developed.[45] In this system where knowledge is crammed, and the ability to recall it is tested, students are sifted during their progression from one educational institution to the next. But here Murakami hints that this process is essentially empty, and that the end point is a state of crystal acquiescence.

[41] 'Toshokan kitan', 215.
[42] This section is missing from the UK picture book version of the story.
[43] 'Toshokan kitan', 221–2.   [44] Wakabayashi, 'Introduction', 20.
[45] Thomas P. Rohlen, 'The Juku Phenomenon: An Explanatory Essay', *Journal of Japanese Studies* 6.2 (1980): 211.

This reading also helps make sense of one of the oddest bits of this already strange library story: the gourmet food the sheep man cooks for the boy. Not only is this food delicious, it is also a fusion of Western and Japanese ingredients, resulting in difficult-to-follow foreign loanwords parading across the page at regular intervals.[46] On the one hand, this technique adds to the sense of incongruity that such elaborate cuisine should be available in a dark cell under a public library. But this juxtaposition of the food, the languages, the dismal circumstances, and the ever-present threat of violence also resonates with philosopher Asada Akira's observations of the 1980s in Japan. For Asada, Japan in that period became a playful utopia characterized by wordplay, parody, and 'childlike games of differentiation'. However, this utopia was underpinned by a rigid ideology of Japaneseness that enabled 'the children to play freely'—one which again harked back to the Emperor system.[47] Thus, the sheep man's food, and by inference the vast range of consumer goods available to the Japanese, is both enticement to and distraction from the violent horror of being inducted into the playful utopia—a process that will leave the subject blissfully empty but susceptible to menacing power structures lurking beneath the surface of the everyday library.

But the boy is not doomed to his fate. At the urging of the beautiful girl, *boku* manages to convince the sheep man to help him escape on the night of the new moon, when, according to the girl, the librarian should be asleep. On that night they make their way back through the labyrinth, only to be greeted by the librarian and a giant dog—the same dog that had in the past bitten the boy and made him so submissive—holding the boy's pet starling in its mouth. The incensed librarian declares that as punishment he will cut the sheep man into pieces and feed him to giant centipedes, while the boy will be fed, vital organs first, to the dog. All is not lost, however, as the starling in the dog's mouth begins to expand, tearing open the dog's jaws and growing to such a size that the librarian is crushed against the wall. The voice of the beautiful girl tells them to flee, and the boy and sheep man leave the building. Finding himself alone, the boy calls for the sheep man, but he is nowhere to be seen. The boy returns home to his mother, who simply greets him good morning and makes him breakfast. Her face, however, appears slightly sadder than usual. The story ends with the death of the boy's mother and the boy lying alone in 'darkness as pitch black as the night of the new moon', now completely alone, thinking of the cell at the bottom of the library.[48]

---

[46] Loanwords are written in Japanese in the phonetic katakana script. Unlike Japanese kanji characters, katakana has no inherent meaning and can thus present difficulties to readers who do not already know the referent.

[47] Akira Asada, 'Infantile Capitalism and Japan's Postmodernism: A Fairy Tale', in *Postmodernism and Japan*, ed. Masao Miyoshi and Harry Harootunian (Durham, NC, and London: Duke University Press, 1989), 276.

[48] 'Toshokan kitan', 248.

That the story should end with his mother's death suggests that, even though he managed to escape, the boy's contact with the symbolic order has changed him fundamentally and irreversibly. He has come of age, but the outcome is separation from his mother and alienation from his objects of desire. He thinks of the sheep man, liberated from the cell beneath the library, but this does not make him happy; instead, the image of the sheep man searching for a place to fit into the world fills him with sadness. If we accept the reading suggested above of the sheep man as a projection of the boy himself, then the boy's ruminations on the fate of the sheep man may reflect the boy's own situation. Murakami's library tale is a bleak assessment of the condition of the subject in the face of power and violence, but is an assessment that can be explained.

Sitting in the background to this discussion, and perhaps contributing to the difference in approach of Tanaka and Murakami to the 1980s, are their respective experiences of the previous two decades. Although only seven years older than Tanaka, Murakami experienced first-hand the turmoil of the 1968 student movement as it tore across Japanese university campuses (Tanaka was only 12 years old at the time). Murakami came of age at a time in Japan when grand narratives of liberation still held the power to motivate large swathes of Japanese youth to action. While the radicals of Murakami's generation held a range of grievances, chief among them was visceral reaction to the normalization of an economistic, material, productivity-driven view of the good life: a view maintained by the ever-present threat of state violence.[49] The powerful cultural output that accompanied this historical moment, and the actions of the students themselves, were all part of a politics of imagination—attempts to look beyond the bureaucratic, capitalist present to see new and different value systems and social arrangements.[50] But Murakami would also have witnessed the internal contradictions and petty squabbles of this movement spill over into factional violence. He would have seen the mass arrests of students in 1969, and watched as the movement became more radical, more violent, and more marginalized in the face of overwhelming state power.[51]

The boy alone, paralysed and in the dark, unable to return to the library to confront what lurks beneath, is allegorical of the experience of Murakami's generation, who clawed at the very foundations of Japan's symbolic order, but came away disillusioned with romantic ideologies of the future and impotent when faced with the forces that structured their everyday experience. Murakami would continue to interrogate this theme of power, the everyday, and the potential

---

[49] Takemasa Ando, 'Transforming "Everydayness": Japanese New Left Movements and the Meaning of their Direct Action', *Japanese Studies* 33.1 (2013): 1–18.
[50] See, for example, Miryam Sas, *Experimental Arts in Postwar Japan: Moments of Encounter, Engagement, and Imagined Return* (Cambridge, MA: Harvard University Press, 2011).
[51] For more see Christopher Perkins, *The United Red Army on Screen: Cinema, Aesthetics and the Politics of Memory* (Basingstoke: Palgrave Macmillan, 2015), ch. 2.

for action in his subsequent novels, in a process which culminated in his opus *The Wind-Up Bird Chronicle* (1995). Yet again he would send his protagonist underground to grapple with the strange and terrifying power structures hidden below the crystalline surface of the everyday, only this time *boku* would emerge triumphant. But it is interesting to think that the path towards this triumph started when a boy simply entered a library to 'borrow some books'. For Murakami, as for writers in many other cultures from at least the time of Jonathan Swift onwards, the library can function as an ideological battle-site, encapsulating much wider literary and societal arguments, and can stage them in a way that finds a global audience.

15

Fantastic Books and Where to Find Them

Libraries in Fairy Tale and Fantasy

Sara Lodge

Libraries are magical places. Like graveyards, they surround us with the tightly packed remains of the dead. Like forests, they are quiet but full of rustling leaves that betoken unseen business. Architecturally, many libraries resemble churches, with high walls, stained-glass windows, carved wooden stalls, and nooks for private reflection. And like religious or mystical sites, libraries often harbour a sense of the numinous. Where silence is allowed to gather, arcane thoughts become visible like motes of dust in sunlight. Two Portuguese libraries—the baroque Joanina Library at the University of Coimbra and the Mafra Palace Library—deliberately contain live bats. These tiny guardians protect the books from insects and are allowed to fly about after sunset, when the credenzas of books are covered with leather shields that collect the bat droppings. Even in buildings where there are no bats, we retain a sense of the magical possibilities that may be let fly in the library, especially after dark.

So it isn't surprising that many works of fairy tale and fantasy invoke libraries. These are places where hidden secrets come to light; where magic lurks, waiting to be released into physical form. That is, after all, what books enable. They provide keys to doors behind which may lie marvels or monsters. With its library and Edgar Allan Poe-derived supernatural librarian, Mr Raven, George MacDonald's 1895 fantasy for adults, *Lilith*, mixes monstrosity and marvel, and in *The Library: A Catalogue of Wonders* Stuart Kells has written enthusiastically about the fantastic 'libraries and scriptoria of Tolkien's Middle-earth'.[1] Yet other literary libraries are just as unsettlingly magical. In Angela Carter's *The Bloody Chamber*, sadomasochistic images in Bluebeard's pornographic library alert his latest bride to his habit of binding and collecting women. In J. K. Rowling's *Harry Potter* series, the Hogwarts Library, presided over by Irma Pince, contains tens of thousands of texts enchanted to prevent damage or defacement, some of which scream when you try to remove them. Books in the fantastical world often occupy a suggestive, uncanny place between being alive and being dead. They are dangerous if not treated with sufficient care.

---

[1] Stuart Kells, *The Library: A Catalogue of Wonders* (Berkeley, CA: Counterpoint, 2017), 122.

In E. Nesbit's 'The Town in the Library', from *Nine Unlikely Tales* (1901), two bored children—Rosamund and Fabian—are left home alone on Christmas Eve by their socialist mother in a kind of quarantine, because she fears they may be coming down with measles and she doesn't want her children giving measles to the poor while she is distributing tea and flannel petticoats. The children find their way into the forbidden top drawers of a bureau and begin building a town out of books:

> They got Shakespeare in fourteen volumes, and Rollin's 'Ancient History,' and Gibbon's 'Decline and Fall,' and 'The Beauties of Literature' in fifty-six fat little volumes, and they built not only a castle, but a town – and a big town – that presently towered above them on the top of the bureau. 'It's almost big enough to get into,' said Fabian, 'if we had some steps.' So they made steps with the 'British Essayists,' the 'Spectator,' and the 'Rambler,' and the 'Observer', and the 'Tatler'; and when the steps were done they walked up them. You may think that they could not have walked up these steps and into a town they had built themselves, but I assure you people have often done it, and anyway this is a true story. They had made a lovely gateway with two fat volumes of Macaulay and Milton's poetical works on top, and as they went through it they felt all the feelings which people have to feel when they are tourists and see really fine architecture.[2]

It is noticeable here, especially to the female reader, that the abandoned children build their town out of books by men: solid and imposing educational texts of the kind that might make very grand gateways and educational steps. But when the children have entered the town they have made out of books, they do not recognize it. They are uncomfortable tourists in their own bibliographic building who experience what people 'have to feel' in the presence of grandeur. They are alienated and, increasingly, trapped.

It turns out that the town in the library is an occupied territory. It contains an army: fifty blue soldiers who were reserved in the forbidden drawers of the bureau for the children's Christmas present. The soldiers requisition food, demanding the candied fruit that, again, the children have looted from the bureau and that was intended to fill their Christmas stockings. Indeed, the children's adventure becomes increasingly nightmarish, acquiring the qualities of a fever dream of the kind one might experience when coming down with measles. For Rosamund and Fabian can't get out of the town in the library they have built. First the soldiers announce, 'We have taken this town, and you are our prisoners. Do not attempt to escape, or I don't know what will happen to you.'[3] Nesbit comments that 'The dungeons were the pigeon-holes of the bureau, and the doors of them were the

[2] E. Nesbit, 'The Town in the Library' in *Nine Unlikely Tales* (London: Benn, 1901), 282.
[3] Nesbit, 'The Town in the Library', 286.

little "Beauties of Literature" – very heavy doors too.'[4] Suggestively, rather than an aesthetic gateway, anthologies such as the 'Beauties of Literature,' selected to educate children's taste, prove to be heavy barriers that lock them in.

Then the children find that, although they have built a town and got into it, inside is 'their own house with the very town they had built – or one exactly like it – still on the library floor'. Every time they try to penetrate the town within the library, within the town with the library, they find that they are 'deeper and deeper into a nest of towns in libraries in houses in towns in libraries in houses in towns in…and so on for always—something like Chinese puzzle-boxes multiplied by millions and millions for ever and ever'.[5] This proto-Borgesian library has become a model of infinite regress. It is a labyrinth of learning that threatens to imprison children in their own home; or, perhaps, in their own heads. Luckily, Rosamund and Fabian do eventually get out of the town in the library and, due to the measles, escape parental punishment for infringing the forbidden bureau.

Nesbit explores some familiar themes here: the idea of forbidden knowledge is biblical, as is the threat of permanent exile that such knowledge can entail. The labyrinth and the library are linked by the notion of the brain as itself labyrinthine, a storehouse of ideas that can replicate infinitely and hide themselves from themselves, until the originating subject loses all certainty as to whether it is the controller or the victim of the thoughts that dominate it. The fantastical library, like the mind's interior, is a zone of power, of secret, guarded, compendious knowledge that has no limits. Yet it is also a potentially threatening space: a form of intellectual hive that respects its own functions, structures, and hierarchies more than the individual. There is a scene of literary combat here that will be a central concern of this chapter, which principally concerns works of imaginative fiction by female authors. 'The Town in the Library' is partly about the relationship between the rule-bound, involuted architecture of the Academy, with its didactic essays, epics, and elegant extracts—in Nesbit's era, predominantly male texts—and the freewheeling female imagination. It contains the seeds of a genre stand-off between History and Fantasy.

Libraries in early twenty-first-century fiction can be just as engrossing as the library in Nesbit's early twentieth-century narrative. The two more modern fantasies to which I now turn, Susanna Clarke's *Jonathan Strange and Mr Norrell* (2004) and Deborah Harkness's trilogy *A Discovery of Witches* (2011–14), both begin and end in a library. Both involve, too, a quest for hidden and forbidden books. Building on elements discerned in Nesbit's story, I want to suggest that they both emerge from a teasing approach to the relationship between History and Fantasy and the way that historical narratives have traditionally marginalized

---

[4] Nesbit, 'The Town in the Library', 289.   [5] Nesbit, 'The Town in the Library', 293.

women, while Fantasy has remained the least respectable, most easily derided, form of fiction in the Academy.

Susanna Clarke's *Jonathan Strange and Mr Norrell* is an exceptionally well-constructed historical novel. It takes place in the period between 1806 and 1816, and many of the events that it chronicles, from the Napoleonic Wars to the madness of George III, are described with great accuracy. The spoken language of the novel, the dress and manners, are beautifully convincing. The book is a testament to the considerable and fruitful reading of its author. History is, here, not merely a scenic backdrop but an inspiration for style. The book revels in elegance and wit. It thoroughly enjoys the dynamic tension between the cultural restraints of the period—in terms of politeness, social class, and linguistic usage— and the extraordinary magical events disclosed by the narrative.

The book begins with a male club, the York Society of Magicians, which is wholly theoretical in its study of magic, one of whose members suddenly asks a commonplace question that is difficult and uncomfortable for the club to hear: why is no practical magic done in England any longer? The answer (which astonishes the club) is that there *is* one practising magician, Mr Norrell. Mr Norrell is academic in temperament, a historian, a bibliophile, and a pedant. He is precise, dry, cautious—but, it turns out, has an overweening ambition to suppress all other modern practitioners of magic. He wants to have a monopoly on knowledge. And he makes all the members of the York Society, but one, sign a contract renouncing their own claims to be called magicians if he, Norrell, can convince them that he is able to practise magic in real life.

Norrell is, as it were, an Augustan magician, and the magical contests he engages in are acerbic battles of wit reminiscent of the age of Pope and Swift. However, when Mr Norrell demonstrates his ability to practise magic to the York Society of Magicians, he does it, tellingly, through bringing all the statues and carvings in York Minster to life. These talking statues reveal the suppressed histories that have been bothering them for the many centuries of their existence: of women murdered and artefacts pillaged, of jealousies and personal wrongs. There is a sudden cacophony in the snowbound cathedral. Magic has released, as fiction also can do, an enlarged picture of history in which minor players are permitted to revise what has previously been recorded and those who were once merely depicted have voices of their own.

Clarke's book will be a story about the competition between Mr Norrell and Jonathan Strange to be the chief practitioner and reviver of English magic. It is a duel, but also a kind of love affair between two men who need each other. For Jonathan Strange is the antithesis of Norrell in his working methods. He is an improviser, an impulsive, instinctive magician who is not restrained by tradition. He is, in fact, a kind of Romantic—it is said that he met Byron—and his youthful brio produces a different kind of textual enchantment. Clarke's novel might be described as a story of magical 'Sense and Sensibility', with male leads.

We discover Mr Norrell in his extraordinary library at Hurtfew Abbey, where we also leave the two magicians at the book's close. Norrell's library is a labyrinth that can only be penetrated by magical means. Even the novice magicians Mr Honeyfoot and Mr Segundus recognize when they visit Hurtfew for the first time that it is an enchanted zone that lies somehow outside of the normal boundaries of space and time:

> Mr Segundus... could never afterwards picture the sequence of passageways and rooms through which they had passed, nor quite decide how long they had taken to reach the library. And he could not tell the direction; it seemed to him as if Mr Norrell had discovered some fifth point of the compass – not east, nor south, nor west, nor north, but somewhere quite different, and this was the direction in which he led them... The bookcases which lined the walls of the room were built of English woods and resembled Gothic arches laden with carving. There were carvings of leaves (dried and twisted leaves, as if the season the artist had intended to represent were autumn), carvings of intertwining roots and branches, carvings of berries and ivy – all wonderfully done. But the wonder of the bookcases was nothing to the wonder of the books. The first thing a student of magic learns is that there are books *about* magic and books *of* magic. And the second thing he learns is that a perfectly respectable example of the former may be had for two or three guineas... and that the value of the latter is above rubies... At Hurtfew all the walls were lined with bookshelves and all the shelves were filled with books. And the books were all, or almost all, old books; books of magic.[6]

Clarke makes the magical library an organic, unplaceable, breathing space. It exists outside of the compass of architectural definition. Its shelves are carved with leaves and fruit. And its books are not merely descriptive of magic as a historical phenomenon. They are *magical books*: books that enable magic to be performed. In this sense they are like living animals rather than taxidermic specimens—they are capable of giving birth. At the end of the novel, the books in this library will briefly be turned into ravens and will rise from the shelves in a huge, wheeling flock.

Clarke draws a distinction between the years before and after 1600. After this time, magic is only described. Before it, there are practising magicians, including women (for example, Catherine of Winchester and Loveday Ingham). Clarke is clearly drawing on a 'before and after' model of the Renaissance, but one in which the predominant atmosphere of post-1600 culture is one of loss. By the time people start to write *about* magic, she asserts, they are no longer practising it.

[6] Susanna Clarke, *Jonathan Strange & Mr Norrell* (London: Bloomsbury, 2005), 12–13.

Many of the early magicians could not speak or write English. This places magic in the realm of the oral tradition, conjuring it as an art ill-served by literacy. Of course, Clarke's account of the loss of magic here draws on traditional stories including Chaucer's and Shakespeare's allusions to the faeries being all gone out of England; it also encompasses our modern knowledge about witch trials and how they destroyed thousands of innocent women across Europe during their peak from the fifteenth to the early seventeenth centuries. But Clarke's distinction between books about magic and books *of* magic is revisionist in its insistence that the book that enables new spells to be made (the recipe book; the grimoire) is rarer, more vital, more valuable than the analytical text. The nature of the library's secret power lies in creativity that retains the potential to spring from ideas harboured indefinitely within the text. Books of magic are not seminal but uterine.

Norrell greedily buys up all the magical books he can find, keeping them out of the hands of Arabella Strange, who has tried to find the money to buy the Duke of Roxburghe's collection at auction. But Norrell can't, in the end, control the magic he tries to catalogue and dominate. The scholar's enchantments fail him, despite his desperate attempts to rule by limiting access to texts and exercising hermeneutic power over them.

Clarke is clearly a bibliophile. Her novel has two hundred footnotes. And her story of Mr Norrell attending the sale of the Duke of Roxburghe's extraordinary library in 1812, to glean its extraordinary magical incunabula, draws on her knowledge of the real Roxburghe collection and the renewed interest in early manuscripts to which it led.[7] But the point here is that her feminized history of 'books *of* magic'—while it plays with notions of revival and restoration current in the eighteenth century—is a story about books as living, open, fictive forms rather than repositories of purely academic knowledge. One of the most significant characters in *Jonathan Strange and Mr Norrell* is Vinculus, a street magician, whose skin is covered in writing: a prophetic text with which he was born and which preserves the words of arch-magician John Uskglass. In the final pages of Clarke's novel, the writing on Vinculus's skin alters completely:

> 'I have changed!' said Vinculus. 'Look!' He took off his coat and opened his shirt. 'The words are different! On my arms! On my chest! Everywhere! This is not what I said before!' Despite the cold, he began to undress....
>
> Childermass [Norrell's servant] dismounted from his horse with feelings of panic and desperation. He had succeeded in preserving John Uskglass's book from death and destruction; and then, just when it seemed secure, the book itself had defeated him by changing....
>
> 'But why should you change all of a sudden? There is no rhyme or reason in it!'

---

[7] Clarke, *Jonathan Strange & Mr Norrell*, 358–63.

'There is every sort of reason,' said Vinculus. 'I was a Prophecy before; but the things that I foretold have come to pass. So it is just as well I have changed – or I would have become a History! A dry-as-dust History!'[8]

In writing Fantasy rather than History, Clarke is consciously exploring the tension between a bibliographic conception of the library as a historical resource, whose primary function is collecting and preserving texts, and a different conception of the library as a host of living cells, barely under control, whose magical subjects retain the power of organisms to speak, charm, fly. In the fantastical text we are not dealing with 'the body in the library' so much as 'the body *is* the library'. Clarke celebrates the possibility of radical revision by making Vinculus's text erase and rewrite itself before the reader's eyes.

The organic, living quality of the magical text is also present in Deborah Harkness's *Discovery of Witches* trilogy. This is a quest narrative. At its heart is a lost book—the Book of Life—that is greatly feared and greatly desired by various constituencies whose members distrust and fear one another: humans; daemons; witches; and vampires.

Our heroine, Diana Bishop, is an academic scholar, a young professor at Yale, who specializes in history of science, specifically alchemical manuscripts: 'my research focused on the period when science supplanted magic – the age when astrology and witch-hunts yielded to Newton and universal laws'.[9] However, Diana is also by heritage a witch. She has chosen to deny and not to explore this facet of herself because her parents—both academic anthropologists and both also witches—were killed in Africa when she was 7. Diana doesn't practise magic, though she does allow herself occasionally to use her supernatural powers to fetch down a heavy tome in the Bodleian Library that is too high for her to reach without a stepladder.

The story, which will involve Diana reclaiming and exploring her birthright as a powerful witch as well as an academic historian, begins and has its conclusion in the Bodleian Library. At the beginning Diana summons up an ancient, illustrated alchemical manuscript, Ashmole 782, that seems to be alive; the book tugs on its call slip, it sighs audibly when she loosens its brass clasps, and the pages are in motion:

Words shimmered and moved across its surface – hundreds of words – invisible unless the angle of light and the viewer's perspective were just right.[10]

[8] Clarke, *Jonathan Strange & Mr Norrell*, 994.
[9] Deborah Harkness, *A Discovery of Witches* (London: Headline, 2011), 9.
[10] Harkness, *A Discovery of Witches*, 12.

Ashmole 782 is an enchanted palimpsest. Several pages have been torn out. The writing has been hidden by a spell. Diana can't decipher it and decides to return it to the stacks. But the magic has been unleashed. This is, it turns out, a book—*the* book—that everyone has been looking for, for centuries. Getting it back, completing it, and understanding it, while evading all those who wish Diana ill, will become the work of the trilogy. The journey will take Diana back in time to the sixteenth century. By the end of it she will understand that the book is a very uncanny artefact indeed. It is made of the skins and blood of hundreds of magical beings and it contains the genomic secret—suppressed by centuries of doctrine— that vampires, daemons, witches, and humans are not separate species but are all related and in certain instances can interbreed. It is, then, a Book of Life in various different senses. It is made of organic material. It contains information that will change the living world of the novel. And it is a prophetic text about a new birth, rather like the Bible. The urtext is not a patriarchal, religious, didactic story but a composite truth about relatedness made up of the bodies of all who have lived it and will live it. Importantly, at the end of the *Discovery of Witches* trilogy, Diana absorbs the book: it becomes an ever-evolving text, written in her body: '*I was the Book of Life*'.[11] Like Vinculus in *Jonathan Strange and Mr Norrell*, her prophetic journey involves a book that belongs not in the exclusive, locked historical domain of the library but in the living and changing domain of her own fertile, female corpus.

In the society of Ray Bradbury's dystopian novel *Fahrenheit 451* (1953), books are outlawed and burned. Book-loving exiles memorize favourite texts in order to preserve them orally: they 'become' the books they love. Susanna Clarke and Deborah Harkness, in their bibliophile fantasies, also create living characters (Vinculus; Diana Bishop) who *are* books. But the role of these characters is not merely to preserve the text they carry but to bear it into the future in a manner akin to the role of a mother bearing children: the material has the host's DNA in it, but its future shape and meaning are fluid and unknowable. Again, here, in their feminist emphasis on the essence of power as creativity rather than ownership, and on writing as innately multivalent, these writers assert a view of the book in history that is much less interested in the *auteur* than in the generative dialogues and fictive futures to which the text gives rise.

During her timewalking journey into the 1590s, Diana discovers that she is a 'weaver', a most unusual kind of witch, with the power to create and to manage the elements of earth, water, wind, and fire. She learns how to harness her abilities from sixteenth-century witches, acquiring the practical wisdom and community of her foremothers and serving the community of women as a midwife and herbalist. She performs alchemical experiments with Mary Sidney, Countess of

---

[11] Deborah Harkness, *The Book of Life*, (London: Headline, 2014), 533.

Pembroke, who is described as a 'paragon of learning' who also 'has a propensity for setting things alight'.[12] Through her *Discovery of Witches* fantasy series, Harkness quietly restores women to the historical picture of early modern science, suggesting what has been omitted in terms of women's wit, witchiness, wickness. The conversation between past and present becomes an explicitly two-way street, where Diana's father (also an academic), who was alive in the 1970s, visits Shakespeare and swaps lines of dialogue with him.

Deborah Harkness is herself an academic, a historian of science and professor of history at the University of Southern California. Like Susanna Clarke, she is writing fantasy from a scholarly background. It is hard not to see the theme of her trilogy (where Diana Bishop learns to accept her powers as a witch rather than a don) as an allegory of Harkness's own move from analytical academic writing toward creative fiction. Her trilogy is both erudite and pokes fun at scholarly conventions and academic jealousies. Matthew Clairmont, the male love interest, is a vampire academic in the Oxford science faculty who at the age of 30 has an impossible publication record: the kind of record you can only build up if you have actually lived for six hundred years. Harkness's books mount an implicit defence of Fantasy not as mere escapism but work that can engage in knowing, knowledgeable dialogue with academic writing. In the final book of the trilogy, Diana has to disobey the rules of the Bodleian Library, which disallow fire of any kind, and let her familiar—a female fire-dragon called Corra—loose in the stacks. I see in this a strong desire to reclaim the library for Fantasy: to assert that it belongs there.

Should women be having to make this argument at this point in history? Perhaps not. But academic prejudice against Fantasy as a genre remains real and sharp-edged. I was present at an academic meeting where a senior creative writer lamented that a couple of students studying creative writing had disappointed the faculty by turning out to be 'fantasists'. The implication was that they had been admitted to the degree under false colours; that what they were doing required less skill and held less aesthetic or social value than 'real' fiction-writing did. The pun also half-suggested that writers of fantasy were delusional. Fantasy still labours under a burden of literary designation that regards it as at worst juvenile and at best niche. Like pornography, it may be damned as too nakedly commercial, too openly concerned with wish fulfilment rather than insight; its technical exigencies are also implicitly viewed by some in the academic community as too loose: one can invent anything; the world is the fantasy writer's dream sequence. While these prejudices remain current, and while financially straitened, cramped modern library administrations become ever keener to replace physical books with digital data, work like that of Clarke and Harkness that assertively

---

[12] Deborah Harkness, *Shadow of Night* (London: Headline, 2012), 245.

locates Fantasy within the tactile space of the library is especially valuable in conjuring the power of manuscript and printed texts as physical, living, magical artefacts. Fantasy has become a quiet advocate for the library—not as dusty depository and study space, but as a place of breathtaking adventure.

The library in the fantasy novel is, however, by no means untouched by the digital universe. In the final book of Harkness's trilogy, the Book of Life copies itself to Diana with the speed and ease of a vast file. In Genevieve Cogman's *The Invisible Library* (2015), The Library for which the heroine works is a repository like a supercomputer that stores data from an infinite number of 'worlds' and the historical time periods within which they operate. Spies from the library are sent on missions into these multiple worlds in order to bring back certain required books that contain unique language usage or other data necessary toward completing the Library's encyclopaedic, pantextual mothership of knowledge. The operational scheme of The Library resembles, in certain respects, that of the Oxford English Dictionary. There is a tension between the individual and the library, whose infinite, multidimensional task across space and time requires subservience (the library workers are branded on their backs, like books) and dwarfs their emotional needs and wishes. However, in *The Invisible Library* many of the texts needed to complete The Library's comprehensive knowledge store are works of fiction; their significance amounts to a metatextual assertion of Fantasy's own power. Again, in this book, the heroine introduces a dragon into the library. While the theoretical suprahuman power of the library may lie in its holdings and bindings (what it contains, collects, requisitions), in Fantasy the library's greatest power is incendiary: the book is an imaginative touchpaper. It should liberate the reader's own creative fire.

In Cressida Cowell's *A Hero's Guide to Deadly Dragons* (2007), the sixth book in her *How To Train Your Dragon* sequence of children's books, her 12-year-old Viking hero, Hiccup Horrendous Haddock the Third, has to break into the Meathead Public Library to steal a book. The book he is after is a tiresome academic tome, *How To Train Your Dragon* by Professor Yobbish, whose dubious wisdom on the topic of dragon-training amounts to only one sentence: 'Yell at it!'[13] The Meathead Public Library (which doesn't allow anyone to borrow books) is, in common with so many libraries in Fantasy, a dark labyrinth that contains monsters, including the Hairy Scary Librarian, who will try to kill anyone he encounters in the stacks.

Uncannily, however, the book Hiccup discovers in the library, which enables his escape, is his *own* book. Before coming to the library, Hiccup had been drafting lines in an exercise book toward a tentative future volume: A Hero's Guide to

---

[13] Cressida Cowell, *How To Train Your Dragon: A Hero's Guide to Deadly Dragons* (London: Hodder, 2007), 97. As in so many fantasy novels by women, the fictional text parodies the supposedly authoritative male 'academic' text: both here are called 'How to Train Your Dragon'.

Deadly Dragons. His father, Chief Stoick the Vast, irritated to have a scribbler rather than a soldier for a son, had confiscated it. In the Meathead Public Library, Hiccup encounters a book with his name on the cover, and the very same title of the book he had been writing. It is *A Hero's Guide to Deadly Dragons* by his ancestor, Hiccup Horrendous Haddock the Second. In discovering that his ancestor had improvised a book with exactly the same title and interests as his own, Hiccup not only finds a literal way out of the library, escaping the wrath of the librarian; he finds permission to be an author himself. As in so many works of Fantasy, the path out of the library turns out to be a path of self-realization. Borrowing books isn't what fantasy libraries are for. In this genre, the book one finds within the library's mute and threatening complexity typically relates to one's inner life: it is a magical, living text—a book that can transform the dead language of knowledge into the living dialogue of action.

This is quintessentially true of Matt Haig's recent bestseller *The Midnight Library* (2020), where the protagonist, Nora Seed, has attempted suicide and is hovering between life and death. She finds herself in the Midnight Library, amongst books that are all the lives she might have lived. She can also consult her Book of Regrets: options that she rejected and subsequently mourned. Nora 'reads' (that is, enters and lives) chapters of her various possible lives. She is permitted to stay in any one of them, if she finds the narrative she likes best. She tries out lives in which she became a champion swimmer, a rock-star singer, an environmentalist working on glacier melt, and an academic philosopher in Cambridge with a husband and daughter. Nora finds interest in all these possible lives; but all of them contain losses and emptiness within their apparent success and fulfilment. None of the imagined narratives fits her perfectly. Indeed, the only way in which she can leave the limbo of the Midnight Library, a collapsing space of infinite regress and infinite regret, is to choose to resume, with renewed wonder and appreciation, the life she had attempted to exit—her messy, unsatisfactory, mediocre, unfinished 'root life' that still has the potential to be anything at all:

> She had to want the life she always thought she didn't. Because just as this library was a part of her, so too were all the other lives. . . . She might have missed those particular opportunities that led her to become an Olympic swimmer, or a traveller, or a vineyard owner, or a rock star, or a planet-saving glaciologist, or a Cambridge graduate, or a mother, or the million other things, but she was still in some way *all* those people.[14]

Haig's book resembles Frank Capra's 1947 film *It's A Wonderful Life*; it has a moral and a therapeutic message for the reader (the protagonist's name, 'Seed', is

---

[14] Matt Haig, *The Midnight Library* (Edinburgh: Canongate, 2020), 269.

almost too pointed). Yet it is also a distinctly modern book. The Internet, where every computer click begets millions of possible pathways, has heightened our sense of the individual as possessing infinite choices, day by day and moment by moment. Online, our stories are constantly renewing themselves like cells, in a process of self-revision that may not end with death. In this digital universe the fantastical library, too, has renewed its meanings. It is still a labyrinth, akin to the brain itself, whose inspiral pathways of infinite resource can be both a wonder and a trap. It is still a place of magic and mystery, where what seemed dead can prove to be living. But in a modern world where too much time is spent on-screen, the library of Fantasy also strongly suggests that books should not be screens, in the sense of constructs that partition and hide us from the raw energy and risk of being and making. The magical books in *Jonathan Strange and Mr Norrell* fly from Hurtfew Library as birds; in *A Discovery of Witches*, the buried truths of the Book of Life must be loosed from Oxford's Bodleian Library into Diana's body to reveal their contemporary valency. Nora Seed must get out of the Midnight Library if she is to live. In all these books, the library is a kind of temporary physical stasis, like reading itself. You can't inhabit it forever. It is a place you must leave, because its infinite scope and obsessive forms of organization paradoxically tend toward entropy. Yet, like reading, the apparent stasis of occupying the fantastical library will work a profound transformation that forever alters your view of the magical world outside.

Coda

Libraries and Political Identities

Alice Crawford, Robert Crawford, and Siân Reynolds

Elias Canetti's 1935 novel *Die Blendung* (translated into English as *Auto da Fé* by Cicely Veronica Wedgwood in 1948) presents a shocking vision of totalitarianism principally through its depiction of scholar Peter Kien's obsession with his vast personal library. *Don Quixote* was one of many books Canetti read as a child, and, as Tania Hinderberger-Burton has indicated, there is a quixotic aspect to Canetti's novel about a man whose 'intellect is seduced by books and [who] can no longer distinguish between books and reality'.[1] Laced with misogyny and violence, *Die Blendung*, as its German title suggests, involves a willed blinding of the protagonist's consciousness towards anything other than the book hoard that comes to dominate his Vienna apartment.

Kien's life's passion has been to immure himself in books. Sitting at his desk, he is conscious that 'the entire wall-space up to the ceiling' is 'clothed in books'. To maximize book space, the only light comes from skylights. Kien has fulfilled 'his dearest wish: the possession of a well-stocked library, in perfect order and enclosed on all sides, in which no single superfluous article of furniture, no single superfluous person could lure him from his serious thoughts'.[2] Already, near this novel's start, that mention of a supposedly 'superfluous person' is menacing in the context of 1930s European totalitarianism. Marina van Zuylen's astute 2018 study *Monomania* progresses from consideration of *Middlemarch*'s Casaubon to the Kien of Canetti's profoundly disconcerting novel. Van Zuylen invokes 'Don Quixote', but shows how Kien becomes 'the great strategist of library art'. Kien, 'like Eliot's Casaubon, uses his knowledge not to grasp the world but to flee from it. Pathologically dependent on a system of classification, he buries himself frantically in the act of possessing and organizing his books to dispel life's complexities.'[3] Perhaps more clearly in retrospect, we can see how this novel deploys the library-obsessed Kien as a paradigm of the totalitarian consciousness.

---

[1] Tania Hinderberger-Burton, 'The Quixotic in Canetti's "Die Blendung"', *Modern Austrian Literature*, 16.3/4 (1983): 174.

[2] Elias Canetti, *Auto da Fé*, trans. C. V. Wedgwood (1946; repr. London: Vintage, 1995), 23.

[3] Marina van Zuylen, *Monomania: The Flight from Everyday Life in Literature and Art* (Ithaca, NY: Cornell University Press, 2018), 146, 141.

Kien's Viennese library, in this tale of books and book burning, becomes a synecdoche for the totalitarian state, just as Kien comes to emblematize the totalitarian individual. Tropes familiar from earlier chapters of the present volume, including the battle of the books, the obsessive scholar, the burning of libraries, are deployed by Canetti in a book which makes the library in some unsettling ways an epitome of a chilling political identity.

It might be assumed that in the following century such an ambitious use of the library as a fictional trope with which to analyse the temper of the nation has been abandoned. Yet, surprisingly perhaps, in several twenty-first-century cultures the library has emerged as a focus for national identity. The present coda to *Libraries in Literature* will focus on three such works: Mikhail Elizarov's *The Librarian* (first published in Russian in 2007, and translated into English by Andrew Bromfield in 2015); Sophie Divry's *The Library of Unrequited Love* (first published in French as *La Cote 400* ['Classmark 400'] in 2010, and translated into English by Siân Reynolds in 2013); and the English novelist Salley Vickers's *The Librarian* (2018). The purpose of this coda is to argue not that these novels derive from Canetti's work, but that they represent in their very different ways a revival of the literary use of the library as a way of examining contemporary personal and political life.

The most shocking of these early twenty-first-century fictions is Elizarov's *The Librarian*. Vital to its design are the writings of a fictitious Soviet-era author, Dmitry Alexandrovich Gromov (1910–81), who is imagined as having spent much of his life in the Donbas region on the borders of Ukraine and Russia. By the time the Ukrainian-raised Russophone novelist Elizarov (b.1973) wrote *The Librarian*, the Donbas had come to be associated with contending oligarchic groups, competing nationalisms, and political thuggery. Elizarov is well aware of this Ukrainian cultural backdrop, though his novel also invokes older, complex literary and popular cultural resonances—from the writings of the experimental twentieth-century poet-novelist Andrei Platonov (who supplies the epigraph to Elizarov's book) to the Soviet-era satirical magazine *Krokodil*. Tellingly, *The Librarian* alludes, also, to the great Russophone Ukrainian Nikolai Gogol's 1835 Gothic tale of a young philosopher's ultimately fatal engagement with monstrous witchery, sex, conflict and all-seeing vision, *Viy*. In *The Librarian* a 27-year-old engineer, Alexei Vyazintsev, realizes (like many others in the novel) that reading the apparently pedestrian works of the largely forgotten Gromov confers on the reader remarkable powers. In the often Gothic and dystopian world of *The Librarian*, heavily armed, thuggish clans fight to possess Gromov's surviving works. These gangs are called 'libraries' or 'reading rooms'; the libraries' members are not just intellectual readers but also such people as men 'shattered by the war in Afghanistan' and 1990s 'retired soldiers who had no wish to betray their Soviet oath'. Along with hard-bitten, witchlike old women and younger female fighters, these people can transform a library 'into a serious combat unit with strict discipline and a security service. The library could turn out up to a hundred fighting men at any time.' These libraries locate 'bibliographies of Gromov', and, alert both to 'the card index' and 'computerization' of 'data', they track down his books to augment their power.[4] Much of Elizarov's narrative is taken up with gory, neo-medieval battles between competing libraries and reading rooms. At times, to anglophone readers these accounts of pitched battles can seem like Tolkien rewritten by Irvine Welsh, but the narrative is suffused with a deep awareness of Soviet-era currents of thought and of the post-Soviet rivalries of competing oligarchic groups—as well as of the transforming power of narrative that is represented by the heavily armed libraries' most treasured books.

Lenin and Stalin are named in Elizarov's novel, but neither Vladimir Putin nor any other contemporary politician is mentioned. It is impossible, however, not to read this violent book (whose events are set around the year 2000) as an account of post-Soviet Russia and other republics of the former USSR, including, not least, war-torn Ukraine. Elizarov's narrative is partly satirical, and the use of terms such as 'library' and 'reading room' is at one level ironic; but there is also a deeper fascination with the power of books and narratives which those libraries and reading rooms represent. On the surface, Gromov's writings may have a pedestrian tone redolent of what was commended by Soviet-era bureaucrats; but, at a deeper level, it is clear that reading those works still conveys to and confers upon their readers remarkable and even superhuman powers. Though political narratives of the state may change, nonetheless these apparently redundant books so treasured by their libraries and librarians continue to articulate a tale of the nation that, whether for good or ill, cannot be renounced. While there may be a sense of nostalgia for aspects of the Soviet-era USSR, and for the heroic energies that resisted fascism during the Great Patriotic War, there is also in *The Librarian* a sense of a deeper, and deeply troubling, mystical articulation of the soul of the nation which the most prized books, and their guardians, represent.

Eventually, after all the other members of his reading room have been eliminated in conflict, the young librarian Alexei Vyazintsev finds himself under the control of another clan in what seems to be an old folks' home populated by grotesque old women headed by the 95-year-old Gorn. Here Alexei is initiated into his new clan and becomes the keeper, the curator of its complete set of Gromov texts. He ends up as a literal version of an 'underground man' (to invoke Dostoevsky's term in *Notes from Underground*), completely immured in a subterranean cell-like room at the bottom of a deep shaft, his job simply to continue reading the texts of the library, keeping alive its values which can confer on the readers such qualities as power, joy, and endurance. At the end of the novel, this young librarian is presented in his 'incarceration' as a 'Curator of the

---

[4] Mikhail Elizarov, *The Librarian*, trans. Andrew Bromfield (London: Pushkin Press, 2015), 15, 18, 19.

Motherland'.[5] Through an allusion to the *Tale of Bygone Years* traditionally ascribed to the monk Nestor, Elizarov conjures up the early twelfth-century Kiev-connected chronicle which narrates the earliest history of the land of Rus.[6] While the librarian Alexei is not a medieval monk, he becomes nonetheless, like Nestor, a keeper of the national soul—but a trapped, immobile one. Like the students from the Soviet-era science fiction film *Moscow-Cassiopeia* (also invoked in the novel's closing pages) who are sent on a vast mission into outer space to contact an alien civilization, the librarian Alexei, isolated in his cell with Gromov's books, is destined to endure—in his case, it seems, forever—in a determined mission whose significance acquires mystical as well as political and cultural resonance.[7]

> What year is it outside now? If the Motherland is free and its borders are inviolate, then the librarian Alexei Vyazintsev is keeping his watch steadfastly in his underground bunker, tirelessly spinning the thread of the protective Veil extended above the country. To protect against enemies both visible and invisible.[8]

However crude and satirical aspects of it may be at times, Elizarov's ambitious, knowing, and haunting fiction *The Librarian* (much lauded in Russia and now translated into at least eleven languages) ultimately transcends satire and presents an image of the library as a powerful, if problematic, resource at the core of a civilization. In an era when libraries can seem threatened as never before, this is an arresting, uncomfortable, and eerily prophetic, vision. This librarian's library is at once potent, essential, and enduring, yet thoroughly and oppressively entrapping.

French writer Sophie Divry's 17,000-word monologue addressed by a librarian to a hapless reader who has been locked in a library overnight is shorter, gentler, and more alert to the politics of gender than Elizarov's *The Librarian*, but Divry's book too works allusively and articulates among other things a sense of national identity and bookish entrapment. Mixing pedagogy and erudition with emotion and humour, as well as some concealed intertextuality, Divry uses the library as a kind of dressing-up box for the roles the narrator/speaker will play. Signalling aspects of French political and cultural identity, her book is also full of contradictions, showing considerable ambivalence about libraries and librarians in general.

The librarian who provides the soliloquy works in a public library in a French provincial town. How the trapped reader has managed to get locked inside the library basement overnight we are not told. This reader is neither named nor even explicitly given any gender markings in French, but most readers of Divry's novella have assumed him to be a man. The librarian—definitely a woman—

---

[5] Elizarov, *Librarian*, 392, 403.   [6] Elizarov, *Librarian*, 396.   [7] Elizarov, *Librarian*, 408.
[8] Elizarov, *Librarian*, 410.

comes across this lost soul before official opening time next morning, and claims she cannot let him out until the security people arrive. Meanwhile, she enlists his (or her) help to do some re-shelving, still carrying on a one-sided conversation, to which her captive audience must listen and occasionally respond, wordlessly. The book works through a series of triggers or references, placed without fanfare in a colloquial, apparently inconsequential, but in fact artfully arranged, stream of words; there are no paragraphs.

On the opening page, the very first book mentioned—because it needs re-shelving—is *Existentialism Is a Humanism*. 'You know, book by Sartre', as the librarian says.[9] This is a clear signal—perhaps warning is a better term—that we are in a French narrative with intellectual ambitions. The Sartre title properly belongs upstairs, with 'the eggheads on the ground floor' (10), in charge of the Philosophy section—while down here, looking after Geography and various practical shelfmarks, the speaker is a humble and low-paid employee. The scene is set for her distinctive philosophical take on libraries and the librarian's life, gradually revealing her as her own woman intellectually. She is acquainted not only with philosophy but with sociology, since the second title mentioned is Émile Durkheim's *The Division of Labour in Society*: 'There it is, shelfmark 301. Next to Suicide' (13). Durkheim is famous for his work on suicide, a suggestive enough reference, but here he is being called upon to explain the division of labour and to sympathize with the angst (if not the suicide) of the 'invisible woman' or—as she calls herself—the 'cultural assembly-line worker' (11). She illustrates this by referring to the soul-destroying task of checking books out. Both Sartre and Durkheim are referenced several times in the book, usually with a sad or bitter undertow. As well as the two analytical disciplines of philosophy and sociology, readers will encounter in the book most of the fields of study a library normally covers and repeatedly have their attention drawn to the narrator's interpretation of the world, in terms of philosophy, sociology, history, and literature.

The narrator's monologue has a central theme: to consider the library itself as an entity, and as a valuable gift to ordinary people. During the first half of the book, she praises a series of 'heroes' of the library, who will recur in different guises throughout. *Primus inter pares* is Melvil Dewey,

> our founding father for all us librarians. Just a little guy from a poor family somewhere in America and he was only twenty-one when he thought up the most famous classification system in the world. Dewey is the Mendeleyev of librarians. Not the Periodic Table of Elements, but the classification of areas of culture. (13)

[9] Sophie Divry, *The Library of Unrequited Love*, trans. Siân Reynolds (London: MacLehose Press, 2013), 9; hereafter page references are supplied in the main text of this coda.

The listener is treated to a short lecture on the Dewey Decimal System interspersed with speculative, slightly barbed remarks about Dewey himself. Order has its faults, indeed, in a novel alert to issues of national, cultural, class, and gender politics. One criticism of Dewey, despite his pioneer status, is that:

> When that fanatic Dewey classified literature, he set up a monument of ethno-centrism: 810, American literature; 820, English literature: two whole divisions for the English-speakers. 830 to 880, European literature: six divisions for the whole of old Europe. And what about the hundreds of other languages in the world? Just one division: 890. Just one heading, see?   (17)[10]

The reason for Divry's novella's original French title—*La Cote 400*—now appears: what stops the speaker sleeping at night is that (in this particular library) Languages have been moved from shelfmark 400 to 800 (Literature), so that the 400 section now has no books. This is a sign that the librarian likes order, despite her generally rebellious nature, and finds it distressing when that order is disturbed—a contradiction that runs throughout. Shelfmark 400 has become a metaphor for the potential emptiness or absences which may lurk inside the library, while Dewey stands in for the American threat to French (or European) culture, of which there are several more mentions. Though the relationship between the library and national identity is far less obtrusive in Divry's text than in Elizarov's, nevertheless this theme is subtly present. In France, as in Ukraine and Russia, the library can be seen as a custodian of national values.

As well as ruminating on Dewey, Divry's Gallic librarian is happy to report that other, rather older library benefactors are French: the seventeenth-century Cardinal Mazarin had 40,000 books in his personal library in Paris, and left them to the public (readers can still go into the Bibliothèque Mazarine in Paris, housed in the same building as the French Academy). Meanwhile, Mazarin's much-less-famous contemporary, the librarian Gabriel Naudé, devised a dozen categories and thirty subcategories, '*Pre-Melvil Dewey!*' the librarian exclaims in italics, 'proving that the Americans didn't invent everything' (29–30).

As part of this assertion of distinctively French culture and praise of order, logically enough the French revolutionaries of 1789 also receive approval. The librarian's own favourite shelfmark is 944.75: history of the French Revolution. She likes it for bringing order to the chaos of laws and measures of the Ancien Régime,

> Because it really needed a good clean-out. Before that it was all privileges, tithes, salt tax, plumed hats. With their holy days for Saint Eustace and Saint Eulalia,

[10] This feature of the Dewey system was later amended, as the librarian admits.

different weights and measures in every parish in France, people speaking dialects nobody could understand ten miles away, it was total chaos.   (33)

But this French librarian's approval is really for the revolutionary policy—at least in theory—of making books widely available. The revolutionaries confiscated books from the émigré aristocracy and the clergy, intending to distribute them to public libraries—and had a project for a Big Catalogue, even if 'they never got round to it' (35).

One final but important French hero here is Eugène Morel—'entirely forgotten today' (39), but responsible for making libraries in France more pleasant places to be in. Morel published a survey of French public libraries in 1908. He proposed that readers be able to borrow books, rather than have to read them on the spot, and that there should be longer opening hours, comfortable seats, special areas for children, good lighting. He also contributed to the founding of the unique L'Heure Joyeuse children's library (still in Paris today).[11] Overall, these and other references scattered throughout the monologue serve as landmarks in the provision of French public libraries, contributing to a philosophy of the local municipal library: it is one of the best things in modern society and necessarily a place of order—even if it can always be improved, and the building may be in need of modernizing. This librarian has not read Durkheim for nothing: her listener is next treated to some sociological analysis of both the library staff and the readers, none of whom come out of her excoriating gaze very well.

Subtly and shrewdly, Divry deploys her librarian protagonist to present a French-accented emotional sociology of the public library. Her sociology of the workplace stems from a political position—anti-authoritarian and incidentally feminist, but with its roots in 1789. This librarian is basically on the side of 'the people' and their right to be educated, and against the rich and powerful. The sociology of the readers is partly determined by the kind of book they want, also analysed in class terms. In the hierarchy of departments, French Literature and History are 'blue-blood aristocracy' and the list traverses several layers, finally reaching 'the proletariat' in the basement: Geography, IT, practical books, dictionaries, travel guides. France's libraries are presented as unequivocally a great cultural good and potentially social equalizers. But readers do not always realize this or appreciate them. Readers can be the enemies of the library, as indeed the librarians can be enemies of the readers. The first reference to readers is decidedly snippy:

---

[11] L'Heure Joyeuse ('The Happy Hour') was founded in 1924 as part of a US-funded initiative. There were only a dozen such in France in 1931. See Annie Renonciat, ed., *Livre mon ami: lectures enfantines 1914–1954*, exhibition catalogue (Paris: Mairie du Ve arrondissement, 1991).

They put books back in the wrong place, they steal them, they muddle them up, they dog-ear them. Some people even tear out pages... It's men that do that every time. And underlining like crazy, that's always men as well. Men just have to make a mark on a book.... (22)

If readers are the proletariat, however, this is perhaps not entirely their fault. They are often cowed by bossy librarians, 'the thought police of the library' (79). Indeed, intimidated readers are often not so much enemies of the library as refugees (though for a mixture of reasons). In winter the library is literally a warm place, 'a real refugee centre' (58). In summer, by contrast, 'the library is full to bursting' with people, looking for reading matter, including serious research students. The librarian has a particularly soft spot for research students, although she is contemptuous of the chosen subject of the one who, it will become clear, is the object of her unrequited love, a history postgraduate called Martin. Alas, to her despair, she has peeked over his shoulder, and found that his thesis is on peasant revolts in the Poitiers region in the reign of Louis XV, a 'kind of a nothing reign' (33).

The students are counterbalanced by 'little old men'—usually with an obsessive interest—but still the library is 'the beating heart of the Great Consolation' (70). What a library should mean to its readers is expressed in a flight of lyricism:

[W]hen we go into a library and look at all those bookcases stretching into the distance, what descends on our soul, if not grace?...Those endless bookshelves reflect back to us an ideal image, the image of the full range of the human mind....Help yourself, it's free.... Oh good grief, for once I was being serious, and I got carried away again. (67)

Where the often dystopian vision of Elizarov's *The Librarian* nevertheless contains a certain nostalgic yearning for the idealism of Soviet-era communism, here in Divry's novella the library is seen as embodying aspirations that are every bit as noble as the noblest aspirations of the French revolutionaries.

There is, however, a downside to the library in Divry's speaker's monologue. The French librarian experiences a feeling of powerlessness in the face of all human knowledge, a theme that can be related to certain French literary and historical traditions. In history, it is connected to the totalizing approach, the desire to embrace all human experience of the past in the 'histoire globale' of the Annales School, associated with Lucien Fèbvre, Fernand Braudel, and others.

For Divry's librarian, daily confronted with thousands of books, embracing all of culture has a frightening effect: 'You never feel so miserable as in a library' (76). This sense of oppression is linked, in the book's second half, to her impossible obsession with the student she knows as 'Martin', the one studying peasant revolts in the Poitiers region in the reign of Louis XV. The two emotions are combined in a passage in which the theme of 'unrequited love' becomes explicit, and in which she apostrophizes him, pointing out that it is 'so stupid reading all those books' because it will be absolutely impossible to read all the library's stock (75).

By the time her breathless monologue winds down, she has begun to describe the library as 'the arena where every day the Homeric battle begins between readers and books. In this struggle, the librarians are the referees' (77). Paradoxically, this at least affords the librarian a choice, which is one way out:

> A barricade has only two sides and I know which side I'm on, comrade. I'm here to help the poor crushed thirsty reader faced with the crushing prestige of the Army of Books. (77)

By now, the mild irritation the librarian has felt at the opening of the novel has become a full-blown lament for a lost life, a lost love, retrieved only by the feeling that she has a role to play. The last ten pages combine longing for Martin 'to actually look at me' (90) with some bitter reflections about the cultural universe, in the shape of Great French Writers, once admired. Maupassant—a favourite author in the early part of the monologue—is later scorned as sexually obsessed. His *Bel-Ami* 'isn't even a novel, it's an ode to male potency as a weapon of domination, allied to money' (87). As for Sartre and Simone de Beauvoir, their complicated relationship is sarcastically analysed, with most sympathy extended to Beauvoir, for whom the speaker expresses fellow feeling at being let down by men. But still, 'with all that suffering and misery and love inside her', Beauvoir managed to write 'her best book', *The Mandarins* ('shelfmark FR BEA'), whereas the lack of love and creativity, but also the overwhelming intellectual burden represented by the library, make the librarian feel 'just a cockroach' (90). The monologue ends with a veritable *cri de coeur*:

> What good will it have been to put shelf-marks on all these books? What good will it have been to spend my entire youth in overheated libraries? Yes, what's the point of Simone de Beauvoir and Eugène Morel if Martin doesn't come? (91–2)

In detail and design *The Library of Unrequited Love* encourages readers to see its library as an articulation of French national identity and history, but its conclusion also prompts thinking about libraries and librarians. Divry's librarian is well aware of the stereotype of the woman librarian—serious, bookish, perhaps frustrated on various levels—and generally a subaltern, rarely having the chance to voice an opinion. Divry has said that she was influenced in part by Patrick Süskind's play *The Double Bass*—about one of the players in the orchestra who rarely gets a starring role, but is essential to the whole.[12] Throughout the

---

[12] Sophie Divry, email to Siân Reynolds, 10 May 2019.

monologue Divry's librarian constantly plays with her listener (and the reader), adopting many roles—bossy, clever, sexy, bitter, dreamy, learned, emotional—which one might therefore interpret as variations on a single theme voiced by an instrumental player.

As in music, there is conflict (the 'Homeric struggle'), requiring some kind of resolution. What is to be done? This librarian criticizes her fellow workers if they lack certain qualities, notably a degree of sympathy with the reader. She insists—echoing Danton's famous sound bite about audacity ('De l'audace, encore de l'audace, toujours de l'audace')—that 'you need kindness, more kindness, always more kindness' (79). In France as elsewhere, librarians have to be jealous guardians of books, and therefore to favour good order—but at the same time they have a responsibility to readers, who, like themselves, are only human. As well as signalling its library's status as an articulation of distinctively French culture, Divry's witty and beguiling novella shows how, under the intellectual hunger and everyday interaction with readers, there lies an existential fear of the overwhelming world of books, and a need for some kind of essential human contact, whether personal or professional. Despite her anguish and disillusion, this 'cultural assembly-line worker' daily returns to the fray: 'it all starts up again every day, I fall for it. The Homeric struggle. Every day I go back into the arena' (91).

Published in 2018, two years after the United Kingdom voted to leave the European Union, Salley Vickers's *The Librarian* is signally different in its cultural and political bearings from both Elizarov's novel of the same title and Divry's novella. Vickers's tale apparently constitutes a paean to a lost world. Written as pro-Brexit Britain dreamed of a return to the splendid isolation of a post-war past, it takes its readers to a 1950s England where the happy functioning of the public lending library signals all is well with the world.

Young, idealistic Sylvia Blackwell, fresh from library school, attempts to make her children's library a catalyst for change in the small, middle-English country town of East Mole. Setting up home in a picturesque country cottage, she overhauls the library's collections, disposing of such mouldering Victorian tomes as *Stories of the Patriarchs* and *The Joys of Obedience*, and replacing them with attractive new twentieth-century titles, including *Emil and the Detectives*, *Mary Poppins*, and *The Borrowers*. Library-school training fresh in her mind, she embarks on a publicity drive to attract new readers and starts a story-time programme for younger children. Like Divry's librarian, Sylvia is a mentor figure who involves herself enthusiastically in her community. She encourages her neighbour's son, 11-year-old Sam Field, to explore the imaginative world of *Treasure Island*, and guides her landlady's granddaughter, timid Lizzie Smith, towards the confidence to pass her eleven-plus examination.

The story, however, follows no easy trajectory towards success. Sylvia's dreams of doing good through her library prove complex and evanescent. Tutored by the librarian, Lizzie Smith does indeed go on to enjoy a grammar school education, but her playmate Sam, whose sharp mind had made his prospects even brighter, crashes out of the system, led astray by his too-close immersion in the swash-buckling world of *Treasure Island*. Sylvia's 'roses-round-the-door' cottage proves in reality to be damp and insanitary, and she leaves East Mole having lost her job, and deep in the misery of a failed love affair.

Salley Vickers's library is, it seems, a metaphor for an impossible dream. The iconography of dreams informs the long first part of the book. Where Elizarov's allusions, like those of Divry, are subtle, Vickers's references to *A Midsummer Night's Dream* are intrusively insistent throughout: Sylvia has acted the part of Bottom in a long-ago school play; Lizzie Smith in her school play is given the parts of first Mustardseed, then Snout, then playwright Peter Quince. Sylvia and her married lover Hugh attend a performance of Elgar's *The Dream of Gerontius* on their first date. The reader's attention is drawn repeatedly to the dream world of *Tom's Midnight Garden*, the 1958 children's classic by Philippa Pearce. '*We are such stuff as dreams are made on*,' thinks Lizzie Smith at the end of the tale, remembering her Shakespeare as she sits with Sam Field in his Sydney apartment, admiring on his wall an Aboriginal painting entitled '*Dream Life*'.[13]

As a children's librarian, Sylvia has longed to open up to her young charges the dream worlds available to them through books. 'Children's authors', she tells Hugh, 'can write about magic, other worlds, and be taken seriously. I mean, suggest somewhere, even if hidden, there's another reality as real as the everyday world we take for granted that enlarges our sense of ordinary reality, gives it more meaning, if you see what I mean?' (123).

It is the central sadness of the story that Sylvia discovers that such dream worlds are not easily attained. Though she has dreamed of using her library to make good things happen, this novel is sinisterly insistent that the library, the librarian, and books in particular are in fact instrumental in making *bad* things happen. Passing 'the black spot' to his unpleasant neighbour Mr Collins, Sam Field becomes not a romantic *Treasure Island* character but a potentially delinquent schoolboy impli-cated in arson. The theft by spoilt 11-year-old Marigold Bell of a copy of Henry Miller's *Tropic of Cancer* from the library's restricted access collection results in lasting trauma for her and her friends, and in Marigold's need for psychiatric treatment years later. Sylvia's lover, Hugh Bell, lies to her that he has read to the end of Dodie Smith's *I Capture the Castle*, confirming the fragility of their love and, eventually, the end of their affair. East Mole library may be, as Sylvia tells her neighbour's little girls at the start of the book, 'a palace full of stories' (38), but it is also a place presided over by the evil, misogynistic Mr Booth, who thwarts her every move, mobilizes the library committee against her, and in the end engineers the closure of the children's library. As an image, the library signals ambivalence.

---

[13] Salley Vickers, *The Librarian* (London: Viking, 2018), 364; subsequent page references are supplied in the main text of this coda.

It can be, as Sylvia longs for it to be, a paradise, opening magic casements into imaginary worlds for eager readers; but it can also be a place where malevolent control is exerted, censorship imposed, and lives frustrated. 'They burned books, didn't they, the Nazis?' says Sylvia's friend Ned (302).

Though shot through with a historically situated nostalgia for the role of post-war lending libraries in Britain, and their importance for a particular generation of children (born, like Vickers, in the 1940s), the novel at this stage recognizes much that was wrong with the world it evokes. Vickers tilts vigorously at the English class hierarchy (Mrs Bird is 'not quite out of the right drawer' to be invited to the Bells' cocktail party (172); Hugh has a 'public school smirk' (281)); she takes up arms firmly, too, against the English eleven-plus system with the iniquities it engendered, notes in passing the marginalization in East Mole society of homosexuals and gypsies, and speaks out clearly against institutional misogyny. The first part of the story is full of mess, mistakes, and misalignments, the lives of Sylvia and her young protégés as complicated by missteps and misdirected love entanglements as those of the characters in *A Midsummer Night's Dream*.

If Sylvia's 'little paradise' of the children's library is a metaphor for that other 'little paradise' of a glorious post-war English past which may have beguiled the 2016 pro-Brexit voters, then Vickers seems to be warning at the end of Part 1 that this paradise is an illusion. The perfect England never existed, just as the reality of East Mole children's library falls so painfully short of Sylvia's imaginings. Nostalgia is a dangerous thing. Realizing this, Sylvia seems to leave East Mole an older and wiser woman.

What, then, to make of the novel's short and strangely dislocated Part 2? Here the focus shifts abruptly to the later life of Lizzie Smith, now the successful children's author Elizabeth Pattern (her role as playwright Peter Quince has been prescient), first on a trip to East Mole to support a campaign against its library's closure, and later on a book-signing tour to Australia where she encounters Sam Field, now a successful geneticist. Where Part 1 has closed on a note of subtlety, posing a question mark over an illusion and suggesting its flaws, Part 2 forces the debate open again. Both children have reached the career dream worlds opened up for them by the librarian. Lizzie Smith, product of the eleven-plus system, is shown enjoying all the fruits of her success; Sylvia's intervention in her education has worked. Sam Field, too, has succeeded, reaching university via his secondary modern and embarking on an academic career 'mainly thanks to Sylvia – or through her, I should say' (360). Vickers drives the point home—as a geneticist, Sam specializes in 'hypercommunication of information' (360), researching the 'junk DNA' which may make it possible for people to intuit things 'they haven't consciously acquired' (360). For him, Tom and Hattie meeting in each other's dreams in *Tom's Midnight Garden* exemplifies this phenomenon— dream worlds *can* be attained, the author seems to insist. If so, the novel might now therefore suggest, the 'little England' dreamed of by the pro-Brexit voter may indeed be realizable again?

Certainly *The Librarian*'s closing Author's Note positions its author squarely on the side of nostalgia. Her list of *Recommended Reading From East Mole Library* will stir happy memories for many older readers and allows us to leave the book with warm thoughts of our own hours with *The Story of the Treasure Seekers*, *Swallows and Amazons*, and *Anne of Green Gables*. It is heart-warming, too, to read Vickers's tribute to the library she visited as a child, and to the librarian who encouraged her; many readers will have had similar experiences and will be happy to be reminded of them. But it is disturbing to be left so unapologetically in the past, with no suggestion of the hundreds of modern children's authors who are still keeping young people's minds invigorated—and bookshop shelves busy— with tales more alluring and relevant to twenty-first-century readers. It is hard not to see her coda as indulgent, a rather clumsy attempt to have it both ways, which makes the novel ultimately a frustrating and unsatisfying read.

In the United Kingdom the EU Referendum vote was very close—51.9 per cent to leave versus 48.1 per cent to remain. A novel which leaves its readers in uncomfortable near-equilibrium, uncertain whether a dream can be achieved or not, is perhaps simply reflecting a British electorate not sure what its dreams are, or what to do next. Vickers's novel may hint at social divisions that will be hard, if not impossible, to heal within the existing framework of the state. Though it leaves such matters largely implicit, her novel, as much as the fictions of Elizarov and Divry, albeit in a very different way, suggests how in the early twenty-first century the library can function in contemporary literature as a synecdoche for wider power struggles not only within the politics of class and gender but also within the complex temperament of a nation.

Works Cited

Adams, James Eli. *A History of Victorian Literature* (Chichester: Wiley-Blackwell, 2012).

Adey, Robert. *Locked Room Murders and Other Impossible Crimes: A Comprehensive Bibliography* (Minneapolis: Crossover Press, 1991).

Aitken, George A. 'Steele's *Ladies Library*'. *The Athenaeum: Journal of English and Foreign Literature, Science, the Fine Arts, Music and the Drama* 2958, Saturday 5 July 1884: 16–17.

Alcott, Louisa May. *Little Women: or, Meg, Jo, Beth and Amy* (Boston: Roberts Brothers, 1868).

Alcott, Louisa May. *Little Women* (1868–9; repr. Boston: Little, Brown: 1934).

Allingham, Margery. *The Police at the Funeral* (1931; repr. London: Vintage Books, 2007).

Altick, Richard. *The English Common Reader: A Social History of the Mass Reading Public 1800–1900* (Chicago: University of Chicago Press, 1957).

Alvarez-Recio, Leticia. 'Translations of Spanish Chivalry Works in the Jacobean Book Trade: Shelton's *Don Quixote* in the Light of Anthony Munday's Publications'. *Renaissance Studies* 33.5 (2018): 691–711.

Ando, Takemasa. 'Transforming "Everydayness": Japanese New Left Movements and the Meaning of their Direct Action'. *Japanese Studies* 33.1 (2013): 1–18.

Andrews, Miles Peter. *The Mysteries of the Castle* (London: J. Woodfall et al., 1795).

Anon. *Dramatic Pieces, Calculated to Exemplify the Mode of Conduct Which Will Render Young Ladies Both Amiable and Happy, When Their School Education is Completed* (London: John Marshall [, c.1785]).

Ardila, J. A. G., ed. *The Cervantean Heritage: Reception and Influence of Cervantes in Britain* (Oxford: Legenda, 2009).

Armstrong, Karen. *The Lost Art of Scripture* (London: Bodley Head, 2019).

Asada, Akira. 'Infantile Capitalism and Japan's Postmodernism: A Fairy Tale'. In *Postmodernism and Japan*, ed. Masao Miyoshi and Harry Harootunian (Durham, NC, and London: Duke University Press, 1989), 273–8.

Asada, Akira. 'A Left Within the Place of Nothingness'. *New Left Review* 5 (2000): 1–26.

Asimov, Isaac. 'Death of a Honey-Blonde'. *The Saint Detective Magazine*, June 1956: 110–25. Repr. as 'What's in a Name?' in *Asimov's Mysteries* (Garden City, NY: Doubleday, 1968), 54–70.

Asimov, Isaac. *Nightfall, and Other Stories* (Garden City, NY: Doubleday, 1969).

Auden, W. H. 'The Guilty Vicarage' (1948). In *Detective Fiction: A Collection of Critical Essays*, ed. Robin W. Winks (London: Prentice-Hall, 1980), 15–24.

Augst, Thomas. 'Introduction: American Libraries and Agencies of Culture'. *American Studies* 42.3 (Fall 2001): 11–12.

Augst, Thomas. 'Faith in Reading: Public Libraries, Liberalism, and the Civil Religion'. In *Institutions of Reading: The Social Life of Libraries in the United States*, ed. Thomas Augst and Kenneth Carpenter (Amherst, MA, and Boston, MA: University of Massachusetts Press, 2007), 148–83.

Austen, Jane. *Northanger Abbey* (1818; repr. Boston: Little Brown, 1903).

Austen, Jane. *Pride and Prejudice*, ed. R. W. Chapman, 3rd rev. ed. (Oxford: Oxford University Press, 1965).

Austen, Jane. Letter to Cassandra Austen, 15 September 1813. In *Jane Austen Letters*, ed. Deirdre Le Faye, 3rd ed. (Oxford and New York: Oxford University Press, 1995), 218.

Austen, Jane. *Northanger Abbey*, ed. Marilyn Butler (London: Penguin, 2003).

Babel, Isaac. *Complete Works*, ed. Nathalie Babel, trans. Peter Constantine (New York: W. W. Norton, 2001).

Bachelard, Gaston. *The Poetics of Space* (Boston: Beacon Press, 1994).

Bacon, Francis. *Of the Advancement and Proficience of Learning*, trans. Gilbert Watts (Oxford: Robert Young & Edward Forrest, 1640).

Bacon, Francis. *Essays or Counsels Civil and Moral, with Other Writings* (London: George Newnes, 1902).

Bacon, Francis. *Works* (London: Newnes, 1902).

Bacon, Francis. *Essays* (London: Oxford University Press, 1966).

Bacon, Francis. *De dignitate et augmentis scientiarum*, Vol. 6 (1623; repr. Turnhout: Brepols Library of Latin Texts—Series B, 2010).

Baenen, Michael A. 'A Great and Natural Enemy of Democracy? Politics and Culture in the Antebellum Portsmouth Athenaeum'. In *Institutions of Reading: The Social Life of Libraries in the United States*, ed. Thomas Augst and Kenneth Carpenter (Amherst, MA, and Boston, MA: University of Massachusetts Press, 2007), 72–98.

Baggs, Chris. 'The Public Library in Fiction: George Gissing's *Spellbound*'. *Library History* 20.2 (July 2004): 137–46.

Baker, Edward. 'Breaking the Frame: Don Quixote's Entertaining Books'. *Cervantes: Bulletin of the Cervantes Society of America* 16.1 (1996): 12–31.

Baker, Kenneth. *On the Burning of Books* (London: Unicorn, 2016).

Baker, Thomas. *An Act at Oxford* (London: Bernard Lintot, 1704).

Baker, William. *The Libraries of George Eliot and George Henry Lewes*, ELS Monograph Series 24 (Victoria, BC: University of Victoria, 1981).

Bakerman, Jane S. 'Renovating the House of Fiction: Structural Diversity in Jane Smiley's *Duplicate Keys*'. *Midamerica* 15 (1988): 111–20.

Barnett, Louise. *Jonathan Swift in the Company of Women* (Oxford: Oxford University Press, 2007).

Barnett, Teresa. *Sacred Relics: Pieces of the Past in Nineteenth-Century America* (Chicago, IL: University of Chicago Press, 2013).

Barrett, Francis. *The Magus, or Celestial Intelligencer; Being a Complete System of Occult Philosophy* (1801; repr. York Beach, ME: Samuel Weiser, 2000).

Barthes, Roland. 'The Death of the Author'. In *Image-Music-Text*, by Roland Barthes, ed. and trans. Stephen Heath (New York: Hill & Wang, 1977), 142–8.

Battles, Matthew. *Library: An Unquiet History* (London: Heinemann, 2003).

Beecher, Catharine, and Harriet Beecher Stowe. *The American Woman's Home; or, The Principles of Domestic Science* (New York: J. B. Ford, 1869).

Behn, Aphra. *Sir Patient Fancy* (London: Richard & Jacob Tonson, 1678).

Behn, Aphra. *The Luckey Mistake* (London: R. Bentley, 1689).

Bellamy, Edward. *Looking Backward, 2000–1887* (Boston and New York: Houghton Mifflin, 1889).

Benjamin, Walter. 'Unpacking My Library'. In *Illuminations*, ed. Hannah Arendt, trans. Harry Zohn (London: Fontana Press, 1992), 61–9.

Benn, Aphra. *Sir Patient Fancy* (London; Richard & Jacob Tonson, 1678).

Benson, L. D., ed. *The Riverside Chaucer*, 3rd ed. (Oxford: Oxford University Press, 1987).

Berkeley, George. *Maxims Concerning Patriotism. By a Lady* (Dublin: [s.n.,] 1750).

Berkeley, George. *The Correspondence of George Berkeley*, ed. Marc A Hight (Cambridge: Cambridge University Press, 2013).

Bernard, William Bayle. *The Tide of Time* (London: Thomas Hailes Lacy, 1859).

Beros, M. 'Bibliomania: Thomas Frognall Dibdin and Early Nineteenth-Century Book-Collecting'. *TXT* 1 (2014): 140–5.

Bett, Doris. *Heading West* (New York: Simon & Schuster, 1995).

Bibliotheca Fanatica; or, The Phanatique Library (n.p.: 1660).

Bodemer, Brett. 'Rabelais and the Abbey of Saint-Victor Revisited'. *Information & Culture* 47.1 (2012): 4–17.

Bond, Donald, ed. *The Spectator*, 5 vols (Oxford: Clarendon Press, 1965).

Borges, Jorge Luis. 'An Autobiographical Essay'. In *The Aleph and Other Stories 1933–1969*, ed. and trans. Norman Thomas di Giovanni in collaboration with the author (New York: E. P. Dutton, 1970), 211–60.

Borges, Jorge Luis. *El idioma de los argentinos* [1928] (Buenos Aires: Espasa Calpe/Seix Barral, 1994).

Borges, Jorge Luis. 'Al espejo', in *La rosa profunda*. In his *Obras completas*, Vol. 3 (Buenos Aires: Emecé, 1996), 109.

Borges, Jorge Luis. 'A Biography of Tadeo Isidoro Cruz (1829–1874)'. In *Collected Fictions*, trans. Andrew Hurley (New York: Viking Penguin, 1998), 212–14.

Borges, Jorge Luis. *Collected Fictions*, trans. Andrew Hurley (New York: Viking Penguin, 1998).

Borges, Jorge Luis. 'Pierre Menard, Author of the *Quixote*'. In *Collected Fictions*, trans. Andrew Hurley (New York: Viking Penguin, 1998), 93–5.

Borges, Jorge Luis. 'The Library of Babel'. In *Collected Fictions*, trans. Andrew Hurley (New York: Viking Penguin, 1998), 112–8.

Borges, Jorge Luis. 'An Investigation of the Word'. In *The Total Library: Non-Fiction 1922–1986*, ed. Eliot Weinberger (London: Allen Lane, 1999), 39.

Borges, Jorge Luis. 'A Profession of Literary Faith'. In *The Total Library: Non-Fiction, 1922–1986*, ed. Eliot Weinberger (London: Allen Lane, 1999), 23–7.

Borges, Jorge Luis. 'Borges and I'. In *The Total Library: Non-Fiction 1922–1986*, ed. Eliot Weinberger (London: Allen Lane, 1999), 324.

Borges, Jorge Luis. *Selected Poems*, ed. Alexander Coleman (London: Allen Lane; and New York: Viking Books, 1999).

Borges, Jorge Luis. 'The Nothingness of Personality'. In *The Total Library: Non-Fiction 1922–1986*, ed. Eliot Weinberger (London: Allen Lane, 1999), 3–9.

Borges, Jorge Luis. 'The Total Library'. In *The Total Library: Non-Fiction 1922–1986*, ed. Eliot Weinberger (London: Allen Lane, 1999), 214–16.

Borges, Jorge Luis. 'Anatomía de mi Ultra' ('Anatomy of My Ultra') [1921]'. In *Jorge Luis Borges: textos recobrados, 1919–1929* (Buenos Aires: Emecé, 2001), 95.

Borges, Jorge Luis. 'Manifiesto del Ultra' ('Ultra Manifesto)'. In *Jorge Luis Borges: textos recobrados, 1919–1929* (Buenos Aires: Emecé, 2001), 86–7.

Borges, Jorge Luis, and Adolfo Bioy Casares. *Boruhesu kai kitan shū* (Tokyo: Shōbunsha, 1976).

Bownas, Geoffrey, and Anthony Thwaite, eds. *The Penguin Book of Japanese Verse* (London: Penguin, 2009).

Bradbury, Ray. *Fahrenheit 451* (New York: Ballantine, 1953).

Bradbury, Ray. 'Bright Phoenix' (1947). *The Magazine of Fantasy and Science Fiction* 24.5 (May 1963): 23–9.

Bramley, Gerald. *A History of Library Education* (New York: Archon Books & Clive Bingley, 1969).

Brantley, Ben. 'Screwball Eggheads Tear Up the Library in "Travesties"'. *New York Times*, (25 April 2018): Section c, 5.

Brewer, John. *The Pleasures of the Imagination* (New York: Farrar, Straus and Giroux, 1997).

Brittain, William. 'The Man Who Read John Dickson Carr' (1965). In *Murderous Schemes: An Anthology of Classic Detective Stories*, ed. Donald E. Westlake (Oxford: Oxford University Press, 1996), 59–65.

Brooks, Shirley. *The Naggletons* (London: Bradbury, Agnew, 1875).

Broome, Adam. *The Oxford Murders* (London: G. Bles, 1929).

Broome, Adam. *The Cambridge Murders* (London: G. Bles, 1936).

Brown, Huntington. *Rabelais in English Literature* (Paris: Société d'édition 'les belles lettres', 1933).

Brown, William Hill. *The Power of Sympathy*, 2 vols (Boston: Isaiah Thomas, 1789).

Browne, Douglas G. *The May Week Murders* (London: Longmans & Co., 1937).

Browne, Thomas. *Religio Medici*, 8th ed. (London: R. Scot et al., 1682).

Browne, Thomas. *Certain Miscellany Tracts* (London: Charles Mearne, 1684).

Brown-Syed, Christopher, and Charles Barnard Sands. 'Some Portrayals of Librarians in Fiction – A Discussion'. *Education Libraries* 21.1–2 (1997): 17–24.

Bukowski, Charles. *War All the Time* (Santa Rosa, CA: Black Sparrow, 1984).

Bullard, Paddy. 'What Swift Did in Libraries'. In *Jonathan Swift and the Eighteenth-Century Book*, ed. Paddy Bullard and James McLaverty (Cambridge: Cambridge University Press, 2013), 64–84.

Bullard, Paddy, and James McLaverty. *Jonathan Swift and the Eighteenth-Century Book* (Cambridge: Cambridge University Press, 2013).

Burns, Grant. *Librarians in Fiction: A Critical Bibliography* (Jefferson, NC: McFarland, 1998).

Burns, Robert. *Letters*, ed. J. De Lancey Ferguson. 2nd ed. ed. J. De Lancey Ferguson and G. Ross Roy, 2 vols. (Oxford: Clarendon Press, 1985).

Burrow, J. W. *The Crisis of Reason: European Thought, 1848–1914* (New Haven: Yale University Press, 2000).

Burton, Robert. *The Anatomy of Melancholy*, ed. Floyd Dell and Paul Jordan-Smith (New York: Tudor, 1955).

Bury, Richard de. *The Philobiblon of Richard de Bury*, trans. Ernest C. Thomas (London: Kegan Paul, Trench & Co., 1888).

Bury, Richard de. *The Philobiblon of Richard de Bury*, ed. Andrew Fleming West, 3 vols (New York: Grolier Club, 1889).

Butler, Samuel. *Hudibras* (London: W. Rogers, 1684).

Byatt, A. S. *Possession* (London: Chatto & Windus, 1990).

Byers, Reid. *The Private Library: The History of the Architecture and Furnishing of the Domestic Bookroom* (New Castle, DE: Oak Knoll Press, 2021).

Cabell, James Branch. *Beyond Life* (1919; repr. New York: R. M. McBride, 1921).

Campbell, James W. P. *The Library: A World History* (London: Thames & Hudson, 2013).

Canetti, Elias. *Auto da Fé*, trans. C. V. Wedgwood (1946; repr. London: Vintage, 1995).

Canfield, Dorothy. 'Hillsboro's Good Luck'. In *Hillsboro People*, by Dorothy Canfield (New York: Holt, 1915), 187–206. Originally pub. in *Atlantic Monthly* 102 (July 1908): 131–9.

Carlyle, Thomas. *On Heroes, Hero-Worship and the Heroic in History*, ed. George Wherry (Cambridge: Cambridge University Press, 1911).

Carlyle, Thomas. *On Heroes, Hero-Worship and the Heroic in History* (1841; repr. London: Oxford University Press, 1963).

Carnegie, Andrew. 'Why Mr. Carnegie Founds Free Libraries'. In *Campaigning for a Public Library: Suggested Material for Newspaper Use and for General Circulation*. (Madison, WI: Wisconsin Free Library Commission, 1906), 7.

Carnegie, Andrew. *Autobiography* (Boston: Houghton Mifflin, 1920).

Cartwright, William. *Comedies, Tragi-comedies, with Other Poems* (London: Humphry Moseley, 1651).

Cavendish, Margaret. *Poems and Phancies* (London: William Wilson, 1664).

Certeau, Michel de. *The Practice of Everyday Life*, trans. Steve Randall, Vol. 1 (Berkeley: University of California Press, 1984).

Cervantes Saavedra, Miguel de. *The History of the Valorous and Wittie Knight-errant, Don-Quixote Of the Mancha*, trans. Thomas Shelton (London: Edward Blount and W. Barret, 1612).

Cervantes Saavedra, Miguel de. *Don Quixote*, trans. Peter le Motteux, 2 vols (London: Dent, 1970).

Chandler, Raymond. 'The Simple Art of Murder' (1944). In *The Art of the Mystery Story*, ed. Howard Haycraft (New York: Carroll & Graf, 1983), 226–9.

Charvat, William. *The Origins of American Critical Thought, 1810–1835* (Philadelphia: University of Pennsylvania Press, 1936).

Chaucer, Geoffrey. *The Riverside Chaucer*, ed. L. D. Benson. 3rd ed. (Oxford: Oxford University Press, 1987).

Chesterton, G. K. 'The Return of Don Quixote'. *The Collected Works of G.K. Chesterton*, Vol. 8 (San Francisco: Ignatius Press, 1999).

Christie, Agatha. *An Autobiography* (London: William Collins, 1977).

Christie, Agatha. *The Body in the Library* (1942; repr. London: HarperCollins, 2016).

Churchill, Winston. *Coniston* (New York: Macmillan, 1907).

Cibber, Colly. *Love Makes a Man* (London: Richard Parker et al., 1701).

Clarke, Susanna. *Jonathan Strange & Mr Norrell* (London: Bloomsbury, 2005).

Clery, Emma J. *The Feminization Debate in Eighteenth-Century England: Literature, Commerce, and Luxury* (Basingstoke: Palgrave Macmillan, 2004).

Close, Anthony J. 'The Legacy of Don Quijote and the Picaresque Novel'. In *The Cambridge Companion to the Spanish Novel*, ed. Harriet Turner and Adelaida López de Martínez (Cambridge: Cambridge University Press, 2003), 15–30.

Coghill, Mrs Harry, ed. *The Autobiography and Letters of Mrs M. O. W. Oliphant* (Edinburgh and London: Blackwood, 1899). Repr. in *The Selected Works of Margaret Oliphant*, ed. E. Jay and J. Shattock, 25 vols (London: Pickering & Chatto, 2011–17), Vol. 6.

Coleman, Wanda. *Bathwater Wine* (Santa Rosa, CA: Black Sparrow, 1998).

Coletti, Theresa. *Naming the Rose: Eco, Signs and Modern Theory* (Ithaca, NY: Cornell University Press, 1988).

Collins, V. H., ed. *Ghosts and Marvels: A Selection of Uncanny Tales from Daniel Defoe to Algernon Blackwood* (London: Oxford University Press, 1924).

Colman, George [the Elder]. *Polly Honeycombe* (London: T. Becket et al., 1760).

Colman, George [the Younger]. *The Iron Chest* (London: Cadell and Davies, 1796).

Conkling, Helen. *Red Peony Night* (Pittsburgh: University of Pittsburgh Press, 1997).

Cook, Daniel. 'Bodies of Scholarship: Witnessing the Library in Late-Victorian Fiction'. *Victorian Literature and Culture* 39.1 (2011): 107–25.

Cook, Daniel. *Reading Swift's Poetry* (Cambridge: Cambridge University Press, 2020).

Cook, Michael. *Narratives of Enclosure in Detective Fiction: The Locked Room Mystery* (London: Palgrave Macmillan, 2011).

Cooley, Martha. *The Archivist* (Boston: Little, Brown, 1998).

Cowell, Cressida. *How To Train Your Dragon: A Hero's Guide to Deadly Dragons* (London: Hodder & Stoughton, 2007).

Cowley, Abraham. *Poems*, ed. A. R. Waller (Cambridge: Cambridge University Press, 1905).

Cox, Michael. *M. R. James: An Informal Portrait* (Oxford: Oxford University Press, 1983).

Crabbe, George. *The Complete Poetical Works*, ed. Norma Dalrymple-Champneys and Arthur Pollard, 3 vols (Oxford: Clarendon Press, 1988).

Crawford, Alice, ed. *The Meaning of the Library: A Cultural History* (Princeton: Princeton University Press, 2015).

Crawford, Robert, ed. *The Scottish Invention of English Literature* (Cambridge: Cambridge University Press, 1997).

Crawford, Robert. 'The Library in Poetry'. In *The Meaning of the Library*, ed. Alice Crawford (Princeton: Princeton University Press, 2015), 176–98.

Cumberland, Richard. *The Natural Son* (London: C. Dilly et al., 1785).

Cunningham, J. V. *Collected Poems and Epigrams* (London: Faber & Faber, 1971).

Daniel, Glyn. *The Cambridge Murders* (London: Gollancz, 1945).

Darnton, Robert. *The Case for Books* (New York: Public Affairs, 2009).

Daskam, Josephine Dodge. *Whom the Gods Destroyed* (New York: Charles Scribner's Sons, 1902).

D'Avenant, William. *The Man's the Master* (London: Henry Herringman, 1669).

D'Avenant, William. *The Tempest* (London: Henry Herringman, 1670).

Davidson, John. *Poems*, ed. A. Turnbull (Edinburgh: Scottish Academic Press, 1973).

Davidson, Lynn. *Islander* (Wellington and Bristol: Victoria University Press and Shearsman, 2019).

Davidson, Peter. *The Idea of North* (London: Reaktion, 2016).

Davies, Owen. *Grimoires: A History of Magic Books* (Oxford: Oxford University Press, 2009).

Davis, Lavinia. *Reference to Death* ([Toronto: Toronto Star,] 1950).

Davis, Richard Harding. *Farces* (New York: Charles Scribner's Sons, 1906).

Delafield, E. M. *Diary of a Provincial Lady* (London: Macmillan, 1930).

Dennison, Lynda, ed. *The Legacy of M. R. James: Papers from the 1995 Cambridge Symposium.* (Donington: Shaun Tyas, 2001).

De Quincey, Thomas. *Letters to a Young Man* (Philadelphia: John Penington, 1843).

Dereske, Jo. *Miss Zukas and the Library Murders* (New York: Avon Books, 1994).

De Tocqueville, Alexis. *Democracy in America*, 2 vols (New York: J. & H. G. Langley, 1841).

Dewey, Melvil. 'The Ideal Librarian'. *Library Journal* 24.1 (1899): 14.

Dibdin, Thomas Frognall. *Bibliomania: or Book-Madness: Containing Some Account of the History, Symptom, and Cure of the Fatal Disease* (London: Printed for Longman et al. by W. Savage, 1809).

Dibdin, Thomas Frognall. *Bibliophobia: Remarks on the Present Languid and Depressed State of the Book Trade* (London: Henry Bohn, 1832).

Dickens, Charles. *Hard Times* (1854; repr. London: Nelson, 1903).

Dickens, Charles. *The Letters of Charles Dickens*, ed. Madeline House and Graham Storey (Oxford: Clarendon Press, 1965–2002).

Dickens, Charles. *David Copperfield* (1850; repr. London: Vintage, 2017).

Dil, Jonathan. 'Writing as Self-Therapy: Competing Therapeutic Paradigms in Murakami Haruki's Rat Trilogy'. *Japan Forum* 22.1–2 (2010): 43–64.

D'Israeli, Isaac. *Curiosities of Literature*, 5 vols (London: John Murray, 1807).

Divry, Sophie. *The Library of Unrequited Love*, trans. Siân Reynolds (London: MacLehose Press, 2013).

Divry, Sophie. Email to Siân Reynolds, 10 May 2019.

Dod, Bernard G. 'Aristoteles latinus'. In *The Cambridge History of Later Medieval Philosophy*, ed. Norman Kretzmann, Anthony Kenny, Jan Pinborg, and Eleonore Stump (1982; repr. Cambridge: Cambridge University Press, 2008), 43–79.

Domier, Sharon. 'From Reading Guidance to Thought Control: Wartime Japanese Libraries'. *Library Trends* 55.3 (2007): 551–69.

Douglass, Frederick. 'My Foreign Travels'. In *Frederick Douglass Papers, Series One: Speeches, Debates and Interviews*, ed. John W. Blassingame, Vol. 5. 1881–95 (New Haven, CT: Yale University Press, 1992), 278–338.

Dove, Rita. *On the Bus with Rosa Parks* (New York: W.W. Norton, 1999).

Duffy, Carol Ann. *Selling Manhattan* (London: Anvil, 1998).

Duncan, Ian. 'Walter Scott and the Historical Novel'. In *The Oxford History of the Novel in English*, Vol. 2. *English and British Fiction 1750–1820*, ed. Peter Garside and Karen O'Brien (Oxford: Oxford University Press, 2015), 312–31.

Duncan, Ian. *Human Forms: The Novel in the Age of Evolution* (Princeton: Princeton University Press, 2019).

Dunn, Douglas. *New Selected Poems* (London: Faber & Faber, 2003).

Dunning, Andrew. 'The Medieval Cartulary Behind a Ghost Story'. British Library: Medieval Manuscripts Blog, 27 August 2017; https://blogs.bl.uk/digitisedmanuscripts/2017/08/the-medieval-cartulary-behind-a-ghost-story.html.

Dutton, Charles. *Murder in a Library* (New York: Dodd, Mead & Co., 1931).

Eco, Umberto. *The Name of the Rose*, trans. William Weaver (London: Vintage Books, 2004).

Ehrenpreis, Irvin. *Swift: The Man, His Works, and the Age*. Vol. 1. *Mr Swift and his Contemporaries* (London: Methuen, 1962).

Eliot, George. *Middlemarch* (1872; repr. Edinburgh: Blackwood, 1881).

Eliot, George. *The Mill on the Floss*, 2 vols (1860; repr. London: Dent, 1930).

Eliot, George. *Middlemarch* (1872; repr. London: Dent, 1969).

Eliot, George. *Middlemarch*, ed. David Carroll (Oxford: Oxford University Press, 1998).

Eliot, George. *The Mill on the Floss*, ed. Gordon Haight (Oxford: Oxford University Press, 2015).

Eliot, T. S. *The Sacred Wood* (1920; repr. London: Methuen, 1960).

Elizarov, Mikhail. *The Librarian*, trans. Andrew Bromfield (London: Pushkin Press, 2015).

Elliott, Margaret A. *The Librarian's Stereotyped Image in Romance Novels, 1980–1995: Has the Image Changed?* Master of Library and Information Science diss., Kent State University (1996).

Ellis, Katharine Ruth. *The Wide Awake Girls in Winsted* (Boston: Little, Brown & Co., 1909).

Ellis, Thomas Sayers. *The Maverick Room* (Minneapolis: Graywolf Press, 2005).

Emerson, Ralph Waldo. *The Complete Works*. Vol. 7. *Society and Solitude*, ed. Edward Waldo Emerson (Boston, MA, and New York: Houghton Mifflin, 1904).

Fallin, Lee. 'Beyond Books: The Concept of the Academic Library as Learning Space'. *New Library World* 117.5/6 (2016): 308–20.

Fante, John. *The Road to Los Angeles* (Santa Barbara, CA: Black Sparrow, 1985).

Ferris, Ina. 'Bibliographic Romance: Bibliophilia and the Book Object'. *Romantic Circles Praxis Series: Romantic Libraries Issue* (University of Maryland, February 2004); https://romantic-circles.org/praxis/libraries/index.html.

Ferris, Ina. 'Book Fancy: Bibliomania and the Literary Word'. *Keats-Shelley Journal* 58 (2009): 33–52.

Ferris, Ina. *Book-Men, Book Clubs, and the Romantic Literary Sphere* (London: Palgrave Macmillan, 2015).

Ferris, Ina, and Paul Keen, eds. *Bookish Histories* (Basingstoke: Palgrave Macmillan, 2009).

Ferster, Judith. *Fictions of Advice: Literature and Politics of Counsel in Late-Medieval England* (Philadelphia: University of Pennsylvania Press, 1990).

Fielding, Penny. 'Reading Rooms: M. R. James and the Library of Modernity'. *Modern Fiction Studies* 46.3 (2000): 749–71.

Fifty Years of Ghost Stories. (London: Hutchinson, 1936).

Flutsch, Maria. 'Girls and the Unconscious in Murakami Haruki's *Kafka on the Shore*'. *Japanese Studies* 26.1 (2006): 69–79.

Folsom, Elizabeth I. 'Natural Selection'. In *As We Are: Stories of Here and Now*, ed. W. B. Pitkin (New York: Harcourt Brace, 1923), 47–72.

Foote, Samuel. *The Author* (London: P. Valliant et al., 1757).

Foote, Samuel. *The Lyar* (London: G. Kearsly et al., 1764).

Forcione, Alban K. *Cervantes, Aristotle, and the Persiles* (Princeton: Princeton University Press, 1970).

Ford, Lionel. *Letter to M. R. James*, 27 December 1887. Cambridge University Library MS Add. 7481 F74.

Forrest-Thomson, Veronica. *Collected Poems and Translations* (Lewes: Allardyce, Barnett Publishers, 1990).

Franklin, Benjamin. *Benjamin Franklin's Autobiography*, ed. Joyce E. Chaplin (New York and London: W. W. Norton, 2012).

Fraser, Bashabi, and Elaine Greig, eds. *Edinburgh: An Intimate City* (Edinburgh: Department of Recreation, Edinburgh City Council, 2000).

'Free Public Libraries'. *New York Times*, 14 January 1872, 4.

Freier, Mary P. 'The Librarian in Rowling's *Harry Potter* Series'. *CLCWeb: Comparative Literature and Culture* 16.3 (2014): 1–9.

Frońska, Joanna. *The Royal Collection of Manuscripts*. British Library: Catalogue of Illuminated Manuscripts; https://www.bl.uk/catalogues/illuminatedmanuscripts/TourRoyalGen.asp.

Fuller, Thomas. *Andronicus* (London: Richard Hall et al., 1661).

Furlong, E. J., and David Berman. 'George Berkeley and *The Ladies Library*'. *Berkeley Newsletter* 4 (December 1980): 4–13.

Gameson, Richard. 'The Image of the Medieval Library'. In *The Meaning of the Library*, ed. Alice Crawford (Princeton: Princeton University Press, 2015), 31–71.

Garon, Sheldon. *Molding Japanese Minds: The State in Everyday Life* (Princeton: Princeton University Press, 1998).

Garrett, George. *The King of Babylon Shall Not Come Against You* (New York: Harcourt, Brace, 1996).

Garside, Peter, James Raven, and Rainer Schöwerling, eds. *The English Novel 1770–1829: A Bibliographical Survey of Prose Fiction Published in the British Isles*, 2 vols (Oxford: Oxford University Press, 2000).

Garve, Andrew. *The Galloway Case* (London: Collins Crime Club, 1958).

Gaselee, Stephen. 'Montague Rhodes James, 1862–1936'. *Proceedings of the British Academy* 22 (1936): 418–33.

'Genjū jiten'. *Yomiuri Shimbun*, 10 March 1975, 7.

Gerhard, Sandra Forbes. *'Don Quixote' and the Shelton Translation* (Madrid: Studia Humanitatis, 1982).

Gifford, Douglas, ed. *Scottish Short Stories 1800–1900* (London: Calder & Boyars, 1971).

Gigante, Denise. *Taste: A Literary History* (New Haven: Yale University Press, 2005).

Gill, Bartholomew. *The Death of an Ardent Bibliophile* (London: Macmillan, 1995).

Gissing, George. *New Grub Street*, 3 vols (London: Smith, Elder, 1891).

Glapthorne, Henry. *Wit in a Constable* (London: F[rancis] C[onstable], 1640).

Godwin, William. *Fleetwood; or, The New Man of Feeling*, ed. Pamela Clemit (London: Pickering, 1992).

Grafton, Anthony, ed. *Rome Reborn: The Vatican Library and Renaissance Culture* (New Haven: Yale University Press, 1993).

Grafton, Anthony. *Commerce with the Classics: Ancient Books and Renaissance Readers* (Ann Arbor: University of Michigan Press, 1997).

Grant, Helen. 'The Nature of the Beast: The Demonology of "Canon Alberic's Scrapbook"'. In *Warnings to the Curious: A Sheaf of Criticism on M. R. James*, ed. S. T. Joshi and Rosemary Pardoe (New York: Hippocampus Press, 2007), 227–37.

Gray, Alasdair. *Unlikely Stories, Mostly* (Edinburgh: Canongate, 1983).

Grimes, Brendan. 'The Library Buildings up to 1970'. In *Essays on the History of Trinity College Library*, ed. Vincent Kinane and Anne Walsh (Dublin and Portland, OR: Four Courts Press, 2000), 72–90.

Grundy, Isobel. *Lady Mary Wortley Montagu: Comet of the Enlightenment* (Oxford: Oxford University Press, 2001).

Haig, Matt. *The Midnight Library* (Edinburgh: Canongate, 2020).

Hallissy, Margaret. 'Reading the Plans: The Architectural Drawings in Umberto Eco's *Name of the Rose*'. *Critique* 42.3 (2001): 271–86.

Hamilton-Honey, Emily. 'Guardians of Morality: Librarians and American Girls' Series Fiction, 1890–1950'. *Library Trends* 60.4 (Spring 2012): 771–2.

Hammond, Brean. 'Swift's Reading'. In *The Cambridge Companion to Jonathan Swift*, ed. Christopher Fox (Cambridge: Cambridge University Press, 2003), 73–86.

Hanegraaff, Walter. *Esotericism and the Academy: Rejected Knowledge in Western Culture* (Cambridge: Cambridge University Press, 2012).

Harford, Lesbia. 'In the Public Library'. *internetPoem.com* website: https://internetpoem.com/lesbia-harford/in-the-public-library-poem/

Harker, Jaime. *America the Middlebrow: Women's Novels, Progressivism, and Middlebrow Authorship Between the Wars* (Amherst: University of Massachusetts Press, 2007).

Harkness, Deborah. *A Discovery of Witches* (London: Headline, 2011).

Harkness, Deborah. *Shadow of Night* (London: Headline, 2012).

Harkness, Deborah. *The Book of Life* (London: Headline, 2014).

Harriss, Will. *The Bay Psalm Book Murder* (New York: Walker & Co., 1983).

Haugen, Louise. *Richard Bentley: Poetry and Enlightenment* (Cambridge, MA: Harvard University Press, 2011).

Hayes, Kevin J. *A Colonial Woman's Bookshelf* (Knoxville, TN: University of Tennessee Press, 1996).

Hays, Mary. *Memoirs of Emma Courtney*, ed. Marilyn Brooks (Peterborough: Broadview Press, 2000).

Haywood, Eliza. *A Wife to be Lett* (London: Dan Browne Jr et al., 1724).

Hazlitt, William. 'On Reading Old Books'. In *The Complete Works of William Hazlitt*, ed. P. P. Howe, Vol. 12 (London: J. M. Dent & Sons, 1931), 220–9.

Hill, Selima. *Violet* (Newcastle: Bloodaxe, 1997).

Hindenberger-Burton, Tania. 'The Quixotic in Canetti's *Die Blendung*'. *Modern Austrian Literature* 16.3–4 (1983): 165–76.

Hoare, Peter, ed. *The Cambridge History of Libraries in Britain and Ireland* (Cambridge: Cambridge University Press, 2006).

Hoberman, Ruth. 'Women in the British Museum Reading Room During the Late-Nineteenth and Early-Twentieth Centuries: From Quasi- to Counterpublic'. *Feminist Studies* 28.3 (Autumn 2002): 489–512.

Hollingshead, Greg. 'Sources for the *Ladies' Library*'. *Berkeley Newsletter* 11 (1989–90): 1–9.

Holmes, Oliver Wendell Sr. 'For the Dedication of the New City Library, Boston'. In *The Writings of Oliver Wendell Holmes*, Vol. 13 (Boston, MA, and New York: Houghton Mifflin, 1891), 181–2.

Holmes, Oliver Wendell Sr. *The Poet at the Breakfast Table* (Boston, MA: Houghton Mifflin, 1900).

Holt, Hazel. *The Cruellest Month* (New York: Penguin, 1991).

Hopkins, Pauline. *Contending Forces: A Romance Illustrative of Negro Life North and South* (New York: Oxford University Press, 1988).

House, Madeline, and Graham Storey, eds. *The Letters of Charles Dickens* (Oxford: Clarendon Press, 1965–2002).

Houston, Alan Craig. *Benjamin Franklin and the Politics of Improvement* (New Haven, CT: Yale University Press, 2008).

Howe, Susan. *The Nonconformist's Memorial* (New York: New Directions, 1993).

Hughes, Martin. 'A Maze of Secrets in a Story by M. R. James'. In *Warnings to the Curious: A Sheaf of Criticism on M. R. James*, ed. S. T. Joshi and Rosemary Pardoe (New York: Hippocampus Press, 2007), 258–78.

Humble, Nicola. *The Feminine Middlebrow Novel 1920s to 1950s*. Rev. ed. (Oxford: Oxford University Press, 2004).

Humble, Nicola. 'Sitting Forward or Sitting Back: Highbrow v. Middlebrow Reading'. *Modernist Cultures* 6.1 (May 2011): 41–59.

Hume, David. 'Of the Rise and Progress of the Arts and Sciences'. In *Essays Moral, Political and Literary*, by David Hume, ed. Eugene F. Miller. Rev. ed. (Indianapolis: Liberty Fund, 1987), 117–37.

Humphreys, K. W. *A National Library in Theory and Practice* (The Panizzi Lectures, 1987) (London: British Library, 1988).

Hunt, Leigh. 'My Books'. In *Essays and Sketches*, ed. R. Brimley Johnson (London: Oxford University Press, 1906), 95.

Hutton, Margaret-Anne. 'Shelving Books? Representations of the Library in Contemporary Texts'. *Comparative Critical Studies* 14.1 (2017): 7–27.

Innes, Michael. *Death at the President's Lodging* (London: Penguin, 1936).

Innes, Michael. *Appleby and Honeybath* (London: Gollancz, 1983).

'International Congress of Women'. *The Times*, 5 July 1899, 10.

'In this busy age there is only time for the best books'. *Popular Science Monthly* 112.1, January 1928: 87.

Irving, Washington. *The Sketch-Book of Geoffrey Crayon, Gent.*, ed. Susan Manning (Oxford: Oxford University Press, 2009).

Irwin, Raymond. *The Heritage of the English Library* (London: George Allen & Unwin, 1964).

Jacquet, Claude. *Joyce et Rabelais* (Paris: Didier, 1972).

James, Felicity. 'Romantic Readers'. In *The Oxford Handbook to British Romanticism*, ed. David Duff (Oxford: Oxford University Press, 2018), 478–94.

James, Henry. *The Bostonians* (London: Macmillan, 1886).

James, M. R. *Casting the Runes: manuscript version*, British Library MS Egerton 3141.

James, M. R. *Letter to family, 13 November 1887*, Cambridge University Library MS Add. 7480 D6/291.

James, M. R. *Letter to family, 17 January 1888*, Cambridge University Library MS Add. 7480 D6/293.

James, M. R. *A Descriptive Catalogue of Manuscripts in the Fitzwilliam Museum* (Cambridge: Cambridge University Press, 1895).

James, M. R. *A Descriptive Catalogue of the Manuscripts other than Oriental in the Library of King's College, Cambridge* (Cambridge: Cambridge University Press, 1895).

James, M. R. 'The Testament of Solomon'. *The Guardian* (Church Newspaper), March 15 1899, 367.

James, M. R. 'Lost Hearts', *Pall Mall Magazine* 7.32 (1895). Repr. in *Ghost Stories of an Antiquary*, ed. M. R. James (London: Edward Arnold, 1904).

James, M. R. *Old Testament Legends: Being Stories out of Some of the Less-Known Apocryphal Books of the Old Testament* (London: Longmans, Green & Co., 1913).

James, M. R. *The Wanderings and Homes of Manuscripts* (London: SPCK, 1919).

James, M. R. *The Lost Apocrypha of the Old Testament: Their Titles and Fragments* (London: SPCK, 1920).

James, M. R. *List of the Manuscripts Formerly Owned by John Dee, with Preface and Identifications* (Oxford: Oxford University Press, 1921)

James, M. R. 'The Testament of Solomon'. *Journal of Theological Studies* 24 (1923): 467–8.

James, M. R. *Eton and King's: Recollections, Mostly Trivial, 1875–1925* (1926; repr. Ashcroft, BC: Ash-Tree Press, 2005).

James, M. R. 'Some Remarks on Ghost Stories'. *The Bookman* (December 1929): 169–72. Repr. in *M. R. James. Collected Ghost Stories*, ed. Darryl Jones (Oxford: Oxford University Press, 2011).

James, M. R. 'Occult Sciences'. *The Ghosts and Scholars M. R. James Newsletter 5* (Subscribers' Supplement) (February 2004).

James, M. R. *Collected Ghost Stories*, ed. Darryl Jones (Oxford: Oxford University Press, 2011).

Jamie, Kathleen. *The Queen of Sheba* (Newcastle: Bloodaxe, 1994).

'Jane Oliver' [obituary]. *The Times*, 8 May 1970, 12.

Jarrell, Randall. *The Complete Poems* (London: Faber & Faber, 1971).

Jarvis, Ewen. 'A Poetics of Intellectual Library Space: A Hidden Story of Natural Growth'. *Double Dialogues* 12 (2010): http://www.doubledialogues.com/article/a-poetics-of-intellectual-library-space-a-hidden-story-of-natural-growth/

Jay, Elisabeth, ed. *The Autobiography of Margaret Oliphant. The Complete Text*. (Oxford: Oxford University Press, 1990).

Jay, Elisabeth. *Mrs Oliphant: 'A Fiction to Herself': A Literary Life* (Oxford: Clarendon Press, 1995).

Jay, Elisabeth, and J. Shattock, ed. *The Selected Works of Margaret Oliphant*, 25 vols (London: Pickering & Chatto, 2011–17).

Jerrold, Walter. *Thomas Hood: His Life and Times* (New York: John Lane, 1909).

Jones, Darryl, ed. *M. R. James. Collected Ghost Stories* (Oxford: Oxford University Press, 2011).

Jones, Russell, and Claire Askew, eds. *Umbrellas of Edinburgh* (Glasgow: Freight, 2016).

Jonson, Ben. *Poems*, ed. Ian Donaldson (London: Oxford University Press, 1975).

Jordan, Thomas. *Fancy's Festivals* (London: Thomas Wilson, 1657).

Joshi, S.T., and Rosemary Pardoe, eds. *Warnings to the Curious: A Sheaf of Criticism on M. R. James* (New York: Hippocampus Press, 2007).

Joyce, James. *A Portrait of the Artist as a Young Man* (1916; repr. London: Jonathan Cape, 1943).

Joyce, James. *Ulysses*. (1922; repr. Harmondsworth: Penguin, 1974).

Kawasaki, Yoshitaka. 'Library History Studies in Japan and the Japan Society for the Study of Library History (JSSLH)'. *Libraries and Culture* 25.1 (1990): 130–7.

Kawasaki, Yoshitaka, et al. 'The Development of Public Libraries in Japan After World War II'. 62nd IFLA General Conference Proceedings, August 1996; https://origin-archive.ifla.org/IV/ifla62/62-kawy.htm.

Kay, Jackie. *Darling: New and Selected Poems* (Tarset: Bloodaxe Books, 2007)

Keery, James. *That Stranger, The Blues* (Manchester: Carcanet, 1996).

Kees, Weldon. *The Collected Poems*, ed. Donald Justice (Lincoln: University of Nebraska Press, 1975).

Kells, Stuart. *The Library: A Catalogue of Wonders: A Love Letter to Libraries and to Their Makers and Protectors* (Melbourne: Text Publishing, 2017).

Kelly, John. *The Married Philosopher* (London: T. Worrall et al., 1732).

Kendrick, Nancy. 'Berkeley's Bermuda Project and *The Ladies Library*'. In *Berkeley Revisited: Moral, Social and Political Philosophy*, ed. Sébastien Charles (Oxford: Voltaire Foundation, 2015), 243–57.

Kenyon, John. *Poems: For the Most Part Occasional* (London: Edward Moxon, 1838).

Kidd, Colin. *The World of Mr Casaubon* (Cambridge: Cambridge University Press, 2014).

Kitchen, Barbara. 'Librarian's Image in Children's Fiction'. Master of Library and Information Science diss., Kent State University (2000).

Klancher, Jon. *The Making of English Reading Audiences* (Madison: University of Wisconsin Press, 1987).

Knight, Stephen. *Crime Fiction 1800–2000* (London: Palgrave Macmillan, 2004).

Knowles, James Sheridan. *The Dramatic Works* (London: Routledge, 1859).

Lamb, Charles. *Essays of Elia* (London: Oxford University Press, 1964).

Langton, Jane. *The Transcendental Murder* (New York: Harper & Row, 1964).

Larkin, Felix M., ed. *Librarians, Poets and Scholars* (Dublin: Four Courts Press, 2007).

Larkin, Philip. *A Girl in Winter* (London: Faber & Faber, 1947).

Larkin, Philip. 'Reputations Revisited'. *Times Literary Supplement*, 21 January 1977, 66.

Larkin, Philip. *Required Writing* (London: Faber & Faber, 1983).

Laux, Dorianne. *Smoke* (New York: BOA Editions, 2000).

Leavis, Q. D. *Fiction and the Reading Public*. (1932; repr. London: Chatto & Windus, 1978).

Lee, Nathaniel. *Caesar Borgia* (London: R. Bentley et al., 1680).

Le Faye, Deirdre, ed. *Jane Austen Letters*. 3rd ed. (Oxford and New York: Oxford University Press, 1995).

Leff, G. 'The *Trivium* and the Three Philosophies'. In *A History of the University in Europe*. Vol. 1. *The Middle Ages*, ed. Hilde de Ridder-Symoens (Cambridge: Cambridge University Press, 1992), 307–36.

Lemarchand, Elizabeth. *Step in the Dark* (London: HarperCollins, 1976).

Lennox, Charlotte. *The Female Quixote*, 2nd ed. 2 vols (London: A. Millar, 1752).

Leonard, Tom, ed. *Radical Renfrew* (Edinburgh: Polygon, 1990).

Leslie, Shane. 'Montague Rhodes James'. In *Warnings to the Curious: A Sheaf of Criticism on M. R. James*, ed. S. T. Joshi and Rosemary Pardoe (New York: Hippocampus Press, 2007), 28–38.

Levine, Joseph M. 'Ancients and Moderns Reconsidered'. *Eighteenth-Century Studies* 15.1 (Autumn 1981): 72–89.

Levine, Joseph M. *The Battle of the Books: History and Literature in the Augustan Age* (London and Ithaca: Cornell University Press, 1991).

Lewis, Sinclair. *Main Street* (New York: [s.n.,] 1920.

'Librarians in Congress'. *The Times*, 6 October 1877, 10.

Light, Alison. *Forever England: Femininity, Literature and Conservatism Between the Wars* (London: Routledge, 1991).

Lloyd, L. J. 'The Ghost Stories of Montague Rhodes James'. *Book Handbook* 4 (1947): 237–53.

Lochhead, Liz. *A Choosing* (Edinburgh: Polygon, 2011).

Lockridge, Frances, and Richard Lockridge. *The Distant Clue* (Philadelphia, PA: Lippincott, 1963).

Lor, C. H. 'The Medieval Interpretation of Aristotle'. In *The Cambridge History of Later Medieval Philosophy*, ed. Norman Kretzmann, Anthony Kenny, Jan Pinborg, and Eleonore Stump (1982; repr. Cambridge: Cambridge University Press, 2008), 80–98.

Loran, Martin. 'An Ounce of Dissension'. In *Pacific Book of Australian SF*, ed. John Baxter (Sydney: Angus & Robertson, 1968), 27–48.

Lubbock, S. G. *A Memoir of Montague Rhodes James* (Cambridge: Cambridge University Press, 1939).

Lyall, Roderick J. 'Robert Henryson's *Morall Fabillis*: Structure and Meaning'. In *A Companion to Medieval Scottish Poetry*, ed. Priscilla Bawcutt and Janet Hadley-Williams (Cambridge: D. S. Brewer, 2006), 89–104.

Lyly, John. *Sapho and Phao* (London: Thomas Cadman, 1584).

Lynch, Deidre. 'Gothic Libraries and National Subjects'. *Studies in Romanticism* 40.1 (2001): 29–48.

Lynch, Deidre. '"Wedded to Books": Bibliomania and the Romantic Essayists'. *Romantic Circles Praxis Series: Romantic Libraries Issue* (University of Maryland, February 2004). https://romantic-circles.org/praxis/libraries/lynch/lynch.html

McCarthy, Muriel and Ann Simmons. *The Making of Marsh's Library: Learning, Politics and Religion in Ireland, 1650–1750* (Dublin and Portland, OR: Four Courts Press, 2004).

McCray, J. Louise. 'Novel-Reading, Ethics, and William Godwin in the 1830s'. *Studies in Romanticism* 59.2 (2020): 209–30.

McCray, J. Louise. '"Peril in the means of its diffusion": William Godwin on Truth and Social Media'. *Journal of the History of Ideas* 81.1 (January 2020): 67–84.

McDayter, Mark. 'The Haunting of St James's Library: Librarians, Literature, and *The Battle of the Books*'. *Huntington Library Quarterly* 66.1/2 (2003): 1–26.

McGowan, Todd. *Psychoanalytic Film Theory and the Rules of the Game* (London: Bloomsbury Academic, 2015).

Mackenzie, Henry. *The Man of Feeling* (1771; repr. Berwick: John Taylor, 1780).

McLamore, Richard V. 'The Dutchman in the Attic: Claiming an Inheritance in *The Sketch-Book of Geoffrey Crayon*'. *American Literature* 72.1 (March 2000): 31–57.

McMillan, Ian. *To Fold the Evening Star: New and Selected Poems* (Manchester: Carcanet, 2016).

McMullen, Haynes. *American Libraries Before 1876* (Westport, CT, and London: Greenwood Press, 2000).

McSeveney, Angela. *Coming Out With It* (Edinburgh: Polygon, 1992).

Madhubuti, Haki R. *Heartlove: Wedding and Love Poems* (Chicago: Third World Press, 1998).

Magrath, Gabriella. 'Library Conventions of 1853, 1876, and 1877'. *Journal of Library History, Philosophy and Comparative Librarianship* 8.2 (April 1973): 52–69.

Mainz, Valerie. *Days of Glory? Imaging Military Recruitment and the French Revolution* (Basingstoke: Palgrave Macmillan, 2016).

Mandal, Antony. *Jane Austen and the Popular Novel* (Basingstoke: Palgrave Macmillan, 2007).

Manguel, Alberto. *The Library at Night* (New Haven: Yale University Press, 2008).

Manguel, Alberto. *The Traveler, the Tower, and the Worm* (Philadelphia: University of Pennsylvania Press, 2013).

Manley, Mary de la Rivière. *Secret Memoirs and Manners of Several Persons of Quality* (London: John Morphew et al., 1709).

Map, Walter. *De Nugis Curialium/Courtiers' Trifles*, ed. and trans. M. R. James; rev. C. N. L. Brook and R. A. B. Mynors (Oxford: Clarendon Press, 1983).

Marcus, Laura. 'The Library in Film: Order and Mystery'. In *The Meaning of the Library*, ed. Alice Crawford (Princeton: Princeton University Press, 2015), 199–219.

Marlowe, Christopher. *Plays and Poems*, ed. M. R. Ridley (London: Dent, 1973).

Marsack, Robyn. 'Remembering Seamus Heaney'. *Poetry Reader* (Scottish Poetry Library) 14 (Winter 2014): 4.

Mason, John. *Princeps Rhetoricus* (London: H. R. [et al.], 1648).

Masterman, J. C. *An Oxford Tragedy* (London: Gollancz, 1933).

May, Thomas. *The Tragedie of Cleopatra Queen of AEgypt* (London: Thomas Walkly, 1639).

Melnyczuk, Askold, ed. *Take Three: Agni New Poets Series: 1* (Minneapolis: Graywolf Press, 1996).

Melville, Herman. *Moby-Dick; or, The Whale*, 2 vols (1851; repr. London: Constable, 1922).

Meredith, Royston. *Mr Steele Detected: Or, the Poor and Oppressed Orphan's Letters to the Great and Arbitrary Mr Steele; Complaining of the Great Injustice Done, to the Publick in General, and to Himself in Particular, by the Ladies Library* (London: John Morphew, 1714).

Merish, Lori. *Sentimental Materialism: Gender, Commodity Culture, and Nineteenth-Century American Literature* (Durham, NC: Duke University Press, 2000).

Metres, Philip. 'Hearing of Alia Muhammed Baker's Stroke', 1970. *poets.org*: https://poets.org/poem/hearing-alia-muhammed-bakers-stroke.

Miller, William, and Gregory Christie. *Richard Wright and the Library Card* (New York: Lee & Low Books, 1997).

Milleret, Jean de. *Entretiens avec Jorge Luis Borges* (Paris: Pierre Belfond, 1967).

Mills, Chester. 'Eliot's Casaubon: the Quixotic in *Middlemarch*'. In *The Cervantean Heritage*, ed. J. A. G. Ardila (London: Legenda, 2009), 176–80.

Milne, A. A. *The Red House Mystery* (1922; repr. OTB E-book Publishing, 2015).

Mitchell, Richard H. 'Japan's Peace Preservation Law of 1925: its Origins and Significance'. *Monumenta Nipponica* 28.3 (1973): 317–45.

Mole, Tom. *The Secret Life of Books* (London: Elliott & Thompson, 2019).

Montagu, Mary Wortley. *The Dean's Provocation for Writing the Lady's Dressing Room* (London: T. Cooper, 1734).

Montaigne. *Complete Essays*, trans. Donald M. Frame (Stanford, CA: Stanford University Press, 1958).

Moody, Nickianne. 'The Boots Booklovers' Libraries'. *Antiquarian Book Monthly* (November 1996): 36–8.

Moore, Thomas. *M. P. or the Blue-stocking* (London: J. Power et al., 1811).

Morrah, Dermot. *The Mummy Case Mystery* (New York: Harper, 1933).

Munford, William Arthur. *A History of the Library Association* (London: Library Association, 1976).

Murakami, Haruki. *Kangarū biyori* (Tokyo: Kōdansha, 1983).

Murakami, Haruki. 'Toshokan kitan'. In *Kangarō biyori*, by Haruki Murakami (Tokyo: Kōdansha, 1986).

Murakami, Haruki. *Murakami Haruki zensakuhin 1979–1989* (Tokyo: Kōdansha,1993).

Murakami, Haruki. *Kafka on the Shore* (London: Harvill, 2005).

Murakami, Haruki. *The Strange Library*, trans. Ted Goossen (London: Harvill Secker, 2014).

Murakami, Haruki. Toshokan kitan (Tokyo: Shinchōsha, 2014).

Murakami, Haruki, and Maki Sasaki. *Fushigi na toshokan* (Tokyo: Kōdansha, 2005).

Murphy, Olivia. *Jane Austen the Reader: The Artist as Critic* (New York: Palgrave Macmillan, 2013).

Murphy, Patrick J. *Medieval Studies and the Ghost Stories of M. R. James* (University Park, PA: Pennsylvania State University Press, 2017).

Murray, Les. *Collected Poems* (Manchester: Carcanet, 1991).

Naudé, Gabriel. *Instructions Concerning Erecting of a Library*, trans. John Evelyn (London: G. Bedle, T. Collins & J. Crook, 1661).

Nesbit, E. 'The Town in the Library'. In *Nine Unlikely Tales*, by E. Nesbit (1901; London: Benn, 1960), 243–66.

'New Fiction'. *Scotsman*, 27 March 1933, 2.

Noble, Jon. 'From Tom Pinch to Highliber Zavora: The Librarian in Fiction'. *Orana* 37.3 (November 2001): 23–8.

Noya, Fumiaki. ' "Sekai no owari to hādoboirudo wandārando" ron: "boku" to "watashi" no dejabyū'. *Kokubungaku* 40.4 (1995): 54.

Nye, Naomi Shihab. *Fuel* (New York: BOA Editions, 1998).

O'Brien, Sean. *The Beautiful Librarians* (London: Picador, 2015).

Odell, Thomas. *The Smugglers* (London: John Clarke et al., 1729).

Oechslin, Werner. ' "Mentalmente architettato" – Thoughts in Physical Form: Immutable or Dynamic? The Case of the Library'. In *Collection, Laboratory, Theatre: Scenes of Knowledge in the 17th Century*, ed. Helmar Schramm, Ludger Schwarte, and Jan Lazardzig (Theatrum Scientiarum (English ed.), Vol. 1) (Berlin: de Gruyter, 2005), 122–45.

Oliphant, Margaret. 'Modern Light Literature – History'. *Blackwood's Magazine* 78 (October 1855): 437–51.

Oliphant, Margaret. 'In Maga's Library: The Old Saloon'. *Blackwood's Magazine* 141 (January 1887): 126–53.

Oliphant, Margaret. *A Memoir of the Life of John Tulloch* (Edinburgh and London: William Blackwood & Sons, 1888).

Oliphant, Margaret. *The Marriage of Elinor* (London: Macmillan, 1892).

Oliphant, Margaret. 'The Library Window'. *Blackwood's Magazine* 159 (January 1896): 1–30. Repr. in *The Selected Works of Margaret Oliphant*, ed. E. Jay and J. Shattock, 25 vols (London: Pickering & Chatto, 2011–17), Vol. 12, 265–99.

Oliphant, Margaret. 'The Land of Suspense'. *Blackwood's Magazine* 161 (January 1897): 131–57.

Oliphant, Margaret. "'Tis Sixty Years Since'. *Blackwood's Magazine* 161 (May 1897): 599–624.

Oliphant, Margaret. *The Autobiography and Letters of Mrs M. O. W. Oliphant*, ed. Mrs Harry Coghill (Edinburgh and London: Blackwood, 1899). Repr. in *The Selected Works of Margaret Oliphant*, ed. E. Jay and J. Shattock, 25 vols (London: Pickering & Chatto, 2011–17), Vol. 6.

Oliphant, Margaret. *Stories of the Seen and Unseen* (Edinburgh and London: Blackwood, 1902).

Oliphant, Margaret. 'La Fenêtre de la Bibliothèque', trans. Marguerite Faguer. In *Les Oeuvres Libres*, (Nouvelle série 128), (Paris: Librairie Arthème Fayard, 1957).

Oliphant, Margaret. *Selected Stories of the Supernatural*, ed. Margaret K. Gray (Edinburgh: Scottish Academic Press, 1985).

Oliphant, Margaret. *A Beleaguered City and Other Stories*, ed. Merryn Williams (Oxford: Oxford University Press, 1988).

Oliphant, Margaret. *The Autobiography of Margaret Oliphant. The Complete Text*, ed. E. Jay (Oxford: Oxford University Press, 1990).

Oliphant, Margaret. *A Beleaguered City and Other Tales of the Seen and Unseen*, ed. Jenni Calder (Edinburgh: Canongate, 2000).

Oliphant, Margaret. *The Selected Works of Margaret Oliphant*, ed. E. Jay and J. Shattock, 25 vols (London: Pickering & Chatto, 2011–17).

Oliphant, Margaret. *The Library Window: A Story of the Seen and Unseen*, ed. Annmarie S. Drury (Peterborough, ON: Broadview Press, 2019).

Oliver, Jane. 'Ann Stafford'. *Times*, 29 September 1966, 14.

Oliver, Jane, and Ann Stafford. *Business as Usual* (London: Collins, 1933).

Ortega y Gasset, José. 'The Mission of the Librarian', trans. James Lewis and Ray Carpenter. *Antioch Review* 21.2 (Summer 1961): 133–54.

Orwell, George. 'Bookshop Memories' (1936). In *The Collected Essays, Journalism and Letters of George Orwell*, ed. Sonia Orwell and Ian Angus, Vol. 1: *An Age Like This, 1920–1940* (Harmondsworth: Penguin, 1971), 273–7.

Osborne, John. *Radical Larkin: Seven Types of Technical Mastery* (Basingstoke: Palgrave Macmillan, 2014).

Ovenden, Richard, *Burning the Books: A History of Knowledge Under Attack* (London: John Murray, 2020).

Paling, Chris. *Reading Allowed: True Stories and Curious Incidents from a Provincial Library* (London: Constable, 2017).

Pardoe, Rosemary. 'Hostanes Magus'. In *The Black Pilgrimage and Other Explorations: Essays on Supernatural Fiction*, by Rosemary Pardoe (King's Norton: Shadow Publishing, 2018), 43–9.

Parks, Stephen. 'George Berkeley, Sir Richard Steele and *The Ladies Library*'. *The Scriblerian* 13.1 (Autumn 1980): 1–2.

Partridge, Christopher, ed. *The Occult World* (London and New York: Routledge, 2016).

Paterson, Alasdair. *On the Governing of Empires* (Exeter: Shearsman, 2010).

Paterson, Don. *God's Gift to Women* (London: Faber & Faber, 1997).

Patrick, Q. *Murder at Cambridge* (New York: Farrar & Rinehart, 1932, © 1933)

Paulson, Ronald. *Don Quixote in England* (Baltimore: Johns Hopkins University Press, 1998).

Peachey, Jenny. *Shining a Light: How People in the UK and Ireland Use Public Libraries and What They Think of Them* (Dunfermline: Carnegie UK Trust, 2017).

Pearl, Nancy. 'Murder by the Book: Biblio-Mysteries'. *Library Journal*, 1 September 2004: 207.

Penzler, Otto. *Bibliomysteries: An Annotated Bibliography of the First Editions of Mystery Fiction Set in the World of Books, 1849–2000* (New York: Mysterious Press, 2014).

Perkins, Chris. 'Flatness, Depth and Kon Satoshi's Ethics'. *Journal of Japanese and Korean Cinema* 4.2 (2012): 119–33.

Perkins, Chris. *The United Red Army on Screen: Cinema, Aesthetics and the Politics of Memory* (Basingstoke: Palgrave Macmillan, 2015).

Pettegree, Andrew, and Arthur der Weduwen, *The Library: A Fragile History* (London: Profile Books, 2021).

Pfaff, Richard William. *Montague Rhodes James* (London: Scolar Press, 1980).

Piper, Andrew. *Dreaming in Books: The Making of the Bibliographic Imagination in the Romantic Age* (Chicago: Chicago University Press, 2009).

Planché, James Robinson. *The Good Woman in the Wood* (London: Thomas Hailes Lacy [, 1852]).

Poe, Edgar Allan. 'The Fall of the House of Usher'. *Burton's Gentleman's Magazine* V/3 (September 1839): 145–52.

Poe, Edgar Allan. 'The Raven'. *American Review* II (February 1845): 143–5.

Poetry Foundation: 'Harriet Staff'. 'A Wanda Coleman Branch of the Los Angeles Public Library?' (2014), https://www.poetryfoundation.org/harriet/2014/12/a-wanda-coleman-branch-of-the-los-angeles-public-library-.

Powell, Neil. *George Crabbe: An English Life 1754–1832* (London: Pimlico, 2004).

Prescott, Anne Lake. *Imagining Rabelais in Renaissance England* (New Haven: Yale University Press, 1998).

Pressman, Jessica. *Bookishness: Loving Books in a Digital Age* (New York: Columbia University Press, 2020).

Preston, Claire. 'Punctual Relations: Thomas Browne's Rhetorical Reclamations'. *Studies in Philology*, 115.3 (Summer 2018): 598–614.

Price, Leah. *The Anthology and the Rise of the Novel: From Richardson to George Eliot* (Cambridge: Cambridge University Press, 2000).

Price, Leah, ed. *Unpacking My Library: Writers and their Books* (New Haven and London: Yale University Press, 2011).

Price, Leah. *How To Do Things With Books In Victorian Britain* (Princeton: Princeton University Press, 2012).

Priestman, Martin. *Detective Fiction and Literature* (London: Macmillan, 1990).

Purcell, Mark. *The Country House Library* (New Haven and London: Yale University Press, 2017).

Pym, Barbara. *An Unsuitable Attachment* (London: Grafton, 1982).

Rabelais, François. *The First Book of the Works of Mr Francis Rabelais, Doctor in Physik, containing Five Books of the Lives, Heroick Deeds, and Sayings of Gargantua, and his Sonne Pantagruel...faithfully translated into English [by Thomas Urquhart]* (London: Richard Baddeley, 1653).

Rabelais, François. *Gargantua and Pantagruel*, trans. Thomas Urquhart and Peter le Motteux, 2 vols (London: Dent, 1966).

Radcliffe, Ann. *The Mysteries of Udolpho* (1794; repr. London: Dent, 1973).

Randolph, Thomas. *Aristippus* (London: John Marriott, 1630).

Randolph, Thomas. *The Muses Looking Glass* (London: William Roybould, 1638).

Raven, James. *London Booksellers and American Customers: Transatlantic Literary Community and the Charleston Library Society, 1748–1811* (Columbia, SC: University of South Carolina Press, 2002).

Rea, Joanne E. 'Joyce and "Master François Somebody"'. *James Joyce Quarterly* 18.4 (Summer 1981): 445–50.

Renonciat, Annie, ed. *Livre mon ami: lectures enfantines 1914–1954*. Exhibition catalogue (Paris: Mairie du Vᵉ arrondissement, 1991).

Reynolds, Frederick. *The Dramatist* (London: T. N. Longman et al., 1793).

Reznikoff, Charles. *The Poems of Charles Reznikoff: 1918–1975*, ed. Seamus Cooney (Boston: David R. Godine, 2005).

Rhodes, Neil. *Shakespeare and the Origins of English* (Oxford: Oxford University Press, 2004).

Riley, Peter. *Against Vocation: Whitman, Melville, Crane, and the Labors of American Poetry* (Oxford: Oxford University Press, 2019).

Ringrose, Jayne. 'The Legacy of M. R. James in Cambridge University Library'. In *The Legacy of M. R. James: Papers from the 1995 Cambridge Symposium*, ed. Lynda Dennison (Donington: Shaun Tyas, 2001): 23–36.

Ríos, Alberto. 'Don't Go Into the Library' (2017). *Poets.org*: https://poets.org/poem/dont-go-library.

Rivers, Isabel. *Books and their Readers in Eighteenth-Century England* (Leicester: Leicester University Press, 1982); Vol. 2 (London: Continuum, 2001).

Roberts, Alexander, and James Donaldson, eds. *The Anti-Nicene Fathers: The Writings of the Fathers Down to A.D. 325*, 10 vols (Peabody, MA: Hendrickson, 1995).

Roberts, Kyle B., and Mark Towsey, eds. *Before the Public Library: Reading, Community, and Identity in the Atlantic World* (Leiden and Boston, MA: Brill, 2008).

Robertson, Randy. 'Swift's *Leviathan* and the End of Licensing'. *Pacific Coast Philology* 40.2 (2005): 38–55.

Rohlen, Thomas P. 'The Juku Phenomenon: An Explanatory Essay'. *Journal of Japanese Studies* 6.2 (1980): 207–43.

Rose, Mark. *Authors and Owners: The Invention of Copyright* (Cambridge, MA; Harvard University Press, 1993).

Ruskin, John. *Sesame and Lilies* (1865; repr. New York: Silver, Burdett & Co., 1900).

Salter, Mary Jo. *A Phone Call to the Future: New and Selected Poems* (New York: Knopf, 2008).

Sas, Miryam. *Experimental Arts in Postwar Japan: Moments of Encounter, Engagement, and Imagined Return* (Cambridge, MA: Harvard University Press, 2011).

Sayers, Dorothy L., ed. *Great Short Stories of Detection, Mystery and Horror* (London: Gollancz, 1928). Pub. in America as *Second Omnibus of Crime*, ed. Dorothy L. Sayers (New York: Coward-McCann, 1932).

Sayers, Dorothy L. *Gaudy Night* (1935; repr. Sevenoaks: Hodder & Stoughton, 1987).

Scott, Walter. 'Maturin's Fatal Revenge'. *Quarterly Review* 3.6 (May 1810): 339–47.

Scott, Walter. *Waverley* (1814; repr. New York: Dutton, 1906).

Scott, Walter. *The Antiquary* (London: Dent, 1923).

Scott, Walter. *Waverley* (London: Penguin, 1981).

Scott, Walter. *Waverley: Or, 'Tis Sixty Years Since* (London: Penguin, 1985).

Scott, Walter. *The Antiquary*, ed. David Hewitt (Edinburgh: Edinburgh University Press, 1995).

Scott, Walter. *Reliquiae Trotcosienses; or, The Gabions of the Late Jonathan Oldbuck Esq. of Monkbarns*, ed. Gerard Carruthers and Alison Lumsden (1830; repr. Edinburgh: Edinburgh University Press, 2004).

Scott, Walter. *Waverley*, ed. P. D. Garside (Edinburgh: Edinburgh University Press, 2007).

Scudéry, Madeleine de. *Ibrahim, ou l'Illustre Bassa, Premiere partie* (Paris: Antoine de Sommaville, 1641).

Scudéry, Madeleine de. *Ibrahim, or, The Illustrious Bassa, An Excellent New Romance*, trans. Henry Cogan (London: Humphrey Moseley et al., 1652).

Sellers, Susan. '"Mischievous to the public interest": The Lady Literate in Arts Diploma and the Admission of Women to the University of St Andrews, 1876–1914'. In *Launch-Site for English Studies: Three Centuries of Literary Studies at the University of St Andrews*, ed. Robert Crawford (St Andrews: Verse, 1997), 107–23.

Shakespeare, William. *The Tempest*, ed. Frank Kermode (London: Methuen, 1964).

Shakespeare, William. *Love's Labour's Lost*, ed. Richard David (London: Methuen, 1968).

Shakespeare, William. *Titus Andronicus*, ed. J. C. Maxwell (London: Methuen, 1968).

Shapiro, Karl. *Creative Glut: Selected Essays*, ed. Robert Phillips (Chicago: Ivan R. Dee, 2004).

Shelton, Thomas, trans. *The History of the Valorous and Wittie Knight-errant, Don-Quixote Of the Mancha*, by Miguel de Cervantes Saavedra (London: Edward Blount and W. Barret, 1612).

Sheridan, Frances Chamberlaine. *The Discovery* (London: T. Davies et al., 1763).

Sheridan, Richard Brinsley. *The Rivals* (London: John Wilkie et al., 1775).

Shillito, Charles. *The Country Book-Club. A Poem* (London: Printed for the author and sold by W. Lowndes et al., 1788).

Shirley, James. *Honoria and Mammon* (London: The Author, 1659).

Sidney, Philip. *The Defence of Poesie* (London: William Ponsonby, 1595).

Silverstein, Norman. 'Deconstructing the Rabelaisian Element of *Finnegans Wake*'. *James Joyce Quarterly* 11.4 (Summer 1974): 414–19.

Smiles, Samuel. *Self-Help; with Illustrations of Character and Conduct* (London: John Murray, 1859).

Smiley, Jane. *Duplicate Keys* (London: Jonathan Cape, 1984).

Smith, Ali. *Public Library and Other Stories* (London: Hamish Hamilton, 2015).

Smith, Charles. *The Writing Desk…from the German of Kotzebue* (New York: Charles Smith, 1801).

Smith, Daniel Starza, Matthew Payne, and Melanie Marshall. 'Rediscovering John Donne's Catalogus librorum satyricus'. *Review of English Studies* 69.290 (June 2018): 455–87.

Smith, Iain Crichton. *New Collected Poems*, ed. Matthew McGuire (Manchester: Carcanet, 2011).

Smollett, Tobias. *The Expedition of Humphry Clinker* (1771; repr. London: Dent, 1968).

Solstad, Dag. *T. Singer*, trans. Tiina Nunnally (New York: New Directions, 2018).

Staikos, Konstantinos. *A History of the Library in Western Civilization* (New Castle, DE: Oak Knoll Press, 2004–12).

Stavely, Susan. 'Don Quixote in Eighteenth-Century England'. *Comparative Literature* 24.3 (Summer 1972): 193–215.

St Clair, William. *The Reading Nation in the Romantic Period* (Cambridge: Cambridge University Press, 2004).

Stern, Gerald. *This Time: New and Selected Poems* (New York: W.W. Norton, 1998).

Stokes, John. *The Forest of Rosenwald* (New York: E. Munden, 1821).

Stoppard, Tom. *Travesties* (London: Faber & Faber, 1974).

Stout, Janis P. 'Dorothy Canfield, Willa Cather, and the Uncertainties of Middlebrow and Highbrow'. *Studies in the Novel* 44.1 (2012): 27–48.

Stowe, Harriet Beecher. *Uncle Tom's Cabin; or, Life Among the Lowly* (London: John Cassell, 1852).

Strecher, Matthew C. 'Magical Realism and the Search for Identity in the Fiction of Murakami Haruki'. *Journal of Japanese Studies* 25.2 (1999): 263–98.

Stuart-Wortley, Emmeline. *Moonshine* (London: W. S. Johnson, 1843).

Sutherland, John. 'Literature and the Library in the Nineteenth Century'. In *The Meaning of the Library*, ed. Alice Crawford (Princeton: Princeton University Press, 2015), 124–50.

Swan, John. *Aye nowyir talkin* (Glasgow: Glasgow District Libraries, 1984).

Swartwout, R. E. *The Boat Race Murder* (London: Grayson & Grayson, 1933).

Swift, Jonathan. *The Lady's Dressing Room* (London: J. Roberts, 1732).

Swift, Jonathan. *Selected Prose and Poetry*, ed. Edward Rosenheim Jr (New York: Holt, Rinehart & Winston, 1968).

Swift, Jonathan. *Gulliver's Travels* (1726; repr. London: Oxford University Press, 1974).

Swift, Jonathan. *A Tale of a Tub and Other Works*, ed. Marcus Walsh. Vol. 1 of *The Cambridge Edition of the Works of Jonathan Swift*, ed. Claude Rawson, Ian Higgins, James McLaverty, and David Womersley (Cambridge: Cambridge University Press, 2010).

Swift, Jonathan. *Gulliver's Travels*, ed. David Womersley; Cambridge Edition of the Works of Jonathan Swift, Vol. 16 (Cambridge: Cambridge University Press, 2012).

Symons, Julian. 'Take That Body Out of the Library!' *Suspense* 3.7 (July 1960): 2–4.

Symons, Julian. *Bloody Murder* (1972; repr. London: Penguin, 1992).

Tanaka, Yasuo. *Nantonaku, kurisutaru* (Tokyo: Kawade bunko, 2014).

Taylor, Alan, ed. *Long Overdue: A Library Reader* (London and Edinburgh: Library Association/Mainstream Publishing, 1993).

Temple, William. *Miscellanea. The Second Part*, 4th ed. (London: Ri. and Ra. Simpson, 1696).

The Ladies Library, 3 vols (London: J. Tonson, 1714).

'The Wide-Awake Girls of [*sic*] Winsted'. *Journal of Education* 70.16 (28 October 1909): 441.

Thomas, Ernest C., trans. *The Philobiblon of Richard de Bury* (London: Kegan Paul, Trench & Co., 1888).

Thomas, Paul L. 'Magical Murakami Nightmares: Investigating Genre Through *The Strange Library*'. In *Haruki Murakami Challenging Authors*, ed. Matthew C. Strecher and Paul L. Thomas (Rotterdam: Sense Publishers, 2016), 47–57.

Thorndike, Lynn. *A History of Magic and Experimental Science*, 8 vols (New York: Columbia University Press, 1923).

Toth, Susan A., and John Coughlan, eds. *Reading Rooms: America's Foremost Writers Celebrate Our Public Libraries with Stories, Memoirs, Essays and Poems* (New York: Doubleday, 1991).

Trachtenberg, Alan. *The Incorporation of America: Culture and Society in the Gilded Age* (1982; repr. New York: Hill & Wang, 2007).

Traugott, John. 'A Tale of a Tub'. In *Modern Essays on Eighteenth-Century Literature*, ed. Leopold Damrosch Jr (Oxford: Oxford University Press, 1988), 3–45.

Treadwell, Michael. 'Swift's Relations with the London Book Trade to 1714'. In *Author/Publisher Relations During the Eighteenth and Nineteenth Centuries*, ed. Robin Myers and Michael Harris (Publishing Pathways) (Oxford: Oxford Polytechnic Press, 1983), 1–36.

Trollope, Anthony. *North America*, 2 vols (London: Chapman & Hall, 1862).

Tyler, Royall. *The Contrast* (Philadelphia: Thomas Wignell, 1790).

Urquhart, Thomas. *The Jewel*, ed. R. D. S. Jack and R. J. Lyall (Edinburgh: Scottish Academic Press, 1983).

Vanbrugh, John. *The Relapse* (London: Samuel Briscoe et al., 1697).

Vaughan, Henry. *Poetry and Selected Prose*, ed. L. C. Martin (London: Oxford University Press, 1963).

Verne, Jules. *Twenty Thousand Leagues Under the Sea* (London: Ward, Lock & Co. [, n.d]).

Vesper, Virginia. *The Image of the Librarian in Murder Mysteries in the Twentieth Century*. Report for Middle Tennessee State University. (Murfreesboro: Middle Tennessee State University, 1994).

Vickers, Salley. *The Librarian* (London: Viking, 2018).

Wakabayashi, Bob Tadashi, ed. *Modern Japanese Thought* (Cambridge: Cambridge University Press, 1998).

Walk in Dread: Tales from 'A Century of Ghost Stories'. (London: Hutchinson, 1970).

Wallack, Lester. *Rosedale* [1863]. In *Davy Crockett and Other Plays*, ed. Isaac Goldberg and Hubert Heffner (Princeton: Princeton University Press, 1940).

Walsh, Jill Paton. *The Wyndham Case* (Leicester: Thorpe, 1994).

Walsh, Marcus. 'Text, "Text", and Swift's *Tale of a Tub*'. *Modern Language Review* 85.2 (1990): 290–303.

Walsh, Marcus. 'Swift's *Tale of a Tub* and the Mock Book'. In *Jonathan Swift and the Eighteenth-Century Book*, ed. Paddy Bullard and James McLaverty (Cambridge: Cambridge University Press, 2013), 101–18.

Walwyn, Brett W. 'M. R. James and Changing Methods of Incunable Description'. In *The Legacy of M. R. James: Papers from the 1995 Cambridge Symposium*, ed. Lynda Dennison (Donington: Shaun Tyas, 2001), 211–17.

Ward, Mrs Humphrey. *Robert Elsmere*, ed. Miriam Elizabeth Burstein (Brighton: Victorian Secrets, 2013).

Warner, Marina. 'The Library in Fiction'. In *The Meaning of the Library*, ed. Alice Crawford (Princeton: Princeton University Press, 2015), 153–75.

Warner, Michael. *The Letters of the Republic: Publication and the Public Sphere in Eighteenth-Century America* (Cambridge, MA: Harvard University Press, 1990).

Webb, Beatrice. *My Apprenticeship* (Harmondsworth, Pelican, 1938).

Webb, James. *The Occult Underground* (La Salle, IL: Open Court, 1974).

Weinberger, Eliot, ed. *The Total Library: Non-Fiction 1922-1986, Jorge Luis Borges*, trans. Esther Allen, Suzanne Levine, and Eliot Weinberger (London: Allen Lane, 1999).

Welch, Theodore F. *Libraries and Librarianship in Japan* (London: Greenwood Press, 1997).

West, Andrew Fleming, ed. *The Philobiblon of Richard de Bury*, 3 vols (New York: Grolier Club, 1889).

Whaley, F. J. *Trouble in College* (London: Skeffington, 1936).

Wharton, Edith. *Summer: A Novel* (London: Macmillan, 1917).

Wharton, Edith. *The House of Mirth* (1905; repr. London: Oxford University Press, 1952).

Wharton, Edith, and Ogden Codman Jr. *The Decoration of Houses* (New York: Charles Scribner's Sons, 1907).

Wheatley, Edward. *Mastering Aesop: Medieval Education, Chaucer and his Followers* (Gainesville, FL: Florida University Press, 2000).

White, T. H. *Darkness at Pemberley* (London: Gollancz, 1932).

Whitechurch, Victor. *Murder at the College* (London: Crime Club/Collins, 1932).

Whitehead, William. *A Trip to Scotland* (London: J. Dodsley et al., 1770).

Whyte, Hamish. *Hannah, Are You Listening?* (Glenrothes: Happen*Stance*, 2013).

Wild, Robert. *The Benefice* (London: R. Janeway, 1689).

Williams, Abigail. *The Social Life of Books: Reading Together in the Eighteenth-Century Home* (London: Yale University Press, 2017).

Williamson, Edwin. *Borges: A Life* (New York: Viking Penguin, 2004).

Wilson, John. *The Cheats* (London: G. Bedell et al., 1664).

Woolf, Virginia. *A Room of One's Own* (1929; repr. London: Grafton Books, 1988).

Wordsworth, William, and S. T. Coleridge. *Lyrical Ballads*, ed. Fiona Stafford (Oxford: Oxford University Press, 2013).

Wotton, William. *Reflections Upon Ancient and Modern Learning* (London: J. Leake for Peter Buck, 1694).

Wright, Richard. *Black Boy: A Record of Childhood and Youth* (New York: Harper, 1945).

Yamane, Yumie. 'Murakami Haruki 'odoru shōjin' ron: boruhesu he no kage'. *Kokubungakukō* 209 (2011): 33.

Yun Lee Too. *The Idea of the Library in the Ancient World* (Oxford: Oxford University Press, 2010).

Zboray, Ronald J., and Mary Saracino Zboray. 'Home Libraries and the Institutionalization of Everyday Practices Among Antebellum New Englanders'. *American Studies* 42.3 (Fall 2001): 63–86.

Zueblin, Charles. *American Municipal Progress* (1902; repr. New York: Macmillan, 1916).

Zuylen, Marina van. *Monomania: The Flight from Everyday Life in Literature and Art* (Ithaca, NY: Cornell University Press, 2018).

Zwicker, Stephen N. 'The Constitution of Opinion and the Pacification of Reading'. In *Reading, Society and Politics in Early Modern England*, ed. Kevin Sharpe and Steven N. Zwicker (Cambridge: Cambridge University Press, 2003), 295–316.

Index

For the benefit of digital users, indexed terms that span two pages (e.g., 52–53) may, on occasion, appear on only one of those pages.